T0295872

NOBEL LECTURES

ECONOMIC SCIENCES

2011 – 2015

Nobel Lectures

Including Presentation Speeches and Laureates' Biographies

Physics

Chemistry

Physiology or Medicine

Economic Sciences

Nobel Lectures

Including Presentation Speeches
and Laureates' Biographies

Economic Sciences

2011 – 2015

Editor

Mats Persson

Stockholm University, Sweden

NEW JERSEY • LONDON • SINGAPORE • BEIJING • SHANGHAI • HONG KONG • TAIPEI • CHENNAI • TOKYO

Published by

World Scientific Publishing Co. Pte. Ltd.
5 Toh Tuck Link, Singapore 596224
USA office: 27 Warren Street, Suite 401-402, Hackensack, NJ 07601
UK office: 57 Shelton Street, Covent Garden, London WC2H 9HE

NOBEL LECTURES IN ECONOMIC SCIENCES (2011–2015)

ISBN 978-981-124-729-3 (hardcover)
ISBN 978-981-124-758-3 (paperback)
ISBN 978-981-124-730-9 (ebook for institutions)
ISBN 978-981-124-731-6 (ebook for individuals)

For any available supplementary material, please visit
https://www.worldscientific.com/worldscibooks/10.1142/12551#t=suppl

Printed in Singapore

PREFACE

The Prize in Economic Sciences (or *The Sveriges Riksbank Prize in Economic Sciences in Memory of Alfred Nobel*, as the official name reads) covers a wide range of social issues, from abstract theory to very practical problems. Each year, that year's Laureates give lectures in Stockholm presenting their work; these lectures can often be rather technical, or at least appear technical to the layman. At the award ceremony, a member of the Prize Committee makes a more accessible, shorter presentation of the work. This volume publishes these non-technical presentations, as well as the original lectures of the Laureates, and (in most cases) also a brief autobiographical sketch of each Laureate.

The 2011 Prize was awarded jointly to *Thomas J. Sargent* and *Christopher A. Sims* "for their empirical research on cause and effect in the macroeconomy". There is a special problem in economics in the sense that experiments cannot normally be performed. In the absence of laboratory data, we therefore have to rely on historical real-world data, but these data most often fail to separate cause and effect. Assume for instance that we want to know how the central bank can affect inflation and GDP by changing the interest rate. The historical data do not tell us in a simple fashion whether an interest rate change made inflation and unemployment change in the following year, or whether expected future changes in inflation and unemployment made the central bank decide to change the interest rate. Sargent and Sims have developed mathematical models of the economy that make it possible to estimate the effect of policy changes; their work has thus had a substantial effect on the actual performance of fiscal and monetary policy.

The 2012 Prize, shared by *Lloyd S. Shapley* and *Alvin E. Roth* "for the theory of stable allocations and the practice of market design," provides a neat example of the interplay between abstract theory and real-world applications. In the 1950s and 1960s, Lloyd Shapley published several papers that established him as one of the world's leading researchers in the field of game theory. A few of these papers provided theoretical solutions to the well-known problem of "matching", i.e., the question of how one could pair two counterparts (for instance, prospective spouses in matrimony, or students and schools in an education system, or homeowners who wish to swap houses in order to improve their living) in an efficient way. The ideas in these papers were used some decades later by *Alvin E. Roth*, who had been assigned the task of improving the matching of tens of thousands of students with hundreds of schools in New York. It turned out that the algorithm suggested by Shapley was not only theoretically elegant, but also practical and applicable to the New York school problem — and to a number of other pressing problems. For instance, Roth has shown how Shapley's models can be practicably used for matching new doctors with hospital internships, for matching donors of human organs with patients in need of a transplant, and for many other applications.

Is it possible to make systematic gains in the stock market? The three 2013 Laureates, *Eugene F. Fama*, *Lars Peter Hansen* and *Robert J. Shiller*, have made significant contributions to answering this question and were awarded the Prize "for their empirical analysis of asset prices". While it was shown theoretically in the 1950s and early 1960s that in an *efficient* asset market no systematic gains can be made (unless you have insider information), Fama pioneered the empirical testing of this theory. In a number of papers from the late 1960s and onwards, he formalized the definitions of "market efficiency" and "systematic gains," and he worked out several tests of whether stock markets are really efficient. The data indicated that the hypothesis of market efficiency cannot in general be rejected, at least not in the short run. Fama's results arose much attention and gave rise to a whole new subfield in economics, namely that of "empirical finance". Within that subfield, Shiller could show that there is actually some predictability of stock prices in the longer run, over 3 to 7 years. Does that mean that stock markets are inefficient after all? Not necessarily; Shiller's results showed that we need better data and more subtle tests, taking the fact into account that investor risk attitudes might change over time. Hansen provided a statistical tool for considering this feature — a tool that has turned out to be useful not only in empirical finance, but also in a number of other fields of economics.

The 2014 Laureate, *Jean Tirole*, was awarded the Prize "for his analysis of market power and regulation". There is a common misperception that economists build their policy prescriptions on the assumption of an idealized world of perfect competition. While this might have been true for 18th century economists (if even then) it is certainly not true for 20th century economists, where the study of market power and monopoly has been one of the most vibrant fields of research. Here the basic question is, how should society regulate large, powerful companies in order to improve the economy's performance to the benefit of the citizens? This question is addressed in the field of "industrial organization". In recent decades, that field has witnessed a remarkable transformation, providing answers to many questions that earlier generations of economists — not to mention governments and regulatory agencies — could not grasp. Alone or in collaboration with colleagues (perhaps most prominently, the late Jean-Jacques Laffont), and with the use of game theory and the economics of information, Tirole has helped transform the field of industrial organization into an important aid for government policy.

Consumption is arguably the most important issue for mankind, at least in poor countries. But even in richer countries, consumption is important for the development of the macroeconomy since it represents the largest part of GDP. The 2015 Prize was awarded to *Angus Deaton* "for his analysis of consumption, poverty, and welfare". He addressed consumption in a number of ways of which the most important concerned the *construction of demand systems* (i.e., sets of equations describing how demand for different goods is affected by prices, incomes and demographic factors), the *development of aggregate consumption over time* (or, similarly, aggregate saving, which is identical to income minus consumption), and the *construction of household surveys* for the collection of consumption data. This broad work has been theoretical and mathematical as well as empirical, mixed with a considerable quantity of knowledge of real-world data and down-to-earth practical detail.

Mats Persson

CONTENTS

Economic Sciences 2011

Thomas J. Sargent and Christopher A. Sims

"for their empirical research on cause and effect in the macroeconomy"

The Sveriges Riksbank Prize In Economic Sciences In Memory of Alfred Nobel

Speech by Professor Per Krusell of the Royal Swedish Academy of Sciences.

Your Majesties, Your Royal Highnesses, Laureates, Ladies and Gentlemen,

Our national economies are continuously exposed to changes in the world around us. Fluctuations in the economic activity of other countries influence foreign demand for our products; variations in the prices of raw materials influence our production costs; technical innovations change the mix of goods and services demanded. Evaluating alternative responses to these sorts of inevitable economic disturbances is a central task for policymakers. How much, for example, would a particular increase in interest rates or decrease in income taxes affect the nation's inflation and employment? And how long before those effects would be realised?

Macroeconomic questions like these are hard to answer, because they are fundamentally social science questions. Unlike natural scientists, economists cannot look for answers by conducting controlled experiments, at least not on whole economies. We must work instead with the data provided by history. In addition, economies do not behave like mechanical, natural science systems. Nature obeys its laws independently of what governments decide, but economies do not, because economies consist of thinking people. Thinking people are also influenced by expectations about the future. For this reason, economies are also influenced by expectations of future policy decisions not yet made. This makes the co-variations observed in historical data hard to interpret. Does a particular historical change in an interest rate explain the subsequent change in the inflation rate? Or is the causality the reverse: did the expected path of inflation generate the interest rate change? In general, how can we distinguish between cause and effect in a macroeconomy?

Thomas Sargent and Christopher Sims have provided powerful tools that can be used with the data to answer that question. They have developed methods that let us precisely distinguish the effect of economic policy changes from the effect of other changes in the economic environment. Their work has illuminated the effects of monetary and fiscal policy not just for researchers but also for central bankers and finance ministers everywhere.

Christopher Sims has focused on the effects of unexpected changes in economic policy. Using a particular form of time series analysis, so-called vector autoregression, he has shown how we can understand the dynamic response of the economy to an impulse like a temporary policy change. Such impulse-response analysis allows us to track how, for example, an unexpected lowering of the interest rate, engineered by a central bank, can affect inflation and employment over time. Based on this contribution, we now know that a lower interest rate implies an immediate, gradual increase in production and employment, with a maximal effect after about two years. But it implies no immediate effect on inflation at all. In fact, inflation only starts to slowly increase roughly a year and a half after the interest rate drop, after which it recedes. What we have learned about this process is critical for central bankers considering alternative changes in interest rates.

Thomas Sargent's research has allowed us to understand the effects of more permanent changes in economic policy, such as a switch to new government budget rules. This kind of analysis requires a different approach because the historical data offer few examples of systematic policy changes. Indeed, some policy changes being considered may never have been used before. Sargent's approach to such analysis relies on certain aspects of the behaviour in the economy being rather constant – at least, not changing when policy changes. Examples of such constant behaviours are how people trade off leisure and work and how firms trade off different kinds of production inputs. Sargent showed how statistical methods could be used to measure these "universal economic constants" in the historical data and how a mathematical model of the economy could be built around them. With such a model, economists and policymakers can now conduct artificial laboratory experiments and investigate the effects of systematic macroeconomic policy changes.

Dear Professors Sargent and Sims,

You have successfully confronted a fundamental challenge facing empirical macroeconomic research: to disentangle cause and effect in historical data. The methods you have developed are now central tools for economic researchers trying to understand how our economies work and how they react to temporary and permanent changes in the economic environment. Because your methods allow us to use historical data to identify the causal effects of changes in economic policy, they have also become indispensable tools for policymakers worldwide. Modern empirical macroeconomic analysis rests on your shoulders.

It is an honour and a privilege to convey to you, on behalf of the Royal Swedish Academy of Sciences, our warmest congratulations. I now ask you to receive your Prize from His Majesty the King.

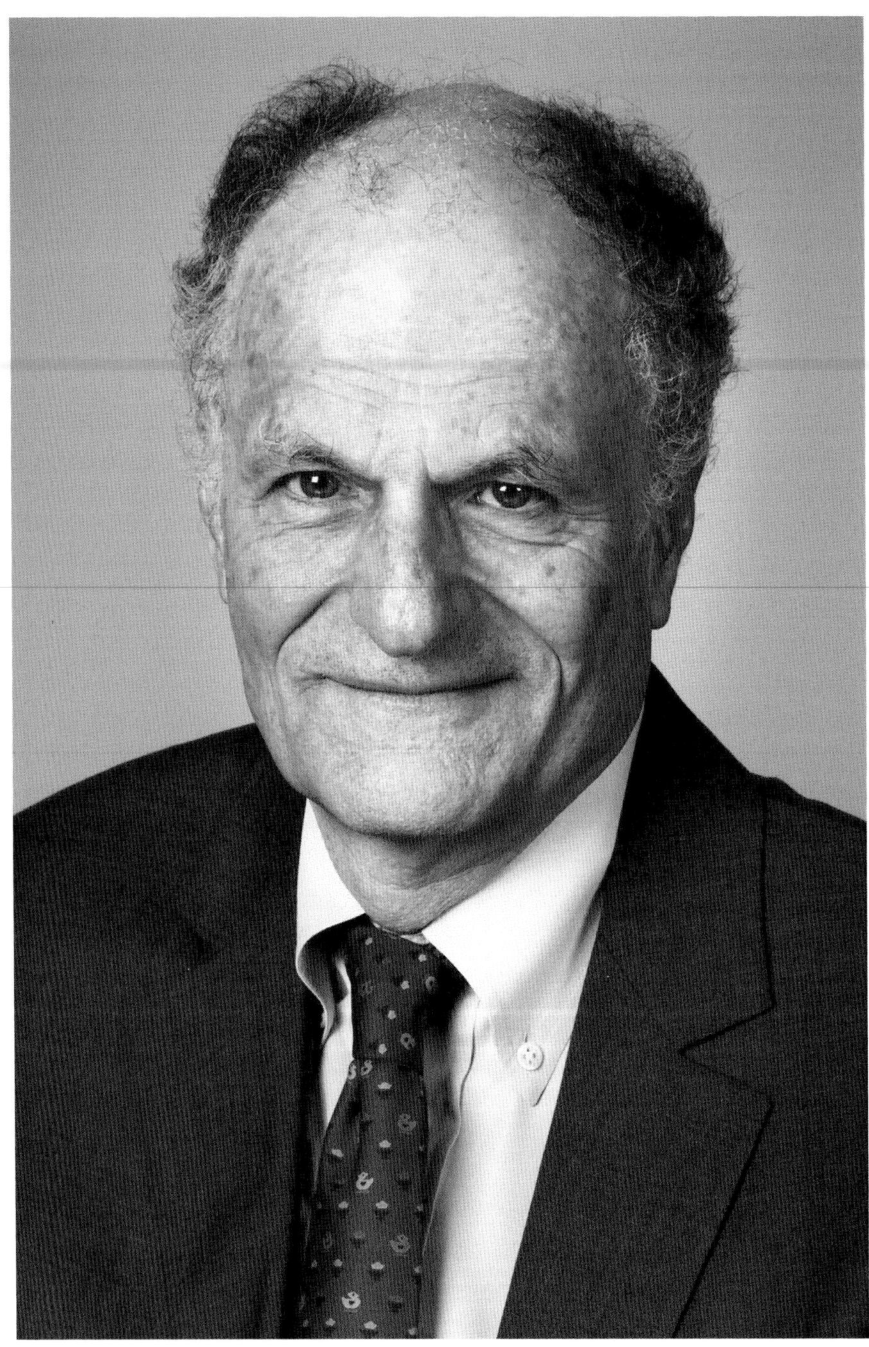

Thomas J. Sargent. © The Nobel Foundation. Photo: U. Montan

Thomas J. Sargent did not submit an autobiography. See https://www.nobelprize.org/prizes/economic-sciences/2011/sargent/facts/

Nobel Lecture: United States Then, Europe Now

Thomas J. Sargent

New York University and Hoover Institution

Under the Articles of Confederation, the central government of the United States had limited power to tax. Therefore, large debts accumulated during the US War for Independence traded at deep discounts. That situation framed a US fiscal crisis in the 1780s. A political revolution—for that was what scuttling the Articles of Confederation in favor of the Constitution of the United States of America was—solved the fiscal crisis by transferring authority to levy tariffs from the states to the federal government. The Constitution and acts of the First Congress of the United States in August 1790 gave Congress authority to raise enough revenues to service a big government debt. In 1790, the Congress carried out a comprehensive bailout of state governments' debts, part of a grand bargain that made creditors of the states become advocates of ample federal taxes. That bailout created expectations about future federal bailouts that a costly episode in the early 1840s proved to be unwarranted.

I. Introduction

I work in a macroeconomic tradition developed by John Muth, Robert E. Lucas Jr., Edward C. Prescott, Finn Kydland, Nancy Stokey, and Neil Wallace. I use macroeconometric methods championed by Lars Peter Hansen and Christopher A. Sims. I interpret macroeconomic history in ways advanced by Irving Fisher, Milton Friedman, Anna Schwartz, and

This is a Nobel Prize lecture delivered in Stockholm on December 8, 2011. I thank George Hall for being my partner in studying the history of US fiscal policy. I thank Anmol Bhandari, Alan Blinder, Alberto Bisin, David Backus, Timothy Cogley, V. V. Chari, George Hall, Lars Peter Hansen, Martin Eichenbaum, Michael Golosov, David Kreps, Robert E. Lucas Jr., Ramon Marimon, Rodolfo Manuelli, Carolyn Sargent, Robert Shimer, Cecilia Parlatore Siritto, Vasiliki Skreta, Richard Sylla, Christopher Tonetti, Eric Young, and Warren Weber for criticizing earlier versions.

Reprinted with permission from *Journal of Political Economy*, 2012, vol. 120, no. 1, pp. 1–40.

François Velde.[1] To illustrate how these research traditions have shaped me, I tell how predicaments facing the European Union today remind me of constitutional decisions the United States faced not once but twice.

I begin with a simple expected present value model for government debt and explain how Hansen and Sargent (1980) used rational expectations econometrics to render this model operational by deducing cross-equation restrictions that characterize how the value of a government's debt depends on statistical properties of the government's net-of-interest surplus. This econometric specification isolates essential determinants of the value of a country's debt or currency. The econometric theory leaves open who chooses the all-important statistical process for the government net-of-interest surplus. In democracies, voters choose. Different outcomes emerge under alternative democratic political arrangements.

A case study illustrates how democracies have balanced conflicting interests. My case study is how the constitutions of the United States have influenced the government net-of-interest surplus process and therefore the value of government debt. I say constitutions, plural, because we Americans have tried two of them, first the Articles of Confederation that were ratified in 1781 and then the US Constitution that was ratified in 1788. Those constitutions embraced two very different visions of a good federal union. The first constitution was designed to please people who preferred a central government that would find it difficult to tax, spend, borrow, and regulate foreign trade. The second served opposite interests. The US framers abandoned a first constitution in favor of a second because they wanted to break the prevailing statistical process for the net-of-interest government surplus and replace it with another one that could service a bigger government debt.[2] Exactly how and why they did that is enlightening: starting in 1789, they rearranged fiscal affairs first and then approached monetary arrangements as an afterthought.

[1] See Muth (1960, 1961), Lucas (1972, 1976), Lucas and Prescott (1971, 1974), Lucas and Stokey (1983), Kydland and Prescott (1977), Hansen and Sargent (1980), Hansen (1982), Sims (1972, 1980), Fisher (1926, chaps. 11, 12), Friedman and Schwartz (1963), and Velde (2009). Fisher (1926, chaps. 11, 12), entitled "Statistical Verification," set out a roadmap for Friedman and Schwartz (1963). Velde and Weber (2000) beautifully formalize and extend an enlightening model of bimetallism created by Fisher. The issues described in this paper have been with us for a very long time. See Conklin (1998) for a description and analysis of sovereign debt issues faced by Spain under Phillip II. For an exquisite example of how theory imitates life, see Velde (2009) for an account of an actual pure change of units monetary experiment that is a key ingredient of the mental experiment analyzed by Lucas (1972).

[2] The term "framers" rather than "founders" or "founding fathers" is more descriptive of how they thought of themselves, namely, as creators of an institutional framework within which their successors would act. See Rakove (1997).

The fiscal institutions of the European Union today remind me of those in the United States under the Articles of Confederation. The power to tax lies with member states. Unanimous consent by member states is required for many important European Union–wide fiscal actions.

Some lessons from US history are these:

1. *The ability to borrow today depends on expectations about future revenues.* Without institutions that provide adequate revenue sources, governments may have neither the current revenue nor the ability, by issuing debt, to pledge future revenues when occasions demanding especially large public expenditures arise. The inability to issue debt comes from the fact that prospective debt holders rationally anticipate that the government will be constrained in its ability to raise enough revenues to service the debt. To provide public goods, even rare ones like surges of defense spending during wars, governments require the flexibility to tap adequate sources of revenue.
2. *Free-rider problems exist for subordinate governments vis-à-vis a central government.* Because there is a classic free-rider problem in paying for public goods, subordinate governments, such as states in the United States or nations in the European Union, cannot be relied on voluntarily to provide revenue to the central government to pay for public goods. Each state has an incentive to refuse, hoping that other states will accept the burden.
3. *Good reputations can be costly to acquire.* In deciding whether or not to pay preexisting debts, governments have strong incentives to default. Their anticipations of default make prospective creditors reluctant to purchase debts in the first place. Governments therefore have incentives to earn reputations that they will pay off their debts in the future. Acquiring such a reputation can be costly because it might well require making apparently unnecessary payments to debts incurred before the current government took office. Compensating such historical debt holders can seem unjust to current taxpayers, but it may be necessary for the long-run health of a republic.
4. *It can help to sustain distinct reputations with different parties.* It is challenging for a government simultaneously to sustain distinct reputations with disparate parties. This challenge manifested itself when the US federal government struggled to confront British trade restrictions from 1790 to 1812 and in the early 1840s when it wanted its actions to send separate nuanced messages to foreign and domestic creditors as well as various state governments.

5. *Confused monetary-fiscal coordination creates costly uncertainties.* Fiscal and monetary policies are always coordinated and are always sustainable, even though they may be obscure. In the beginning, the United States coordinated them by adopting a commodity money standard and restricting states' and banks' ability to create fiduciary monies. Other arrangements are possible. You can have a monetary union without having a fiscal union. You may want a fiscal union even though you do not want a monetary union. Obscure coordination arrangements increase uncertainty in markets and among ordinary citizens.

II. The Math

A basic theory about how creditors value a government's debt starts with a sequence of one-period budget constraints $g_t + b_t = T_t + R^{-1}b_{t+1}$, or

$$b_t = s_t + R^{-1}b_{t+1}, \quad t \geq 0,$$

where $R > 1$ is the gross return on one-period inflation-indexed government debt, b_t is the stock of one-period pure discount (zero coupon) inflation-indexed bonds issued at $t - 1$ and falling due in period t, and g_t, T_t, and $s_t = T_t - g_t$ are government expenditures net of interest payments on the debt, total tax collections, and the government net-of-interest surplus, respectively. Iterate the government budget constraints for $t \geq 0$ backward to get

$$b_t = -R(s_{t-1} + Rs_{t-2} + \cdots + R^{t-1}s_0) + R^t b_0, \quad t \geq 1,$$

which states that large government *debts* come from accumulating big government *deficits* $-s_{t-j}$, $j = 1, \ldots, t$, as well as rolling over any initial debt b_0. But sustaining large government debts requires prospects of big government *surpluses* in the future. To appreciate this, iterate the budget constraints for $t \geq 0$ forward to get

$$b_t = \sum_{j=0}^{\infty} R^{-j} s_{t+j},$$

which states that the value of government debt equals the discounted present value of current and future government surpluses. Recognizing that future surpluses can be forecast only imperfectly induces us to replace s_{t+j} with $E_{t-1}s_{t+j}$, where $E_{t-1}(\cdot)$ temporarily denotes the public's forecast based on time $t - 1$ information known by prospective bondholders at time $t - 1$ to be pertinent for forecasting future surpluses. (Remember that these one-period bonds are purchased at time $t - 1$ and redeemed at time t, so it is information at time $t - 1$ that is pertinent for valuing bonds that mature at t.) Then the value of government debt becomes

$$b_t = \sum_{j=0}^{\infty} R^{-j} E_{t-1} s_{t+j}. \quad (1)$$

To get practical implications from the bond pricing equation (1) requires a theory about how people forecast the present discounted value of the government surpluses dedicated to servicing its debt. In situations like this, Hansen and Sargent (1980) joined Muth (1960, 1961), Lucas and Prescott (1971, 1974), and Lucas (1972, 1976) in applying the economist's venerable device of modeling decisions as optimization problems (see also Sargent 1971, 1977, 1979). When the decision is to choose a sequence of forecasts, this approach is said to impose *rational expectations*.[3] Evidently, optimal forecasts depend on the statistical properties of the object to be forecast.

Suppose that the actual process for the government surplus is the first component of an $m \times 1$ vector stochastic process y_t that is governed by a moving average representation, so that $s_t = e_s y_t$, where e_s is a selection vector and

$$y_t = \sum_{j=0}^{\infty} C_j w_{t-j}, \quad (2)$$

where $\{w_t\}$ is an m-dimensional martingale difference sequence and the information set J_t known to prospective bondholders at t is generated by $w_t, w_{t-1}, \ldots$. Assume that $Ew_t w_t' = I$. Here w_t constitutes "news" that arrives at time t. Following Hansen, Roberds, and Sargent (1991), it is convenient to write the first equation of (2) as

$$s_t = \sum_{j=0}^{\infty} \sigma_j w_{t-j} = \sigma(L) w_t, \quad (3)$$

where L is the lag operator meaning $L^j w_t = w_{t-j}$ and $\sigma(L) = \sum_{j=0}^{\infty} \sigma_j L^j$. Assume that the spectral density matrix $S_y(\omega) = C(e^{-i\omega})C(e^{i\omega})^T$ has full rank m for almost all $\omega \in (-\pi, \pi]$, a condition equivalent with y being stochastically nonsingular.[4]

It is revealing to compute the value of bonds under rational expectations in two steps by applying an argument that invokes the law of iterated expectations. First, temporarily give bond purchasers "too much" information by replacing the subjective expectation $E_{t-1}(s_{t+j}) \equiv E(s_{t+j}|J_{t-1})$ in equation (1) with $E(s_{t+j}|J_t)$, the mathematical expectation of s_{t+j} condi-

[3] Muth (1960, 1961) began this approach. Situations in which those people who most influence prices forecast optimally can themselves be the outcomes either of long experiences from individuals' statistical learning processes (see Bray and Kreps 1987; Marcet and Sargent 1989) or else of a competitive process that somehow encourages the survival of the fittest (Blume and Easley 2006). See Sargent (2008) for implications for macroeconomics.

[4] Stochastic nonsingularity means that no component of y can be expressed exactly as a linear combination of past, present, and future values of other components of y.

tional on the history of shocks w_t, w_{t-1}, ... in equation (2). Under this expanded information assumption, Hansen and Sargent (1980) showed in another context that[5]

$$b_t = \sum_{j=0}^{\infty} \kappa_j w_{t-j}, \tag{4}$$

or

$$b_t = \kappa(L) w_t,$$

where

$$\kappa(z) = \frac{z\sigma(z) - R^{-1}\sigma(R^{-1})}{z - R^{-1}}, \tag{5}$$

where z is a scalar complex variable and $\kappa(z)$ is the z-transform of the $\{\kappa_j\}$ sequence.[6] Next, to reduce information to the set w_{t-1}, w_{t-2}, ... actually available to prospective bondholders when they purchase the bonds at time $t-1$, we follow Hansen et al. (1991), who establish that the requirement that b_t be measurable with respect to time $t-1$ information J_{t-1} information implies that $\kappa_j = \kappa(0) = 0$, which in light of equation (5) requires that[7]

$$\sigma(R^{-1}) = 0. \tag{6}$$

Equation (6) has a natural economic interpretation: it states that the present value of the moving average coefficients for the net-of-interest surplus must equal zero. This condition renders the value of debt maturing at t measurable with respect to J_{t-1}.

Equations (2), (3), (4), (5), and (6) encode cross-equation restrictions that are hallmarks of rational expectations econometrics: the coefficients κ_j that tell the response of debt b_t to past shocks w_{t-j} are nonlinear functions of the discount factor R^{-1} and the coefficients σ_j in the moving average representation for the net-of-interest surplus s_t.[8]

Equations (2), (3), (4), (5), and (6) illustrate much of the logical structure and empirical power of rational expectations econometrics:[9]

- Current and lagged values of all components of the shock vector

[5] Hansen et al. (1991) extend this formula to handle the interesting case in which the first difference of s_t is a linear combination of a stationary vector process y_t like (2). See Hansen (2011) and Hansen and Sargent (2013) for further generalizations.

[6] The numerator of $\kappa(z)$ is designed to contain a zero that cancels the pole at R^{-1}, i.e., the zero in the denominator at R^{-1}. This makes the Taylor series and Laurent series expansions of $\kappa(z)$ coincide.

[7] Related measurability requirements play a key role in Aiyagari et al. (2002).

[8] See Sargent (1981) for the role of those cross-equation restrictions in other contexts.

[9] This is the theme of the papers in the volume about rational expectations econometrics edited by Lucas and Sargent (1981), especially the introductory essay. Hansen (1982) and Hansen and Sargent (1991) extended and refined rational expectations econometrics.

w_t that impinge on future surpluses s_{t+j} appear in the debt valuation equation (4).

- The shock response coefficients κ_j in equation (4) for the value of debt would change if government policy were permanently to alter the σ_j's in (3) that characterize the stochastic process for the government surplus. This technical finding is the heart of the influential critique of pre–rational expectations econometric evaluation procedures forcefully stated by Lucas (1976). Section III below argues that George Washington and Alexander Hamilton understood that to increase the value of US government debt they would have to break the stochastic process (3) for $\{s_t\}$ that had prevailed in the United States in the 1780s.
- The same basic theory applies when there are prospects for default. For example, each period, suppose that there is a probability $\pi \in (0, 1)$ that the government will write off a fraction $\phi \in (0, 1)$ of its debt.[10] Let $\tilde{R}^{-1}$ be the discount factor applying to default-free debt. Then a "certainty equivalent" discount factor R^{-1} that compensates a risk-neutral creditor for holding default-prone debt is

$$R^{-1} = \tilde{R}^{-1}[(1 - \pi) + \pi(1 - \phi)]. \tag{7}$$

With this adjustment to the discount factor, the preceding theory applies. Bigger haircuts ϕ and higher probabilities of default π lower the discount factor R^{-1} and thereby reduce the value of the debt.[11]

- Hansen et al. (2007) opened the way to extending the theory to incorporate variable discount factors that can absorb some of the effects of the news shocks w_t.
- Important technicalities impede linking our theory to vector autoregressions. Shocks in vector autoregressions for y_t must be in the Hilbert space spanned by $y_t, y_{t-1}, \ldots$ (see Sims 1980). These so-called fundamental shocks emerge from constructing the Wold moving average representation for y_t that is associated with the limit of a sequence of finite-order vector autoregressions as the lag length is driven to $+\infty$. Hansen et al. (1991) show that the internal logic of the present value equation (1) and the associated restriction $\sigma(R^{-1}) = 0$ imply that the moving average (2) is not a Wold representation because the shocks $w_t, w_{t-1}, \ldots$ span a larger space than the linear space spanned by $y_t, y_{t-1}, \ldots$, and so the w_t shocks are not what would be recovered by running a vector autoregres-

[10] I assume that ϕ and π are constant and do not depend on the stochastic process for the net-of-interest surplus s_t.

[11] Arellano (2008) used related ideas to model sovereign risk.

sion. Hansen et al. (1991) discuss substantial implications of this fact for extracting econometrically testable implications from the theory.[12]

A. *Need for More Economic Theory?*

This piece of economics-plus-statistical forecasting theory forms the essence of the pricing model used by prospective buyers and sellers of government debt.[13] For the purposes of those buyers and sellers, it is enough to have a good-fitting statistical model of the stochastic process (3) governing the government surplus.

But for other purposes, a statistical model alone is inadequate. The model formed by equations (2), (3), (4), (5), and (6) is superficial because the government surplus process $\{s_t\}$ is itself the outcome of a political decision process.[14] The model summarizes but does not purport to explain the statistical properties of the surplus process (2)–(3) in terms of the balance of conflicting interests that actually created it.

Economic theory goes deeper by analyzing contending economic and political forces that actually produce a statistical regime. In economic theory, an agent is a constrained optimization problem. A model consists of a collection of constrained optimization problems. Theories of general equilibrium, games, and macroeconomics acquire power by deploying an equilibrium concept whose role is to organize disparate choice problems by casting them within a coherent environment.[15] In the presence of one or more large players—governments in this case—decisions of some agents typically impinge on the constraint sets of others and therefore on their incentives to make subsequent decisions. In such cases, the statistical process that represents an equilibrium outcome emerges jointly with agents' beliefs about what would happen in situations that they never face. Beliefs about those events have important

[12] Thus, there is a subtle relationship between the present value theory described in this section and causality in the sense of Granger (1969) and Sims (1972).

[13] It is highly simplified relative to papers that embody standard practice today. In particular, the assumption that the interest rate is risk-free and constant is a big oversimplification. See Lucas (1978), Harrison and Kreps (1979), Eaton and Gersovitz (1981), Hansen and Singleton (1983), Hansen and Richard (1987), Hansen and Jagannathan (1991), and Arellano (2008) and references that they cite and that cite them for extensions of the basic model that relax that assumption about the interest rate.

[14] The adjective "superficial" is descriptive, not critical.

[15] Kreps (1997) describes common features of the equilibrium concepts used in theories of games and general equilibrium. To understand the empirical observations in the US case study presented later in this paper might require going beyond this equilibrium concept to incorporate improvisation and adaptation in new ways that Kreps indicates at the end of his paper.

influences on outcomes that do happen.[16] Chari and Kehoe (1990), Stokey (1991), and Bassetto (2005) have explored and applied notions of equilibrium appropriate to situations in which a large government interacts with many atomistic private agents.

I will not formally use a single such model in the rest of this paper. But broad insights from this class of models shape virtually everything I detect in the fiscal and monetary history of the United States.

B. *A Humbling Message?*

Macro models use the standard equilibrium concept to produce statistical processes for things like the government surplus as outcomes. This is a powerful method for "explaining" objects like $\{s_t\}$. But the equilibrium concept can disable someone who proposes to improve outcomes. Why? Because the equilibrium already contains the best responses of all decision makers, including any government agents who inhabit the model.[17] Assuming that an equilibrium that explained the historical data can also be expected to "work" in the future puts a model builder in the position of not being able to recommend changes in policy precisely because he has understood the forces that have led policy makers to do what they do. The model builder's way of understanding them is to say that they were optimizing. And giving advice would imply that he thinks that they were not optimizing or were not well informed.[18]

C. *Modeling Reforms*

By an *environment*, economic theorists mean a list of agents, a specification of actions available to every agent, a timing protocol telling who acts when, and an information flow telling what is known, and when and by whom it is known. Some changes in an environment can amount to changes in institutions, for example, reassigning particular decisions

[16] Fudenberg and Levine (1993) and Sargent (2008) and the references there describe and apply notions of self-confirming equilibrium, a type of rational expectations equilibrium in which possibly erroneous beliefs about events that do not happen in equilibrium still have big effects on observed equilibrium outcomes.

[17] Goethe said it this way: "So divinely is the world organized that every one of us, in our place and time, is in balance with everything else."

[18] The issue of whether equilibrium models are normative or positive was raised at a general level by Sargent and Wallace (1976) and more specifically in the context of interpreting vector autoregressions by Sargent (1984).

The only time I saw Milton Friedman speechless was at a dinner party at Stanford in the mid-1980s. His close friend George Stigler trapped Friedman by asking him two questions. First, Stigler asked whether Friedman consulted for private businesses. Friedman said no, that because businessmen had more information and had already optimized, he had nothing useful to tell them. Then Stigler said, "Well that makes sense to me Milton, but then why are you always telling governments what to do?"

to an independent central bank or assigning particular taxes exclusively to states or exclusively to a central government within a federal system. This concept of equilibrium ties our hands by asserting that if you want to change outcomes, such as the government surplus process mentioned above, then you have to reform institutions, which can mean agreeing on a new constitution. This is subversive. Nevertheless, that is what economic theory teaches. George Washington and Alexander Hamilton knew it, and that is why they led a second political revolution, this one against the Articles of Confederation. They redesigned American institutions partly because they did not like the (equilibrium) $\{s_t\}$ process and the implied value of government debt that the Articles of Confederation regime had fostered.

III. The United States

Acknowledging that I lack anything approaching a complete model but highly prejudiced by a *class* of equilibrium models, I now pursue an informal pattern recognition exercise to organize historical events that occurred in the United States and that remind me of choices being faced now as Europe struggles to manage a common currency.[19] I see the authors of the Constitution in 1787 and the architects of our federal government's institutions and policies in 1790–92 to be wrestling with the implications of the government budget constraint (1), an equation that preoccupies both the United States and some European states today.[20]

A. *Victorious but in Default*

The United States emerged from the US War for Independence in 1783 with big debts and a constitution that disabled the US central government. The Articles of Confederation established a Continental Congress and an executive weak beyond the sweetest dreams of a contemporary American advocate of small government. The articles worked as intended to restrain the central government from taxing and spending. That outcome served the interests of some US citizens but not of others. It was not good for the Continental Congress's creditors. The Continental Congress lacked powers adequate to service its substantial foreign

[19] Maybe it is a pattern *imposition* exercise. I did not select facts out of the blue. You cannot get anywhere accepting a complete "democracy of facts," as Borges (1962) illustrated in his story about Funes the Memorius, who refused to impose patterns because he wanted to account for everything. My exercise amounts to pattern recognition with strong preconceptions. Prejudices help because data are limited.

[20] The remainder of this paper relies on empirical evidence assembled for Hall and Sargent (n.d.).

and domestic debts. To levy taxes, the central government required unanimous consent of 13 sovereign states.[21] To finance the war, the Continental Congress had printed IOUs in the forms of non-interest-bearing paper money ("bills of credit") as well as interest-bearing debt.[22] So had each of the 13 states. After the war, the states could levy taxes to service at least parts of their interest-bearing debts.[23] The central government could not. It regularly pleaded for contributions from the states, with at most limited success.[24] An outcome was that continental debts traded at deep discounts, and so did debts of many states. Paper currencies depreciated markedly.[25] Deprived of tax revenues, the Continental Congress tried to roll over its maturing debt and to pay interest falling due by borrowing more.[26] This became increasingly difficult as the 1780s unfolded. Ultimately, the Continental Congress stopped paying its creditors and watched interest payments in arrears grow in the form of new IOUs called "indents." Authority to levy tariffs, the most remunerative potential source of tax revenues, resided in the states. In 1781 and 1783, the Continental Congress asked the 13 states to ratify amendments to the Articles of Confederation that would have allowed it to impose a continental import duty whose proceeds were to be devoted entirely to servicing the continental debt. Each time, 12 states approved, but one state did not (Rhode Island the first time, New York the second), killing the amendments (see McDonald 1985, 170–71).

[21] Cournot (1897, chap. 9) constructed a model of a monopolist that buys complementary inputs from *n* monopolists. That model can be reinterpreted to explain how decision making by consensus leads to very inferior outcomes.

[22] Bills of credit were small-denomination circulating paper notes. They were not legal tender. Before the revolution, American colonies had issued paper notes declared to be legal tender, but the British government had prohibited them from being legal tender in an act of 1764.

[23] See Wood (2009) for an account of differing states' debt positions and how this fed into the politics. Also see Elkins and McKitrick (1993) for a comprehensive account of the political struggles associated with creating and running US institutions during the Washington administration.

[24] Mailath and Postlewaite (1990) and Chari and Jones (2000) explain why decentralized systems with voluntary participation cannot be relied on to provide public goods.

[25] The continental currency eventually declined to 1/40 or 1/100 of its initial value, but that inflation in the paper currency is not revealed by aggregate price indexes. David and Solar (1977, 17) report an authoritative price index for the United States during this period. An interesting thing about their series is that because the unit of account was in specie, the depreciation of the paper continental currency does not show up. It is an interesting contrast that during the US Civil War, the paper greenback displaced specie as the unit of account in most states that remained in the Union. California and Oregon were exceptions. Their courts refused to enforce the federal legal tender law, and they stayed on a specie standard.

[26] This ignites the dynamics that underlie the unpleasant arithmetic of Sargent and Wallace (1981).

B. Trade Policies

In the 1780s under the Articles of Confederation, the United States had 13 tariff policies and 13 trade policies. The states' main trading partner, Great Britain, discriminated against American shipping and American goods. Britain had done less of that before the revolution, but a foreseeable consequence of victory in the American revolution was that the 13 American states would be excluded from the British imperial trading system. Occasionally individual American states sought to retaliate against British discrimination, but their efforts were always undermined by neighboring states.[27] The British could play one US state against another.

C. Crisis and a Second Revolution

Milton Friedman said that countries confront problems only after they have become crises. In the 1780s, the huge interest-bearing debts and currencies that had been issued to finance the war set the stage for a prolonged fiscal crisis from the point of view of the government's creditors, if not its taxpayers. Measured at par (but not at the deeply discounted values then prevailing in the market), the ratio of continental plus state debt to GDP stood at about 40 percent, a massive debt at a time when the government could raise at most only a small percentage of GDP in taxes. About two-thirds of this debt had been incurred by the Continental Congress, the rest by the 13 states.[28] Sometimes fiscal crises have provoked political revolutions that renegotiate past promises and resettle accounts among taxpayers and government creditors, as they did in France in 1789 and the United States in 1787–88.[29]

IV. Restructuring Fiscal Institutions

To rearrange powers and incentives, the framers scrapped the original constitution, the Articles of Confederation, and wrote an entirely new one better designed to protect US government creditors.[30] The US Constitution realigned incentives and authorities in ways that (*a*) let the central government devote enough tax revenues to service debts that

[27] See Rakove (1997, chap. 2) and Irwin (2009) for the history and Cournot (1897, chap. 9) for the theory.

[28] Hamilton (1790) estimated that at the beginning of 1790, the total debt at par stood at $79 million, of which $25 million was owed by the states and $12 million was owed to foreigners.

[29] Sargent and Velde (1995) see the French Revolution through the lens of the government budget constraint.

[30] There is a grain of truth in a controversial interpretation of the framers' motives authored by Beard (1913).

the Continental Congress and the states had issued to pay for the war and (*b*) gave the central government exclusive authority to tax and regulate US international trade. That gave the federal government the tools to implement a national trade policy that could deter British discrimination against US citizens.

In the early days of the United States, the government budget constraint linked debt service capacity very closely to trade policy. That tariffs were the main source of federal revenues confronted the country with a choice that framed US politics from 1789 to 1815. Britain was the main potential trading partner of the United States. Raising revenues to fund US debt required sizable and reliable trade volumes with Britain, even if that meant restraining US reactions to British discrimination against US goods and ships. But because Washington and Hamilton and the Federalists put a high priority on faithfully servicing the US government's debt and thereby earning the United States a reputation for paying its bills, they made preserving a difficult peace with Britain a cornerstone of their policy. So they refrained from retaliating against British trade restrictions. Later, because they wanted to retaliate against British trade restrictions, Jefferson and Madison and the Republicans were willing to imperil trade volumes with Britain and to sacrifice federal tariff revenues. They were willing to do that even if it affected US creditors adversely. Irwin (2009) describes how choices about these tradeoffs can explain political outcomes in the United States both in the 1790s when the Federalists protected trade and peace and also after 1805 when the Republicans jeopardized trade and peace first with an embargo and then with the War of 1812 against Britain.[31]

A. *Reorganizing Fiscal Affairs*

Hamilton and the first Congress reorganized fiscal affairs first.[32] Dates reflect priorities. Congress created the Treasury Department on September 2, 1789, a Bank of the United States on February 25, 1791, and a US mint in the Coinage Act of April 2, 1792. On September 21, 1789, the Congress directed newly appointed Secretary of Treasury Alexander Hamilton to prepare a plan for "an adequate provision for the public credit." Hamilton delivered his *Report on Public Credit* to Congress on January 14, 1790. Congress accepted Hamilton's recommendations, including his proposal to nationalize the states' debts, in the Acts of August

[31] A theme of Wills (2002) is that James Madison overestimated the damage that an embargo could inflict on Britain and that he underestimated the damage that it would do to American commerce and the ties that bound New England to the Union.

[32] See Sylla (2009) for a comprehensive account and interesting interpretation of Hamilton's plans. Also see Wright (2008).

4 and August 5, 1790.[33] Those acts set out a detailed plan for rescheduling continental debt by selling a set of securities that Congress designed with Hamilton's advice. These new debts promised to pay specific sequences of payoffs denominated in a unit of currency called a "dollar," which in August 1790 was a silver coin issued by Spain.

Hamilton (1790) told Congress that honoring the Continental Congress's original promises to pay would drive down *prospective* returns on government debt by raising *ex post* returns relative to what had been expected during the 1780s when continental debt had traded at deep discounts.[34] He also argued that prospective returns could be lowered if private traders would come to regard government debt as a fully trusted obligation to the bearer, increasing its liquidity. Confirming Hamilton's expectations, discounts on continental and state bonds evaporated when news spread about the pro-administration outcome of the debate.[35]

B. *Discrimination and Liquidity*

An especially fascinating part of Hamilton's report is his response to James Madison's proposal to discriminate among current owners of continental bonds according to when they had purchased them (see Hamilton 1790). Motivated by concerns about fairness, Madison wanted to take away inordinate capital gains from people who had purchased continental bonds at discount; he also wanted to compensate former owners who had sold them at discount. Hamilton convinced Congress that such ex post discrimination would adversely affect the beliefs of

[33] Acts of the First Congress, second session, included the Act of August 4, 1790, making provision for the debt of the United States; the Act of August 5, 1790, to provide more effectually for the settlement of accounts between the United States and the individual states; and the Act of August 19, 1790, making further provision for the payment of the debts of the United States.

[34] Remember formula (7) for the discount factor.

[35] Hamilton had altered creditors' views about the government's "type." The situation of the new government in the United States in 1789 reminds me of an example about sovereign default in Bassetto (2005, sec. 4). Assume that a government with a dubious fiscal record leaves office and is replaced by a new government that is perfectly credible and dedicated to repay the debt. Despite the best intentions, whether or not the new government defaults is still influenced decisively by the private agents' beliefs. If they persist with beliefs that the new government will default, they will demand prohibitive interest rates, rendering even a well-meaning government eventually unable to meet its obligations at those rates. So to succeed the new government will have to implement good economic policies and also benefit from good (or lucky?) "expectations management," whatever that means. See Bassetto (2006).

prospective purchasers of government debt and would thereby damage liquidity and trust in the market for bearer government bonds.[36]

C. *Federal Bailout of States*

The United States began with a comprehensive bailout of the individual states when on August 4, 1790, the US Congress accepted Alexander Hamilton's proposal to nationalize (or "assume") states' debts. That completed a negotiation begun at the constitutional convention when authority to tax imports had been transferred from the states to the federal government. In exchange for acquiring that most important revenue source, the federal government agreed to bail out the states, a decision that realigned creditors' interests away from states and toward the federal government.[37] By converting creditors of the states into creditors of the central government, Hamilton converted those bondholders into advocates of a federal fiscal policy that devoted a substantial share of the proceeds of a revenue-raising tariff to servicing those bonds. A stated justification for nationalizing the states' debts was that most of them had been incurred to finance states' contributions to the national War for Independence. The US Treasury set up a system designed to account for each state's contributions to the Glorious Cause and to compensate them accordingly. It would have been prudent for subsequent lenders to appreciate that Congress had reasoned that it was states' contribution to that national enterprise that justified the 1790 bailout. Investors should not have interpreted it as a promise to bail out states in the future no matter what, but apparently some of them did, to their eventual regret (please see Sec. VI below).

D. *Why Pay?*

The government institutions that they designed and the decisions that Congress and the president made in 1790 and 1791 confirm that the framers intended fully to honor the debts that they had inherited from the Continental Congress. Making good on the promises originally made

[36] Although the Congress defeated Madison's proposal for discrimination, a related idea returned to affect the Madison administration two decades later during the War of 1812. Dewey (1912, 134) describes an act of March 24, 1814, that required the government retroactively to offer more favorable terms to previous creditors if subsequent issues garnered lower market prices.

Proposals to discriminate among creditors often surface during negotiations to reschedule debts. For example, there are proposals for private holders of Greek government debt to take substantial voluntary haircuts while nonprivate creditors are to be paid in full.

[37] McDonald (1985, 166–67) describes how in the early 1780s Superintendent of Finance Robert Morris tried but failed to organize the Continental Congress's domestic creditors as a nationalizing force.

to continental and state debt holders to finance the US War for Independence meant disappointing other expectations and breaking promises at least implicitly made about other dimensions of fiscal policy, for example, to keep taxes low. The deep discounts at which continental debts traded in the mid-1780s reflected traders' anticipations of those low-tax policies. Why, then, did the framers choose to keep some promises (ones to its creditors that had apparently already been substantially discounted) by breaking other promises (those to continental taxpayers) that had been protected by the Articles of Confederation?[38] If, as seems appropriate, we regard 1787 or 1789 as a new beginning—"time 0" in models of Ramsey plans and recursive mechanism design—then Ramsey models in the representative agent tradition of Lucas and Stokey (1983), Chari, Christiano, and Kehoe (1994), and Jones, Manuelli, and Rossi (1997) will not help us to answer that question. Those models typically advise a government to default on all initial public debts and thereby impose that least distorting of taxes, an unforeseen capital levy.[39] Other revolutionaries have done that,[40] but not the US framers. Their purpose in realigning authorities and interests was to affirm that a "deal is a deal," at least as far as concerned obligations to the government's creditors, if not to taxpayers.

To understand why Hamilton and Washington and other framers wanted to pay, we have to take into account heterogeneities of economic situations and consequent conflicting interests (see Meltzer and Richard 1981) as well as reputational considerations that are absent from these Ramsey models. The purposes for which those initial debts were incurred, the identities of the individual creditors, and the perceived adverse consequences of default all mattered in ways neglected at least by the three representative agent Ramsey models cited above.[41] Such Ram-

[38] The "why pay?" question has been sharply posed by Bulow and Rogoff (1989) and Kletzer and Wright (2000).

[39] Sometimes they have also done whatever they could to acquire net claims on the private sector in order to finance future expenditures efficiently. Paal (2000) describes how the Hungarian communists deliberately reset time 0 after World War II and acquired claims on the public by restarting the monetary system.

[40] Lenin and Trotsky and their admirers in Eastern Europe did that. The leaders of the French Revolution in 1789 did not, instead struggling valiantly for years to service the prerevolution debt until circumstances eventually forced them into a substantial default in 1797. See Sargent and Velde (1995).

[41] American politics and policies toward debt management in the aftermath of the US War for Independence differed strikingly, e.g., from those in Germany after World War I. Domestic creditors owned most of a very large government debt that Germany had accumulated during World War I, but then the Versailles treaty imposed big further debts on the German government in the form of huge and uncertain reparations payments to some of the victors. Politics in the United States after the War for Independence differed from those in Germany after World War I because the US foreign debt had come from the benevolence and trust of friends in France and Holland who had sent us resources during the war, not the vengeance of foreign powers that had defeated us, as was true in Germany. A hyperinflation produced consequences that allowed Germany to escape most

sey models help explain government policies after some political revolutions, but not those of the United States in 1789.

In paying those continental and state obligations, Secretary of Treasury Hamilton wanted the federal government to gain enduring access to domestic and international credit markets. That would expand options for financing temporary surges in government expenditures by borrowing, thereby allowing his successors to moderate the contemporary tax increases needed to finance those surges.[42] He also asserted that an outstanding stock of government debt earning a relatively risk-free return would foster the development of domestic credit markets, which he thought would be a boon to commerce and industry.[43]

E. *Monetary Arrangements*

Only after fiscal policy had been set on course in the Acts of August 4 and August 5, 1790, did Hamilton and the Congress then turn to monetary policy. Hamilton presented his report proposing a Bank of the United States on December 14, 1790, and his report proposing that the United States mint US silver and gold coins only on January 28, 1791. It was widely presumed that the United States would follow leading European countries in embracing a commodity money standard. So the remaining monetary policy decisions for the framers simply involved choices of coin sizes and of a seigniorage rate for the mint.[44]

F. *A National Bank?*

After a tense debate during which James Madison argued that a federally chartered monopoly bank would be unconstitutional, the Congress

of those reparations payments, albeit at the cost of tremendous collateral damage in the form of a massive redistribution away from German nominal creditors to German nominal debtors as the value of the German mark depreciated from its pre–World War I value by a factor of 10^{12} by November 1923. Sargent (1982) describes how Germany abruptly ended its hyperinflation by using a version of the simple theory (1) for valuing government debt. Before November 1923, the most important component of Germany's government surplus process s_t was an inflation tax. The hyperinflation was arrested by adopting policies that adjusted government expenditures and taxes, along with fortifying a central bank that would refuse to levy the inflation tax.

[42] That is, he wanted the option to issue debt in the fashion made explicit by Secretary of the Treasury Albert Gallatin in his 1807 report to Congress (see Dewey 1912, 128), a policy later formalized in the tax-smoothing models of Barro (1979) and Aiyagari et al. (2002)

[43] See Krishnamurthy and Vissing-Jorgensen (2010) and references cited there for modern arguments about good effects fostered by a stock of safe government debt. See Brewer (1989) and North and Weingast (1989) for accounts of the flexibility that the government of Britain had achieved by successfully implementing fiscal institutions that Hamilton admired. An implication of Bassetto (2005, 2006) is that even with good institutions and well-intentioned policy makers, sometimes there are multiple equilibria, and we need luck or skill to select among them.

[44] They set the seigniorage rate to zero, a decision called "free coinage."

awarded an exclusive 20-year federal charter to a Bank of the United States.[45] The bank was mostly privately owned and mostly operated in the interests of its private shareholders, though it did serve as fiscal agent of the federal government and as a depository for federal revenues. It also issued bank notes that circulated as currency and were convertible into specie on demand. It issued notes only in exchange for short-term loans to the federal government or very short-term commercial loans promising low risk. It avoided real estate and other long-term and risky loans. In these ways, it could be said to implement the "real-bills" regime of Adam Smith (1806), whose writings on the subject very probably influenced Hamilton.[46]

G. A Mint

The framers seem to have regarded monetary policy as a sideshow to be tidied up only after a sound fiscal policy had been secured. The Act of August 4, 1790 (1 Statutes, 138), had prescribed detailed procedures for funding US and states' debts. New federal IOUs were to be denominated in dollars, which on August 4, 1790, meant Spanish dollars because at that time there were no US dollars. In a report on coinage delivered in May 1791, Hamilton proposed that the United States manufacture a silver dollar defined to have the same silver content as a Spanish dollar.[47] The Mint Act of April 2, 1792, accepted Hamilton's recommendations virtually intact by creating a US dollar. In terms of the fundamental determinant of its value, namely, its metal content, the US dollar was a copy of the Spanish dollar, the only difference being that it had American and not Spanish "advertisements" stamped on its

[45] Madison changed his mind when, serving as president 20 years later, the bank's charter came up for renewal and opponents of the bank brought up Congressman Madison's 1791 arguments to use against his administration's request to renew the bank's charter. Although he changed sides, Madison was on the losing side both times, as Congress refused to renew the bank's charter in 1811, causing the United States to finance the War of 1812 with its long-standing fiscal agent having just been abolished and scrambling to improvise alternative arrangements for acquiring short-term credit. Whether to have a national bank serving as fiscal agent of the federal government is something that statesmen such as James Madison and Henry Clay changed their minds about, and so did the country. The charter of the first Bank of the United States was not renewed in 1811, and neither was the charter of the second bank in 1836.

[46] Smith's real-bills doctrine stresses benefits from permitting a government-owned or private financial intermediary to issue circulating notes that are backed by safe evidences of private indebtedness. To Smith, "real" meant relatively risk-free. Smith pointed to efficiency gains that could be gathered by allowing paper notes backed by safe private evidences of indebtedness to circulate and displace precious metals that would otherwise serve as media of exchange. See Sargent and Wallace (1982) for an analysis of pros and cons of the real-bills doctrine.

[47] Section 9 of the Act of April 2, 1792, states that each dollar is "to be of the value of a Spanish milled dollar as the same is now current."

sides. In terms of essential economic forces, whether or not the United States actually issued these dollars was incidental.[48]

H. Outcomes

The Appendix displays important outcomes in graphs of data taken mostly from early reports of the US Treasury. Deep discounts on the continental debt evaporated, and the federal government successfully rescheduled its debt (again see eq. [7] for the discount factor). Tariffs constituted virtually all federal revenues. About 2 percent of GDP was collected in federal taxes annually during the 1790s. About 40 percent of those revenues were used to service the debt. Under Hamilton and his Federalist successors, the debt was serviced and the principal rolled over, but substantial economic growth allowed the debt/GDP ratio to decline more or less continuously until the War of 1812, except for an increment used to finance some of the $15 million paid to Napoleon Bonaparte for Louisiana.[49] In 1790, a big "fiscal space" (see Ghosh et al. 2011) for the United States was provided by prospects for rapid population and economic growth, prospects that were realized in the 25 years after 1790.

V. Following Through?

Timing protocols that prevail in a democratic society open enduring issues about the roles of commitments, precedents, and reputations. Expectations about *future* governments' decisions influence prices and quantities *today*, but today's citizens and policy makers cannot bind future citizens to prescribed courses of action.[50] Decisions made in 1790 and 1791 were just the beginning of the great American fiscal and

[48] The US mint functioned as European mints typically did in those days. The mint stood ready to sell on demand at a fixed price, but did not purchase, gold or silver coins in exchange for gold or silver bullion, respectively. If you wanted to purchase coins from the mint, you took your bullion to the mint. The mint assayed the metal and then forged and stamped coins that it returned to you. If you wanted to melt the coins to retrieve the bullion, you could melt them yourself or you could export or sell the coins to private parties for specie.

[49] To put the magnitudes in perspective, at par value, the total continental and state debt that Hamilton rescheduled in 1790 was about $79 million, which at that time was about 40 percent of GDP, an estimate subject to substantial uncertainty. The Louisiana Purchase was a good bargain for the United States.

[50] Kydland and Prescott (1977) delineated this tension. See Klein and Rios-Rull (2003), Debortoli and Nunes (2007), and Klein, Krusell, and Rios-Rull (2011) for a small sample of an important literature in macroeconomics that uses Markov perfect equilibria to study quantitatively how outcomes under a sequential timing protocol differ from those under a timing protocol that awards a government the ability to choose once and for all. See Battaglini and Coate (2008) for a political-economic equilibrium under a sequential voting protocol.

monetary adventure. Conjectures about how their successors would complete or modify their plans vitally concerned the framers.[51] They had sought to create institutions (timing protocols?) and precedents (reputations?) that they hoped would limit subsequent choices in ways that would induce their successors to choose good public policies. Subsequent US history witnessed tax revolts (an armed rebellion against the federal government in 1794 western Pennsylvania when farmers protested a federal excise tax on whisky) and tariff and trade regulation revolts (in 1814 when New England states threatened to dissolve the Union, and in the early 1830s when President Jackson faced down John C. Calhoun and South Carolina during the nullification crisis). Struggles over how much the federal government should tax and spend and regulate continued until the US Civil War and beyond.

It is useful at this point to mention examples of how an administration's decisions interacted with those of its predecessors and those of its successors.

A. *Federal and State Paper Monies?*

The authors of the Constitution and their supporters abhorred paper money and the sorry state to which American domestic, if not foreign, credit had been reduced. That attitude set the stage for a debate at the constitutional convention about which powers over monetary standards to assign to state and federal governments and which to deny them. Delegates to the convention agreed to prohibit *state* governments from issuing bills of credit or otherwise make a paper currency a legal tender.[52] What about the *federal* government? Preliminary drafts of the Constitution had given the federal Congress the right to issue bills of credit. Thus, even though the convention had already agreed explicitly to forbid states from issuing paper money, on the morning of August 16, 1787, the eighth clause of the seventh article in the draft of the Constitution said that "the legislature of the United States shall have the power to borrow money and emit bills on the credit of the United States." Madison's notes of the convention's proceedings on August 16, 1787, record a debate about a motion to strike out the clause authorizing Congress to emit bills of credit. The motion carried 9 states to 2.

[51] At the convention on June 26, 1787, James Madison (1956) said, "In framing a system which we wish to last for ages, we shd. not lose sight of the changes which ages will produce." In 1811 Secretary of the Treasury Albert Gallatin told Congress, "To meet these loans in the future we must depend on coming prosperity and the wisdom of successors; that is, favorable circumstances and rigid economy" (quoted in Dewey 1912, 129).

[52] Article I, Sec. 10, includes the following restrictions: "No State shall enter into any Treaty, Alliance, or Confederation; grant Letters of Marque and Reprisal; coin Money; emit Bills of Credit; make any Thing but gold and silver Coin a Tender in Payment of Debts."

Three contributions to the August 16 debate especially fascinate me. (1) James Wilson's clear statements stressing the ex ante advantages in terms of promoting credit to be reaped by denying future government decision makers the authority to take actions that would occasionally tempt them ex post; (2) George Mason's and Edmund Randolph's statements urging the convention to appreciate the advantages of reserving for future decision makers enough flexibility to deal with contingencies of a kind that could not be foreseen in 1787; and (3) Madison's remark that withholding the authority to make government bills of credit legal tender would be sufficient to restrain potential abuses.[53]

Partly influenced by their understanding of that August 16, 1787, debate, during the first three-quarters of the nineteenth century, many Americans believed that the framers had intended to shut the door on the federal government's issuing a paper legal tender and that the fact that the majority of the delegates did not go further and explicitly prohibit the federal government from issuing bills of credit simply reflected the constitutional convention delegates' presumption that powers not explicitly awarded should be understood to be denied to Congress.[54] An extensive review of the documentary record convinced Bancroft (1886) that the framers' intent was clearly not to allow Congress to make a paper currency a legal tender.[55]

B. *What Kind of Currency Union?*

Before 1789, the 13 states already had joined a currency union. All used the Spanish dollar. Article 1, Section 8, of the US Constitution gives the federal Congress the exclusive power "to coin Money, regulate the Value thereof, and of foreign Coin, and fix the Standard of Weights and Measures." As we saw in Section V.A, the Constitution expressly prohibited states from issuing paper currency, and most believed that prohibition extended to the federal government. The federal government only mod-

[53] See Bancroft (1886) for histories of legal tender acts in colonial America and of the framers' aversion to making paper monies legal tender. Madison stood true on this matter. As president from 1809 to 1817, he presided over an administration that issued federal bills of credit to finance most expenditures for the War of 1812 but did not make them legal tender.

[54] Sustaining this tradition, the Confederacy did not make its paper currency a legal tender.

[55] Bancroft's review of the evidence was prompted by what he regarded as the Supreme Court majority's flagrant disregard of the historical record in deciding the 1884 legal tender case *Juilliard v. Greenman.* The court reasoned that because Congress had the power to pay debts, it could do so by any means not expressly prohibited by the Constitution; that little attention needed to be paid the debates and votes at the constitutional convention because it was difficult to glean a consensus from them; that Congress's power to borrow money included the power to issue obligations in any appropriate form, including hand-to-hand currency; and that the authority to issue legal tender notes accompanied the right of coinage (see Dewey 1912, 366–67).

estly and temporarily circumvented that implicit limitation by allowing the Bank of the United States to issue circulating notes in exchange for short-term government debts.[56] It took longer for the states to circumvent the restriction.[57] In January 1837, in *Briscoe v. Bank of Kentucky*, the majority of the US Supreme Court, including newly appointed Chief Justice Taney, decided that state-chartered and state-owned banks had the right to issue paper bank notes (see Howe 2007, chap. 11). The real-bills reasoning of Adam Smith (1806) and Sargent and Wallace (1982) or the Modigliani-Miller reasoning of Wallace (1981) indicates how this decision effectively disarmed the Article I, Section 10, prohibition against states' issuing bills of credit by allowing state banks to purchase state bonds with their circulating bank notes. After that and until Congress taxed them out of existence during the Civil War, a multitude of currencies circulated within and across states during what has been mislabeled a "free-banking era."[58] Many such currencies circulated simultaneously with fluctuating rates of exchange that reflected probabilities that state-chartered bank notes could be converted on demand into specie. So before the US Civil War from 1861 to 1865, we had a currency union in one sense: the precious metals were the unit of account throughout the Union. But in another sense we did not: we had multiple currencies that presented citizens with choices about holding currencies bearing different risks and returns. There was no lender of last resort, no deposit insurance, and no presumption of federal bailouts of banks' depositors. All that stood behind those notes was the prudence of bank managers promoted by what Bagehot (1920) called the "preservative apprehension" of owners of bank notes.[59]

So if the framers intended to establish a currency union, they had at best mixed success, at least before the Civil War. And if they had wanted a currency union, it apparently would have been based on a commodity

[56] Congress refused to renew the bank's charter in 1811.

[57] Actually, some state-chartered banks were issuing notes before Congress chartered the first Bank of the United States.

[58] Free banking—in the sense of free entry—did not prevail. Most banks had to have state charters. Many of those state bank charters contained explicit provisions requiring the bank to make loans to the state or to buy bonds issued to fund canals, railroads, or turnpikes. Most of the assets that these banks purchased with notes were loans and discounts. However, banks that operated under so-called free-banking laws were required to purchase state bonds to back their notes.

[59] See Rolnick and Weber (1983, 1984). With multiple private media of exchange bearing different and fluctuating rates of return, issuers usually accepted (but did not redeem) the demand liabilities of others. An outcome was that issuers typically wanted to redeem and clear notes issued by other banks in order to augment their holdings of specie (or "lawful money"). From the 1820s to the 1850s, the Suffolk Bank of Boston successfully administered a private note-clearing operation for banks from all over New England. The Suffolk Bank managed a private "currency union" in the sense that notes of New England banks circulated at par throughout the region. See Weber (2009).

money, not a managed fiat currency like the one we have in the United States today.

I now turn to continuing controversies about the scope of the fiscal union that the framers established in August 1790.

VI. What Kind of Fiscal Union?

From the start of the republic in 1789 until the Civil War, Americans continued to dispute the proper scope and magnitude of federal tax, spend, transfer, and regulation policies. Interests that coalesced around the great Whig statesman Henry Clay's American System in the 1830s advocated federal expenditures on infrastructure projects—roads, canals, railroads, universities—public goods that they argued merited national fiscal support. A coalition of interests with strong support in the southern states blocked most such measures.[60] McPherson (1988, sec. III, chap. 14) documents how the Thirty-Seventh Congress (1861–62) seized the occasion of the secession of most slave states to reorder the federal union along lines that fulfilled many of Clay's goals. On July 1, 1862, the Congress passed the Internal Revenue Act, which among other things imposed the first federal income tax. On that same day, the Congress passed the Pacific Railroad Act awarding public lands and federal loans to companies that would construct intercontinental railroads. On July 2, 1862, Congress passed the Morrill Act awarding grants of federal land for establishing what came to be known as land grant colleges.[61] Earlier, similar legislation had been defeated by a Democratic Party, now decimated by the loss of its core to the Confederacy, that had wanted a weaker federal union than Clay and Lincoln. The seceding states expressed those preferences when they wrote a Confederate Constitution that in important ways more closely resembled the Articles of Confederation than the US Constitution. It took 4 years of awful civil war to force rebels to accept not only Abraham Lincoln's interpretation of what it meant for all men to have been "created equal" but also the type of federal union that Hamilton and Washington had begun and that Abraham Lincoln preserved and extended.

Another federal bailout of the states?—A sequel to Hamilton's 1790 bailout of the states' debts provides another example of how fiscal crises can provoke enduring institutional changes, this time at the level of individual states.[62] Today, many US state constitutions require state govern-

[60] Those southern interests were enthusiastic about using federal resources to pursue military adventures, such as the war in Mexico opposed by Abraham Lincoln and other Whigs, through which the United States acquired territories for building additional slave states and senators.

[61] The Congress also passed a law granting federal land to settlers ("homesteaders").

[62] One of Milton Friedman's favorites was a "law of unintended consequences."

ments to balance their budgets annually. Before the 1840s, state constitutions of US states did not impose year-by-year balanced budgets. Adams (1887) tells how, in response to adverse fiscal occurrences in the late 1830s and early 1840s, many states rewrote their constitutions to require balanced budgets annually.[63] Here is the story.

During the 30 years after 1789, citizens debated whether the federal government should or could finance public infrastructure projects. Before the Civil War, they decided that it could not. In response to a string of presidential vetoes of public works appropriations, state governments assumed responsibility for public works projects. After 1829, many state governments ran large government deficits, substantial parts of which were justified at the time because they were said to be deficits on capital account, not current account. The logic was that those state bonds had been issued to help finance public or private infrastructure projects. People advanced the theory that those bonds would be self-financing because ultimately they would promote growth and larger state government tax receipts in the forms of fees or taxes on increased land values. Belief in that theory allowed state bonds to be sold widely. Some were purchased by Europeans who were partly convinced by the self-finance theory and who also apparently mistakenly understood them to carry as much investor protection as federal bonds, which had earned a good reputation through a sustained record of having been honored after the wars of independence and 1812. And investors in state bonds knew that the federal government had comprehensively bailed out state debts at the beginning of the republic. Also, Article IV, Section 1, of the US Constitution mandates strong protection for owners of state debts: "Full Faith and Credit shall be given in each State to the public Acts, Records, and judicial Proceedings of every other State. And the Congress may by general Laws prescribe the Manner in which such Acts, Records and Proceedings shall be proved, and the Effect thereof." But foreign investors in state bonds may not have noticed weakened investor protection created by the Eleventh Amendment to the Constitution, passed in 1793 after a citizen of one state had taken a grievance against another state into a federal court. The Eleventh Amendment disarms the investor protection originally guaranteed by Article I, Section 1, by stating, "The Judicial power of the United States shall not be construed to extend to any suit in law or equity, commenced or prosecuted against one of the United States by Citizens of another State, or by Citizens or Subjects of any Foreign State."

For European and other bondholders, the story did not end happily. During a recession at the end of the 1830s, many states defaulted (see

[63] Those new constitutions thereby mandated that states forgo the efficiency gains of tax smoothing delineated by Barro (1979) and Aiyagari et al. (2002).

Scott 1893; Ratchford 1941). European bondholders then learned that the Eleventh Amendment deprived them and other creditors of American states of protection in federal courts. During the 1840s, Congress debated but ultimately rejected proposals for the federal government to pay those state debts. During the congressional debates, advocates of a bailout recited the precedent set by Hamilton's 1790 bailout of the states. But opponents successfully argued that Hamilton had bailed out state debts incurred for a glorious national purpose, while the debts of the early 1840s had been incurred for disparate causes to finance local projects. That and other arguments led Congress to refuse to bail out the state debts.

This episode cost the United States a hard-earned high-quality reputation for all US government debt, federal as well as state, and cast long reputational shadows in two directions. It seems that the international bond markets' response to these state bond failures did not immediately include an inclination to adopt a nuanced view that discriminated finely between the creditworthiness of federal and state authorities. For years, the reputation of federal credit in Europe suffered along with that of the states.

But the Congress's decision not to bail out the states had other, arguably more beneficial, consequences for the country. A legacy of the Congress's decision was that in the 1840s more than half of the US states rewrote their state constitutions to require year-by-year balanced budgets. This is yet another example of fiscal crises that have produced the lasting institutional changes that we sometimes call revolutions.[64]

Did the Congress do the right thing in refusing to assume those state debts? There is a strong case to be made that it did: at the cost of temporarily sacrificing the federal government's hard-earned good reputation with international creditors who were unable or unwilling to distinguish between the repayment records of federal and state governments, that decision succeeded in establishing a strong reputation of

[64] See Wallis and Weingast (2005). As noted, the Eleventh Amendment to the US Constitution stated that state debts cannot be enforced in federal courts. However, debts of municipal corporations and counties are enforceable in state and federal courts. Adams (1887) claimed that this system of arrangements for protecting investors and the balanced budget restrictions in state constitutions explain the marked shift in expenditures and debts from states to local and municipal and county governments during the nineteenth century. Wallis (2000, 2001) has effectively taken up this theme.

The story does not end here. Section 4 of the Fourteenth Amendment to the US Constitution says, "The validity of the public debt of the United States, authorized by law, including debts incurred for payment of pensions and bounties for services in suppressing insurrection or rebellion, shall not be questioned. But neither the United States nor any State shall assume or pay any debt or obligation incurred in aid of insurrection or rebellion against the United States, or any claim for the loss or emancipation of any slave; but all such debts, obligations and claims shall be held illegal and void." The Fourteenth Amendment strives simultaneously to protect the reputation of federal debt and to eradicate the reputation of state debts issued by Confederate states.

the federal government vis-à-vis the states. The Congress told the states not to expect the federal government to backstop their profligacy.[65] To put the point bluntly, if by bailing out those state debts the federal government had set up expectations that it would back up state loans in the future, that would have exposed the United States to adverse consequences such as ones that Kareken and Wallace (1978) warned about in another context, namely, the insurance of financial institutions. Kareken and Wallace taught that underpriced government insurance of deposits of inadequately regulated financial intermediaries provides incentives for those intermediaries to become as big as possible and as risky as possible. That will almost surely put the government into the position of eventually having to bail them out. Therefore, Kareken and Wallace said that if you want to extend deposit insurance, you had better regulate financial intermediaries' portfolios. Extending and applying the Kareken and Wallace logic to federal bailout of states, in exchange for offering such insurance, a federal bailout of the states would have set the United States on the road to extended federal control of states' fiscal policies. And where would that have ended? With federal control of cities too?[66] Without Congress's 1840s refusal to bail out the states, it is probable that those state constitutions would never have been rewritten to mandate year-by-year balanced budgets.

VII. Lessons for Now?

For the type of government we had under the Articles of Confederation in the 1780s—a weak fiscal union unlikely to pay its creditors what they had been promised—those deeply discounted continental bonds had been fairly priced in the 1780s. Hamilton and Washington had set out to change the government's "type" by realigning interests in ways that would induce the United States to pay what it had promised earlier and would promise later. And Hamilton wanted the market to price the bonds accordingly (via formula [7] for the discount factor again). Hamilton set out to manipulate current and prospective public creditors' expectations about whether the government would honor its bonds the only way he knew: by creating a fiscal union with institutions and interests aligned in ways that would increase the actual probability that the federal government would pay. The framers' purpose in creating

[65] See Fudenberg and Kreps (1987) for how difficult it can be to sustain distinct reputations with multiple parties. Another example of this difficulty might be that in the arrangements and decisions that it had set up to pay federal and state debts in the 1790s, the United States led by the Federalists in the 1790s had set precedents that inadvertently created expectations on the part of state creditors that it would backstop their profligacy.

[66] Related issues may return to the United States soon: will the federal government bail out high-debt states? Should state income tax be deductible on federal tax returns, thereby administering a transfer from the frugal states to the profligate states?

that fiscal union was not primarily to facilitate a monetary union, a distinct project about which they revealed substantial ambivalence in their subsequent indecision about whether to charter a national bank or whether instead to foster competition among private currencies issued by state-chartered banks.

In terms of fiscal arrangements, the European Union today has features reminiscent of the United States under the Articles of Confederation. The power to tax lies with the member states. Unanimous consent by member states is required for many important European Union–wide fiscal actions. Reformers in Europe today seek to redesign these aspects of European institutions, but so far the temporal order in which they have sought to rearrange institutions has evidently differed from early US experience in key respects. The United States nationalized fiscal policy first, and for the US framers, monetary policy did not mean managing a common fiat currency, or maybe even having a common currency at all. The European Union has first sought to centralize arrangements for managing a common fiat currency and until now has not wanted a fiscal union. And to begin its fiscal union, the United States carried out a comprehensive bailout of the government debts of the individual states. So far, at least, the European Union does not have a fiscal union, and few statesmen now openly call for a comprehensive bailout by the European Union of the debts owed by governments of the member states.

Especially because of the contentious and obscure state of politics influencing monetary and fiscal policy in the United States today, an American is certainly not qualified to advise European citizens about what lessons, if any, to draw from the story about how the United States created a fiscal union. To ferret out useful lessons, it would be important to identify circumstances in Europe now that match those of the United States then and circumstances that differ. The United States created its fiscal union at a time when the vast majority of people worked and lived on farms and when a substantial minority were slaves. People were much poorer then than now. Life expectancies were so very much shorter then than now that few working people lived long enough or ever earned enough to be able to stop working much before they died. Doctors and medicine often did more harm than good, so it was probably better that most people could not afford them. Deferred compensations, mostly for military service (pensions) but also some for land confiscated from Native Americans, were the only legal entitlements to government-financed transfer payments. Most people could not vote. The federal government was small, and it redistributed only a small fraction of GDP. In peacetime in the first two decades of the United States, federal expenditures averaged 1 or 2 percent of GDP, and in the beginning in the 1790s the federal government allocated 40 percent of its tax revenues to servicing the federal debt. The government debt that the Congress and president nationalized in 1790 had been incurred for a widely endorsed national cause.[67] And 50 years later, when Congress refused another massive federal bailout of state debts, its actions proved that the purpose for which those state debts had been incurred mattered.

Many of these circumstances differ in Europe today. Unlike the central government of the United States then, the European Union itself does not have a large debt; instead, the troublesome debts that the market discounts are all obligations incurred by subordinate governments. People live longer, and most do not work on farms. They retire for substantial periods of their lives, and many do not start working until much later in their lives than those early Americans did. There are large public expenditures on education. Medicines and doctors make people healthier and older. Families are weaker. Government-financed safety nets and retirement and medical systems are pervasive and absorb substantial fractions of national budgets. Government regulations of labor markets have changed—slavery is gone; there are minimum wages, unemployment and disability compensation arrangements, and employment protection laws. These differ in their generosity and strength across EU states.[68] Are there greater differences in these institutions and peoples' skills and preferences across EU member states today than there were in the United States then? In some ways, US member states were much more diverse, for example, in attitudes toward slavery. But in terms of the fraction of GDP that citizens in different states wanted the federal government to consume or redistribute, there was probably much more agreement across member states then than there is in the United States today. Then, beyond redistributing from taxpayers to government creditors, the federal government's redistributional activities were minimal. Some proponents of a fiscal union in Europe today may want more redistribution and some opponents may want less.

There are lessons for the United States now. The government budget constraint and a pricing equation for government debt always prevail. The message of the unpleasant arithmetic of Sargent and Wallace (1981) is that with a responsible fiscal policy—one that sustains present value government budget balance with zero revenues from the inflation tax—it is easy for a monetary authority to sustain low inflation; but with a profligate fiscal policy, it is impossible for a monetary authority to sustain low inflation because the intertemporal government budget then implies that the monetary authority must sooner or later impose a sufficiently large inflation tax to finance the budget. In this sense, monetary

[67] The Tories had either left or remained quiet.

[68] Ljungqvist and Sargent (2008) study how differences in these features of social safety nets across countries and continents can account for different outcomes for unemployment in the face of common changes in the microeconomic environment.

and fiscal policies cannot be independent. They must be coordinated. There are simple and transparent devices for coordinating fiscal and monetary policies.[69] Other more obscure ways are also possible, like one that seems to prevail in the United States today.

Appendix

Outcomes in Graphs

Figures A1, A2, A3, A4, A5, A6, A7, A8, A9, and A10 show some of the fiscal outcomes of the policies that Washington and Hamilton designed.

Figures A1 and A3 show federal revenues by source from 1790 to 1820, both relative to GDP and per capita, respectively. These figures confirm that customs duties were the dominant source of federal revenues. Notice how much those revenues suffered when, during Madison and Jefferson's embargo in 1808 and 1809, the United States did eventually use trade policy to retaliate against the British. Today, Hamilton is sometimes characterized as someone who advocated a big state, but that has to be put in the context of the 1790s when, as figure A1 shows, a "big state" advocate wanted to raise about 2 percent of GDP in federal revenues and to use much of those revenues to service federal debt. Hamilton and Washington's policy of forbearance toward the British during the 1790s was designed to protect federal revenues and to avoid the outcomes that Madison and Jefferson's policy eventually temporarily brought about. Figures A2 and A4 show the composition of federal expenditures, both relative to GDP and per capita, respectively. Evidently, throughout the period, a large fraction of expenditures went to servicing the federal debt.

Figure A5 shows the ratio of the net-of-interest federal deficit to GDP, and figure A6 shows the debt to GDP ratio, where debt is being valued at par. Figure A7 shows the growth rate of GDP and the inflation rate. Both of these figures should be viewed as subject to substantial measurement errors. Figure A8 shows the composition of the federal debt. The figure shows how the domestic unfunded debt was converted into instruments described in the Act of August 4, 1790, and how rapidly the Treasury managed to carry out that successful debt restructuring. Notice the debt that was issued to help purchase the Louisiana Territory in 1803.

Figures A9 and A10 show per capita real GDP and per capita nominal GDP,

[69] Milton Friedman may have appeared abruptly to have changed his mind about how to coordinate monetary and fiscal policy, but if you look at it more deeply, he really didn't. Friedman recommended two apparently diametrically opposed ways to coordinate monetary and fiscal policy. Friedman (1953) recommended that the monetary authority use open-market operations to purchase 100 percent of all government debt. That put responsibility for money growth squarely on the shoulders of the fiscal authorities. To control money growth, he recommended that fiscal authorities balance the budget over the business cycle. In Friedman (1960), he reversed himself and instead recommended a version of the famous rule that the monetary authority commit itself to print government-issued fiat money at k percent per period no matter what, thereby committing itself to finance at most a small fraction of any government deficit.

See Sims (2001) for some pros and cons of "dollarization" as a coordinating device.

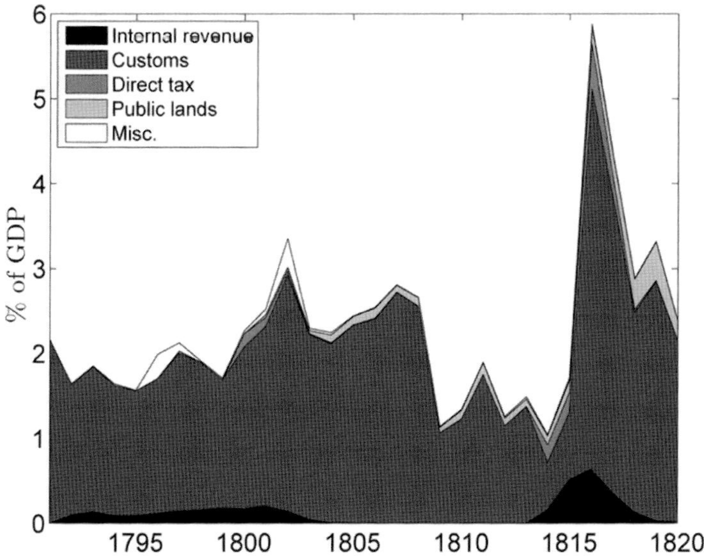

Fig. A1.—Composition of federal revenues by source

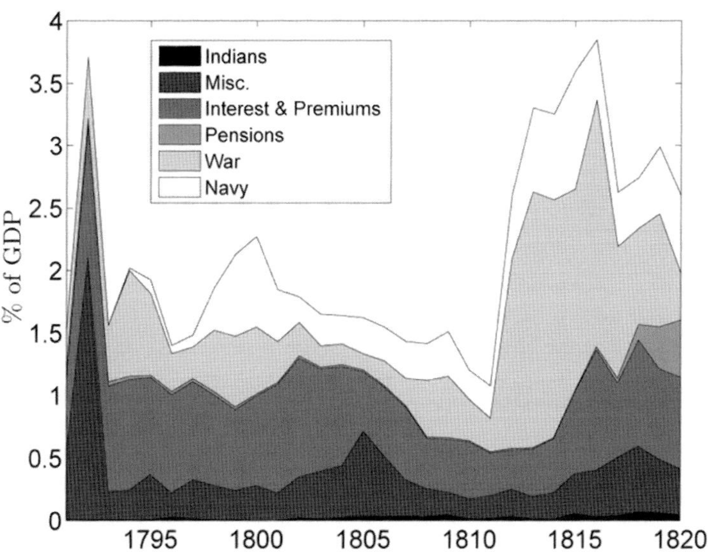

Fig. A2.—Composition of federal expenditures by type

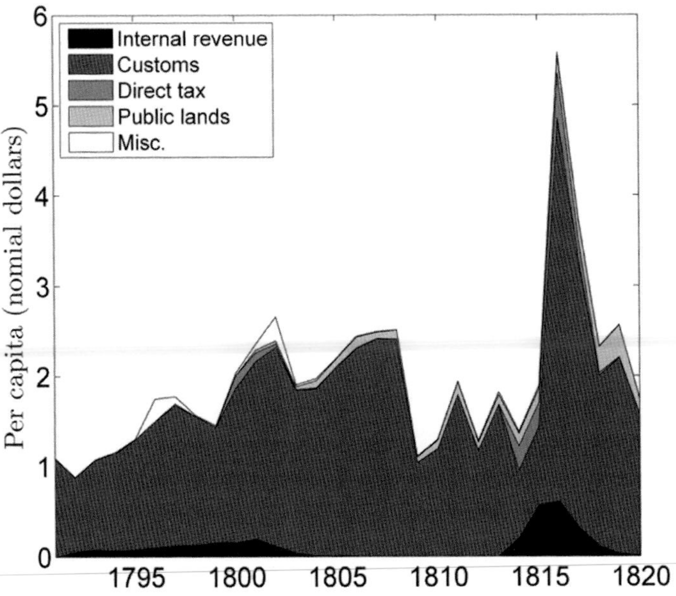

Fig. A3.—Per capita composition of federal revenues by source

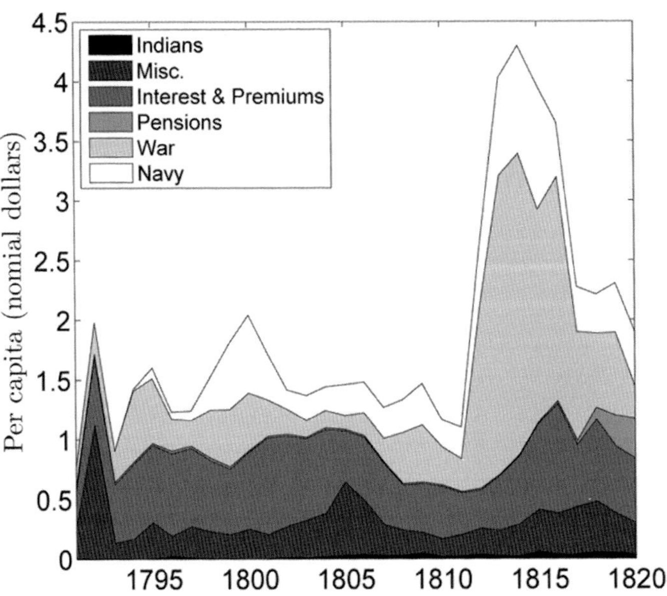

Fig. A4.—Per capita composition of federal expenditures by type

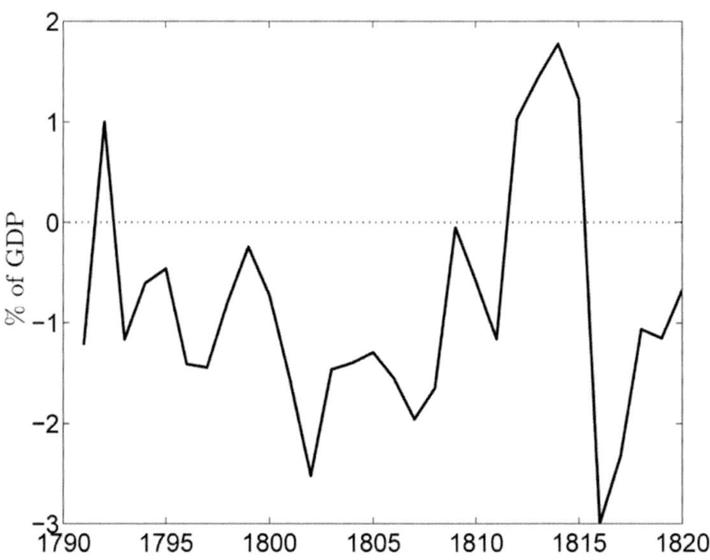

FIG. A5.—Primary deficit to GDP ratio

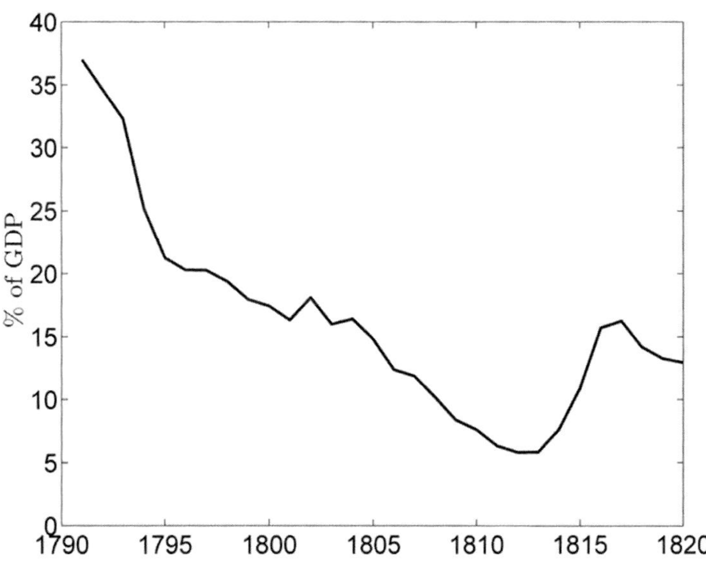

FIG. A6.—Par value debt to GDP ratio

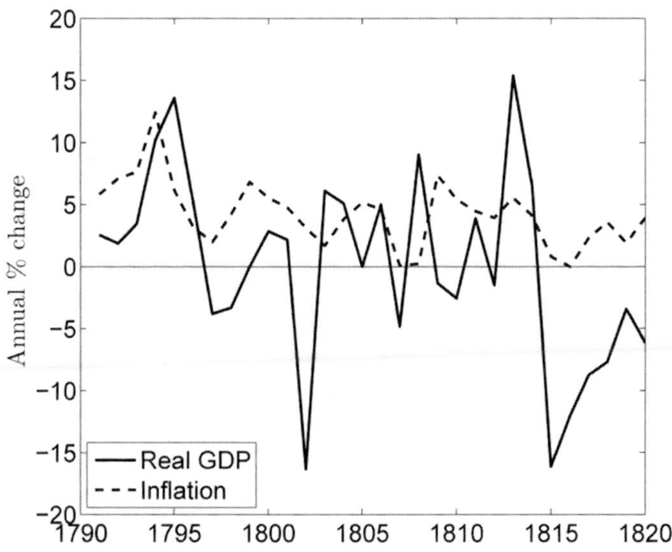

Fig. A7.—Annual inflation and real GDP growth

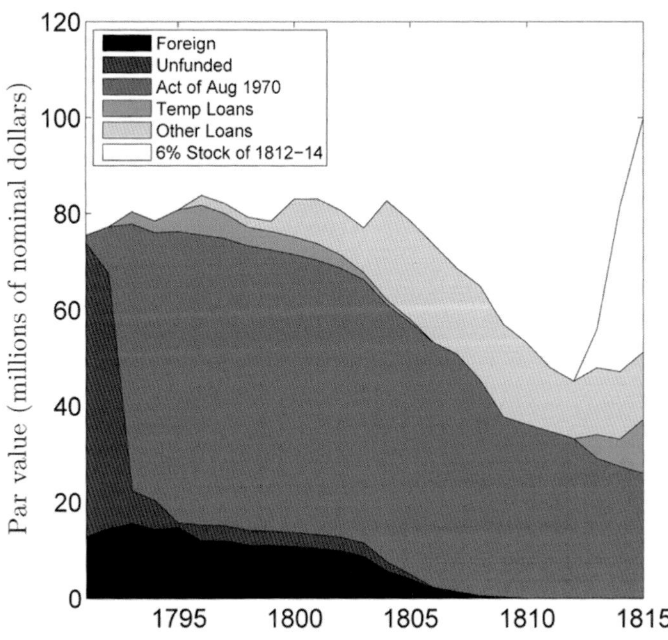

Fig. A8.—Composition of the debt outstanding by type of obligation

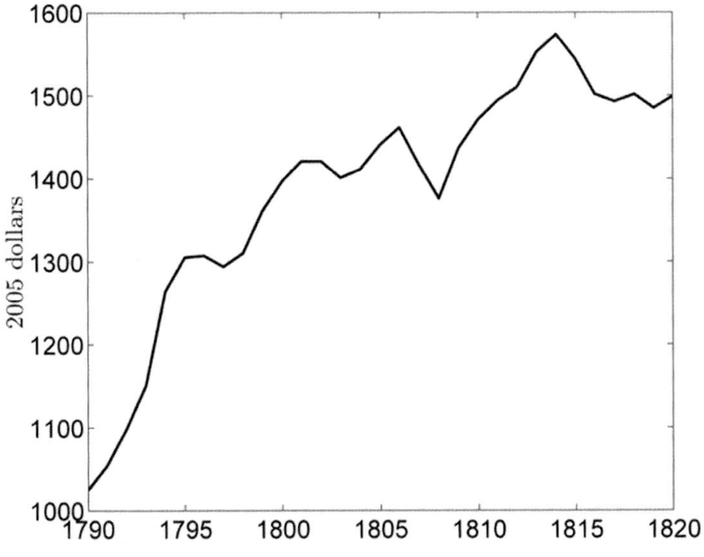

Fig. A9.—Per capita real GDP (2005 dollars)

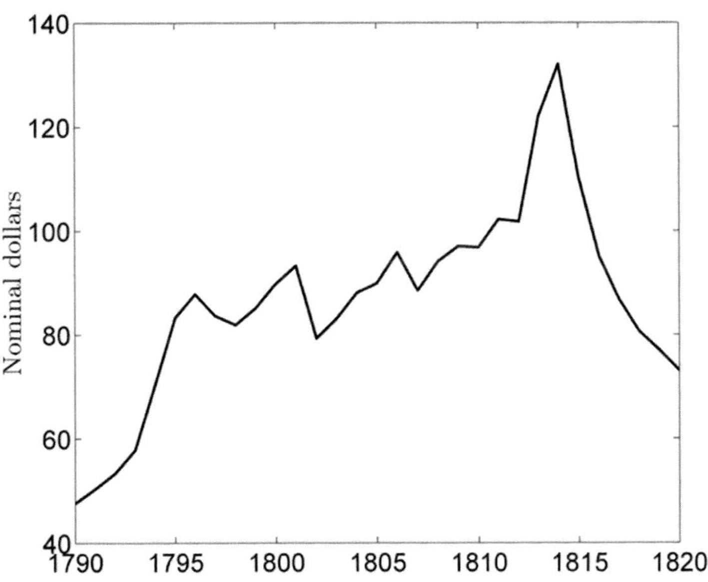

Fig. A10.—Per capita nominal GDP

again both probably subject to substantial measurement errors. Evidently, the debt to GDP ratio shrank over the period mainly through growth in GDP.

Data Sources

The data in these graphs come from the following sources. Figure A1: Revenue: *Annual Report of the Secretary of the Treasury on the State of the Finances for the Year 1870* (Washington, DC: Government Printing Office, 1870), table K, Statement of the Receipts of the United States from March 4, 1789, to June 30, 1870, by Calender Years to 1843, and by Fiscal Years (Ending June 30) from That Time (pp. XXVI–XXVIX). Nominal GDP: Louis Johnston and Samuel H. Williamson, "What Was the U.S. GDP Then?" *MeasuringWorth* (http://www.measuringworth.org/usgdp/, 2010). Figure A2: Expenditures: *Annual Report of the Secretary of the Treasury on the State of the Finances for the Year 1870* (Washington, DC: Government Printing Office, 1870), table L, Statement of the Expenditures of the United States from March 4, 1789, to June 30, 1870, by Calender Years to 1843, and by Fiscal Years (Ending June 30) from That Time (pp. XXX–XXXI). Nominal GDP: Same as figure A1. Figures A3 and A4: Same revenue and expenditure data as in figures A1 and A2. Population: US Bureau of the Census, *Historical Statistics of the United States, Earliest Times to the Present*, millennial ed. (New York: Cambridge University Press, 2006), table Aa7 (the numbers include slaves); also from *Measuring Worth*. Figure A5: Hall and Sargent (n.d.) calculated the primary deficit using the revenue and expenditure data cited above. Nominal GDP: Same as in figures A1 and A2. Figure A6: Debt: *Annual Report of the Secretary of the Treasury on the State of the Finances for the Year 1870* (Washington, DC: Government Printing Office, 1870), table H, Statement of the Outstanding Principal of the Public Debt of the United States on the 1st of January of Each Year, from 1790 to 1842, Inclusive (p. XXV). Figure A7: GDP deflator and real GDP growth from *Measuring Worth*. Figure A8: Reports of the Secretary of the Treasury of the United States: Report on the Finances, December 1815, table C, Statement of the Public Debt on the 1st day of January, in Each of the Years, from 1791 to 1815 Inclusive (pp. 47–50), http://fraser.stlouisfed.org/docs/publications/treasar/AR_TREASURY_1815.pdf. Figures A9 and A10: From *Measuring Worth*.

References

Adams, Henry C. 1887. *Public Debts: An Essay in the Science of Finance*. New York: Appleton.

Aiyagari, S. Rao, Albert Marcet, Thomas J. Sargent, and Juha Seppala. 2002. "Optimal Taxation without State-Contingent Debt." *J.P.E.* 110 (6): 1220–54.

Arellano, Cristina. 2008. "Default Risk and Income Fluctuations in Emerging Economies." *A.E.R.* 98 (3): 690–712.

Bagehot, Walter. [1873] 1920. *Lombard Street: A Description of the Money Market*. New York: Dutton.

Bancroft, George. 1886. *A Plea for the Constitution of the U.S. of America: Wounded in the House of Its Guardians*. New York: Harper.

Barro, Robert J. 1979. "On the Determination of the Public Debt." *J.P.E.* 87 (5): 940–71.

Bassetto, Marco. 2005. "Equilibrium and Government Commitment." *J. Econ. Theory* 124 (1): 79–105.

———. 2006. "Fiscal Policy and Price Stability: The Case of Italy, 1992–98." *Chicago Fed Letter,* no. 233 (December).

Battaglini, Marco, and Stephen Coate. 2008. "A Dynamic Theory of Public Spending, Taxation, and Debt." *A.E.R.* 98 (1): 201–36.

Beard, Charles A. 1913. *An Economic Interpretation of the Constitution of the United States.* No. beard1913 in History of Economic Thought Books, Archive for the History of Economic Thought, McMaster Univ.

Blume, Lawrence, and David Easley. 2006. "If You're So Smart, Why Aren't You Rich? Belief Selection in Complete and Incomplete Markets." *Econometrica* 74 (4): 929–66.

Borges, Jorge Luis. 1962. *Labyrinths.* New York: New Directions.

Bray, Margaret, and David M. Kreps. 1987. "Rational Learning and Rational Expectations." In *Arrow and the Ascent of Modern Economic Theory,* edited by George Feiwel, 597–625. New York: New York Univ. Press.

Brewer, John. 1989. *The Sinews of Power: War, Money and the English State, 1688–1783.* London: Unwin Hyman.

Bulow, Jeremy, and Kenneth Rogoff. 1989. "Sovereign Debt: Is to Forgive to Forget?" *A.E.R.* 79 (1): 43–50.

Chari, V. V., Lawrence J. Christiano, and Patrick J. Kehoe. 1994. "Optimal Fiscal Policy in a Business Cycle Model." *J.P.E.* 102 (4): 617–52.

Chari, V. V., and Larry E. Jones. 2000. "A Reconsideration of the Problem of Social Cost: Free Riders and Monopolists." *Econ. Theory* 16 (1): 1–22.

Chari, V. V., and Patrick J. Kehoe. 1990. "Sustainable Plans." *J.P.E.* 98 (4): 783–802.

Conklin, James. 1998. "The Theory of Sovereign Debt and Spain under Philip II." *J.P.E.* 106 (3): 483–513.

Cournot, Augustin. 1897. *Researches into the Mathematical Principles of the Theory of Wealth.* New York: Macmillan.

David, Paul A., and Peter Solar. 1977. "A Bicentenary Contribution to the History of the Cost of Living in America." In *Research in Economic History,* vol. 2, edited by Paul Uselding, 1–80. Greenwich, CT: JAI.

Debortoli, Davide, and Ricardo Nunes. 2007. "Political Disagreement, Lack of Commitment, and the Level of Debt." Manuscript, Univ. Pompeu Fabra.

Dewey, Davis R. 1912. *Financial History of the United States.* 4th ed. New York: Longmans, Green.

Eaton, Jonathan, and Mark Gersovitz. 1981. "Debt with Potential Repudiation: Theoretical and Empirical Analysis." *Rev. Econ. Studies* 48 (2): 289–309.

Elkins, Stanley, and Eric McKitrick. 1993. *The Age of Federalism.* New York: Oxford Univ. Press.

Fisher, Irving. 1926. *The Purchasing Power of Money: Its Determination and Relation to Credit, Interest, and Crises.* New York: Macmillan.

Friedman, Milton. 1953. "A Monetary and Fiscal Framework for Economic Stability." In *Essays in Positive Economics,* edited by Milton Friedman, 133–56. Chicago: Univ. Chicago Press.

———. 1960. *A Program for Monetary Stability.* New York: Fordham Univ. Press.

Friedman, Milton, and Anna Jacobson Schwartz. 1963. *A Monetary History of the United States, 1867–1960.* Princeton, NJ: Princeton Univ. Press.

Fudenberg, Drew, and David M. Kreps. 1987. "Reputation in the Simultaneous Play of Multiple Opponents." *Rev. Econ. Studies* 54 (4): 541–68.

Fudenberg, Drew, and David K. Levine. 1993. "Self-Confirming Equilibrium." *Econometrica* 61 (3): 523–45.

Ghosh, Atish R., Jun I. Kim, Enrique G. Mendoza, Jonathan D. Ostry, and Mahvash S. Qureshi. 2011. "Fiscal Fatigue, Fiscal Space and Debt Sustainability in Advanced Economies." Working Paper no. 16782, NBER, Cambridge, MA.

Granger, C. W. J. 1969. "Investigating Causal Relations by Econometric Models and Cross-Spectral Methods." *Econometrica* 37 (3): 424–38.

Hall, George, and Thomas J. Sargent. n.d. "A Fiscal History of the United States." Monograph in preparation.

Hamilton, Alexander. 1790. *Report on Public Credit*. Presented to Congress, January 9.

Hansen, Lars Peter. 1982. "Large Sample Properties of Generalized Method of Moments Estimators." *Econometrica* 50 (4): 1029–54.

———. 2011. "Dynamic Valuation Decomposition with Stochastic Economies." Fisher-Schultz lecture, Univ. Chicago.

Hansen, Lars Peter, J. Heaton, J. Lee, and N. Roussanov. 2007. "Intertemporal Substitution and Risk Aversion." In *Handbook of Econometrics*, vol. 6, pt. 1, edited by James J. Heckman and Edward E. Leamer, 3967–4056. Amsterdam: Elsevier.

Hansen, Lars Peter, and Ravi Jagannathan. 1991. "Implications of Security Market Data for Models of Dynamic Economies." *J.P.E.* 99 (2): 225–62.

Hansen, Lars Peter, and Scott F. Richard. 1987. "The Role of Conditioning Information in Deducing Testable Restrictions Implied by Dynamic Asset Pricing Models." *Econometrica* 55 (3): 587–613.

Hansen, Lars Peter, William Roberds, and Thomas J. Sargent. 1991. "Time Series Implications of Present Value Budget Balance and of Martingale Models of Consumption and Taxes." In *Rational Expectations Econometrics*, edited by Lars Peter Hansen and Thomas J. Sargent. Boulder, CO: Westview.

Hansen, Lars Peter, and Thomas J. Sargent. 1980. "Formulating and Estimating Dynamic Linear Rational Expectations Models." *J. Econ. Dynamics and Control* 2 (1): 7–46.

———, eds. 1991. *Rational Expectations Econometrics*. Boulder, CO: Westview.

———. 2013. *Risk, Uncertainty, and Value*. Princeton, NJ: Princeton Univ. Press, forthcoming.

Hansen, Lars Peter, and Kenneth J. Singleton. 1983. "Stochastic Consumption, Risk Aversion, and the Temporal Behavior of Asset Returns." *J.P.E.* 91 (2): 249–65.

Harrison, J. Michael, and David M. Kreps. 1979. "Martingales and Arbitrage in Multiperiod Securities Markets." *J. Econ. Theory* 20 (3): 381–408.

Howe, Daniel Walker. 2007. *What Hath God Wrought: The Transformation of America, 1815–1848*. New York: Oxford Univ. Press.

Irwin, Douglas A. 2009. "Revenue or Reciprocity? Founding Feuds over Early U.S. Trade Policy." In *Founding Choices: American Economic Policy in the 1790s*, edited by Douglas A. Irwin and Richard Sylla, 89–120. Chicago: Univ. Chicago Press (for NBER).

Jones, Larry E., Rodolfo E. Manuelli, and Peter E. Rossi. 1997. "On the Optimal Taxation of Capital Income." *J. Econ. Theory* 73 (1): 93–117.

Kareken, John H., and Neil Wallace. 1978. "Deposit Insurance and Bank Regulation: A Partial-Equilibrium Exposition." *J. Bus.* 51 (3): 413–38.

Klein, Paul, Per Krusell, and José-Victor Rios-Rull. 2011. "Time-Consistent Public Policy." Manuscript, Univ. Minnesota.

Klein, Paul, and José-Victor Rios-Rull. 2003. "Time-Consistent Optimal Fiscal Policy." *Internat. Econ. Rev.* 44 (4): 1217–45.

Kletzer, Kenneth M., and Brian D. Wright. 2000. "Sovereign Debt as Intertemporal Barter." *A.E.R.* 90 (3): 621–39.
Kreps, David M. 1997. "Economics—the Current Position." *Daedalus* 126 (1): 59–85.
Krishnamurthy, Arvind, and Annette Vissing-Jorgensen. 2010. "The Aggregate Demand for Treasury Debt." Working paper, NBER, Cambridge, MA.
Kydland, Finn E., and Edward C. Prescott. 1977. "Rules Rather Than Discretion: The Inconsistency of Optimal Plans." *J.P.E.* 85 (3): 473–91.
Ljungqvist, Lars, and Thomas J. Sargent. 2008. "Two Questions about European Unemployment." *Econometrica* 76 (1): 1–29.
Lucas, Robert E., Jr. 1972. "Expectations and the Neutrality of Money." *J. Econ. Theory* 4 (2): 103–24.
———. 1976. "Econometric Policy Evaluation: A Critique." *Carnegie-Rochester Conf. Ser. Public Policy* 1 (1): 19–46.
———. 1978. "Asset Prices in an Exchange Economy." *Econometrica* 46 (6): 1429–45.
Lucas, Robert E., Jr., and Edward C. Prescott. 1971. "Investment under Uncertainty." *Econometrica* 39 (5): 659–81.
———. 1974. "Equilibrium Search and Unemployment." *J. Econ. Theory* 7 (2): 188–209.
Lucas, Robert E., Jr., and Thomas J. Sargent, eds. 1981. *Rational Expectations and Econometric Practice.* Minneapolis: Univ. Minnesota Press.
Lucas, Robert E., Jr., and Nancy L. Stokey. 1983. "Optimal Fiscal and Monetary Policy in an Economy without Capital." *J. Monetary Econ.* 12 (1): 55–93.
Madison, James. 1956. *Notes of Debates in the Federal Convention of 1787.* New York: Norton.
Mailath, George, and Andrew Postlewaite. 1990. "Asymmetric Information Bargaining Problems with Many Agents." *Rev. Econ. Studies* 57:351–67.
Marcet, Albert, and Thomas J. Sargent. 1989. "Convergence of Least Squares Learning Mechanisms in Self-Referential Linear Stochastic Models." *J. Econ. Theory* 48 (2): 337–68.
McDonald, Forrest. 1985. *Novus Ordo Seclorum: The Intellectual Origins of the Constitution.* Lawrence: Univ. Kansas.
McPherson, James. 1988. *Battle Cry of Freedom.* New York: Oxford Univ. Press.
Meltzer, Allan H., and Scott F. Richard. 1981. "A Rational Theory of the Size of Government." *J.P.E.* 89 (5): 914–27.
Muth, John F. 1960. "Optimal Properties of Exponentially Weighted Forecasts." *J. American Statis. Assoc.* 55 (290): 299–306.
———. 1961. "Rational Expectations and the Theory of Price Movements." *Econometrica* 29:315–35.
North, Douglass C., and Barry R. Weingast. 1989. "Constitutions and Commitment: The Evolution of Institutions Governing Public Choice in Seventeenth-Century England." *J. Econ. Hist.* 49 (4): 803–32.
Paal, Beatrix. 2000. "Destabilizing Effects of a Successful Stabilization: A Forward-Looking Explanation of the Second Hungarian Hyperinflation." *Econ. Theory* 15 (3): 599–630.
Rakove, Jack M. 1997. *Original Meanings: Politics and Ideas in the Making of the Constitution.* New York: Vintage.
Ratchford, Benjamin Ulysses. 1941. *American State Debts.* Durham, NC: Duke Univ. Press.
Rolnick, Arthur J., and Warren E. Weber. 1983. "New Evidence on the Free Banking Era." *A.E.R.* 73 (5): 1080–91.

———. 1984. "The Causes of Free Bank Failures: A Detailed Examination." *J. Monetary Econ.* 14 (3): 267–91.

Sargent, Thomas J. 1971. "A Note on the 'Accelerationist' Controversy." *J. Money, Credit and Banking* 3 (3): 721–25.

———. 1977. "The Demand for Money during Hyperinflations under Rational Expectations: I." *Internat. Econ. Rev.* 18 (1): 59–82.

———. 1979. "A Note on Maximum Likelihood Estimation of the Rational Expectations Model of the Term Structure." *J. Monetary Econ.* 5 (1): 133–43.

———. 1981. "Interpreting Economic Time Series." *J.P.E.* 89 (2): 213–48.

———. 1982. "The Ends of Four Big Inflations." In *Inflation: Causes and Effects*, edited by Robert E. Hall, 41–98. Chicago: Univ. Chicago Press (for NBER).

———. 1984. "Autoregressions, Expectations, and Advice." *A.E.R.* 74 (2): 408–15.

———. 2008. "Evolution and Intelligent Design." *A.E.R.* 98 (1): 5–37.

Sargent, Thomas J., and François R. Velde. 1995. "Macroeconomic Features of the French Revolution." *J.P.E.* 103 (3): 474–518.

Sargent, Thomas J., and Neil Wallace. 1976. "Rational Expectations and the Theory of Economic Policy." *J. Monetary Econ.* 2 (2): 169–83.

———. 1981. "Some Unpleasant Monetarist Arithmetic." *Fed. Reserve Bank Minneapolis Q. Rev.* 5 (Fall).

———. 1982. "The Real-Bills Doctrine versus the Quantity Theory: A Reconsideration." *J.P.E.* 90 (6): 1212–36.

Scott, William A. 1893. *The Repudiation of State Debts: A Study in the Financial History of Mississippi, Florida, Alabama, North Carolina, South Carolina, Georgia, Lousiana, Arkansas, Tennessee, Minnesota, Michigan, and Virginia.* New York: Crowell.

Sims, Christopher A. 1972. "Money, Income, and Causality." *A.E.R.* 62 (4): 540–52.

———. 1980. "Macroeconomics and Reality." *Econometrica* 48 (1): 1–48.

———. 2001. "Fiscal Consequences for Mexico of Adopting the Dollar." *J. Money, Credit and Banking* 33 (2): 597–616.

Smith, Adam. 1806. *An Inquiry into the Nature and Causes of the Wealth of Nations.* 3 vols. Edinburgh: Greech.

Stokey, Nancy L. 1991. "Credible Public Policy." *J. Econ. Dynamics and Control* 15 (4): 627–56.

Sylla, Richard. 2009. "Financial Foundations: Public Credit, the National Bank, and Securities Markets." In *Founding Choices: American Economic Policy in the 1790s*, edited by Douglas A. Irwin and Richard Sylla, 59–88. Chicago: Univ. Chicago Press (for NBER).

Velde, François R. 2009. "Chronicle of a Deflation Unforetold." *J.P.E.* 117 (4): 591–634.

Velde, François R., and Warren E. Weber. 2000. "A Model of Bimetallism." *J.P.E.* 108 (6): 1210–34.

Wallace, Neil. 1981. "A Modigliani-Miller Theorem for Open-Market Operations." *A.E.R.* 71 (3): 267–74.

Wallis, John Joseph. 2000. "American Government Finance in the Long Run: 1790 to 1990." *J. Econ. Perspectives* 14 (1): 61–82.

———. 2001. "A History of the Property Tax in America." In *Property Taxation and Local Government Finance*, edited by Wallace Oates. Cambridge, MA: Lincoln Inst. Land Policy.

Wallis, John Joseph, and Barry R. Weingast. 2005. "Equilibrium Impotence: Why the States and Not the American National Government Financed Economic Development in the Antebellum Era." Manuscript, Hoover Inst., Stanford, CA.

Weber, Warren E. 2009. "Clearing Arrangements in the United States before the Fed." Manuscript, Fed. Reserve Bank Minneapolis.

Wills, Garry. 2002. *James Madison.* New York: Times Books.

Wood, Gordon. 2009. *Empire of Liberty: A History of the Early Republic, 1789–1815.* Oxford History of the United States. Oxford: Oxford Univ. Press.

Wright, Robert E. 2008. *One Nation under Debt: Hamilton, Jefferson, and the History of What We Owe.* New York: McGraw Hill.

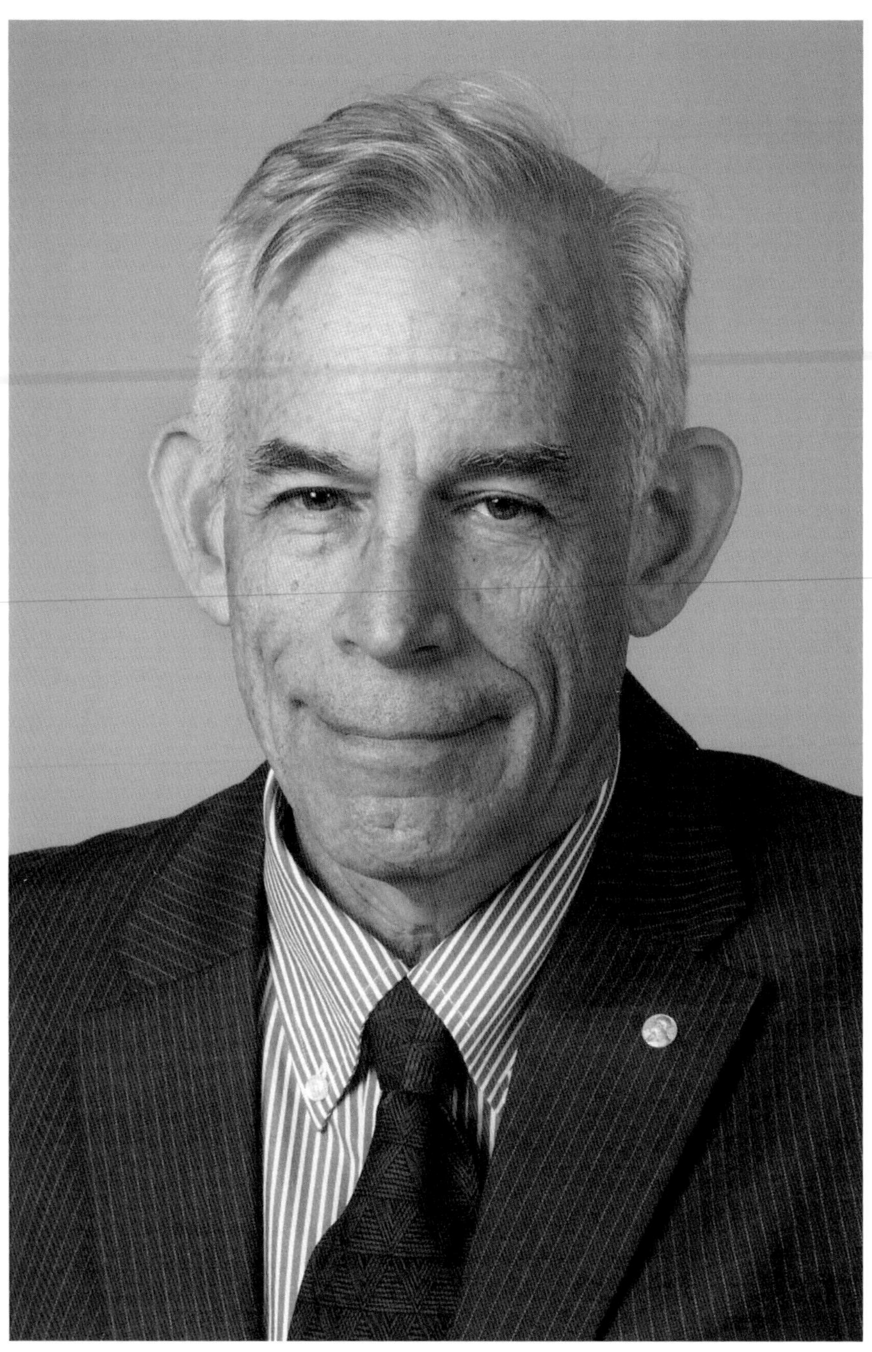

Christopher A. Sims. © The Nobel Foundation. Photo: U. Montan

Christopher A. Sims

My grandfathers were both immigrants to the US, one from Estonia, then part of the Russian empire, and the other from England. The Estonian, William Morris Leiserson, was Jewish. He fled Estonia in 1890 at the age of seven, through a forest in the dark of night, with his mother and two brothers. The family is not sure why they had to flee. It could have been because of a pogrom, or it could have been because of political activities of my great grandfather. Many Jews were fleeing Russia at the time. William's father was meant to join them after they reached the US, but was not seen again. One of William's older brothers, Louis, owned one of the shirtwaist companies in New York that were the site of the famous 1909 strike by the ILGWU, and William worked there as a youth. His formal education in public schools ended at the age of 14, but he read widely and attended public lectures in New York. At the age of 21 he went to Wisconsin, where he persuaded John R. Commons, the institutional economist, to take him on as a student despite his having no high school diploma. He later attended Columbia University in New York for his PhD work. He went on to teach at Antioch College and to become one of the first members of the US National Labor Relations Board, and then served on the National Mediation Service. He married Emily Bodman, whose family had many generations of roots in New England, and had seven children, one of them my mother, Ruth. Ruth, besides raising three children, headed the Connecticut League of Women Voters for a time and served two terms as First Selectman (similar to a mayor) of the town of Greenwich, Connecticut. She was the first woman, and the first Democrat in many decades, to be elected to that position.

My father Albert's father James was an English immigrant who worked as an itinerant manager of textile factories in New England, brought in to turn around poorly performing factories (at a time when the industry was declining). He died at a relatively young age. His wife Minnie Love was also an immigrant, from Northern Ireland, and she, too, died at a young age, leaving seven children to manage their own household, which they did successfully. Albert went to

Michigan State University and received a masters degree in public administration from Syracuse University. He worked in the US State Department, then as vice president of the College Board in New York.

Two of my uncles, Mark and Avery Leiserson, were professors. Mark was a labor economist, first at Yale, then at the World Bank. Avery spent most of his career at Vanderbilt University and served a term as president of the American Political Science Association. Both of them, and my grandfather "Billy" Leiserson, loved intellectual argument. I remember being greeted by grandpa, when I was about seven years old, with a twinkly eye and "Well, Chris, what do you think of the present situation of the country?" This was not an isolated incident. This was his standard greeting for grandchildren. Mark prodded me regularly, from about age 13 onward, to study economics. He gave me von Neumann and Morgenstern's *Theory of Games* for Christmas when I was in high school. When I took my first course in economics, I remember arguing with him over whether it was possible for the inflation rate to explode upward if the money supply were held constant. I took the monetarist position. He questioned whether I had a sound argument to support it. For years I thought he was having the opposite of his intended effect, and I studied no economics until my junior year of college. But as I began to doubt that I wanted to be immersed for my whole career in the abstractions of pure mathematics, Mark's efforts had left me with a pretty clear idea of an alternative.

While I was born in Washington DC (in 1942), from the ages of about five to seven I lived in Germany. My father had been part of the military government while in the Army, then switched to the State Department and brought the family over. We lived in Berlin and in Kronberg, near Frankfurt. At the time, I spoke some German, though I subsequently almost entirely forgot it. After returning to the US, we lived in Hollin Hills, Virginia for a few years, then moved to Greenwich, Connecticut when I was 11. I finished my schooling there and graduated from Greenwich High School in 1959. In high school I played football (third string linebacker, most of the time) and trombone in the band. I had a memorable math teacher in high school, Steven S. Willoughby, who later became president of the National Council of Teachers of Mathematics.

My undergraduate education was at Harvard, where I majored in mathematics, worked in a political group opposing nuclear testing and proliferation, played club rugby and weekend soccer, and played trombone in the band. My honors thesis generalized Khinchin's version of the coding theorem of information theory to infinite-memory channels. Engineers who were roped into reading the thesis tried to convince me to enter graduate school in electrical engineering. In some of my recent research I have found a way to connect information theory to economics.

My first year of graduate study was at UC Berkeley, where I took Microeconomic Theory from Dan McFadden, econometrics from Dale Jorgenson, and Monetary Economics from Richard Lipsey, inspiring teachers. McFadden posed problems that were only *nearly* impossible, from which I learned a lot. He taught micro as largely a set of corollaries of convex analysis. He later told me that this was in the period before he learned how to teach, for which I think I am grateful. Lipsey taught economics as a set of open questions and gave students the sense that they might be finding answers. Jorgenson gave off an almost electric sense of energy and confidence in the power of the rapidly developing field of econometrics.

I moved back to Harvard in my second year of PhD study. My adviser there was Hendrik Houthakker, who largely gave me free rein. I decided to study, empirically, embodied technological change. As I thought I was nearing completion of the work on my model, Henk insisted that I should be able to formulate it in continuous time, then derive the discrete time version from the continuous time version. This was harder than I think Henk realized, and led me to learn a great deal of real analysis in a short time. John Chipman, then visiting Harvard, was the only person I found who not only understood the issues I was dealing with, but could point me to relevant mathematical literature. John urged me to consider the Minnesota department, but Harvard was about to hire Zvi Griliches and Dale Jorgenson, so I decided to stay at Harvard as an assistant professor for two years.

In February 1967, a few months before completing my dissertation work, I married Catherine Sears. We postponed our honeymoon trip to the summer because of dissertation work, and then had to repostpone it because the work kept not finishing. We ended up with a rapid road trip to the Rocky Mountains in September. We arrived and pitched our tent in the dark, in the rain, and awoke to find our tent door flap frozen shut. Cathie, who had not camped before, has remained skeptical of camping trips ever since – even though the weather in the Rockies was better after that morning. Our son Ben arrived two years later, shortly before we moved on to Minneapolis.

Tom Sargent and I knew each other slightly as graduate students at Harvard. We had both come across the issue of interpreting two-sided distributed lag regressions, and we talked about it on the phone once or twice. I had accepted a position for the next year at Minnesota, and my recollection is that I had heard that Neil Wallace and Jack Kareken at Minnesota were enthusiastic about hiring

Tom, and that I was encouraging Tom to go to Minnesota during our telephone conversations. Tom, on the other hand, has said he is sure I proposed his name to Minnesota. In any case it was for me tremendous good fortune that he and I arrived at Minnesota at about the same time. He was and is a gifted teacher, whose students emerged both well trained and enthusiastic and confident about research. I was at Minnesota for 20 years, most of them with Tom as a colleague. Though Neil Wallace, Tom, Ed Prescott and I were seen by many outside Minnesota as a package of "fresh-water" innovators, from inside the Minnesota department we seemed to ourselves to represent sharply distinct viewpoints. We argued, and stimulated each other and our students. Actually much of the "arguing" was implicit, in the conflicting advice we sometimes gave our shared PhD students.

Our two younger children, Jody and Nancy, were born in Minneapolis and both live there now. We spent the entire 20 years in the same house in South Minneapolis, in a neighborhood where the single block-length of our street housed dozens of children. Summer evenings regularly involved "duck-duck grey-duck" and kickball games with street corners as bases.

My first econometrics and statistics courses (a statistics course from Dempster and econometrics courses from Hendrik Houthakker and Lester Taylor, all while an undergraduate at Harvard) did not devote much attention to Bayesian approaches. I had looked at, but not read through Raiffa and Shlaifer's book on decision theory and read some of Pratt's articles that took a Bayesian perspective. As I started graduate school I think I had the impression that the difference between Bayesian and frequentist approaches was mainly semantics, with little implication for practical data analysis. Another student at some point showed me the standard "rare disease" example, in which a 99% confidence interval, while having 99% pre-sample coverage probability, fails to contain the truth in 99% of the cases where the test is positive for the disease. I still remember puzzling over the example. It changed my thinking. It was not until I started analyzing the discrepancy between Bayesian and frequentist approaches to possibly non-stationary time series models that I became convinced that the distinction between the two approaches was important enough in a wide enough class of applications that teaching should always start from the Bayesian perspective. Since then, my teaching at every level has started from a Bayesian perspective, teaching non-Bayesian approaches as side topics.

In macroeconomics, my thinking was of course influenced by my two colleagues Sargent and Wallace, who were part of the core group fomenting the "rational expectations revolution" in macroeconomics. My own research made little use of rational expectations theory at first, focusing instead on using simpler, minimal theory to find the effects of policy by analyzing time series data. This is not because I was opposed to rational expectations ideas – I thought they represented an advance. I just thought the "revolution" aspect of it, in particular the deprecation of the ideas and efforts of the Keynesian econometricians, was overdone. My own work involved criticizing the statistical underpinnings of the Keynesian econometric models, but I viewed them as flawed but important, not worthless. I found the story that those Keynesian models had led to the inflation of 1970s implausible, unsupported by evidence, and recent research seems to confirm that.

While at Minnesota I heard Michael Woodford give a talk, one part of which laid out how the government's intertemporal budget constraint can be regarded as determining the price level. This set me to thinking and writing about the theory of price determination in models that treated both monetary and fiscal policy explicitly, a major part of my research from then on. In this theoretical work I made regular use of a rational expectations framework, which was by that time standard.

After Sargent left Minnesota, the department began to have internal disagreements about whether econometrics was an essential part of graduate training in economics. Many of the most interesting dissertations I helped supervised had been joint projects with Sargent, and his teaching had instilled an interest in careful quantitative research in Minnesota students. I decided it might be more interesting to work elsewhere, and settled on Yale. There I took a relatively bigger role in macro teaching and a relatively smaller one in econometrics teaching. Yale also had internal divisions, in this case over hiring macroeconomists who worked in the rational expectations framework. After nine years there, Princeton, which had a stellar collection of macro and monetary economists in Michael Woodford, Ben Bernanke, and Alan Blinder, and one of the best time series econometricians in Mark Watson, looked attractive, and I moved there. Soon Lars Svensson joined the Princeton faculty. For a few years, the research environment there, with constant interaction and discussion of theory and policy and shared responsibility for advising students, was as good or better than the early days at Minnesota.

Ten years ago, my wife Cathie, who had ridden horses extensively when she was younger, decided to take up riding again, and eventually bought a horse. I thought I should learn to ride to keep up with her. Riding turned out to be a great pleasure for me, and eventually I, too, bought a horse.

Cathie and I now have four grandchildren, aged two to ten, two living in Minneapolis, two in Los Alamos, New Mexico. We visit them regularly, and were happy that all four, with their parents, joined us in Stockholm for the Nobel ceremony.

STATISTICAL MODELING OF MONETARY POLICY AND ITS EFFECTS

Prize Lecture, December 8, 2011

by

CHRISTOPHER A. SIMS

Princeton University, Princeton, NJ, USA.

The science of economics has some constraints and tensions that set it apart from other sciences. One reflection of these constraints and tensions is that, more than in most other scientific disciplines, it is easy to find economists of high reputation who disagree strongly with one another on issues of wide public interest. This may suggest that economics, unlike most other scientific disciplines, does not really make progress. Its theories and results seem to come and go, always in hot dispute, rather than improving over time so as to build an increasing body of knowledge. There is some truth to this view; there are examples where disputes of earlier decades have been not so much resolved as replaced by new disputes. But though economics progresses unevenly, and not even monotonically, there are some examples of real scientific progress in economics. This essay describes one – the evolution since around 1950 of our understanding of how monetary policy is determined and what its effects are. The story described here is not a simple success story. It describes an ascent to higher ground, but the ground is still shaky. Part of the purpose of the essay is to remind readers of how views strongly held in earlier decades have since been shown to be mistaken. This should encourage continuing skepticism of consensus views and motivate critics to sharpen their efforts at looking at new data, or at old data in new ways, and generating improved theories in the light of what they see.

We will be tracking two interrelated strands of intellectual effort: the methodology of modeling and inference for economic time series, and the theory of policy influences on business cycle fluctuations. The starting point in the 1950s of the theory of macroeconomic policy was Keynes's analysis of the Great Depression of the 1930s, which included an attack on the Quantity Theory of money. In the 30s, interest rates on safe assets had been at approximately zero over long spans of time, and Keynes explained why, under these circumstances, expansion of the money supply was likely to have little effect. The leading American Keynesian, Alvin Hansen, included in his (1952) book *A Guide to Keynes* a chapter on money, in which he explained Keynes's argument for the likely ineffectiveness of monetary expansion in a period of depressed output. Hansen concluded the chapter with, "Thus it is that modern countries place primary emphasis on fiscal policy, in whose service monetary policy is relegated to the subsidiary role of a useful but necessary handmaiden."

The methodology of modeling in the 1950s built on Jan Tinbergen's (1939) seminal book, which presented probably the first multiple-equation, statistically estimated economic time series model. His efforts drew heavy criticism. Keynes (1939), in a famous review of Tinbergen's book, dismissed it. Keynes had many reservations about the model and the methods, but most centrally he questioned whether a statistical model like this could ever be a framework for testing a theory. Haavelmo (1943b), though he had important reservations about Tinbergen's methods, recognized that Keynes's position – doubting the possibility of any confrontation of theory with data via statistical models – was unsustainable. At about the same time, Haavelmo published his seminal papers explaining the necessity of a probability approach to specifying and estimating empirical economic models (1944) and laying out an internally consistent approach to specifying and estimating macroeconomic time series models (1943a).

Keynes's irritated reaction to the tedium of grappling with the many numbers and equations in Tinbergen's book finds counterparts to this day in the reaction of some economic theorists to careful, large-scale probability modeling of data. Haavelmo's ideas constituted a research agenda that to this day attracts many of the best economists to work on improved successors to Tinbergen's initiative.

Haavelmo's main point was this: Economic models do not make precise numerical predictions. Even if they are used to make a forecast that is a single number, we understand that the forecast will not be exactly correct. Keynes seemed to be saying that once we accept that models' predictions will be incorrect, and thus have "error terms", we must give up hope of testing them. Haavelmo argued that we can test and compare models, but that to do so we must insist that they include a characterization of the nature of their errors. That is, they must be in the form of probability distributions for the observed data. Once they are given this form, he pointed out, the machinery of statistical hypothesis testing can be applied to them.

In the paper where he initiated simultaneous equations modeling (1943a), he showed how an hypothesized joint distribution for disturbance terms is transformed by the model into a distribution for the observed data, and went on to show how this allowed likelihood-based methods for estimating parameters. After discussing inference for his model, Haavelmo explained why the parameters of his equation system were useful: One could contemplate intervening in the system by replacing one of the equations with something else, claiming that the remaining equations would continue to hold. This justification of – indeed definition of – structural modeling was made more general and explicit later by Hurwicz (1962).

Haavelmo's ideas and research program contained two weaknesses that persisted for decades thereafter and at least for a while partially discredited the simultaneous equations research program. One was that he adopted the frequentist hypothesis-testing framework of Neyman and Pearson. This framework, if interpreted rigorously, requires the analyst not to give probability distributions to parameters. This limits its usefulness in contributing to analysis of real-time decision-making under uncertainty, where assessing the likelihood of various parameter values is essential. It also inhibits combination of information from model likelihood functions with information in the beliefs of experts and policy-makers themselves. Both these limitations would have been overcome had the literature recognized the value of a Bayesian perspective on inference. When Haavelmo's ideas were scaled up to apply to models of the size needed for serious macroeconomic policy analysis, the attempt to scale up the hypothesis-testing theory of inference simply did not work in practice.

The other major weakness was the failure to confront the conceptual difficulties in modeling policy decisions as themselves part of the economic model, and therefore having a probability distribution, yet at the same time as something we wish to consider altering, to make projections conditional on changed policy. In hindsight, we can say this should have been obvious. Policy behavior equations should be part of the system, and, as Haavelmo suggested, analysis of the effects of policy should proceed by considering alterations of the parts of the estimated system corresponding to policy behavior.

Haavelmo's paper showed how to analyze a policy intervention, and did so by dropping one of his three equations from the system while maintaining the other two. But his model contained no policy behavior equation. It was a simple Keynesian model, consisting of a consumption behavior equation, an investment behavior equation, and an accounting identity that defined output as the sum of consumption and investment. It is unclear how policy changes could be considered in this framework. There was no policy behavior equation to be dropped. What Haavelmo did was to drop the national income accounting identity! He postulated that the government, by manipulating "G", or government expenditure (a variable not present in the original probability model), could set national income to any level it liked, and that consumption and investment would then behave according to the two behavioral equations of the system. From the perspective of 1943 a scenario in which government expenditure had historically been essentially zero, then became large and positive, may have looked interesting, but by presenting a policy intervention while evading the need to present a policy behavior equation, Haavelmo set a bad example with persistent effects.

The two weak spots in Haavelmo's program – frequentist inference and unclear treatment of policy interventions – are related. The frequentist framework in principle (though not always in practice) makes a sharp distinction between "random" and "non-random" objects, with the former thought of as repeatedly varying, with physically verifiable probability distributions. From the perspective of a policy maker, her own choices are not "random", and confronting her with a model in which her past choices are treated as "random" and her available current choices are treated as draws from a probability distribution may confuse or annoy her. Indeed economists who provide policy advice and view probability from a frequentist perspective may themselves find this framework puzzling.[1] A Bayesian perspective on inference makes no distinction between random and non-random objects. It distinguishes known or already observed objects from unknown objects. The latter have probability distributions, characterizing our uncertainty about them. There is therefore no paradox in supposing that econometricians and the public may have probability distributions over policy maker behavior, while policy makers themselves do not see their choices as random. The problem of econometric modeling for policy advice is to use the historically estimated joint distribution of policy behavior and economic outcomes to construct accurate probability distributions for outcomes conditional on contemplated policy actions not yet taken. This problem is not easy to solve, but it has to be properly posed before a solution effort can begin.

I. KEYNESIAN ECONOMETRICS VS. MONETARISM

In the 1950s and 60s economists worked to extend the statistical foundations of Haavelmo's approach and to actually estimate Keynesian models. By the mid-1960s the models were reaching a much bigger scale than Haavelmo's two-equation example model. The first stage of this large scale modeling was reported in a volume with 25 contributors (Duesenberry, Fromm, Klein, and Kuh, 1965), 776 pages, approximately 150 estimated equations, and a 50 × 75cm foldout flow chart showing how sectors were linked. The introduction discusses the need to include a "parameter" for every possible type of policy intervention. That is, there was no notion that policy itself was part of the stochastic structure to be estimated. There were about 44 quarters of data available, so without restrictions on the covariance matrix of residuals, the likelihood function would have been unbounded. Also, in order to obtain even well-defined single-equation estimates by standard frequentist methods, in each equation a large fraction of the variables in the model had to be assumed not to enter. There was no analysis of the shape of the likelihood function or of the model's implications when treated as a joint distribution for all the observed time series.

The 1965 volume was just the start of a sustained effort that produced another volume in 1969, and then evolved into the MIT-Penn-SSRC (or MPS) model that became the main working model used in the US Federal Reserve's policy process. Important other work using similar modeling approaches and methods has been pursued in continuing research by Ray Fair described e.g. in his 1984 book, as well as in several central banks.

While this research on large Keynesian models was proceeding, Milton Friedman and Anna Schwartz (1963b, 1963a) were launching an alternative view of the data. They focused on a shorter list of variables, mainly measures of money stock, high-powered money, broad price indexes, and measures of real activity like industrial production or GDP, and they examined the behavior of these variables in detail. They pointed out the high correlation between money growth and both prices and real activity, evident in the data over long spans of time. They pointed out in the 1963b paper that money growth tended to lead changes in nominal income. Their book (1963a) argued that from the detailed historical record one could see that in many instances money stock had moved first, and income had followed. Friedman and Meiselman (1963) used single-equation regressions to argue that the relation between money and income was more stable than that between what they called "autonomous expenditure" and income. They argued that these observations supported a simpler view of the economy than that put forward by the Keynesians: monetary policy had powerful effects on the economic system, and indeed that it was the main driving force behind business cycles. If it could be made less erratic, in particular if money supply growth could be kept stable, cyclical fluctuations would be greatly reduced.

The confrontation between the monetarists and the Keynesian large scale modelers made clear that econometric modeling of macroeconomic data had not delivered on Haavelmo's research program. He had proposed that economic theories should be formulated as probability distributions for the observable data, and that they should be tested against each other on the basis of formal assessments of their statistical fit. This was not happening. The Keynesians argued that the economy was complex, requiring hundreds of equations, large teams of researchers, and years of effort to model it. The monetarists argued that only a few variables were important and that a single regression, plus some charts and historical story-telling, made their point. The Keynesians, pushed by the monetarists to look at how important monetary policy was in their models, found (Duesenberry, Fromm, Klein, and Kuh, 1969, Chapter 7, by Fromm, e.g.) that monetary policy did indeed have strong effects. They argued, though, that it was one among many policy instruments and sources of fluctuations, and therefore that stabilizing money growth was not likely to be a uniquely optimal policy.

Furthermore, neither side in this debate recognized the centrality of incorporating policy behavior itself into the model of the economy. In the exchanges between Albert Ando and Franco Modigliani (1965) on the one hand, and Milton Friedman and David Meiselman on the other, much of the disagreement was over what should be taken as "autonomous" or "exogenous". Ando and Modigliani did argue that what was "autonomous" ought to be a question of what was uncorrelated with model error terms, but both they and their adversaries wrote as if what was controlled by the government was exogenous.

Tobin (1970) explained that not only the high correlations, but also the timing patterns observed by the monetarists could arise in a model where erratic monetary policy was not a source of fluctuations, but he did so in a deterministic model, not in a probability model that could be confronted with data. Part of his story was that what the monetarists took as a policy instrument, the money stock, could be moved passively by other variables to create the observed statistical patterns. I contributed to this debate (1972) by pointing out that the assumption that money stock was exogenous, in the sense of being uncorrelated with disturbance terms in the monetarist regressions, was testable. The monetarists regressed income on current and past money stock, reflecting their belief that the regression described a causal influence of current and past money stock on current income. If the high correlations reflected feedback from income to money, future money stock would help explain income as well. It turned out it did not, confirming the monetarists' statistical specification.

The monetarists' views, that erratic monetary policy was a major source of fluctuations and that stabilizing money growth would stabilize the economy, were nonetheless essentially incorrect. With the right statistical tools, the Keynesians might have been able to display a model in which not only timing patterns (as in Tobin's model), but also the statistical exogeneity of the money stock in a regression, would emerge as predictions despite money stock not being the main source of fluctuations. But they could not do so. Their models were full of unbelievable assumptions[2] of convenience, making them weak tools in the debate. And because they did not contain models of policy behavior, they could not even be used to frame the question of whether erratic monetary policy behavior accounted for much of observed business cycle variation.

II. WHAT WAS MISSING

Haavelmo's idea, that probability models characterize likely and less likely data outcomes, and that this can be used to distinguish better from worse models, fits neatly with a Bayesian view of inference, and less comfortably with the Neyman-Pearson approach that he adopted. Since standard statistics courses do not usually give a clear explanation of the difference between Bayesian and frequentist inference, it is worth pausing our story briefly to explain the difference. Bayesian inference aims at producing a probability distribution over unknown quantities, like "parameters" or future values of variables. It does not provide any objective method of doing so. It provides objective rules for updating probability distributions on the basis of new information. When the data provide strong information about the unknown quantities, it may be that the updating leads to nearly the same result over a wide range of possible initial probability distributions, in which case the results are in a sense "objective". But the updating can be done whether or not the results are sensitive to the initial probability distribution.

Frequentist inference estimates unknown parameters, but does not provide probability distributions for them. It provides probability distributions for the behavior of the estimators. These are "pre-sample" probabilities, applying to functions of the data before we observe the data.

We can illustrate the difference by considering the multiplier-accelerator model that Haavelmo[3] used to show that probability-based inference on these models should be possible. Though it is much smaller than the Keynesian econometric models that came later, at the time many fewer data were available, so that even this simple model could not have been sharply estimated from the short annual time series that were available.

The model as Haavelmo laid it out was

$$C_t = \beta + \alpha Y_t + \varepsilon_t \tag{1}$$
$$I_t = \theta(C_t - C_{t-1}) + \eta_t \tag{2}$$
$$Y_t = C_t + I_t. \tag{3}$$

He assumed $\varepsilon_t \sim N(0,\sigma_c^2)$ and $\eta_t \sim N(0,\sigma_i^2)$ and that they were independent of each other and across time. He suggested estimating the system by maximum likelihood.

He intended the model to be useful for predicting the effect of a change in government spending G_t, though G_t does not appear in the model. This was confusing, even contradictory. We will expand the model to use data on G_t in estimating it. He also had no constant term in the investment equation. We will be using data on gross investment, which must be nonzero even when there is no growth, so we will add a constant term. Our modified version of the model, then, is

$$C_t = \beta + \alpha Y_t + \varepsilon_t \tag{1´}$$
$$I_t = \theta_0 + \theta_1 (C_t - C_{t-1}) + \eta_t \tag{2}$$
$$Y_t = C_t + I_t + G_t \tag{3´}$$
$$G_t = \gamma_0 + \gamma_1 G_{t-1} + \nu_t. \tag{4}$$

We will confront it with data on annual real consumption, gross private investment, and government purchases from 1929 to 1940.[4]

The model does not make sense if it implies a negative multiplier – that is if it implies that increasing G within the same year decreases Y. It also does not make sense if γ_1, the "accelerator" coefficient, is negative. Finally, it is hard to interpret if γ_1 is much above 1, because that implies explosive growth. We therefore restrict the parameter space to $\theta_1 > 0$, $\gamma_1 < 1.03$, $1 - \alpha(1 + \theta_1) > 0$. The last of these restrictions requires a positive multiplier. The likelihood maximum over this parameter space is then at

α	β	θ_0	θ_1	γ_0	γ_1
0.566	166	63.0	0.000	10.7	0.991

Note that the maximum likelihood estimator (MLE) for θ_1 is at the boundary of the parameter space. At this value, the investment equation of the model makes little sense. Furthermore, the statistical theory that is used in a frequentist approach to measure reliability of estimators assumes that the true parameter value is not on the boundary of the parameter space and that the sample is large enough so that a random sample of the data would make finding the MLE on the boundary extremely unlikely.

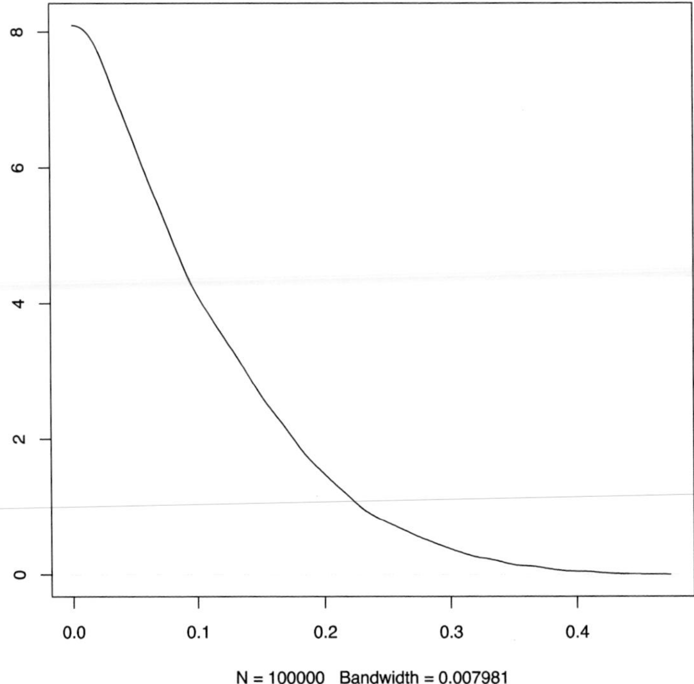

Figure 1. θ_1 probability density.

A Bayesian approach to inference provides a natural and reasonable result, though. The probability density over the parameter space after seeing the data is proportional to the product of the likelihood function with a prior density function. If the prior density function is much flatter than the likelihood, as is likely if we began by being very uncertain about the parameter values, the likelihood function itself, normalized to integrate to one, characterizes our uncertainty about the parameter values. With modern Markov Chain Monte Carlo methods, it is a straightforward matter to trace out the likelihood and plot density functions for parameters, functions of parameters, or pairs of parameters. Under a flat prior, the density function for γ_1 has the shape shown in Figure 1. While the peak is at zero, any value between 0 and 0.25 is quite possible, and the expected value is 0.091. The system's dynamics with $\theta_1 = 0.2$ would be very different from dynamics with θ_1 close to zero. So the data leave substantively important uncertainty about the value of θ_1 and do not at all rule out economically significant accelerator effects. The within-year multiplier in this model, that is the effect of a unit change in G_t on Y_t, is $1/(1-\alpha\ (1+\theta_1))$. Its flat-prior posterior density is shown in Figure 2. Note that the maximum likelihood estimate of the multiplier, shown as a vertical line in the figure, is 2.30, well to the left of the main mass of the posterior distribution. This occurs because the multiplier increases with θ_1, and the MLE at zero is unrepresentative of the likely values of θ_1.

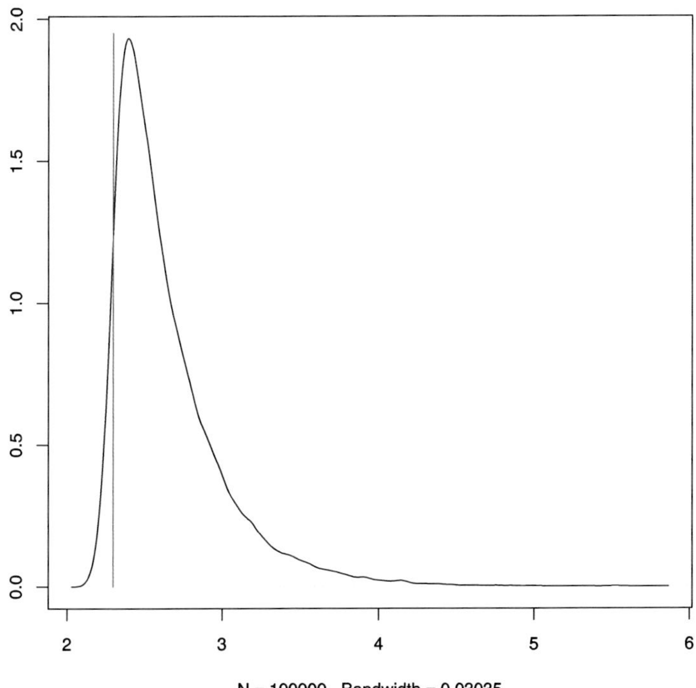

Figure 2. Probability density of multiplier.

In calculating the "multiplier" here, I am looking at the impact of a change in G_t, in the context of a model in which G_t is part of the data vector for which the model proposes a probability distribution. There are several ways of thinking about what is being done in this calculation. One is to say that we are replacing the "policy behavior equation" (4) by the trivial equation $G_t = G^*$, holding the other equations fixed, and considering variations in G^*. Another, equivalent, way to think of it is that we are considering choosing values of ν_t, the disturbance to the policy equation. The latter approach has the advantage that, since we have an estimated distribution for ν_t, we will notice when we are asking about the effects of changes in ν_t that the model considers extremely unlikely.[5] While there is nothing logically wrong with asking the model to predict the effects of unlikely changes, simplifying assumptions we have made in setting up the model to match data become more and more questionable as we consider more extreme scenarios.

Neither of these ways of looking at a multiplier on G is what Haavelmo did in his hypothetical policy experiment with the model. In fact he did not calculate a multiplier at all. He instead suggested that a policy-maker could, by setting G (which, recall, was not in his probability model), achieve any desired level Y^* of total output. He recognized that this implied the policy-maker could see ε_t and η_t and choose G_t so as to offset their effects. He noted that under these assumptions, the effects of changes in Y^* on C_t and

I_t could be easily calculated from equations (1) and (2). He said that what he was doing was dropping the accounting identity (3) and replacing it with $Y_t = Y^*$, but one cannot "drop" an accounting identity. What he was actually doing was replacing an implicit policy equation, $G_t \equiv 0$, with another, $G_t = Y^* - C_t - I_t$, while preserving the identity (3´). Since policy-makers probably cannot in fact perfectly offset shocks like η_t and ε_t, and since they are more likely to have seen themselves as controlling G_t than as directly controlling Y_t, this policy experiment is rather artificial.

If Haavelmo had tried to fit his model to data, he would have had to confront the need to model the determination of his policy variable, G_t. My extension of Haavelmo's model in (1´)-(4) specifies that lagged values of C_t and I_t do not enter the G_t equation (4) and that the disturbance of that equation is independent of the other two disturbances. This implies, if this equation is taken as describing policy behavior, that G_t was determined entirely by shifts in policy, with no account being taken of other variables in the economy. This would justify estimating the first two equations in isolation, as Haavelmo suggested. But in fact the data contain strong evidence that lagged C_t and I_t do help predict G_t.[6] If the model was otherwise correct, this would have implied (quite plausibly) that G_t was responding to private sector developments. Even to estimate the model properly would then have required a more complicated approach.

This discussion is meant only as an example to illustrate the difference between frequentist and Bayesian inference and to show the importance of explicitly modeling policy. It is not meant to suggest that Haavelmo's model and analysis could have been much better had he taken a Bayesian approach to inference. The calculations involved in Bayesian analysis of this simple model (and described more fully in the appendix) take seconds on a modern desktop computer, but at the time Haavelmo wrote were completely infeasible. And the model is not a good model. The estimated residuals from the MLE estimates show easily visible, strong serial correlation, implying that the data have richer dynamics than is allowed for in the model.

In large macroeconomic models it is inevitable that some parameters – some aspects of our uncertainty about how the economy works – are not well-determined by the data alone. We may nonetheless have ideas about reasonable ranges of values for these parameters, even though we are uncertain about them. Bayesian inference deals naturally with this situation, as it did with the prior knowledge that γ_1 should be positive in the example version of Haavelmo's model. We can allow the data, via the likelihood function, to shape the distribution where the data are informative, and use pre-data beliefs where the data are weak.

When we are considering several possible models for the same data, Bayesian inference can treat "model number" as an unknown parameter and produce post-sample probabilities over the models. When a large model, with many unknown parameters, competes with a smaller model, these posterior probabilities automatically favor simpler models if they fit as well as more complicated ones.

The models the Keynesians of the 1960s were fitting were orders of magnitude larger than Haavelmo's, with many hundreds, or even thousands, of free "parameters" to be estimated. Asking the data to give firm answers to the values of these parameters was demanding a lot, too much, in fact. The statistical theory that grew out of Haavelmo's ideas, known as the Cowles Foundation methodology, provided approximate characterizations of the randomness in estimators of these parameters, on the assumption that the number of time series data points was large relative to the number of parameters being estimated, an assumption that was clearly untrue for these models. It was frequentist theory, and therefore insisted on treating unknown quantities as non-random "parameters". To provide reasonable-looking estimates, modelers made many conventional, undiscussed assumptions that simplified the models and made ad hoc adjustments to estimation methods that had no foundation in the statistical theory that justified the methods.[7]

The result was that these models, because they included so many ad hoc assumptions that were treated as if they were certain a priori knowledge and because they were estimated by methods that were clearly dubious in this sort of application, were not taken seriously as probability models of the data, even by those who built and estimated them. Measures of uncertainty of forecasts and policy projections made with the models were not reliable.

III. NEW EVIDENCE AND NEW MODELING IDEAS

While the Keynesian modelers were working on their unwieldy large models, and while Friedman and Meiselman and Anderson and Jordan (1968) were estimating single-equation models explaining income with money, other economists were estimating single equations explaining money with income and interest rates. These latter were labeled "money demand" equations. If, as my 1972 paper implied, M did in fact behave in the regressions of income on money like a legitimate explanatory variable, it seemed likely that the empirical money demand equations were mis-specified. So Mehra (1978) set out to check whether that was so. He found, surprisingly, that that equation also passed tests of necessary conditions that income and interest rates were explaining money causally. The only way to reconcile these results was to put the variables together in a multiple-equation model to study their dynamics.

In my 1980a paper I estimated such a model, as a vector autoregression, or VAR, the type of model I was suggesting in "Macroeconomics and Reality" (1980b). VAR's are models of the joint behavior of a set of time series with restrictions or prior distributions that, at least initially, are symmetric in the variables. They include, for example, restrictions on lag length – the same restrictions on all variables in all equations – or prior distributions favoring smooth evolution of the time series in the model. Of course to make the results interesting, they require some interpretation, which brings in economic theory at least informally. In the 1980a paper I included data on interest rates, production, prices, and money. The results showed clearly that much of the variation in money stock is predictable from past values of the interest rate, particularly so after World War II. Furthermore, a considerable part of the postwar variation in the interest rate was in turn predictable based on past values of industrial production. Since interest rates were in fact a concern of monetary policy makers, this made it hard to argue that money stock itself was an adequate representation of policy or to argue that money supply variation consisted largely of erratic mistakes. If monetary policy was in part systematic and predictable historically, it was no longer clear that shutting down its variation would reduce business cycle fluctuations.

Of course in the 1970s there was increased attention to modeling policy behavior from another side. The rational expectations hypothesis was applied to macroeconomic models. It required that models that included explicit expectations of the future in behavioral equations should base those expectations on the full model's own dynamic structure. A simple version of a rational expectations model was already common in studies of financial markets: the "efficient markets" hypothesis stated that excess returns on assets should be approximately unpredictable, as otherwise there would be profit opportunities from trading on the predictable returns. This meant that the kind of test I had applied to the money-income regressions would tend to imply that any asset price from a smoothly functioning market "causes" movements in any other publicly observable variable. Some economists (Fischer Black, in particular, in conversation with me) thought from the start that money appeared to have a unidirectional causal impact on income in the monetarist regressions for the same reason that stock prices would, and that the result was therefore not strong support for the monetarist causal interpretations of those regressions. But neither the monetarist nor the Keynesian models at the time implied that quantity of money had the same kind of properties as an asset price. While my 1980a paper and subsequent work with VAR models made clear that monetary policy responded to the state of the economy and that the money stock was predictable in a model including interest rates, an explicit theoretical model that validated Fischer Black's intuition arrived later in my 1989 paper, which showed that a monetary policy of making interest rates respond positively to the growth rate of the money stock would lead to an apparent causal ordering from money to income, even in a model with negligible effects of monetary policy on real variables.

Another main conclusion from applying the rational expectations hypothesis was that a model of policy behavior was required to accurately model expectations in the private sector. Since the large Keynesian models had devoted no attention to careful modeling of policy behavior, they could not easily take this criticism into account. While the emphasis from this viewpoint on modeling policy behavior was valuable, the effect on policy modeling of the rational expectations "critique" of the large Keynesian models was for a few decades more destructive than constructive.

Some of the early proponents of rational expectations modeling, such as Sargent (1973), presented it as implying cross-equation restrictions on models that were otherwise similar in structure to the then-standard ISLM models. But even in the small model Sargent used in that article, estimating the complete system as a model of the joint time series behavior was not feasible at the time – he used the model to derive single equations that he estimated and used to test implications of rational expectations. Maximum likelihood estimation of complete systems embodying rational expectations at the scale needed for policy modeling was not possible.

Probably even more important to the inhibiting effect on policy-oriented econometric inference was the emphasis in the rational expectations literature on evaluating non-stochastic alterations of a policy rule within the context of a rational expectations model. The intuition of this point could easily be made clear to graduate students in the context of the Phillips curve. If one accepted that only surprise changes in the price level had real effects, then it was easy to show that a negative correlation between unemployment and inflation might emerge when no attempt was made to control unemployment by manipulating inflation (or vice versa), but that there might nonetheless be no possibility of actually affecting unemployment by deliberately changing the inflation rate, assuming those deliberate changes were anticipated. If one thought of the Phillips curve in this story as standing in for a large Keynesian model, the implication was that what policy makers actually did with econometric models – use them to trace out possible future paths of the economy conditional on time paths for policy variables – was at best useless and at worst might have been the source of the US inflation of the 1970s. This story was widely believed, and it supported a nearly complete shutdown in academic economists' interest in econometric policy modeling.

There was in fact no empirical support for this story. The Phillips curve negative correlation of unemployment with inflation did indeed disappear in the 1970s, but this quickly was reflected in Keynesian empirical policy models, so those models implied little or no ability of policy to reduce unemployment by raising inflation. Rising inflation was not a deliberate attempt to climb up a stable Phillips curve. I would support this argument, which is no doubt still somewhat controversial, in more detail if this essay were about the evolution of macroeconomics generally, but for current purposes, we need only note the effect of the story on research agendas: few economists paid attention to the modeling tasks faced by the staffs of monetary policy institutions.

The emphasis on changes in rules as policy experiments was unfortunate in another respect as well. As we have noted, it was a major defect in Haavelmo's framework and in the simultaneous equation modeling that followed his example that policy changes were always modeled as deterministic, coming from outside the stochastic structure of the model. Recognition of the importance of modeling policy behavior ought to have led to recognition that policy changes should be thought of as realizations of random variables, with those random variables modeled as part of the model's structure. Instead, the mainstream of rational expectations modeling expanded on Haavelmo's mistake: treating policy changes as realizations of random variables was regarded as inherently mistaken or contradictory; attention was focused entirely on non-stochastic, permanent changes in policy behavior equations, under the assumption that these equations had not changed before and were not expected to change again after the intervention.[8]

Large econometric models were still in use in central banks. New data continued to emerge, policy decisions had to be made, and policy makers wanted to understand the implications of incoming data for the future path of the economy, conditional on various possible policy choices. Modelers in central banks realized that the frequentist inference methods provided by the Cowles Foundation econometric theorists were not adapted to their problems, and, in the absence of any further input from academic econometricians, reverted to single-equation estimation. No longer was any attempt made to construct a joint likelihood for all the variables in the model. There were attempts to introduce rational expectations into the models, but this was done in ways that would not have been likely to stand up to academic criticism – if there had been any.[9]

Vector autoregressive models were not by themselves competitors with the large policy models. They are statistical descriptions of time series, with no accompanying story about how they could be used to trace out conditional distributions of the economy's future for given policy choices. In my earliest work with VAR's (1980a; 1980b) I interpreted them with informal theory, not the explicit, quantitative theoretical restrictions that would be needed for policy analysis. It was possible, however, to introduce theory explicitly, but with restraint, so that VAR's became usable for policy analysis. Blanchard and Watson (1986) and my own paper (1986) showed two different approaches to doing this. Models that introduced theoretical restrictions into VAR's sparingly in order to allow them to predict the effects of policy interventions came to be known as structural vector autoregressions, or SVAR's.

IV. CONSENSUS ON THE EFFECTS OF MONETARY POLICY

By 1980 it was clear that money stock itself was not even approximately a complete one-dimensional measure of the stance of monetary policy. Interest rates were also part of the picture. Policy makers in the US and most other countries thought of their decisions as setting interest rates, though perhaps with a target for a path of money growth in mind. They were also concerned about the level of output and inflation, trying to dampen recessions by lowering rates and restrain inflation by raising rates. But there are many reasons why interest rates, money, output and prices are related to output and inflation other than the behavior of monetary policy makers. Interest rates tend to be higher when inflation is high, because lenders require to be compensated for the loss in value of the loan principal through inflation. Interest rates will change when the real rate of return to investment changes, which can happen for various reasons not related to monetary policy. Private sector demand for money balances can shift, because of financial innovation or fluctuating levels of concern about liquidity. Untangling these patterns of mutual influence to find the effects of monetary policy is inherently difficult and can at best produce results that leave some uncertainty.

In my 1986 paper, I attempted this untangling by a combination of strategies. I postulated that interest rate changes could affect private sector investment decisions only with a delay, and also that the Federal Reserve could not, because of delays in data availability, respond within the quarter to changes in output or the general level of prices. The model also included an attempt to identify a money demand equation, using two different sets of additional restrictions. The effects of monetary policy identified this way were quite plausible: a monetary contraction raised interest rates, reduced output and investment, reduced the money stock, and slowly decreased prices. The effects on output of unpredictable disturbances to monetary policy were non-trivial, but accounted for only a modest fraction of overall variability in output. That the responses emerged as "reasonable" was in fact part of the identification strategy. The precise zero-restrictions on some coefficients were interacting with qualitative views as to what a response to a monetary policy contraction should look like.

This pattern of results turned out to be robust in a great deal of subsequent research by others that considered data from other countries and time periods and used a variety of other approaches to SVAR-style minimalist identification. A summary of some of this research appeared in Leeper, Sims, and Zha (1996). It was widely accepted as a reasonable quantitative assessment of how monetary policy changes affect the economy.

SVAR's that isolated an equation for monetary policy behavior could be used for making conditional policy projections, but they did not become widely used as the main model in central bank policy discussions. Future policy is not the only future event that policy makers like to condition on in making projections. Scenarios involving high or low commodity prices due to supply disruptions, high or low productivity growth, decline in the value of the dollar, fiscal policy changes, etc. are often important to policy discussion. Since SVAR's were limiting themselves to isolating monetary policy, treating the rest of the economy as a single "black box" system, they could not easily provide these types of conditional forecasts. Whether accurate or not, the existing large scale models could at least provide answers.

Christiano, Eichenbaum, and Evans (2005) developed a complete dynamic, stochastic general equilibrium model (DSGE), in which all disturbances and equations had economic interpretations and reflected assumed optimizing behavior, yet which also could reproduce the pattern of responses to a monetary policy shock that had emerged from SVAR models. Extending their work,[10] Frank Smets and Raf Wouters (2007; 2003) showed that the model could be used to form a likelihood function and that formal Bayesian inference to estimate the parameters and characterize uncertainty about them was possible. They could compare their models to VAR's and SVAR's, and they showed that their models were competitive with VAR's in terms of fit to the data. They thus finally delivered on Haavelmo's project: a macroeconomic model usable for policy analysis that was in the form of an asserted probability distribution for the data. It could be compared in fit to other models, and proposed improvements to it could be evaluated on the basis of their effects on the full system, not just one equation. Central bank research staffs around the world recognized the potential value of this type of model, and many have since developed models of this type. In some cases this type of model has become the main model used in policy discussions.

V. ARE WE THERE YET?

Haavelmo advocated formulating economic models as probability models not as an end in itself, but because he saw this as the only way it would be possible to test models against one another and thereby make progress. We now have, in Bayesian DSGE models, the first step in Haavelmo's program. But these models in their current form are ripe for improvement, in several directions.

The recent financial crash and recession was not predicted by the DSGE models. Predictions from probability models by construction will be subject to error. It is therefore not the existence of the errors, or even their size, that is a problem; it is that the errors in the forecasts from the DSGE's (and standard SVAR's, for that matter) were of a size that the models' probability structures implied should almost never occur. That too many large errors occur, compared to the predictions of the models, was verifiable before the recent crisis, even though the scale of errors in the recent crisis was greater. Recognizing the true likelihood of large errors in economic models is a technical challenge, which is one reason they received little attention from modelers. Perhaps more important was that unusually large errors are by definition rare events. It is therefore not possible for the historical data by some mechanical statistical procedure to generate a probability model for the large errors. That is, the role of prior distributions will be important in modeling these errors and uncertainty about them will be great. An approach based on the usual tools of frequentist, large-sample-approximate econometrics will not suffice.

A related gap in the current crop of DSGE's is that they are nearly all based on linearization around a steady-state growth path. Users of the models are well aware that the models therefore are likely to become unreliable in the face of large deviations of the economy from its trend line. Large disturbances push us well off the trend line, however, and we need to identify and model the important nonlinearities that then arise.

Already many economists are working at integrating more financial data and more complete models of the financial sector into DSGE models, in hopes that these improvements will help avoid another crash like that of 2008, or failing that make policy choices in the wake of such a crash more accurately apparent. Equally important, in fact probably more important looking ahead, is extending DSGE's to more accurately model fiscal dynamics. The Bayesian DSGE's mostly do not model, or do not model accurately, national debt, the connection of deficits to debt, and the wealth effects on private sector behavior of debt and expected future fiscal policy. These aspects of the economy are central to current policy discussions.

The existing DSGE's are mainly variants on the Christiano, Eichenbaum and Evans model. This is a "micro-founded" model, in which inertia and stickiness, instead of being injected into the model in a purely ad hoc way, are pushed one level down, into the constraints of optimizing representative agents. But these micro foundations are in many instances clearly at odds with empirical micro evidence or common sense. Price stickiness, for example, is modeled by assuming that there is a constraint or a cost associated with changing a nominal price, and that firms setting prices are all individually negligible in size. Everyone understands that actual industries are nearly always characterized by wide divergences in firm size, with a few large firms being strategically important. Everyone understands that the "cost" of changing a nominal price or the constraint that nominal prices can only be changed at times whose occurrence the firm cannot control are at best a strained metaphor. If one thinks of DSGE's as a set of stories that make economists and policy-makers more comfortable with policy projections that basically reproduce what would be implied by SVAR's, the implausibility of the micro-foundations of the DSGE's are of secondary importance. But when the models are used to evaluate welfare effects of alternative policies, these issues become more important. It is unlikely that macroeconomic models that are explicitly built up from micro data will be feasible in the near future. But it is feasible to experiment with variations on the inertial mechanisms in the Christiano, Eichenbaum and Evans framework, investigating whether other specifications can fit as well and might have different policy implications.

Existing DSGE's are too tightly parameterized. The Smets and Wouters US model (2007) for example uses data on seven variables and has 37 free parameters, about five per "equation", which is a parameter density that is probably lower than characterized the large-scale Keynesian models of the 60s and 70s. The result is that Bayesian VAR's fit better than the DSGE's, by a substantial margin.[11] The DSGE's could be made to fit better by adding parameters allowing more dynamics in the disturbances or more flexible specifications of various sources of inertia. Since we think of the theory in these models as at best approximate, though, a more promising approach may be that of DelNegro and Schorfheide (2004), extended by DelNegro, Schorfheide, Smets, and Wouters (2007), who use a DSGE as the source for a prior distribution on the parameters of a SVAR. In their procedure the result can in principle be nearly identical to the DSGE, if the DSGE fits the data well. Park (2010) has extended the Del Negro/Schorfheide framework to make it more realistically reflect uncertainties about identification. This approach to modeling, since it does not treat the DSGE as directly explaining the data, makes using the model's microtheory for evaluating welfare effects of policy impossible. But as I've noted above, this may be all to the good. And use of the model to trace out the distribution of the future of the economy conditional on various sources of disturbance remains possible, and likely more accurate than using the DSGE model directly.

VI. CONCLUSION

Despite some early confusion about how to bring macroeconomic time series data to bear on the issue, the controversy between Keynesian and Quantity Theory views of the effects of standard monetary policy is at least for the time being largely resolved. Interest rate changes engineered by open market operations do have substantial effects on the economy, both on real output and inflation. Erratic shifts in monetary policy are not the main source of cyclical variation in the economy. The quantity of money is not a good one-dimensional index of monetary policy. Effects of monetary policy on output are fairly quick; effects on inflation take longer to play out. The methods of inference that have been developed in resolving these issues have brought us close to realizing Haavelmo's goals for a scientific approach to macroeconomics.

Nonetheless, there remain uncertainties even about the new consensus view, and the models now at the frontier still contain major gaps. Much remains to be done.

APPENDIX: INFERENCE FOR THE HAAVELMO MODEL

The model defined by (1´)–(4) is in the form of a slightly non-standard simultaneous equations model:

$$\Gamma_0 z_t = \phi + \Gamma_1 z_{t-1} + \zeta_t, \tag{5}$$

with

$$\Gamma_0 = \begin{bmatrix} 1 & 0 & -\alpha & 0 \\ -\theta_1 & 1 & 0 & 0 \\ -1 & -1 & 1 & -1 \\ 0 & 0 & 0 & 1 \end{bmatrix}, \begin{bmatrix} 0 & 0 & 0 & 0 \\ -\theta_1 & 0 & 0 & 0 \\ 0 & 0 & 0 & 0 \\ 0 & 0 & 0 & \gamma_1 \end{bmatrix},$$

$$\phi = \begin{bmatrix} \beta \\ \theta_0 \\ 0 \\ \gamma_0 \end{bmatrix}, z_t = \begin{bmatrix} C_t \\ I_t \\ Y_t \\ G_t \end{bmatrix}, \zeta_t = \begin{bmatrix} \varepsilon_t \\ \eta_t \\ 0 \\ \nu_t \end{bmatrix}.$$

The non-standard aspect of the model is that the covariance matrix of ζ_t is constrained to be diagonal. The simultaneous equations literature that emerged from Haavelmo's insights treated as the standard case a system in which the joint distribution of the disturbances was unrestricted, except for having finite covariance matrix and zero mean. It is interesting that Haavelmo's seminal example instead treated structural disturbances as independent, as has been the standard case in the later structural VAR literature.

Likelihood-based inference is straightforward, if we condition on the initial (1929) observation. The distribution of ζ_t is Normal, with a diagonal covariance matrix, i.i.d. across t. So the log pdf of $\zeta_{1930},\ldots,\zeta_{1940}$ is

$$-10\log\sigma_{\varepsilon} - 10\log\sigma\eta - 10\log\sigma_{\nu} - \frac{1}{2}\sum_t \frac{\varepsilon_t^2}{\sigma_{\varepsilon}^2} - \frac{1}{2}\sum_t \frac{\eta_t^2}{\sigma_{\eta}^2} - \frac{1}{2}\sum_t \frac{\nu_t^2}{\sigma_{\nu}^2}. \tag{6}$$

To arrive at the log likelihood, we first substitute $C_t + I_t + G_t$ for Y_t to reduce the system to three variables and three equations. Then we write the shocks as functions of the parameters and the data, using (5) and multiply by the Jacobian of the transformation from the data vector z_t to the shock vector ζ_t, which is

$$\left|\Gamma_0^*\right|^T,$$

where Γ_0^* is the contemporaneous coefficient matrix from the 3×3 version of the system solved to eliminate Y_t.

The likelihood can be integrated analytically with respect to the three η parameters. The integration treated the prior on these parameter as flat in $1/\sigma_{\varepsilon}^2$, $1/\sigma_{\eta}^2$ and $1/\sigma_{n}^2u$. With those parameters integrated out, the resulting function of the six parameters α, β, θ_0, θ_1, γ_0, and γ_1 can be treated as a marginal posterior pdf for those parameters.

The maximum likelihood estimates displayed in the text are arrived at by numerical maximization of this marginal posterior. (Thus they are probably somewhat different from the values of those parameters at the joint likelihood peak, were maximization over the σ parameters and the other six jointly.) To generate the full posterior distribution, a random walk Metropolis algorithm was used, with jump distribution $N(0, \Omega)$, where Ω was 0.3 times a crude estimate of the second derivative of the log posterior density near its peak. The crude estimate was just that produced as the approximate inverse-Hessian during the likelihood maximization computation. Despite the maximum of the posterior pdf being on the boundary, both the maximization and the MCMC iterations converged fairly easily. 100,000 draws were used for the MCMC computations. The coefficients α and β in the consumption function showed effective sample sizes (using the **coda** package for R) of 297 and 284, while for the other parameters the effective size was over one thousand.

REFERENCES

Anderson, L. C., and J. L. Jordan (1968), "Monetary and Fiscal Actions: A Test of Their Relative Importance in Economic Stabilization," *Federal Reserve Bank of Saint Louis Review*, pp. 11–24.

Ando, A., and F. Modigliani (1965), "The Relative Stability of Monetary Velocity and the Investment Multiplier," *American Economic Review*, 55(4), 693–728.

Blanchaed, O.J., and M.W. Watson (1986), "Are Business Cycles All Alike?," in *The American Business Cycle: Continuity and Change*, ed. by R. Gordon, pp. 123–156, University of Chicago Press, Chicago, Illinois.

Christiano, L., M. Eichenbaum, and C. Evans (2005), "Nominal Rigidities and the Dynamics Effects of a Shock to Monetary Policy," *Journal of Political Economy*, 113(1), 1–45.

Delnegro, M., and F. Schorfheide (2004), "Priors from General Equilibrium Models for VARs," *International Economic Review*, 45, 643–673.

Delnegro, M., F. Schorfheide, F. Smets, and R. Wouters (2007): "On the Fit and Forecasting Performance of New Keynesian Models," *Journal of Business and Economic Statistics*, 25(2), 123–162.

Duesenberry, J. S., G. Fromm, L. R. Klein, and E. Kuh, eds. (1965), *The Brookings Quarterly Econometric Model of the United States*. Rand Mc-Nally.

— eds. (1969), *The Brookings Model: Some Further Results*. Rand McNally.

Fair, R. C. (1984), *Specification, Estimation, and Analysis of Macroeconometric Models*, Harvard University Press.

Friedman, M., and D. Meiselman (1963), "The Relative Stability of Monetary Velocity and the Investment Multiplier in the United States, 1897–1958," in *Stabilization Policies*, Commision on Money and Credit.

Friedman, M., and A. J. Schwartz (1963a), *A Monetary History of the United States, 1867–1960*, Princeton University Press.

Friedman, M., and A. J. Schwartz (1963b), "Money and Business Cycles," *The Review of Economics and Statistics*, 45(1), 32–64.

Haavelmo, T. (1943a), "The statistical implications of a system of simultaneous equations," *Econometrica*, 11(1), 1–12.

— (1943b), "Statistical Testing of Business-Cycle Theories," *The Review of Economics and Statistics*, Vol. 25, No.1 (Feb., 1943), pp. 13–18, published by: The MIT Press Stable. URL: http://www.jstor.org/stable/1924542.

— (1944), "The Probability Approach in Econometrics," *Econometrica*, 12 (supplement), iii–vi + 1–115. Hansen, A. H. (1952), *A Guide to Keynes*, McGraw-Hill, New York; Toronto; London.

Hurwicz, L. (1962), "On the Structural Form of Interdependent Systems," in *Logic, Methodology and Philosophy of Science*, pp. 232–239, Stanford University Press, Stanford, CA.

Keynes, J. M. (1939), "Professor Tinbergen's method," *Economic Journal*, 49(195), 558–577, book review.

Leeper, E. M., C. A. Sims, and T. Zha (1996), "What Does Monetary Policy Do?," Br*ookings Papers on Economic Activity*, (2), 1–78.

Leeper, E. M., and T. Zha (2003), "Modest Policy Interventions," *Journal of Monetary Economics*, 50(8), 1673–1700.

Liu, T.-C. (1960), "Underidentification, Structural Estimation, and Forecasting," *Econometrica*, 28(4), pp. 855–865.

Mehra, Y. P. (1978), "Is Money Exogenous in Money-Demand Equations," *The Journal of Political Economy*, 86(2), 211–228.

Park, W. Y. (2010), "Evaluation of DSGE Models: With an Application to a Two-Country DSGE Model," Discussion paper, Princeton University, http://www.sef.hku.hk/~wypark/.

Samuelson, P. A. (1939), "Interactions Between the Multiplier Analysis and the Principle of Acceleration," *Review of Economics and Statistics.*

Sargent, T. J. (1973), "Rational Expectations, the Real Rate of Interest, and the Natural Rate of Unemployment," *Brookings Papers on Economic Activity*, 1973(2), 429–480.

— (1984), "Autoregressions, Expectations, and Advice," *American Economic Review*, 74, 408–15, Papers and Proceedings.

Sims, C. A. (1972), "Money, Income, and Causality," *The American Economic Review*, 62(4), 540–552.

— (1980a), "Comparison of Interwar and Postwar Business Cycles: Monetarism Reconsidered," *American Economic Review*, 70, 250–57.

— (1980b), "Macroeconomics and Reality," *Econometrica*, 48, 1–48.

— (1986), "Are Forecasting Models Usable for Policy Analysis?," *Quarterly Review of the Minneapolis Federal Reserve Bank*, 10, 2–16.

— (1987), "A rational expectations framework for short-run policy analysis," in *New approaches to monetary economics*, ed. by W. A. Barnett, and K. J. Singleton, pp. 293–308, Cambridge University Press, Cambridge, England.

— (1989), "Models and Their Uses," *American Journal of Agricultural Economics*, 71, 489–494.

— (2002), "The Role of Models and Probabilities in the Monetary Policy Process," *Brookings Papers on Economic Activity*, 2002(2), 1–62.

Smets, F., and R. Wouters (2003), "An Estimated Dynamic Stochastic General Equilibrium Model of the Euro Area," *Journal of the European Economic Association*, 1, 1123–1175.

— (2007), "Shocks and frictions in US business cycles: a Bayesian DSGE approach," *American Economic Review*, 97(3), 586–606.

Tinbergen, J. (1939), *Statistical testing of business-cycle theories*, no. v. 1–2 in Publications: Economic and financial, League of Nations, Economic Intelligence Service, http://books.google.com/books?id=E8MSAQAAMAAJ.

Tobin, J. (1970), "Money and Income: Post Hoc Ergo Propter Hoc?," *The Quarterly Journal of Economics*, 84(2), 301–317.

(ENDNOTES)

1 An example of a sophisticated economist struggling with this issue is Sargent (1984). That paper purports to characterize both Sargent's views and my own. I think it does characterize Sargent's views at the time, but it does not correctly characterize my own.

2 This fact, which everyone in some sense knew, was announced forcefully by Liu (1960), and much later re-emphasized in my 1980b paper.

3 Haavelmo's model differs from the classic Samuelson (1939) model only in using current rather than lagged income in the consumption function.

4 We use the chain indexed data, which did not exist when Haavelmo wrote. We construct Y as $C + I + G$, since the chain indexed data do not satisfy the accounting identity and we are not using data on other GDP components.

5 This is the point made, with more realistic examples, by Leeper and Zha (2003).

6 I checked this by fitting both first and second order VAR's.

7 For example, two-stage least squares was widely used to estimate equations in these models. According to the theory, the more exogenous and predetermined variables available, the better the (large-sample) properties of the estimator. But in these models there was an embarrassment of riches, so many instruments that two-stage least squares using all of them reduced to ordinary least squares – the same method Tinbergen used pre-Haavelmo. So in fact, the modelers used fewer instruments, without any formal justification.

8 I argued against this way of formulating policy analysis at more length in 1987.

9 I surveyed the state of central bank policy modeling and the use of models in the policy process in a 2002 paper.

10 The work by Christiano, Eichenbaum and Evans circulated in discussion paper form for years before its final publication.

11 Smets and Wouters report in their tables only marginal likelihoods for Bayesian VAR's that are at least slightly worse than the marginal likelihood of th DSGE. In footnote 13, however, they report that a BVAR with a different prior produces a log marginal likelihood better than that of the DSGE by 9.2 in log units, a substantial advantage in fit for the BVAR.

Economic Sciences 2012

Alvin E. Roth and Lloyd S. Shapley

"for the theory of stable allocations and the practice of market design"

The Sveriges Riksbank Prize In Economic Sciences In Memory of Alfred Nobel

Speech by Professor Torsten Persson of the Royal Swedish Academy of Sciences.

Your Majesties, Your Royal Highnesses, Laureates, Ladies and Gentlemen,

It is important to make the right choices in life. In many critical situations, however, such as among options for school, university, profession or spouse, it is not enough to choose. You also have to be chosen. The key question in this kind of matching is: who gets what?

In August 2011, a 66 year-old man in Livingston, New Jersey, gets a new kidney. The donor is a complete stranger, a 44 year-old man from Riverside, California, who offers his left kidney as a genuinely altruistic gesture. The recipient's niece is prepared to donate one of her kidneys to her uncle, but belongs to the wrong blood group. Instead, the niece is asked to donate her kidney to an unknown woman in Wisconsin, whose ex-boyfriend in turn donates one of his kidneys to another anonymous patient in Pittsburgh. The chain does not come to an end until 60 coordinated transplants have taken place across the entire United States. Four days before Christmas Eve, a 30th patient with chronic kidney failure, a 45 year-old man in Chicago, resumes a normal life after a difficult year of dialysis.

This success story reflects not only achievements in nephrology, but also innovative research in matching theory. Thirty kidneys can be allocated among thirty patients in an almost infinite number of ways. But only a few of these potential matches are truly great, because the human body is so prone to reject foreign organs.

It was only eight years ago that Alvin Roth and his colleagues published their first scientific study on the most efficient way to manage the benevolence of organ donors. The following year, in collaboration with physicians, they established the first centre for matching kidney donors with patients: the New England Program for Kidney Exchange.

At this point in time, Roth was not a novice in the field of matching. In 2003, he had been commissioned to redesign the annual procedure which matches more than 90,000 prospective high-school students in New York with hundreds of schools – a problem with a staggering number of potential solutions. The outcome was so successful that several other metropolises adopted similar systems for school choice. In the mid-1990s, Roth had already been asked to reconstruct the clearinghouse which each year pairs 20,000 new doctors with hospital internships throughout the U.S.

The story of matching theory goes back much further, however. Exactly 50 years ago, the mathematician David Gale wrote a letter to some of his colleagues about a tricky mathematical problem. Assume that a large number of students are to be accepted at a much smaller number of universities. Is there always a stable matching, whereby each student will be admitted by the university she ranks the highest among those which are willing to accept her, and vice versa for the universities? Lloyd Shapley replied by return mail. He not only proved that the answer is "yes", but also proposed a specific algorithm that always results in a stable solution in similar, two-sided matching problems. Several decades later, this is precisely the algorithm Roth built upon when he reformed both the clearinghouse for new doctors and school choice in New York.

In the 1970s, Shapley solved another abstract problem, that of one-sided matching. If a number of individuals each own a house, is there any specific procedure which permits them to exchange houses up to a point where no further improvement is possible, given their housing preferences? Shapley's elegant solution demonstrates that this is indeed the case. Three decades later, Roth built precisely on this result in his work on chains for kidney exchange.

Dear Professors Roth and Shapley,

Professor Shapley: Your contributions to cooperative game theory are legendary among game theorists and economists. You and David Gale are the founders of matching theory, and the deferred-acceptance algorithm you discovered is the cornerstone on which theory and applications rest.

Professor Roth: Your innovative work comprises theory, empirical evaluation, laboratory experiments, and design of actual markets where prices cannot be used, for ethical or legal reasons. It is this feedback between theory and practice that makes market design such a flourishing field.

You have never worked together. But together your contributions constitute one of those unexpected journeys, from basic research motivated by sheer curiosity, to practical use for the benefit of mankind. It is an honour and a privilege to convey to you, on behalf of the Royal Swedish Academy of Sciences, our warmest congratulations. I now ask you to receive your Prize from His Majesty the King.

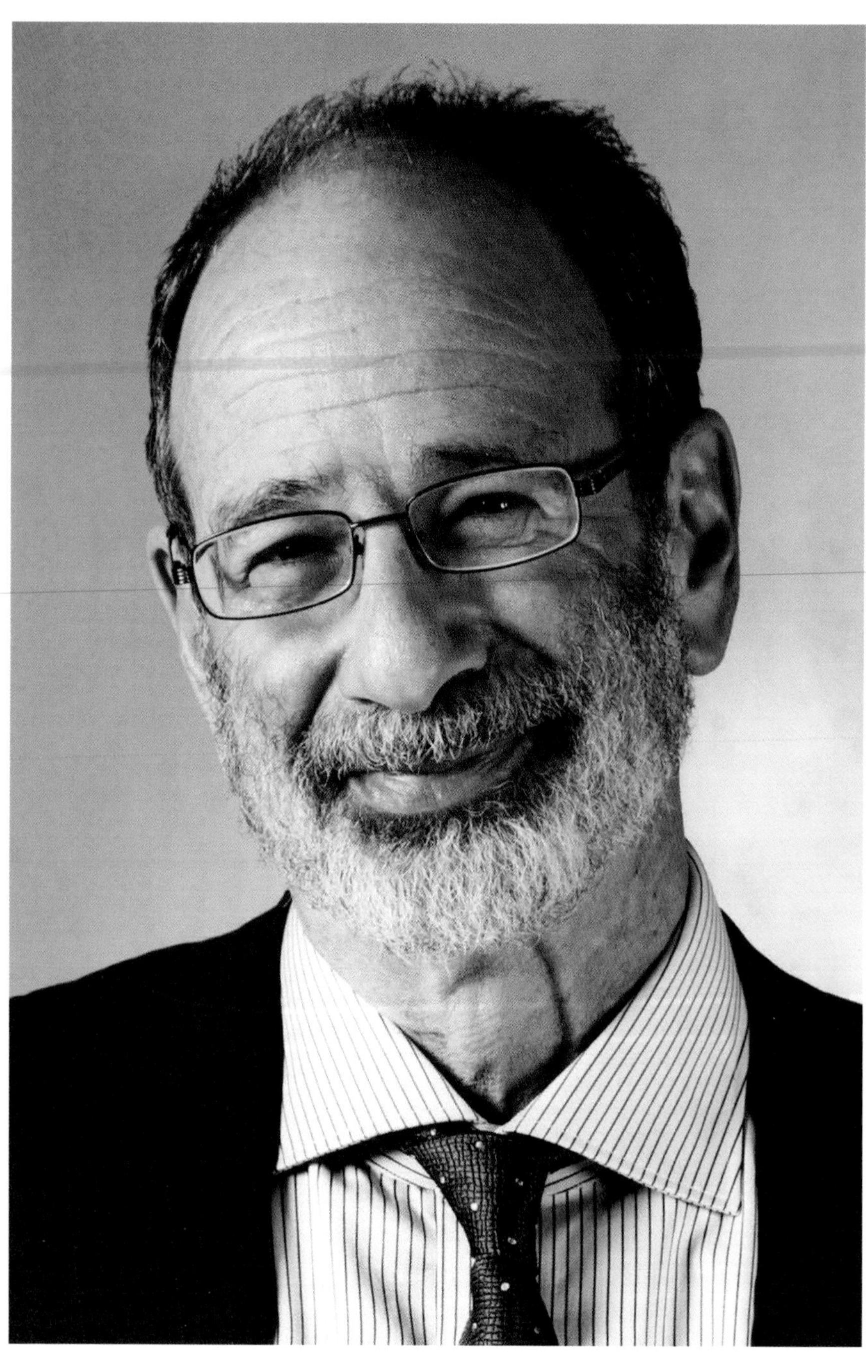

Alvin Roth. © The Nobel Foundation. Photo: U. Montan

Alvin Roth

I was born on December 18, 1951 in the New York City borough of Queens. My parents, Ernest and Lillian, were both public high school teachers of a subject that is probably no longer taught, called Secretarial Studies, which focused on typing and taking dictation via two methods of *shorthand stenography*, Pitman and Gregg. Their students were young women planning to go directly to work as secretaries after high school.

Not long after I was born, science became very fashionable in the United States, following the launch of the Sputnik satellite by the Soviet Union in 1957. I have an early memory of sitting in class listening to a radio broadcast of the launch of an American satellite, maybe one of the Explorer satellites in early 1958, when I was in first grade. That, plus the fact that my older brother Ted thought we should be scientists, was enough to convince me that science could be a career.

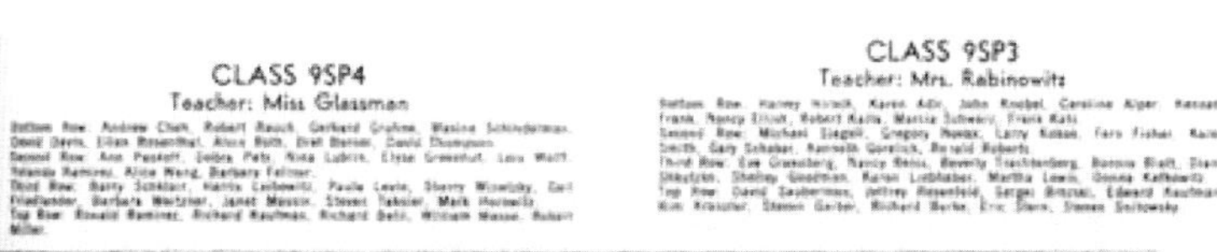

FIGURE 1. Some of my old friends tell me I haven't changed a bit since the 9th grade.

I decided to do research in game theory after taking a class from Michael Maschler, who was visiting Stanford from the Hebrew University of Jerusalem. Bob Wilson agreed to be my advisor and rescued me from having what looked to be a very short academic career after I failed one of my Ph.D. qualifying exams. He was on sabbatical that year, but met with me regularly once a week for an hour. In memory, our meetings followed a kind of script: I would spend a while explaining to him why I hadn't made progress that week, and then he would spend a while telling me not to be discouraged. Then I would describe some roadblock to further progress, and he would, as we finished our meeting, recommend a paper for me to read. Because his recommendations had always been very much on target, I would go straight from his office to the library and start to read the paper. As I did, I would think, this time Bob made a mistake, this paper has nothing to do with my problem. But then, somewhere in the middle of the paper would be a lemma or remark that helped me get around that roadblock …

My dissertation concerned the then popular models of games with transferable utility, and explored a generalization of the stable sets of outcomes that von Neumann and Morgenstern had proposed as "solutions" of such games. The progress of game theory has included the thorough exploration of a number of dead ends, and this eventually turned out to be one of them. But it gave me some tools (I proved a fixed point theorem on lattices), and an enduring interest in game theory.

FIGURE 2. At Columbia University, around 1970.

I applied for jobs in OR and math departments, and was about to take a job in a math department – I had already decided which one – when, at the last minute, I got a phone call from Bill Zangwill, who was putting together an operations research group in the business school at the University of Illinois at Urbana-Champaign. I was completely relaxed at the campus interview, since I figured I already knew what job I was going to take. While I was visiting Illinois, I suggested that, were I to come, I would like a joint appointment in Economics, since that seemed where the most interesting problems for game theory were to be found. I flew home and found a telegram on my front door, saying that a formal offer was on the way. And so I became at least a nominal part-time economist early in my career.

I was fortunate to also follow Ted in attending the Science Honors Program at Columbia University, which offered classes to junior high school and high school students on Saturdays. I thrived there, and I entered Columbia's engineering school in the Fall of 1968 when I was 16, without having graduated from high school.

At Columbia, I spent a lot of time practicing Shotokan karate, which was very satisfying and which taught me that I could work harder than I had thought. I also found time to study Operations Research, which seemed to me to offer the promise of bringing scientific methods to the organization of at least some parts of human activity. After graduating from Columbia I moved to Stanford University in 1971 to pursue my Ph.D. in what was then Stanford's Department of Operations Research.

As I prepared to leave California for Illinois, I paid a visit to Lloyd Shapley at the Rand Corporation in Santa Monica to tell him about my work. I recall a pleasant visit, in which he correctly conjectured how the proof of my fixed point theorem worked, and (if I recall correctly) ended with him driving me to the airport in his station wagon. Around that time, on a visit home to New York, I also visited Oskar Morgenstern at New York University to tell him about my work on von Neumann-Morgenstern solutions. I visited him several more times over the next three years, at NYU and once at his home in Princeton. My discussions with Morgenstern were always non-technical: he would reminisce about people, and I would tell him what I was working on. I sometimes felt a little like Columbus reporting back to Queen Isabella about the new lands that had been discovered in her name; Morgenstern appeared to be entertained by the fact that young people were working on game theory, and pointed out more than once that it had not always been so.

My arrival at Illinois is memorable for two psychologists I met there in my first year. The first, in the first weeks after my arrival, was my colleague Keith Murnighan. We were both new assistant professors in 1974. He had just received his Ph.D. in social psychology from Purdue. One of our senior colleagues suggested we would enjoy talking to each other, and we did, so much so that we decided to do some experiments together, on the kinds of games I had studied in my dissertation. Experiments were newer to me than game theory was to him, but over the course of the next decade we taught each other how to do experiments that would say something useful about game theory. He and I remember our early interactions differently, but we both agree that our first papers took many drafts to converge. Eventually we wrote a dozen papers together, exploring various aspects of game theory including the game theoretic predictions made by theories such as Nash's (1950) "solution" to the problem of determining the outcome of two-person bargaining. (Game theory was young, and many things that today would be called models of behavior, or kinds of equilibrium, were optimistically called "solutions," following von Neumann and Morgenstern.) Keith and I, together with my graduate student Mike Malouf and our colleague Francoise Schoumaker, developed some experimental designs (such as binary lottery games, see Roth and Malouf, 1979, or probabilistically terminated repeated games, see Roth and Murnighan, 1978) that remain in use today. In 1978 I also took a semester leave at the Economics Department at Stanford, where I taught a course whose lecture notes became my first book, *Axiomatic Models of Bargaining* (Roth, 1978). Axiomatic theories of the kind initiated by Nash were beautiful, and I enjoyed pushing the theory forward, but their failure to account for the kinds of behavior we observed so clearly in experiments convinced me that these too were a dead end for economics.

We published some of those early experiments in psychology journals, which in retrospect reflects my misunderstanding of how experimental economics was going to develop. Psychologists had already done some experiments motivated by game theory, but by and large they had not controlled for the kinds of things that game theorists felt were needed to provide clear tests. I imagined that if we could demonstrate experimental designs that controlled for the things that seemed important to game theorists, psychologists might then proceed to test game theoretic predictions in the laboratory in a way that would be convincing to game theorists. But psychologists have their own agendas, and it quickly became clear that economists could not rely on a division of labor with psychologists, we would have to do for ourselves the experiments whose results we were curious to know.

I had the early opportunity at Illinois to teach a graduate course in game theory, and as I prepared my lectures I realized I didn't understand as well as I would like many of the things I had been taught. My attempts to understand these things better led not only to my theoretical papers about Nash's solution, but also to a set of papers about the Shapley value, which had been given an axiomatic foundation when introduced by Shapley (1953). I found that I could not convincingly explain some of the axioms to my students. Instead, I ended up writing a short series of papers in which I explored the idea of formalizing the Shapley value as a utility function for playing a game, so that a decision maker who was a utility maximizer could compare the option of playing a particular position in a given game with other opportunities. The tools for doing this, initiated by Shapley, have not gracefully generalized to the models of games we now mostly consider, but the usefulness of being able to evaluate the prospect of playing a game remains, and how to do that remains an open question. (I also eventually edited a volume of papers on the Shapley value, which we presented to Lloyd at a conference in honor of his 65th birthday and which came out as Roth, 1988.)

Two of my other explorations of models formulated by Shapley began streams of work which have continued throughout my career. In 1974, in the first issue of the first volume of the new *Journal of Mathematical Economics*, Shapley and Herb Scarf (Shapley and Scarf, 1974) explored a simple abstract model of exchange without money, in which each trader was endowed with a single unit of an indivisible good, which they called a "house," and each player had preferences over all the houses. They also introduced the "top trading cycles algorithm," which they attributed to David Gale, for using the preferences of the players to find a set of trades that would result in an allocation in the core: i.e. a set of trades among all the players such that no coalition of players could have done better by going off and trading among themselves. Andy Postlewaite had also arrived as a new assistant professor at Illinois in 1974, and he and I explored the model further (Roth and Postlewaite, 1977), from the point of view of understanding the structure of the core, given the known preferences of the players, a point of view that characterized what was then called cooperative game theory. But I had already begun to think that if one wanted to necessary to elicit the preferences of the players. In a subsequent paper (Roth, 1982a) I showed that the top trading cycles algorithm had the potential to do that in a reliable way, since it would make it safe for players to reveal their true preferences and would never reward a player who mis-stated his preferences.

I had already begun to think about the problem of making it safe for participants to reveal their preferences in connection with the very different kind of clearinghouse that was already in use for organizing the labor market for new American medical doctors. I don't recall how I first heard about that clearinghouse, but I do remember calling the medical librarian (the medical school was in Chicago) and asking her to send me copies of the documents sent to participants in the clearinghouse, which in those days was called the National Intern and Resident Matching Program (NIRMP). Those documents described briefly how the clearinghouse worked: how residency programs advertised their job descriptions, doctors applied for interviews, residency programs interviewed applicants and rank order lists of residency programs were then collected from doctors, and rank order lists of doctors from residency programs, and combined into a match. The documents made what seemed to me to be a surprising claim, namely that the clearinghouse was designed in such a way that everyone – employers and applicants – did best if they submitted rank order lists that corresponded to their true preferences. As I began to explore the history of this medical match, I found that an early algorithm for turning the rank order lists into a matching of applicants to positions had been replaced after it was noticed that it didn't have this property. It had been replaced in the early 1950s by an algorithm that I was able to show was essentially equivalent to the 'deferred acceptance algorithm' proposed and studied by Gale and Shapley (1962), in their seminal paper "College Admissions and the Stability of Marriage." Gale and Shapley showed that such an algorithm could always produce a matching that was stable in the sense that no applicant and position would both prefer one another to [one of those to] whom they were matched.

In a paper called "The Economics of Matching: Stability and Incentives," I showed that there were not any mechanisms that would always both produce a stable matching and make it completely safe for all firms and workers to reveal their true preferences. But the deferred acceptance algorithm could make it completely safe – a "dominant strategy" – for *applicants* to submit a rank order list that ranked jobs according to the applicant's true preferences. Some of these ideas were 'in the air' and were also discovered by others: Dubins and Freedman (1981) also showed that the deferred acceptance algorithm could make it safe for applicants to reveal their true preferences and Bergstrom and Manning (1983, unpublished) also showed that no stable matching mechanism could do this for both sides of the market.

Some measure of how much economics has changed in the last decades can be glimpsed from the reaction my paper received when I submitted it to the

Journal of Political Economy sometime around 1980. The editor, George Stigler, wrote me a polite letter in which he said that he could see that the paper was interesting and important, but that, except for the title, it wasn't about economics at all. He didn't think that a clearinghouse was a marketplace if it didn't use adjustments in prices/wages to clear the market.

That paper was eventually published in *Mathematics of Operations Research* (Roth, 1982b), and it marked the beginning of my broader interest in "matching markets" – which are precisely the many important markets, labor markets among them, in which price adjustment alone doesn't clear the market. Loosely speaking, these are markets that have application procedures, or selection criteria or other institutions, and in which you cannot simply choose what you want (even if you can afford it), but also have to be chosen.

Meanwhile, my relationship with another psychologist was also developing: I met and courted my wife Emilie, who was pursuing her Ph.D. in cognitive psychology at the University of Illinois' famous psychology department. We met while folk dancing and were married in 1977. When she finished her Ph.D. in 1980 we moved about 25 miles West of Champaign-Urbana to the metropolis of Farmer City, Illinois (population about 2000), which was half way between the University of Illinois and Illinois State University, where she briefly taught. But we were only there for two years, after which the search for two jobs led us to Pittsburgh in 1982.

I began a long and happy sojourn in the Economics Department at the University of Pittsburgh (game theory was beginning to become firmly established in economics, and it had not yet thrived in Operations Research). Emilie began work at the Research and Development Center of the Westinghouse Corporation. The work that she and her colleagues did there gave rise to the new discipline that is today called Cognitive Engineering, which focused on understanding the kinds of information that people need to solve the problems they face, and making sure that this information is available to them, for example in control panels designed to help operate power plants, and deal with emergencies as they arise. Her work has since branched out to the design of many other things, and she likes to point out that I followed her into design.

"Design" is a noun as well as a verb, and in Pittsburgh I continued to look in detail at the design of the medical match, and the conditions in the market for new doctors that had given rise to it in the early 1950s. One of the problems that had plagued the labor market for new doctors in the first half of the 20th century was that competition for good students and for good jobs gradually caused positions to be offered earlier and earlier, until eventually medical students and hospitals were arranging the first post-graduation jobs of medical students two years before they graduated from medical school. Not only did this mean that jobs were being arranged so early that important information on the quality of the match was missing, but job offers were made at different times, and decisions about whether to accept offers were demanded very quickly, so that medical students often had little opportunity to compare different potential positions. The labor market clearinghouse that was organized in the early 1950s solved both these market failures, and my 1984 paper analyzed its design, and pointed to some difficulties it was then facing as a consequence of the growing number of medical students who were married to each other and who wished to find two positions in the same vicinity. This history of that market made clear how a clearinghouse that produced stable matchings had played a critical role in making the market thick, so that lots of potential matches could be considered together, and in dealing with the congestion that had arisen in the less centralized marketplaces that preceded it.

As I began to study the history of other labor markets I found that the "unraveling" of annual markets, in which each year offers are made earlier, and in which there is little opportunity to compare offers, is not so rare. My student Xiaolin Xing and I wrote a paper documenting this in over a dozen markets (Roth and Xing, 1994). It became clear that the timing of transactions was also important in understanding how markets and marketplaces work. Timing is important not just in terms of the date at which transactions take place, but also in terms of how much time they can take, and Xiaolin and I studied the congestion that can result when a marketplace doesn't give participants enough time to evaluate as many of the transactions as they would like, in connection with difficulties that were being experienced in the market for clinical psychologists which was then run by telephone on a specified day (Roth and Xing, 1997).

While at Pittsburgh I also continued my theoretical and empirical investigation of stable matchings and clearinghouses. I also began to hire postdoctoral fellows, and with one of them, Marilda Sotomayor (who was introduced to me by David Gale) I wrote a monograph (Roth and Sotomayor, 1990) that helped introduce much of what was then known on the subject to a wider audience of economists. On the empirical side, I studied a set of medical clearinghouses that had been organized in different regions of Britain's National Health Service to deal with the unraveling of their markets for newly graduated doctors (Roth, 1990 and 1991). Those clearinghouses, some of which succeeded and some of which failed, helped provide a kind of natural experiment to clarify how the design of a marketplace could influence the operation of a market.

Pittsburgh became an important center of experimental economics, and my colleague John Kagel (with whom I had earlier edited the *Handbook of Experimental Economics* (Kagel and Roth, 1995) and I were able to use a laboratory experiment to further illuminate the importance of how the clearinghouses were designed. We compared the performance of the failed clearinghouse design used in Newcastle and Birmingham with the successful design used in Edinburgh, under laboratory conditions that controlled away all the many other differences that exist between those three cities and their medical labor markets (Kagel and Roth, 2000).

It was becoming increasingly clear that how participants learned about the strategic environment would be an important part of market design, and my own understanding of some of the issues was helped by a series of papers that Ido Erev and I wrote about the learning behavior that we observed in experiments (e.g. Erev and Roth, 1995 and 1998). At Pittsburgh I was also able to continue studying bargaining behavior in the laboratory, with Jack Ochs and Bob Slonim (Ochs and Roth, 1989; Slonim and Roth, 1998).

My first chance to put market design into practice came in a phone call from Bob Beran, the director of the medical clearinghouse that was by then called the National Resident Matching Program (reflecting changes in the structure of medical practice that had led "internships" to give way to "residencies" even in the first year of postgraduate employment). The Match was already receiving very able technical assistance from Elliott Peranson, whom I had met previously, and Beran was now calling to ask if I would agree to direct the redesign of the underlying match algorithm, to address an emerging crisis of confidence in a way that would be consistent with changes that had taken place in the underlying conditions in the market for new doctors.

I still recall vividly that my gut reaction was "why me?" as I took that first call. I knew of course why I was a natural for him to call; I had written papers on the medical labor market and the history of the match, and a book on matching. But I also knew that the only things in the book that applied directly to the task I was being asked to undertake were the counterexamples. The book was about simple models of matching, and was full of theorems framed in terms of things that would always happen or could never be achieved: e.g. "the set of stable outcomes is always nonempty," or "there doesn't exist any stable matching mechanism that always makes it a dominant strategy for everyone to state their true preferences." Complications were addressed by counterexamples, such as showing that when there are two-career households in the market, the set of stable matchings could be empty. In my role as a theorist, it had been enough to note that couples therefore presented a hard problem. In my new role as a market designer, they would become my problem.

I worked closely with Peranson, and we together developed the algorithm that continues today to run the "main match" for new residents (Roth and Peranson, 1999). Peranson is an entrepreneurial matchmaker, and the Roth-Peranson algorithm has since been adopted by a number of clearinghouses for more senior medical positions, and for other labor markets in (mostly) health care professions, including the market for clinical psychologists that I had studied as a congested decentralized market. In the course of that collaboration, and in my subsequent collaborations on market design, I have found that my tastes in theory have changed accordingly. I no longer just want to know that some features of the market might cause problems: I am also interested in learning more about how big those problems might be, how frequently they might be encountered, and how to work around them.

In Pittsburgh I taught courses both in experimental economics and in game theory. The 1974 Shapley and Scarf paper was among those I taught regularly in my game theory class, and students always expressed unease that the indivisible goods that were being traded, without the use of money, were called "houses." It happens that the University of Pittsburgh Medical Center was then one of a small number of very active transplant centers, due in large part to the pioneering efforts of Pitt surgeon Thomas Starzl to overcome immunological barriers to transplantation. And in 1990 kidney transplantation was in the news as another surgeon, Joseph Murray, shared the Nobel Prize in medicine, for having performed the first successful kidney transplant (between identical twins) and for his subsequent work in overcoming immunological barriers between donors and patients. In my class notes from around that time show that I started referring not just to "houses" but to "kidneys" as indivisible goods that could be traded among patient-donor pairs to obtain better matches. I didn't yet imagine that this would one day be a practical design problem (the first actual kidney exchange was still in the future), but kidney exchange gave me an easy answer to students' questions about why money could not be used: it had been against American law since 1984 to buy or sell organs for transplantation.

Pittsburgh is also where our sons Aaron and Ben were born, in 1984 and 1991, and the ease of raising a family there made it hard to leave. (A word of advice for parents: pay attention! Childhood moves fast. As I write this in early 2013, our younger son is in graduate school, and our older son is a professor of computer science ...) It was hard to leave Pittsburgh, but as our older son was preparing to enter high school (and hence change schools in any event) we moved to Boston in 1998, where I took a position at Harvard, dividing my time equally between the Department of Economics and the Harvard Business School.

At Harvard I occupied two offices and crossed the Charles River twice almost every day, as I would walk from HBS to Economics and then back to get on my bike or in my car for the trip home. It was a short walk, but it sometimes felt like a big change in perspective. As a market designer I was glad to be able to work on both sides of what sometimes seemed like a wide river, between theory and practice, and simple abstraction and messy detail.

One of the first markets I began to study in earnest after arriving at Harvard was the market for top law school graduates who seek prestigious work for a year or two as law clerks to appellate court judges. This is a market that has frequently unraveled (Xiaolin Xing and I had written about it) and just as frequently has tried new rules in an effort to have hiring commence only after law students had completed at least two years of law school. Together with my colleagues Chris Avery and Christine Jolls, and Judge Richard Posner, we surveyed judges and applicants and considered possible solutions (Avery, Jolls, Posner and Roth, 2001 and 2007), as the market struggled and failed to find a homegrown design that would work.

FIGURE 3. Ben, Aaron, Emilie and Al in 2008.

Around that time I also began to study, with Axel Ockenfels, the very different way that timing played a crucial role in the auctions run on eBay. The design of their auctions included an ending rule that elicited a lot of bidding in the final minutes and even seconds of many auctions. We studied, in the field and later (with Dan Ariely) in the lab, how small changes in auction design elicited big changes in bidder behavior (Roth and Ockenfels, 2002; Ariely, Ockenfels and Roth, 2005).

Not long after, Paul Milgrom came for a two year visit, on leave from Stanford, and he and I together taught what may have been the first class in Market Design, in 2000 and again in 2001. Teaching with Paul was a thrilling experience, and helped shaped my views of how the field might develop. Some of those views are in two "manifestos" that I wrote, "The Economist as Engineer ..." (Roth, 2002) and "What Have We Learned from Market Design" (Roth, 2008).

My first Ph.D. student at Harvard was Muriel Niederle, who arrived at Harvard the year before I did, and together with fellow student Stefano DellaVigna peppered me with emails urging me to accept Harvard's offer and assuring me that I'd have no trouble attracting students there. (Indeed, one motivation for moving was the attraction of being able to help educate Harvard students, who would in turn help establish experimental economics and market design more firmly in economics.) She and I began to study the market for gastroenterologists, which was experiencing unraveling like the law clerk market. After studying the gastro market in a series of papers in both economics and medical journals, we were able to help the Yale gastroenterologist Debbie Proctor convince her colleagues to adopt some novel guidelines giving applicants the ability to change their minds if they accepted very early offers, and this helped moderate the pressure to unravel sufficiently so that a successful clearinghouse could operate (see e.g. Niederle and Roth, 2003a,b, 2004 and 2009; Niederle Proctor and Roth, 2006 and 2008). The gastro market underlines what in my experience has been a general rule in market design: for a design to successfully pass from conception to adoption and implementation, it is necessary to have a talented insider who can help us (the economists) understand in detail the market and its problems, and who can take a leading role in explaining and persuading and in implementing institutional changes.

My opportunity to design school choice systems began in 2003 with a phone call from Jeremy Lack at the New York City Department of Education. He knew of my work on the medical match, and wondered if similar efforts might help reorganize the dysfunctional, congested system then used to match students to high schools. Together with Parag Pathak, then a graduate student at Harvard but now a Professor at MIT, and Atila Abdulkadiroğlu, who was then a professor at Columbia, we studied the problem and found ways to adapt a deferred-acceptance clearinghouse that solved the congestion problem and others. It fell to Neil Dorosin, who was director of high school operations at NYC-DOE to implement the new system. He went on to found the nonprofit Institute for Innovation in Public School Choice, which Atila, Parag and I have supported in spreading this technology to a growing number of American cities. But the first city to which we turned our attention after New York was Boston. Atila and Tayfun Sönmez had written a paper about the school choice system used in Boston, and it opened the door for us all to be invited to study the system from the inside, and eventually to redesign the choice algorithm used to implement Boston's school choice goals (see Abdulkadiroğlu and Sönmez, 2003; Abdulkadiroğlu et al., 2005a,b and 2009).

In 2000, the first kidney exchange in the United States took place at Rhode Island Hospital, and my class notes on top trading cycles started to seem to have practical potential to organize such exchanges. When Utku Ünver (who had been my Ph.D. student at Pitt) visited Harvard in 2002, I suggested that we teach a class on kidney exchange. We posted our notes on the web and Tayfun Sönmez, who was Utku's colleague at Koç, read them and suggested that we collaborate. The time zone difference between Istanbul and Boston made it seem as if we were working around the clock. When we finished, we had designed an algorithm both for kidney exchange among patient-donor pairs and for integrating these exchanges with non-directed donors, such as deceased donors (and a growing number of living donors) who aren't part of a pair with a particular intended recipient. We sent a draft of our first paper (Roth, Sönmez and Ünver, 2004) to many surgeons, but initially only one, Frank Delmonico responded. We helped Frank form the New England Program for Kidney Exchange. My colleagues and I (especially, more recently, Itai Ashlagi) have since collaborated with a number other kidney exchange networks, including the Alliance for Paired Donation, founded by an innovative surgeon, Mike Rees, whom we helped to develop new ways of arranging exchanges, including long non-simultaneous chains (Roth et al., 2006 and Rees et al., 2009).

While kidney exchange has now helped thousands of patients with incompatible donors receive transplants of life saving compatible kidneys, many other avenues will still need to be explored, as the number of people waiting for kidney transplants has continued to grow. With my student Judd Kessler I have started to explore ways of increasing deceased donation (Kessler and Roth, 2012 and 13a,b)

In thinking about these issues, I have become eager to understand the quite widespread reluctance to consider monetary markets for kidneys, which are illegal almost everywhere in the world. Economists need to better understand popular attitudes towards all sorts of economic transactions. My 2007 paper "Repugnance as a Constraint on Markets" was my first effort in this direction, but it remains a subject well worth exploring, and of importance well beyond medical issues.

At Harvard I was involved in other market design efforts, both of clearinghouses (for Teach for America, and for field assignments for HBS MBA students with Clayton Featherstone, and for freshman and junior seminars for undergraduates with Steve Leider), and for decentralized markets (such as the signaling mechanism for the market for new Ph.D. economists; see Coles et al., 2010). Decentralized marketplaces face design issues just as much as centralized ones do, and I anticipate that this will be a next frontier in market design.

In the summer of 2012 Emilie and I sold our house and moved to California, where I took up a position at Stanford, after 14 years at Harvard. It was a difficult decision, but we were empty-nesters, and we felt ready for a new adventure. I was 60, and to retire gracefully from Harvard my age plus years of service needed to add up to 75, and so it was that when the call came from the Economics Prize Committee it found us in California, at 3:30 in the morning. I was on leave from Harvard but already teaching at Stanford, as a visitor until I turned 61 in December and became the Gund Professor of Economics and Business Administration Emeritus at Harvard and the McCaw Professor of Economics at Stanford. One of the big attractions of coming to Stanford is that I get to be the colleague of several of my students, including Muriel Niederle, Mike Ostrovsky and Fuhito Kojima, whose dissertations I advised at Harvard, and of my advisor Bob Wilson, who remains active as an emeritus professor. Having students, and being one, form some of the important relationships in an academic life.

The call from the Economics Committee was followed by several hectic months, with some difficult decisions involving the allocation of scarce, indivisible resources, since laureates are only allowed to invite fourteen guests to the main festivities. (Allocation of scarce goods is hard; someone should study it …). In addition to family, our guests included both economists and non-economists who had played important roles in some of the markets I had helped design. Assembling the group made it even clearer that market design is an outward facing part of economics.

Now, still in the near-aftermath of all that excitement, I am working on getting back to work. The Nobel is a very famous prize indeed, widely covered in the press, and the nicest part of the avalanche of emails and other contacts that result from that has been that many old friends have made contact, some of whom I hadn't been in touch with since childhood. It turns out that a Nobel is also followed by other recognitions, and perhaps the most unexpected of these is that the Japan Karate Association in Tokyo has now made me an honorary 7th-degree black belt, something that, given my athletic abilities, is even more unimaginable than being an Economic Sciences Laureate.

FIGURE 4. The final slide from my Prize lecture.

REFERENCES

1. Abdulkadiroğlu, Atila, Parag A. Pathak, and Alvin E. Roth, "The New York City High School Match," *American Economic Review*, Papers and Proceedings, 95, 2, May 2005, 364–367.
2. Abdulkadiroğlu, Atila, Parag A. Pathak, and Alvin E. Roth, "Strategy-proofness versus Efficiency in Matching with Indifferences: Redesigning the NYC High School Match," *American Economic Review*, 99, 5 (December), 2009, 1954–1978.
3. Abdulkadiroğlu, Atila, Parag A. Pathak, Alvin E. Roth, and Tayfun Sönmez, "The Boston Public School Match," *American Economic Review*, Papers and Proceedings, 95, 2, May 2005, 368–371.

4. Abdulkadiroğlu, Atila, and Tayfun Sönmez, "School Choice: A Mechanism Design Approach," *American Economic Review*, 93, 3, June 2003, 729–747.
5. Ariely, Dan, Axel Ockenfels, and Alvin E. Roth, "An Experimental Analysis of Ending Rules in Internet Auctions," *Rand Journal of Economics*, 36, 4, Winter 2005, 891–908.
6. Avery, Christopher, Christine Jolls, Richard A. Posner, and Alvin E. Roth, "The Market for Federal Judicial Law Clerks," *University of Chicago Law Review*, 68, 3, Summer 2001, 793–902.
7. Avery, Christopher, Christine Jolls, Richard A. Posner, and Alvin E. Roth, "The New Market for Federal Judicial Law Clerks," *University of Chicago Law Review*, 74, Spring 2007, 447–486.
8. Bergstrom, T. and R. Manning (1983), "Can Courtship be Cheatproof?" unpublished, http://escholarship.org/uc/item/5dg0f759
9. Coles, Peter, John H. Cawley, Phillip B. Levine, Muriel Niederle, Alvin E. Roth, and John J. Siegfried, "The Job Market for New Economists: A Market Design Perspective," *Journal of Economic Perspectives*, 24, 4, Fall 2010, 187–206.
10. Dubins, L.E. and D.A. Freedman (1981), "Machiavelli and the Gale-Shapley algorithm, "*American Mathematical Monthly*, 88, 485–94.
11. Erev, Ido and A.E. Roth, "Predicting how people play games: Reinforcement learning in experimental games with unique, mixed strategy equilibria," *American Economic Review*, 88, 4, September 1998, 848–881.
12. Gale, D. and L. S. Shapley (1962), "College admissions and the stability of marriage," *American Mathematical Monthly*, 69: 9–15.
13. Kagel, J.H. and A.E. Roth (editors), *Handbook of Experimental Economics*, Princeton University Press, 1995.
14. Kagel, John H. and A.E. Roth, "The dynamics of reorganization in matching markets: A laboratory experiment motivated by a natural experiment," *Quarterly Journal of Economics*, February, 2000, 201–235.
15. Kessler, Judd B. and Alvin E. Roth, "Organ Allocation Policy and the Decision to Donate," *American Economic Review*, Vol. 102 No. 5 (August 2012), 2018–47.
16. Kessler, Judd B. and Alvin E. Roth,"Don't Take 'No' For An Answer: An experiment with actual organ donor registration," working paper, February 2013a.
17. Kessler, Judd B. and Alvin E. Roth, "Organ Donation Loopholes Undermine Warm Glow Giving: An Experiment Motivated by Priority Loopholes in Israel," working paper, February 2013b.
18. Nash, John F. Jr. (1950), "The Bargaining Problem," *Econometrica* 18 (2): 155–162.
19. Niederle, Muriel, Deborah D. Proctor, and Alvin E. Roth, "What will be needed for the new GI fellowship match to succeed?"*Gastroenterology*, January, 2006, 130, 218–224.
20. Niederle, Muriel, Deborah D. Proctor, and Alvin E. Roth, "The Gastroenterology Fellowship Match - The First Two Years," *Gastroenterology*, 135, 2 (August), 344–346, 2008.

21. Niederle, Muriel and Alvin E. Roth, "Relationship Between Wages and Presence of a Match in Medical Fellowships," *JAMA. Journal of the American Medical Association*, vol. 290, No. 9, September 3, 2003a, 1153–1154.
22. Niederle, Muriel and Alvin E. Roth, "Unraveling reduces mobility in a labor market: Gastroenterology with and without a centralized match," *Journal of Political Economy*, 111, 6, December 2003b, 1342–1352.
23. Niederle, Muriel and Alvin E. Roth, "The Gastroenterology Fellowship Match: How it failed, and why it could succeed once again," *Gastroenterology*, 127, 2 August 2004, 658–666.
24. Niederle, Muriel and Alvin E. Roth, "Market Culture: How Rules Governing Exploding Offers Affect Market Performance," *American Economic Journal: Microeconomics*, 1, 2, August 2009, 199–219.
25. Ochs, J. and Roth, A.E., "An Experimental Study of Sequential Bargaining," *American Economic Review*, Vol. 79, 1989, 355–384.
26. Rees, Michael A., Jonathan E. Kopke, Ronald P. Pelletier, Dorry L. Segev, Matthew E. Rutter, Alfredo J. Fabrega, Jeffrey Rogers, Oleh G. Pankewycz, Janet Hiller, Alvin E. Roth, Tuomas Sandholm, Utku Ünver, and Robert A. Montgomery, "A Non- Simultaneous Extended Altruistic Donor Chain," *New England Journal of Medicine*, 360;11, March 12, 2009, 1096–1101.
27. Roth, A.E., *Axiomatic Models of Bargaining*, Lecture Notes in Economics and Mathematical Systems #170, Springer Verlag, 1979.
28. Roth, A.E., "Incentive Compatibility in a Market with Indivisible Goods," *Economics Letters*, Vol. 9, 1982a, 127 132.
29. Roth, A.E., "The Economics of Matching: Stability and Incentives," *Mathematics of Operations Research*, Vol. 7, 1982b, 617 628.
30. Roth, A.E., "The Evolution of the Labor Market for Medical Interns and Residents: A Case Study in Game Theory," *Journal of Political Economy*, Vol. 92, 1984, 991 1016.
31. Roth, A.E. (editor), *The Shapley Value: Essays in Honor of Lloyd S. Shapley*, Cambridge University Press, 1988.
32. Roth, A.E., "New Physicians: A Natural Experiment in Market Organization," *Science*, 250, 1990, 1524–1528.
33. Roth, A.E., "A Natural Experiment in the Organization of Entry Level Labor Markets: Regional Markets for New Physicians and Surgeons in the U.K.," *American Economic Review*, vol. 81, June 1991, 415–440.
34. Roth, Alvin E., "The Economist as Engineer: Game Theory, Experimental Economics and Computation as Tools of Design Economics," Fisher Schultz lecture, *Econometrica*, 70, 4, July 2002, 1341–1378.
35. Roth, Alvin E., "Repugnance as a constraint on markets," *Journal of Economic Perspectives*, 21 (3), Summer 2007, 37–58.
36. Roth, Alvin E. "What have we learned from market design?" Hahn Lecture, *Economic Journal*, 118 (March), 2008, 285–310.

37. Roth, A.E. and I. Erev, "Learning in Extensive-Form Games: Experimental Data and Simple Dynamic Models in the Intermediate Term," *Games and Economic Behavior*, Special Issue: Nobel Symposium, vol. 8, January 1995, 164–212.
38. Roth, A.E. and Malouf, M.K., "Game Theoretic Models and the Role of Information in Bargaining," *Psychological Review*, Vol. 86, 1979, 574 594.
39. Roth, A.E. and Murnighan, J.K., "Equilibrium Behavior and Repeated Play of the Prisoners' Dilemma," *Journal of Mathematical Psychology*, Vol. 17, 1978, 189–198.
40. Roth, Alvin E. and Axel Ockenfels, "Last-Minute Bidding and the Rules for Ending Second-Price Auctions: Evidence from eBay and Amazon Auctions on the Internet," *American Economic Review*, 92 (4), September 2002, 1093–1103.
41. Roth, A.E. and E. Peranson,"The Redesign of the Matching Market for American Physicians: Some Engineering Aspects of Economic Design," *American Economic Review*, 89, 4, September 1999, 748–780.
42. Roth, A.E. and Postlewaite, A. "Weak Versus Strong Domination in a Market with Indivisible Goods," *Journal of Mathematical Economics*, Vol. 4, August 1977, 131–137.
43. Roth, Alvin E., Tayfun Sönmez and M. Utku Ünver, "Kidney Exchange," *Quarterly Journal of Economics*, 119, 2, May 2004, 457–488.
44. Roth, Alvin E., Tayfun Sönmez, M. Utku Ünver, Francis L. Delmonico, and Susan L. Saidman, "Utilizing List Exchange and Undirected Good Samaritan Donation through 'Chain' Paired Kidney Donations," *American Journal of Transplantation*, 6, 11, November 2006, 2694–2705.
45. Roth, A.E. and M. Sotomayor, *Two-Sided Matching: A Study in Game-Theoretic Modeling and Analysis*, Econometric Society Monograph Series, Cambridge University Press, 1990.
46. Roth, A.E. and X. Xing, "Jumping the Gun: Imperfections and Institutions Related to the Timing of Market Transactions," *American Economic Review*, 84, September 1994, 992–1044.
47. Roth, A.E. and X. Xing, "Turnaround Time and Bottlenecks in Market Clearing: Decentralized Matching in the Market for Clinical Psychologists," *Journal of Political Economy*, 105, April 1997, 284–329.
48. Shapley, Lloyd S., "A Value for n-person Games." In *Contributions to the Theory of Games, volume II*, by H.W. Kuhn and A.W. Tucker, editors. Annals of Mathematical Studies v. 28, pp. 307–317. Princeton University Press, 1953.
49. Shapley, Lloyd and Scarf, Herbert, 1974. "On cores and indivisibility," *Journal of Mathematical Economics*, Elsevier, vol. 1 (1), pages 23–37, March.
50. Slonim, R. and A.E. Roth,"Learning in High Stakes Ultimatum Games: An Experiment in the Slovak Republic," *Econometrica*, 66, 3, May 1998, 569–596.

The Theory and Practice of Market Design

Prize Lecture, December 8, 2012

by Alvin E. Roth
Harvard University, Cambridge, MA, USA, Harvard Business School, Boston, MA, USA.

Preamble, to Lloyd Shapley:

Lloyd, when I began studying game theory, your work touched every part of it and shaped it and you were an inspiration—not just for me, but for the whole generation of game theorists who followed you. It is a great honor for me to share this prize with you.

I want to tell you about the theory and practice of market design, which is work that is still very much in progress. I should say personally that I am delighted to be recognized for work that we are still very much engaged with. Many of my colleagues are here in the audience and they are all waiting for me to get back to work.

The citation that the prize committee chose was "for the theory of stable allocations and the practice of market design." So the plan of my talk today is to tell you how stable allocations of the kind that Lloyd just spoke to us about connect to some of the most important markets that we are involved in—the matching markets that determine what schools we go to, and what jobs we get, and maybe who we are married to.

I also want to tell you about some additional theory that goes along with the theory of stable matchings, which helps us make game theory a practical tool for fixing markets when they are broken. And then I want to tell you about some of the applications. The ones I will talk about are job markets, school choice, and kidney transplantation of a certain sort.

Let us start by thinking about what markets and marketplaces do. How do they work, and how do they fail? And how can we fix them when they are broken?

When we think about markets, we often think about commodity markets. Commodity markets can be arm's length and anonymous. When you are buying 100 shares of stock on the New York Stock Exchange, you don't have to apply to buy, you don't have to convince the seller that you will take good care of those stocks. You don't have to worry about whether the seller took good took care of them when he had them. There is no courtship. The price does all the work. The New York Stock Exchange discovers a price at which supply equals demand.

But, in lots of markets, prices don't do all the work.

For example, I have been teaching at Harvard, and now I am teaching at Stanford. Those are both selective American universities. It is expensive to go to them, tuition costs a lot, but that is not what determines who gets to attend. Stanford doesn't raise its tuition until just enough students remain who want to attend. Even though tuition is expensive, it is low enough so that lots of people would like to be Stanford students. And then Stanford chooses the ones they would like.

So, universities don't rely on prices alone to determine who gets what. Labor markets also don't rely on prices alone, and labor markets and college admissions are more than a little like courtship and marriage. That is why the marriage metaphor is a good one because you can't just choose what you want. You also have to be chosen. You can't just tell Stanford that you're coming—they have to admit you.

You can't just tell Google that you are showing up for work. They have to hire you. And of course, it works that way on both sides. Yale can't just tell students to come to Yale. Yale has to compete for students with Harvard and Stanford. Google can't just hire who they want. Google has to compete for employees with Facebook.

So, matching markets are markets in which you can't just choose what you want (even if you can afford it), you also have to be chosen. College admissions and labor markets are two-sided matching markets, where both sides have preferences.

This is where we stand on the shoulders of Gale and Shapley's 1962 paper that Lloyd just told us about. My colleagues and I have also followed up on another paper, which I won't talk about since Lloyd didn't get to it—the Shapley and Scarf paper from 1974. Those two papers did something similar.

They defined a notion of stability. In the two-sided matching problem that Lloyd just told us about, a stable matching is one where there are not two people who are not matched to each other but who would both prefer to be matched to each other than who they are matched to. That's a specialization of the more general idea of the *core* that Lloyd introduced in game theory. If an outcome is in the core, then there is no coalition of players that can go off on their own and do better than they could do in the marketplace.

That is going to be an essential idea for marketplace design. One of the tasks of a market designer is to create a marketplace that people want to come and transact in. They should not be able to do better by transacting outside of the marketplace. The core is a very important formulation of this idea. (Stability was explored explicitly in terms of the core in the Shapley and Scarf, 1974 paper.)

Let me remind you of the deferred acceptance algorithm, which Lloyd just talked to us about, because I want to emphasize that it gets an outcome in the core—as he told us—but I also want to talk about some of its other properties.

Here is a representation of that algorithm that is suitable for thinking of it as a centralized clearing house.

- Step 0: students and schools **privately** submit preferences to a clearinghouse
- Step 1: Each student "applies" to her first choice. Each school **tentatively** assigns its seats to its applicants one at a time in the order of the school's preferences/priorities over students. Any remaining applicants are rejected.
- ...
- Step k: Each student who was rejected in the previous step applies to her next choice if one remains. Each school considers the students it has been holding together with its new applicants and **tentatively** assigns its seats to these students one at a time **in preference/priority order***. Any remaining applicants are rejected.
- The algorithm terminates when no student application is rejected, and each student is (finally) given her current tentative assignment.

Think of a centralized clearinghouse for matching students to schools, in which we ask students and schools to tell us their preferences. We ask the families and the students, "What is your first choice school, what is your second choice, what is your third choice? Write it down." And we say to the schools, "Rank order the students." Maybe the school principals have preferences as they do in New York, or maybe the schools have priorities for different students, established by the school district.

---

* Note that schools take no account of the step of the algorithm at which a student applied.

We take these preferences that have been submitted, and process them in a computer. We look at the students' preferences, and in the computer algorithm we have each student apply to her first choice. In this first step some schools get lots of applications, from the people who apply to those schools as their first choice.

But the schools don't immediately accept the people who applied. If they get more applications than they have spaces, the schools immediately reject those who they can't fit in, keeping—not yet rejecting—those that they prefer, i.e. not immediately rejecting those students who are highest on the school's preferences or priorities among those who have applied so far. That is, each school has its own preference, or priority list, and it keeps the highest priority students who have applied, and it rejects the rest.

But it doesn't accept those students yet, it just doesn't reject them, while it waits to see who else will apply. And every student who has been rejected goes ahead and applies to their next choice school. Every school looks at the new applications together with the old ones—the ones that have not been rejected yet. It orders them in terms of its preferences or priorities. It keeps the ones it likes best and rejects the rest without prejudice about when they applied.

So, you can be a highly preferred student, but you apply and get rejected by your first choice. Next you apply to some school as your second choice, and you can now bump someone who applied to it as their first choice and was not initially rejected—but now they will be rejected because there is not space for both of you, and you have higher priority.

That is how the algorithm works. At each step, any student who has been rejected applies to his next choice. Each school looks at the people who have applied so far, keeps the best ones who have applied so far, and rejects the rest. And the algorithm stops only when no student is rejected anymore, which must eventually happen because no student applies twice to any school. When the algorithm stops, the schools finally admit all the students whose applications they are holding. That is why Gale and Shapley ('62) called this a *deferred acceptance algorithm*, since acceptances are deferred until the end, when all applications have ceased.

What does it mean for the algorithm to result in a stable match? It means there isn't a student and a school, not matched to each other who would rather be matched to each other. Suppose I am a student, and I end up matched to my third choice school. The matching would be unstable if my second choice school would rather have me than someone who they have been matched with, because I would prefer my second choice to my third choice, which is what I have got. If they also preferred me, we would be a blocking pair. We would be able to get together and produce a better match for ourselves, instead of accepting the match produced by the clearinghouse.

How do we know that doesn't happen? Well, the only time I get a chance to apply to my third choice school, according to this algorithm, is when my second choice school has already rejected me because they are full, and they have a full class of students they prefer to me.

So, if I am in my third choice school, it means that although I would prefer to be in my second choice, my second choice would not prefer to have me, and that is why the outcome is stable.

So the deferred acceptance algorithm finds a matching that is stable with respect to the preferences of the students and of the schools. How does the market find out those preferences? One of the questions you have to ask as a market designer is, "If you are going to set up a clearinghouse, and you are going to ask people to tell you their preferences, are they going to want to tell you their preferences, or are they going to want to tell you something else?"

That is, when you say to people, "Tell me your preferences," a natural reaction is, "What are you going to use that information for?" And if you are a parent dealing with a school system you might be reluctant to tell the school district your preferences if they are not going to make it safe for you to do so. When I started to look at two-sided markets in the 1980s, I showed that in fact it is impossible for a stable matching mechanism to always make it safe for everyone to reveal their true preferences.

But remember this is an algorithm with one side that proposes or applies, and one side that accepts and rejects. It turns out that it is completely safe for the side doing the proposing to reveal their true preferences—they can't come to harm by revealing their true preferences.

Let me give you an idea of how you could come to harm with a different algorithm.

When Atila Abdulkadiroğlu and Tayfun Sönmez first looked at the Boston school system, they found there an algorithm that tried to give as many people as possible their first choice. That sounds pretty good! That sounds like a sensible thing for a school system to try to do. But it turns out to make it unsafe for families to reveal their true preferences.

Think of an immediate acceptance algorithm instead of a deferred acceptance algorithm. The algorithm starts the same way—every student applies to their first choice school, and every school accepts as many of the kids who have applied as it can, rejecting the rest, using its own preference list to decide who to accept and who to reject. And then every student who was rejected applies to his or her second choice school. But, this is an immediate acceptance algorithm, and the children who were not rejected on the first step were immediately accepted. So it could be that you have really high priority at your second choice school, but your second choice school is already full. It is filled with people who applied to it as their first choice. And there lies the problem.

If you are not careful which school you list as your first choice, and if you fail to be admitted to the school you say is your first choice, you may find that your second choice has already been filled with people who said it was their first choice. Therefore, it might not be safe for you to tell the school district what your true preferences are because if you don't get your first choice, there is a good chance you will not get your second choice. And then your third choice will be filled with people who listed it as their first or second choice, and now you might fall right through to the bottom.

So, it is unsafe to reveal your preferences in the immediate acceptance algorithm, because that algorithm makes it important to list as your first choice a school that you have a high chance of getting admitted to, and as your second choice a school that has a good chance of not having all its places filled immediately. The deferred acceptance algorithm avoids forcing families to bear these kinds of strategic uncertainties precisely by deferring the acceptances. What makes the immediate acceptance algorithm unsafe is that you can lose your place in a school if you don't list it first. But in the deferred acceptance algorithm, because the schools don't decide who to accept until they see everyone who is going to apply, if you don't get your first choice, you still have just as much chance of getting your second choice as if you had listed it as your first choice. And that is part of the proof that allows you to see why it becomes safe, a *dominant strategy*, for students to state their true preferences in the student-applying deferred acceptance algorithm.

So far we have been talking about theory. Let me tell you how this opens a window on how marketplaces work. I will have to tell you a little bit about how American doctors get their first jobs and what happened over the first fifty years of the 20th century.

Before 1900, doctors graduated from medical school and immediately began to practice medicine. Around 1900, the customary first job of doctors started to be a supervised clinical position in a hospital, called an internship or a residency. Medical graduates looked for their first job at around the time they graduated from their four years of medical school training.

These are very important jobs for doctors—a residency is a bit like graduate school—it shapes your future career. And they are very important jobs for hospitals, because the interns and residents are a big part of a teaching hospital's labor force. So, there started to be competition by hospitals to get good interns and residents. One form this competition took was hospitals started to make offers a little earlier than their principal competitors. And pretty soon, instead of having lots of people trying to get jobs around June of the last year of medical school, medical students found that they were getting offers earlier in the year from hospitals, and the hospitals didn't give them a lot of time to decide. Instead of a thick market, with a lot of employers trying to hire at the same time, there started to be a lot of little thin markets in which a student would get an offer and, without knowing what other offers might come, have to decide yes or no, without being able to compare it to other offers.

These offers started getting earlier and earlier. By the 1930s, the standard time at which American doctors were getting their first jobs was around New Year of their last year of medical school, around the middle of the fourth year of medical school. This caused some distress to the hospitals because it meant hiring was taking place before information was available that would determine students' class standing, their grades in their fourth year of medical school, and things like that. But, the hospitals (and the students) could not stop themselves. Editorials in the medical journals from that time say, "Hiring is getting pretty early, let's not make it any earlier," and everyone agreed that was a good goal.

However by 1940, the standard time that American doctors were getting hired was two years before graduation. That's really inefficient because it turns out lots of information is missing. Not only can't hospitals tell who the good doctors are, the doctors can't tell which jobs they want.

After two years of medical school you might want to be a surgeon, because you got an A in anatomy. But you have not yet had any surgical experience. If the job market is going in the summer of your second year, you are a top student, you get a top surgery job—and only later in your third year, do you discover that you faint at the sight of blood, and that it will be just terrible to be a surgeon. So, there were big inefficiencies in going so early. The market was losing important information about match quality.

Eventually, the medical schools intervened. The medical schools are a third party: They are not the hospitals or the doctors. In 1945, they decided to help control the date at which offers were made, by not releasing any information about students before a certain date. No transcripts, no letters of reference. It had been risky to hire students two years before they graduated, but it was really risky to hire people without knowing any of their grades, or even if they were really medical students.

This succeeded in controlling the date at which offers were made, and then as it became clear that the date was under control, it was moved back from the second year, into the third year, and into the fourth year again.

But another problem developed, now that everyone was making offers at around the same time. There was congestion—there were lots of potential offers to be made, and not that much time to make them.

In 1945 the rules said that offers to students should remain open for ten days. What happened in 1945? There you are, a graduating medical student in 1945, and you get an offer from your third choice hospital. And your second choice hospital says to you, "You are on our waiting list, you are close to getting an offer. If someone turns us down, we will make you an offer. So, don't do anything in a hurry." And you are not in a hurry because you have ten days. So you wait, and, while everyone waits, the waiting lists don't move.

So on the tenth day, you have an offer from your third choice hospital and you are on the waiting list of your second choice. That was a formula for a chaotic tenth day. Some people accepted their third choice, and then later in the day, they accepted their second choice when they got that offer. And if they took a little while to tell their third choice that they were not coming, everybody on the third choice's waiting list had already accepted another position, and then that hospital was very unhappy.

So, to avoid the problems of the tenth day, in 1946 the rule was changed, so that it required that offers be open only for eight days.

You are starting to be market designers already, and you can see that that is not going to solve the problem. There is a problem, but that won't be the solution to it.

By 1950, the hospitals rejected twelve hours as too long to leave offers open, so there was an explicit exploding offer environment in which you would get an offer on the phone and have to say yes or no immediately, because the hospital would say to you, "we have to move down our waiting list, we know that it moves fast."

And then the participants in this market did a remarkable thing. They got together and developed, partly by trial and error, a centralized clearinghouse, with the outward form I have told you about. They asked people for their preferences.

Hospitals submit preferences over the students they have interviewed. Students submit their preferences over the hospitals, more specifically over the residency programs at which they interviewed. And. . .it worked. It was a voluntary program, but pretty soon, everyone was getting matched through the clearinghouse.

When I started to study this in a 1984 paper, I found that this 1950s algorithm was different from but equivalent to Gale and Shapley's deferred acceptance algorithm with hospitals proposing.

So, this market went from being a really chaotic market for the first fifty years of the twentieth century, to being a very orderly market for the next twenty-five years at least. What did the trick was the adoption of a centralized clearinghouse that used something equivalent to the deferred acceptance algorithm.

This was a first among many observations that started to make me think about how marketplaces work, and what they are supposed to do, and how they can fail. This market had been failing. And the way it had been failing from 1900 to 1945, was it had failed to provide thickness. It had failed to bring everyone to the marketplace at the same time so that there would be lots of opportunities available.

In 1945, it proved possible to assemble a thick market—everyone was available at the same time—but there was congestion. It took time to process offers, and people were waiting. Therefore if you were a hospital, you could not make as many offers as you might like. You wanted to make offers and get them accepted or rejected so you could move down your waiting list, but people were holding your offers. You could not move down your waiting list, so you could not make as many offers as you wanted to and as you needed to get to a good match. So, to work well, a marketplace not only has to be thick, it has to be able to deal with congestion. And finally, a marketplace has to be safe and simple to participate in.

In a clearinghouse organized by the deferred acceptance algorithm, if you can get people to wait for and join the central clearinghouse, then it solves the thickness problem without running into congestion, because you can make all those waiting lists move really fast. In the 1950s they ran the medical resident clearinghouse on card-sorting machines; today it is run on computers.

It is safe and simple in the sense that it is safe to submit your true preferences if you are on the proposing side of this market. (It turns out, because the market is a large one, it is quite safe to submit your true preferences whichever side of the market you are on.)

One way you can tell that the stability of the final outcome is important is by looking at clearinghouses around the world. This is not a very common form of market organization, but it is not non-existent, so we can learn from the experience of a number of labor market clearinghouses.

So I started studying different clearinghouses, and whether or not they produced stable matchings in terms of the stated preferences. One of the things you see on the list here is that often, when they produce stable matchings, they also succeed: they are still in use and they stopped unraveling. The first line is the National Resident Matching Program, the American market I just told you about.

Market	**Stable**	**Still in use (stopped unraveling)**
NRMP	yes	yes (new design in '98)
Edinburgh ('69)	*yes*	*yes*
Cardiff	*yes*	*yes*
Birmingham	*no*	*no*
Edinburgh ('67)	*no*	*no*
Newcastle	*no*	*no*
Sheffield	no	no
Cambridge	no	yes
London Hospital	no	yes
Medical Specialties	yes	yes (~30 markets, **1 failure**)
Canadian Lawyers	yes	yes (Alberta, no BC, Ontario)
Dental Residencies	yes	yes (5) (no 2)
Osteopaths (< '94)	no	no
Osteopaths (≥ '94)	yes	yes
Pharmacists	yes	yes
Reform rabbis	yes (first used in '97–98)	yes
Clinical psych	yes (first used in '99)	yes
Lab experiments	yes	yes
(Kagel&Roth *QJE*, 2000)	no	no

It turns out that in various regions of the British National Health Service the market for new medical graduates unraveled in the 1960s much as the American market for new doctors had in the 1940s. A Royal Commission was formed and said, "Do what the Americans do." But the only thing that was described in the American medical literature was that there was a clearinghouse. So every region of the British National Health Service adopted a different kind of clearinghouse, and some were stable, and some were not. They provided something like a small natural experiment.

Those markets are part of a small data set; it is certainly not as comprehensive as we might like. But by and large, when we see clearinghouses that produce stable matchings, they succeed. And when we see unstable matchings, they mostly fail. There are some exceptions, in particular the two markets at

Cambridge and London hospitals, which each matched students from a single medical school to a single hospital and succeeded despite being unstable.

We would like better evidence than this. We use a lot of tools in market design, because to understand existing markets and marketplaces, design new ones, and actually get things implemented, you have to attack the problem from all directions. One of the tools we use is laboratory experimentation.

So, on this list there is a market with twenty-five thousand positions a year (the NRMP); and other markets with a couple of hundred positions, such as the regional markets in Britain. And at the bottom of the list are some experimental markets with a dozen positions, in the laboratory. In the lab we can look at a stable algorithm and an unstable algorithm and see that the difference really affects the success of the clearinghouse.

So, experiments fit nicely on this list; they are one of the tools of market design. They would not carry the day alone: we would not convince medical administrators to implement a stable algorithm just because we found it worked well in the lab. But experiments amplify and help us understand what we are seeing in the field data, and they also help us communicate it.

The way I got involved in redesigning the medical match was I got a telephone call in 1995. Elliott Peranson, who is here today, was involved—he is a matchmaker, he was involved in helping administer the match and I think he put the doctors on to me. They were having some problems with new features in the medical environment—not just married couples, but let me tell you about married couples.

In the 1950s there were almost no women medical students in the United States. Today fifty percent of American medical students are women. In the 1970s, when the figure was around 10%, the market started to run into some trouble, with married couples not always taking the assignments they got in the match. The reason was that the clearinghouse was treating married couples as if they were not married.

That was not working well for married couples because they would get positions that were far apart, or even when they got positions that were close together they might not be getting assignments they liked, since they were not asked what *pairs* of positions they wanted. This means the algorithm being used, which found stable matchings when applicants were all single, was not finding stable matchings any more.

If my wife and I get two jobs in Boston, but one is a good job, and one is a bad job, we are not going to be happy. (As those of you who are married know, the iron law of marriage is that you cannot be happier than your spouse.) We would be happier in New York, with two pretty good jobs. So, until the clearinghouse started asking married couples for their preferences over pairs of jobs, it didn't have a chance of getting stable matchings, in terms of the preferences of married couples. The clearinghouse eventually did allow couples to express their preferences over pairs of jobs, but there remained other problems.

Elliott Peranson and I redesigned the algorithm so that it dealt more gracefully with married couples, and with other kinds of situations in which individuals might need two positions, and other features of the medical market that made some choices complements rather than substitutes. Because Elliott is such a matchmaking entrepreneur, there are dozens of healthcare markets that today use our algorithm in labor clearinghouses. And Muriel Niederle and I have worked on clearinghouses to help fix problems that arise in markets that come later in the career of doctors. She is here today too.

Another recent application is that school districts are starting to use clearinghouses that employ deferred acceptance, and this is close to what Lloyd and David thought of in their 1962 article. Just as Elliott is the "Johnny Appleseed" of clearinghouses in healthcare, Neil Dorosin, who is also here, is the "Johnny Appleseed" of school choice algorithms that are stable. Neil was the director of high school operations in New York City when we first met him, when we were involved in helping to redesign the way New York City high school students are assigned to schools. That was with Atila Abdulkadiroğlu and Parag Pathak, who are also here.

New York City had a semi-centralized system that handled admissions and waiting lists through the mail. For example they would send to a high school student a letter that said, "Congratulations, you have been admitted to two high schools, tell us which one you want." And only when they got that letter back could they look at the vacancies that had been created and then admit some more people.

That was a congested process. There are almost 90,000 students a year who enter New York City high schools, and just before school began about 30,000 of them had not been admitted anywhere and had to be assigned administratively to schools they had not expressed a preference for. We helped New York develop a stable clearinghouse and almost immediately that 30,000 number went down to 3,000.

Different school districts have had different problems. Boston schools used an immediate acceptance algorithm of the kind I told you about that made it unsafe for parents to reveal their true preferences to the school district. And so we helped Boston Public Schools implement a deferred acceptance algorithm as well, that made it safe for families to list their true preferences. That is a technology that has now started to spread to other school districts. Atila and Parag and Neil and I and lots of education professionals in each of these cities have started to make that a technology that is accessible to more and more families in the United States.

Let me move to a very different kind of market and tell you about kidney exchange. It is one of the exciting markets that we deal with. You each have two kidneys. And if you are as healthy as you look, you could remain healthy with just one. But kidney disease is a deadly disease, and transplantation is the treatment of choice. So you might know someone who has kidney disease, and because you're healthy, you could donate a kidney to someone you love.

But sometimes you are healthy enough to donate a kidney, but you can't donate it to the person you love, because of some kind of incompatibility. The figure shows a simple blood type incompatibility.

Donor 1 would love to give her kidney to Recipient 1, who needs one, but Donor 1 has blood type A and Recipient 1 has blood type B, and that is not going to work. There is another patient-donor pair who have the same problem in reverse.

This is what opens up the possibility of exchange. The B blood type patient could get the B blood type kidney from the donor in Pair 2. And at the same time, the donor in Pair 1 can give an A kidney to Recipient 2. So, that is an exchange – that is a kind of thing economists are good at, thinking about exchange, and how it can be organized.

The question was how to develop a marketplace to allow transplantation to occur when otherwise it would not have. This is work done with a number of people, with my colleagues Tayfun Sönmez, and Utku Ünver, and Itai Ashlagi

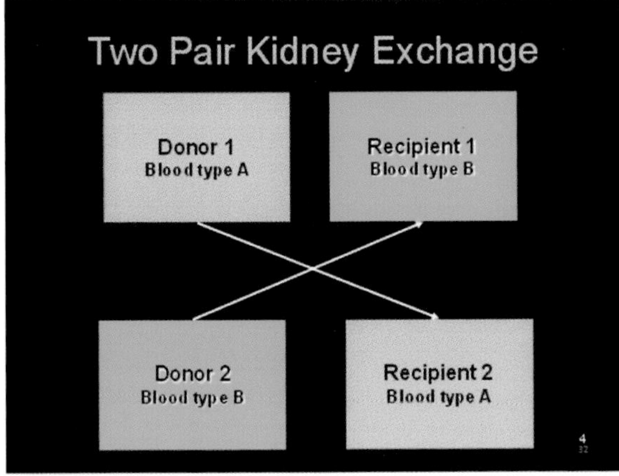

FIGURE 1.

who is here, and with many medical professionals, including Mike Rees—a surgeon whom I will tell you more about and who is here today, too, and Frank Delmonico, who we helped to start the New England Program for Kidney Exchange.

There is congestion in kidney exchange. Here is a picture taken during a pair of surgeries—one nephrectomy—taking a kidney out, and one transplant—putting a kidney in—in Cincinnati, Ohio.

I am in the yellow gown, keeping my hands out of the way, so no one hands me anything. In the bucket is a kidney. Behind me is another operating room you can't see, just steps away, where the nephrectomy took place, moments before. A surgeon and kidney exchange pioneer named Steve Woodle is in the striped cap, and at the same time these surgeries are going on, this donor's patient, and this recipient's donor are at Mike's hospital in Toledo, Ohio undergoing the same set of operations.

When I say at the same time, I mean literally at the same time. The surgical teams got the patients anesthetized, they did the initial incisions, and then they got on their cell phones and they said, "We're ready to go here. Are you ready?"

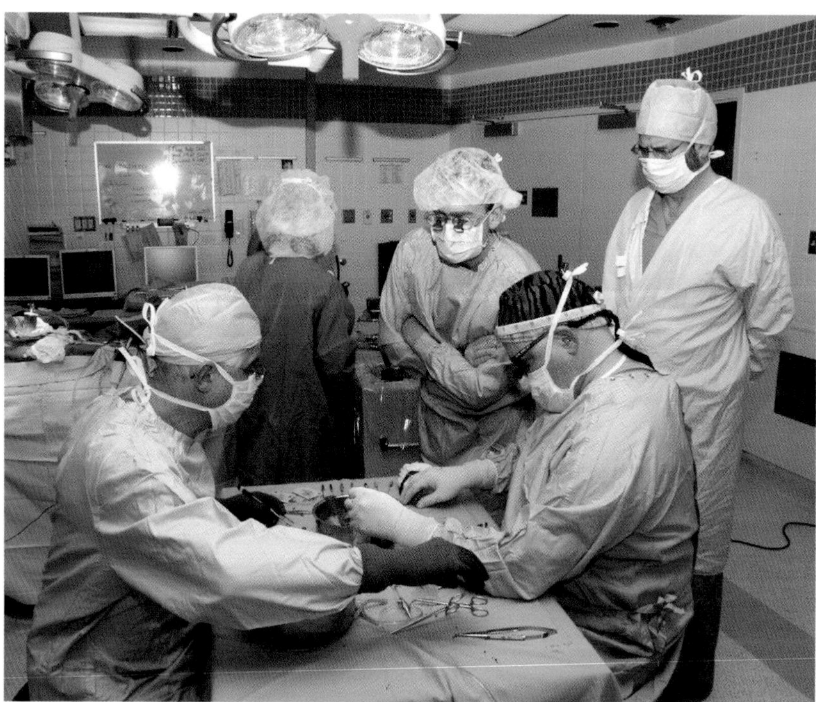

FIGURE 2.

The reason they do the surgeries simultaneously is that you cannot contract on a kidney in the United States. It is illegal to give valuable consideration for an organ for transplantation. That mostly means you can't buy and sell organs, but it also means it is hard to enforce any kind of agreement such as 'today we give you a kidney and tomorrow you give us a kidney.'

So, these operations go on at the same time. That causes congestion because to do this simple two-way exchange you need four operating rooms and four surgical teams, because you have to do two nephrectomies and two transplants at the same time. So, it is already logistically hard to do even the simplest kind of two-pair exchange.

We could do more transplants if we could do larger exchanges. A three-way exchange skirts the "double coincidence" that Jevons told us makes barter exchanges so difficult. That is, sometimes patients can be included in a three-way exchange even if there were no-two way exchanges in which they could take part. To do a three-way exchange simultaneously requires six operating rooms and six surgical teams.

When we initially started, we could only muster four operating rooms and surgical teams at a time. Nowadays, six is not so hard, but you can see that if we were trying to get an even longer exchange, it might be really hard to muster the resources.

But kidney exchange can be done not just in shorter and longer cycles. It can also be done in chains that begin with non-directed donors. Deceased donors are non-directed, they don't have a particular patient in mind, and there is an increasing number of living non-directed donors who want to donate a kidney and don't have a particular patient in mind. One question is, "How many transplants can a non-directed donor facilitate?" When our surgical colleagues were doing all the surgeries simultaneously, we would only have six people in such a chain—three donors and three recipients. But Mike Rees took the initiative in conducting the first non-simultaneous chain, that was reported in an unusual article in the *New England Journal of Medicine* that was a collaboration between surgeons and market designers. Mike led the way in what has become standard practice in kidney exchange. The idea is that a chain initiated by a non-directed donor can be arranged so that each patient-donor pair gets a kidney before they give one. So the cost of a broken link isn't nearly as great as it would be if some pair underwent a nephrectomy and then failed to receive a kidney themselves. The cost of that kind of breach would be not only that they had undergone a surgery that they didn't need and that didn't help them, but that they would no longer have a kidney to exchange in the future, and to avoid that is why we still do cyclic exchanges simultaneously.

Of course in a non-simultaneous chain you have to rely on people who say that they are going to give a kidney next Tuesday to do so. You cannot compel them. But it turns out that this has worked pretty well in practice.

So the chain reported in that paper had twenty people in it—ten nephrectomies and ten transplants at the time it was reported. That chain continued subsequently. The reason there can be a lot of people in it and not just a few is that the congestion has been avoided because these chains can now be done non-simultaneously. The marketplace now allows more exchanges, more transplants to be done because you don't have to assemble all of the operating rooms at the same time.

There have been larger chains, such as one with sixty people in it, thirty nephrectomies and thirty transplants. The same transplants could not be done via a set of small exchanges. The reason has to do with the fact that compatibility graphs that record which patients can take which kidneys have become sparse, as we have a growing proportion of patients who are "highly sensitized," which is to say that they have developed antibodies to many human proteins, and so are immunologically incompatible with most kidneys. Sparse graphs contain very few cycles, but many long chains. And that is why these long chains we are seeing are proving so useful. Itai Ashlagi, who is here today, has been leading the study of those long chains and why they occur and how they can best be managed.

So, why do we have to do kidney exchange, instead of just buying kidneys from willing sellers? My colleague Gary Becker at the University of Chicago has argued that there is no shortage of kidneys, since everyone has two, so there is a surplus. The problem he says, and he is far from alone in this position, is that we are just not mobilizing them properly: the prices, set by law at zero, are too low.

But it turns out a lot of people think it is a terrible idea to buy and sell kidneys, the kind of bad idea that only bad people have. It is against the law here in Sweden. It is against the law in the United States. It is officially illegal in just about every country in the world except for the Islamic Republic of Iran to buy and sell kidneys. There is a legal market in Iran, and there are black markets in many places, and "gray markets" in some where the laws are less than clear.

Which things can and should be bought and sold is an interesting subject that I have written a bit about. I call a transaction "repugnant" if some people would like to do it, and other people don't think they should. So kidney sales are a repugnant transaction. We could talk about repugnant transactions for a long time. But I won't talk about them here, except to say it is an important subject. It turns out there are lots of things we are reluctant to buy and sell. We are reluctant to use money as the tool to decide who gets what. As social scientists,

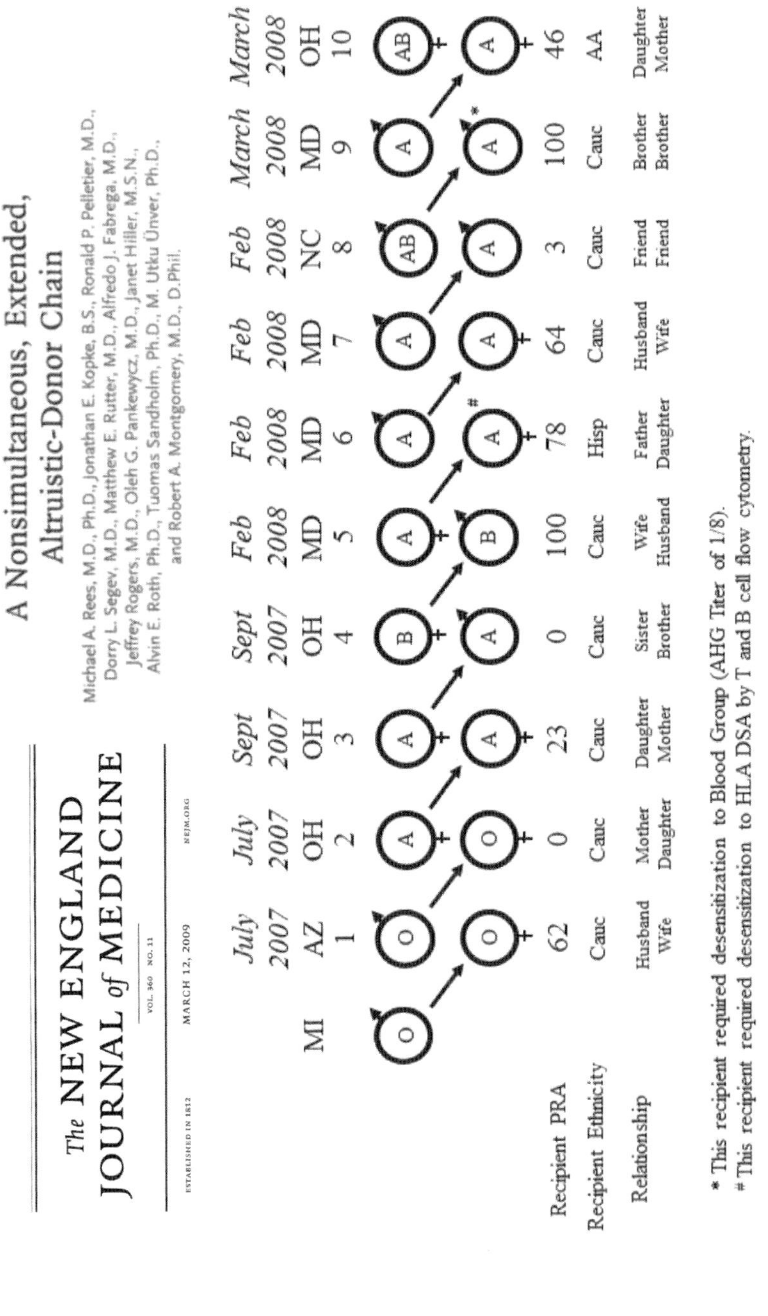

The NEW ENGLAND JOURNAL of MEDICINE

ESTABLISHED IN 1812 VOL. 360 NO. 11 MARCH 12, 2009 NEJM.ORG

A Nonsimultaneous, Extended, Altruistic-Donor Chain

Michael A. Rees, M.D., Ph.D., Jonathan E. Kopke, B.S., Ronald P. Pelletier, M.D., Dorry L. Segev, M.D., Matthew E. Rutter, M.D., Alfredo J. Fabrega, M.D., Jeffrey Rogers, M.D., Oleh G. Pankewycz, M.D., Janet Hiller, M.S.N., Alvin E. Roth, Ph.D., Tuomas Sandholm, Ph.D., M. Utku Ünver, Ph.D., and Robert A. Montgomery, M.D., D.Phil.

		July 2007	July 2007	Sept 2007	Sept 2007	Feb 2008	Feb 2008	Feb 2008	Feb 2008	March 2008	March 2008
	MI	AZ	OH	OH	OH	MD	MD	MD	NC	MD	OH
		1	2	3	4	5	6	7	8	9	10
	O	O	A	A	B	A	A	A	AB	A	AB
		O	O	A	A	B	A#	A	A	A*	A
Recipient PRA		62	0	23	0	100	78	64	3	100	46
Recipient Ethnicity		Cauc	Cauc	Cauc	Cauc	Cauc	Hisp	Cauc	Cauc	Cauc	AA
Relationship		Husband Wife	Mother Daughter	Daughter Mother	Sister Brother	Wife Husband	Father Daughter	Husband Wife	Friend Friend	Brother Brother	Daughter Mother

* This recipient required desensitization to Blood Group (AHG Titer of 1/8).
# This recipient required desensitization to HLA DSA by T and B cell flow cytometry.

FIGURE 3.

I think we need to understand that better. There are things about people's perceptions of markets that economists have not yet spent enough time trying to understand.

What are some next steps for market design? Well, it was easy for us to study markets that used centralized clearinghouses, and in many cases, those are the markets we have helped build, centralized clearinghouses for kidney exchange, for school choice, for labor market clearinghouses. But most markets are organized in a less centralized way than via a clearinghouse, and so part of market design is thinking about rules of engagement. What should the rules be in various kinds of decentralized marketplaces? How should offers be made? How long should they be open? What happens if you accept an offer and later you change your mind? How do you get information about preferences? When we talked about clearinghouses, I said to you that it is possible to organize a clearinghouse so that it is safe for people to reveal their preferences. But in most markets no one will ever ask you your preferences.

You are not American doctors, so you are probably not going to go through a clearinghouse when you look for a job; you will go through application and selection procedures. No one will ever really ask you, "Are we your first choice?" And if they did, you might say, "Of course you are," and say that to everyone who asks you, but that would not be critical in deciding who gets what.

One of the markets that is just getting underway right now in December is the market for new Ph.D. economists in North America. One bit of market design that my colleagues and I did in that market is institute a signaling mechanism—a mechanism by which applicants can send a limited number of signals of interest to employers, to help break through the congestion that arises because it is so cheap to apply nowadays. Most employers looking for certain kinds of economists get applications from all those economists who are on the market.

So, for each job, employers get many, many applications, and the question is how to sort among them, which ones should you pay attention to? The problem is similar to those that you might see on dating websites, which some of my students and colleagues have studied as well.

The problem on a dating website is that women with attractive pictures get many, many emails from men, saying, "How about me?" If they get too many to look at, then they just ignore most of them. And if the men are finding that most of their emails are ignored, then they start sending more emails, reflecting more superficial investigations and less information about match quality.

Muriel Niederle and Soohyung Lee and some colleagues intervened in a dating website on which people were sending lots of emails: they gave people just a few of what they called 'virtual roses'. You could send many emails, but you couldn't send as many roses as you wanted, because you had a strictly limited supply, so if someone got an email that had a rose attached, they knew it was special, and worth paying attention to. Interventions like that helped convey information about matches, just as we found in the economics job market.

Similarly, in a lot of decentralized markets we have looked at, we find that helping convey information, and helping preserve options, for example by allowing people who accept early offers to change their mind, helps the market work better.

A market designer has to think a lot about what constitutes a free market. We just went through an election in the United States and our politicians like to talk about free markets or regulated markets as if these are entirely different things.

I think a useful way to think about free markets is that a free market is a market with rules and institutions that let it operate freely. When we talk about a wheel that can rotate freely, we don't mean a wheel that is unconnected to anything else. We mean a wheel that has an axle, and well-oiled bearings. I think that is a good metaphor for a free market. A free market needs institutions that let it work well. Markets like the New York Stock Exchange have lots of rules—they're not laissez-faire markets, they have rules about when they open in the morning, and when they close in the afternoon, and these help keep the market thick. And they have rules that have the force of law, like rules against insider trading that you can go to jail for violating, and those rules are intended to make it safe for ordinary investors to participate in the market.

So, what makes the New York Stock Exchange work well is a good set of rules. And that is how we should be thinking about free markets—markets with a set of rules that allow them to work freely.

Market design is an ancient human activity, but only recently have contemporary economists focused attention on it and started to take an active role. As economists have started to work as engineers, we find ourselves using a collection of tools to investigate particular markets and marketplace designs.

Game theory is the central tool, and it is a combination of strategic and coalitional models that used to be called "non-cooperative" and "cooperative" game theory, but I think that distinction is not useful anymore. We don't use coalitional and strategic models to study different kinds of games, we use them to ask different questions about the same game, like, "Is the outcome stable?" and "Is it safe to reveal your preferences?"

We need to make lots of careful observations of actual markets and how they work and how they fail. If you are a game theorist, *rules are data*. When we look at markets, we want to know what are their rules and how are those rules changing over time, and what kinds of behavior are people trying to make rules against?

And often, when we are trying to design a market, there's a deadline by which time the design has to be completed and implemented, for example by the time students need to go to school next year. So sometimes we are working beyond our deeply reliable scientific knowledge, and then we use tools such as computation to help us look at the data and try to understand what is going to happen if we implement a particular market design. As I already indicated, controlled experiments are useful in this effort too—especially when you are looking at a new design for which there is not as yet any field evidence about how it would work. Controlled experiments are also useful when you are looking at field data and trying to understand what they mean.

Let me close by saying that market design is a team sport. And it is a team sport in which it is hard to tell who are theorists or practitioners because it blurs those lines.

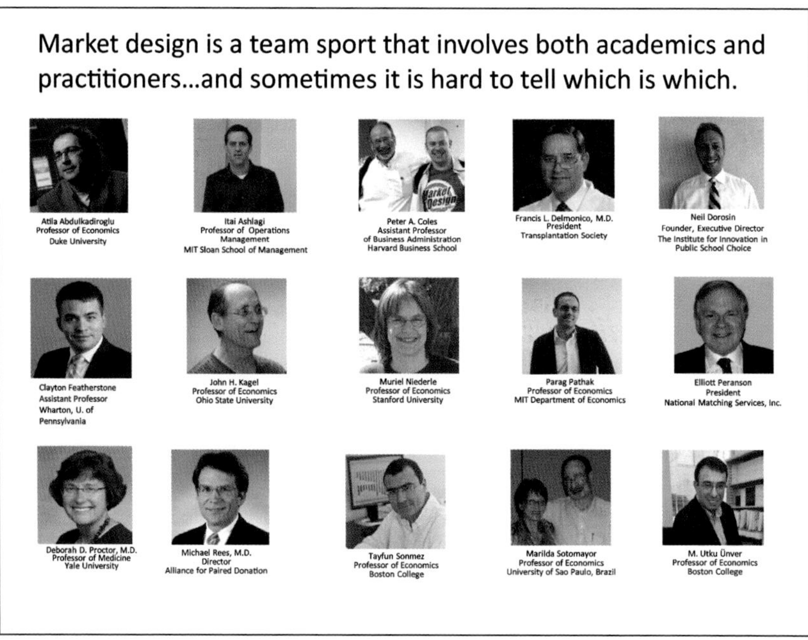

FIGURE 4.

Here are some of my colleagues, with whom I have worked on designing, getting adopted and implementing various marketplaces. Some of them are economists and some of them are not. There are kidney surgeons there and educators, and a matchmaker, and some of them are here to join in this wonderful party with us this week.

Thank you.

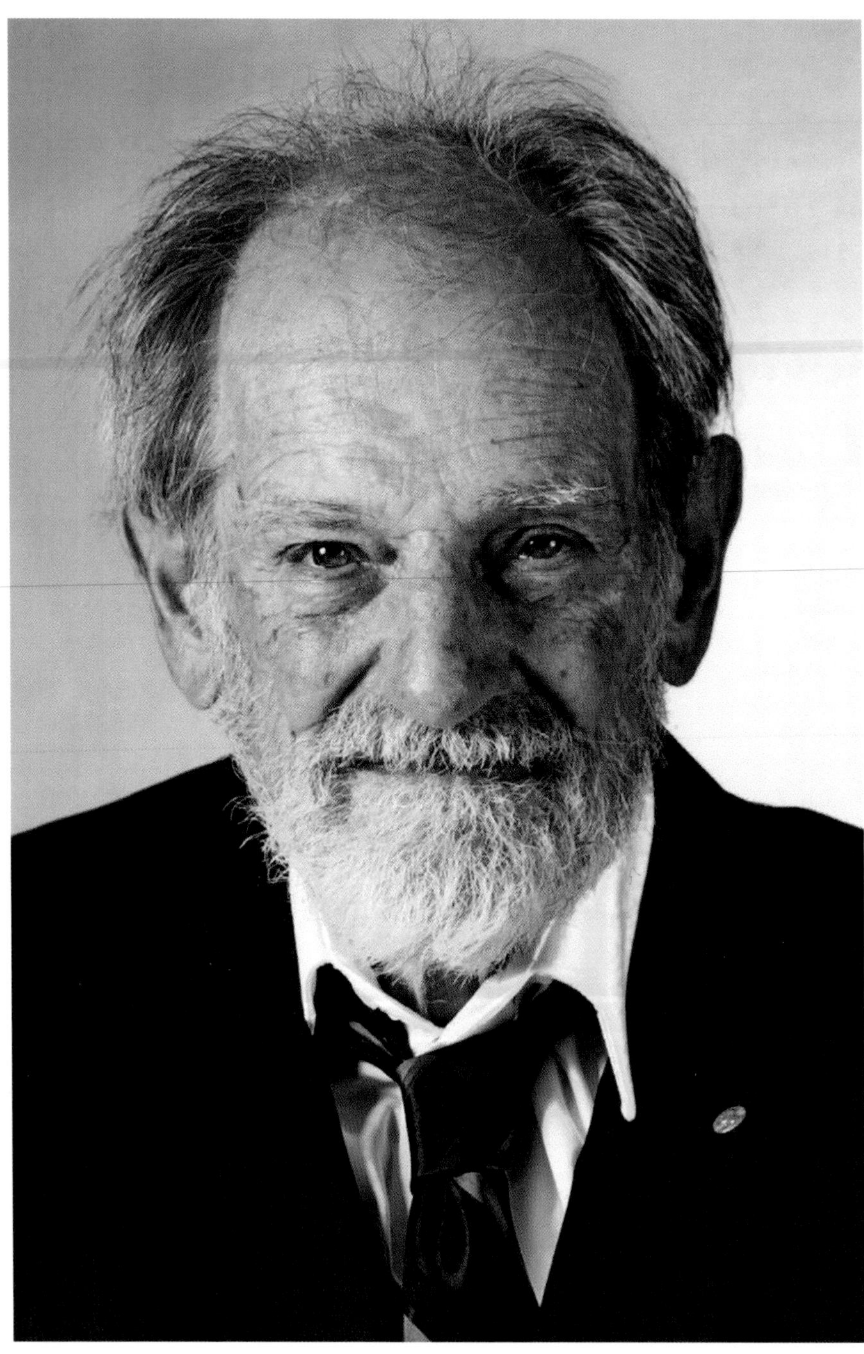

Lloyd S. Shapley. © The Nobel Foundation. Photo: U. Montan

Lloyd S. Shapley

My grandfather, Harlow Shapley, was a noted astronomer. He worked at the 100-inch telescope on Mt. Wilson in Pasadena, California, where he did some important work, most notably determining that the sun was not located at the center of the galaxy, but rather, out on the fringes. His first three children were born in Pasadena, but then in 1920, he was appointed director of the Harvard Observatory, and moved back east.

My father was born on June 2, 1923, in Cambridge, Massachusetts, into a scientific family, the fourth of five children. He grew up in the director's residence at the Harvard Observatory, where he showed an early talent in mathematics.

FIGURE 1. 1929 from left: brothers Alan and Willis, father Harlow, mother Martha holding baby brother Carl, and sister Mildred. Six year old Lloyd is in front.

I had two brilliant, straight-A students for brothers, and I guess my sister ... was rather bright, too. Nevertheless, we would play mathematical games sometimes around the house, play with cards and multiply them, do things like that. So I had this kind of boost from trying to out-excel my brothers, who were four and six years older than I was, and I did fairly well. So I had a family reputation of being the math whiz.

He attended Philips Exeter Academy, then attended Harvard as an undergraduate, where he did well in mathematics and less well in almost every other subject. Then in the middle of his junior year, in 1943, he was drafted, and spent nearly three years in the army.

My father has told me many times of his experience after getting drafted. He was shipped down to North Carolina for boot camp. They also sent him to weather school, and trained him as a weather observer, plotting weather on maps and interpreting them.

Then he and his group were put on a train, which ran them across the country. They spent some time at a base near San Diego, then were put on a troop transport (a converted ocean liner), which sailed out of San Diego towards an unknown destination.

Using his watch and crude home-made navigational instruments, my father plotted the ship's position on a world map posted in the troops' quarters. The ship went due south for days, past the equator, to about 50 degrees south, then turned west, staying well clear of the Japanese presence in the Pacific.

FIGURE 2. Lloyd Shapley in the Army, 1943.

At one point an officer reprimanded him for plotting and publicizing the "secret" position, so after that he took the map down, but continued plotting the position, and some weeks later, correctly named their first stop as Hobart, Tasmania. They finally disembarked in India, then after a long train ride, they flew over the Himalayas on DC-3s, finally arriving in central China.

He also told me of a letter he wrote home. Everything was, of course, censored, so he couldn't even let his family know where he was. To let them know he composed a realistic sounding letter mentioning things like his "Uncle Charlie" – things which wouldn't attract the censors' attention, but would signal to the family that the meaning of the letter wasn't in the words (there was never an "Uncle Charlie" in that family). Back home, his brother Willis figured it out, reading the first letter of each line: "C-H-I-N-A."

My father was in the Army Air Corps, assigned to a secret air base in western China, a weather station which not only made weather observations, it also intercepted broadcasts. This work also involved a certain amount of cryptoanalysis, breaking the codes used in intercepted broadcasts. He was put onto that because he had a high score on the army's mathematical aptitude test.

The bombers had to shuttle bombs and fuel over from India, and about every two weeks they had enough fuel ready and could make a raid on Japan. The planes couldn't wait on the ground in China, since they were in range of the Japanese bombers. Because of this, they needed to know if the weather would be good three days in advance over the target area. The fronts moved down from Siberia, across China and to Japan. The weather center intercepted broadcasts from the Soviets and the Japanese, and even the US Navy in the Pacific. They needed masses of data because the quality was often very poor. So they accumulated all the data they could, plotted it out on the maps, and made long-range forecasts, and then sent it out to all the air fields within range on a particular day.

My father managed to break the Soviet weather code, which provided them with a lot more reliable data. For this he received a Bronze Star, promotion to corporal, and a raise of $4 a month. I remember him mentioning that the pay increase seemed to him at the time to be the most important part.

He was discharged right after VJ Day, and within a few months he returned to Harvard for the spring semester. He finished up in June of 1947, though he was class of 1944 for alumni purposes. (We received a bulletin from his class a few months ago – my father is the sixth member of the Harvard class of 1944 to receive a Nobel Prize.) But he didn't graduate at that point:

I didn't get my degree in '47. I finished all the requirements for the degree, but the last semester I also failed two courses ... I took four courses over the load you take, and I failed two, and maybe got a couple of A's in the other courses. The math courses I was generally good at, and music courses sometimes. So they said, "No, you're on probation. We can't give a degree to someone on probation. If you survive for a year, you'll get the degree next year" ... So I wasn't all that gung-ho about Harvard. My performance at Harvard hadn't been that much. Of course, a great deal of education takes place in a person hanging around – of course, I'd hung around Harvard beforehand.

He had been a math major at Harvard, and done well (he was twice a member of the Putnam team). But he didn't have any focus on any particular area of mathematics at that point. Out of the Army, out of college, he didn't really know what he was going to do.

I ended up not poised to go to graduate school. I didn't know what I was going to do. I was a big music lover, but I had no technical skills there. So I even went to a course at the Union Conservatory one summer before I went off.

He did send out some job applications, one of which was to RAND. And without a formal interview, he was hired. And it turned out RAND was just right for him.

I'm not all that disciplined in getting places on time or going to bed when I should so that I can get up when I should. And RAND is sort of nice – it's open all the time, twenty-four hours. People work at night, late, and you can just go in there.

At that time, the mission of RAND was very open. It was set up by the Air Force to keep in contact with the scientific community, to get scientists to see and solve problems before a war made the solutions urgent.

So the military felt that, yes, we should keep in touch with the scientists after the war ... "So let's just not give them an assignment. Give them some money and say, 'You think of some problems and tell us about it.'" It was a kind of wide-open contract with the Air Force. This led to people like [John] Williams putting together a rather motley crew of people ... And he hired crazy students from the math department, me.

At RAND, a group decided to look at game theory. They set up a seminar, meeting weekly, and they would work through a chapter of *Theory of Games and Economic Behavior*. This book had been originally published in 1944, creating a branch of mathematics to use for economics – that is, to study and analyze situations with multiple actors.

... this was reasonably soon after the publication of Theory of Games and Economic Behavior, John von Neumann and Oskar Morgenstern's opus, a big

thing. I think it was published in '47, a so-called second edition, which simply has an appendix added, which they didn't have finished in time before. So it had appeared and had not made much of a splash, got big reviews and von Neumann, anyway, was well-known in mathematics already. But nothing had happened beyond that.

As a result of these seminars, my father spent some time working with Roger Snow, another young mathematician, on a problem raised by the book, how to find all the solutions to a matrix game.

We made some progress, and finally I guess I broke it, but Roger was also working on it. So it turned out to be Shapley-Snow ... This was a work of mathematics where I had not really even read very many math papers as published and didn't have any clear concept that I was doing anything special except solving a problem.

Von Neumann read it and became very enthusiastic, because there had been very few papers at that point which had responded to *Theory of Games.*

So, von Neumann, partly, I guess, for his own ego, said, "I want to encourage this work," even though he was really not working on game theory anymore. He was working on computer ideas mostly. So he wants to encourage it. So it came back a big rave review or maybe a letter .... von Neumann was all excited about this, and he'll publish it, and he'll sponsor it in any journal you name, and so on.

So at that point, my stock went up, and Roger's went up. At least these two kids – and there weren't all that many of us around – had something enough to get a real pro like von Neumann interested. So, of course, stop everything else while we write this paper and send it off. This is my first contribution, Shapley-Snow. I call it my piece, really, though I mean it's helpful to have Roger in the thing, but he kept saying, "You write it, and I'll read it."

So that was the real start of my father's career in game theory.

My father was at RAND less than two years before he headed off to graduate school at Princeton, though during the summers he worked at RAND as a consultant. The time at Princeton was vital to his development as a mathematician.

I had a lot of mathematical – I learned an awful lot of math. I just learned a lot of math at Princeton and I really got educated mathematically.

At Princeton, his dissertation was "*Additive and Nonadditive Set Functions,*" done with Albert Tucker. While there he published several other papers, including one called "A Value for *n*-person Games," which introduced what is known as the "Shapley Value," a solution concept in game theory, which has become a major part of the field.

One of the early works was this thing which led to the Shapley Value. It was called the Shapley Value, so my name is an adjective for that solution concept. In that case, I can sort of trace the ancestry of how did I think of it. But more specifically, one can look at the – what's the word? Not paradigm. But anyway, the layout of the field as defined by von Neumann and Morgenstern exactly where, when they decided to do this, you could have done something else, and this would lead to the Shapley Value. So I can sort of provide a foundation for my work by following their arguments up to a certain point and then saying, "No, this is more important." Sometimes you can use a unique answer. If you insist on uniqueness, you have to give up something else and then a different way. So it was a kind of rank and file. Sometimes it was rather neat that way.

Very soon after he developed the Shapley value, in considering applications, he worked with Martin Shubik on applying it to the measurement of power in voting situations. This led to an item that became known as the Shapley-Shubik Power Index. They, as two unknown graduate students, one in mathematics and the other in economics, had the temerity to submit this paper to the leading journal in Political Science, and much to the surprise of all concerned it was accepted in a few weeks.

My father found he enjoyed (and was very good at) doing research – coming up with problems, solving them, proving theorems, and writing and publishing papers. Once he had his degree, he was set for doing academic work – however, he was not really interested in teaching. Largely because of that, he returned to RAND, rather than taking a job as a mathematics professor at a university. He kept doing mathematics, proving theorems, and publishing for years.

Though his specialty was game theory, the so-called mathematics of economics, my father has never done economics. He has told me his only real exposure to the field was his collaborations with his good friend Martin Shubik, a classmate from Princeton and a long-time professor of economics at Yale. He told me last year, "Shubik would talk to me for a while, then I would go and explain to him what he had just said."

My father also kept in contact with others of his classmates from Princeton. One of these was David Gale, who was at Brown University in 1961. They communicated by mail – long distance telephone calls were expensive and rare.

One day, a letter arrived from Gale framing a problem of choosing roommates. If you have two groups, with each individual having different preferences, is there a way to come up with a set of stable pairings of one from each group? Gale suspected there wasn't a way to make a stable solution, but couldn't prove it.

The way my father describes it, he received the letter around noon, spent some time thinking, wrote up the solution (There *was* a stable solution, and this is how you come up with it), and mailed it back to Gale later that afternoon.

This solution, the deferred matching algorithm, became the paper "College Admissions and the Stability of Marriage," published in 1962. My father has described how two reviewers rejected it before it was finally published, probably for being too simple – it's a mathematical paper which contains no equations. As stated in the paper:

The argument is carried out not in mathematical symbols but in ordinary English; there are no obscure or technical terms. Knowledge of calculus is not presupposed. In fact, one hardly needs to know how to count.

Yet any mathematician will immediately recognize the argument as mathematical ...

Yet the deferred matching algorithm has turned out to be a major tool in game theory and economics, notably for how Alvin Roth applied it to school admissions.

Even though the mission of RAND was basically military, my father was seldom pressured to work in that direction.

RAND was never really trying to pull me into ... war-gaming things or that sort of problem, but the great thing about RAND for me is they let me do what I wanted. I succeeded in doing what I wanted ... I eventually was getting National Science Foundation (NSF) grants, which were supporting me at RAND and not really drawing on RAND ... I stayed at RAND for maybe ten years longer than I would have otherwise, because almost all my support came from there. NSF grants which helped me to do research on whatever it was, that attracted me at that time.

From 1952 until around the late 1970s he had a considerable collaboration with Shubik on the applications of game theory to economics beginning with a note on Solutions on N-Person Games with Ordinal Utilities. His basic work on the core of a game prompted Shubik to consider the convergence of the core to the competitive equilibrium in an exchange economy modeled as market game with side-payments. They generalized the convergence of both the core and the Shapley value to the competitive equilibrium and further work led to a generalization in the form of "Market Games" utilizing the concept of balanced sets of coalitions. This led to a deep understanding of how cooperative game theory solutions related to the competitive equilibria of exchange economies. They also applied the core concept to an economy with externalities. Their investigation of a classical economic example illustrating the emergence of competition led to The Assignment Game and the role of marginal pairs of traders.

Having completed their investigation of the relationship between cooperative game solutions with many agents and the competitive equilibria of an exchange economy, they observed that although Cournot in the 19th century had suggested the relationship between the noncooperative equilibrium and the competitive equilibrium in an open economy, this result had not been generalized to account for a closed economy. A basic economic model was suggested by Shubik, but it took much work and care to tighten this to a clean mathematical model suitable for generalization. The key observation was that the use of money arose naturally in the model in the strategic form of a game. They called the resulting general class of games "Strategic Market Games."

My father was interested in several aspects of voting throughout his career. With Irwin Mann in 1962, he determined the voting power of the several states in the 51-party voting game known as the Electoral College (used to elect American presidents). He also suggested an approach to evaluating a presidential election, treating it as a game among several million voters. This eventually led to results which showed that the voters of medium-sized states have the lowest voting power in the country.

Another interesting question dealt with the optimal assignments of "weights" to voters – optimal in the sense that a "correct" result is most likely to be obtained. In this case, my father and Bernard Grofman in 1984 determined a formula to assign voters weights based on their likelihood of making a correct decision.

My father also worked with Guillermo Owen on analyzing voting in a "political" situation, using an approach called "spatial games." In this case, voters are assigned ideal positions in a multidimensional space, as well as weights, and the outcomes of the game are also points in this space. These games require players to form coalitions to come up with more favorable outcomes. The value of an outcome to a voter is based on the distance between the voter's ideal position and the location of the outcome – the closer the two points, the more the outcome is worth to that voter.

Working with Yale economist Herbert Scarf, my father described a system where large, indivisible items (such as houses) could be exchanged in an optimal way, building on earlier work by David Gale on top trading cycles. This was published as "On Cores and Indivisibility" in 1974, and the system described led directly to Alvin Roth's work on kidney exchanges.

In 1974, he and Robert Aumann coauthored the book *Values of Non-Atomic Games*; it concerns games with many players, who impinge significantly on the outcome only when they form large coalitions, but not as individuals. Examples are national elections or large economies or markets.

Another collaboration with Aumann concerned perfect equilibria in repeated games; it is a sharpening of the Folk Theorem, which was cited by the Nobel Committee when presenting Aumann with the 2005 prize.

Over the years, my father also did important work in the development of the core, the development of stochastic games, abstract side-payment games, potential games, oceanic games, convex games, and other fields. Most of these, and the above, involve some extremely complex mathematics, a world apart from "College Admissions and the Stability of Marriage," with its simple logical reasoning. But the common thread is that he was solving mathematical problems.

By the late 1970s, my father realized that he was the only one left doing game theory at RAND. His colleagues had retired, or gone to various universities. So he quietly put the word out that he would be open to offers. He really only had two institutions on his list – UCLA and Stanford – but he got offers from all over the world. When the offer finally came from UCLA, he accepted it, and moved there in the fall of 1981.

Teaching didn't appeal to me at all, but academic research did ... there was a big reentry on the teaching basis when I came to UCLA ... The plus was I had some graduate students who I could really train and imbue with my knowledge, whatever it is. Most of my colleagues in game theory, they have generations of students of students. I had nothing like that. But the other side is I have to teach students, which I've learned to do, but I don't know how to do it very well. So I'm not a big teacher, no. Research is my thing.

FIGURE 3. Lloyd and Marian Shapley, 1980.

It was a joint appointment – in the math department to teach math to math students, and in the economics department to teach math to economics students. So despite being a professor of economics, he has never taught economics.

At a conference in June of 1987, my father included in his remarks, "Yesterday was my birthday. I feel like I'm a million years old." Then he added, "Base two, of course." The mathematicians got the joke. A year later, Alvin Roth published a book, *The Shapley Value: Essays in Honor of Lloyd S. Shapley* which begins by saying it is "... in honor of the 1000001st (binary) birthday of Lloyd S. Shapley."

In his 20 years at UCLA, my father had a number of outstanding graduate students, several of whom are now established professors and have their own students.

FIGURE 4. Lloyd, Peter (son) and Richard (grandson) Shapley visiting Mildred Shapley Matthews (his sister) in Pasadena in 2009.

Though he retired from UCLA in 2001, he has tried to remain active in the field since then, collaborating with former students and attending conferences.

Game theory, I think, was made for me, because I was always messing around with great big game-like models, the sort of thing that now they call "Dungeons and Dragons." I used to do that with my friends in school and so on. So I maybe had that mentality, too, but also the mathematical push, because this was a kind of mathematics that I had generated, quite apart from the way it's applied. I've always enjoyed the mathematics of it ...

The problem I get on, from whatever source, if it starts out mathematical interest, I'll follow through to the end. If there's simply an interesting application, well, maybe someone else can do it. I'm right in there in that close equation. The mathematical discovery is the really exciting part. You create conjectures, but you discover results. I think that's the way. I don't consider mathematics – you don't create facts. Of course, the facts are always there, but you discover them.

Game theory ... spreads out so quickly into so many different fields. Once you get multiple decision-makers in the same model, all kinds of things can happen. So there's almost never been a time, after the very beginning of that seminar at RAND that first couple of months, where there was not a game theory problem ahead of me, in front of me somewhere to see. It's also not only unexplored but unstructured, because I think my main contributions here, the big thing – someone wrote a preface in my book with papers on my sixty-fifth birthday – and he, I think correctly, said that for many years I set the agenda for the field by my work. In other words, I was sort of trying to cover the problems that I could see, so I'm building the theoretical structure as well as working on it.

FIGURE 5. Lloyd and Peter Shapley at the Grand Hotel, Stockholm, December 2012.

NOTE

*This is a biography of my father, Lloyd Shapley, based on various sources and discussions with him over the years. Most of the quotes (in italics) are from an interview he did about 20 years ago concerning the RAND Corporation**, where he spent much of his career. I also received assistance from Professors Martin Shubik, Robert Aumann, and Guillermo Owen, and my brother Christopher Shapley. — *Peter Shapley*

**Interview, February 9, 1994. Joint Oral History Project on the RAND Corporation. Archives Division, National Air and Space Museum, Smithsonian Institution, Washington, DC.

Lloyd S. Shapley died on 12 March 2016.

Allocation Games—the Deferred Acceptance Algorithm*

Prize Lecture, December 8, 2012

by Lloyd S. Shapley
University of California, Los Angeles, CA, USA

My work is in a branch of mathematics called "game theory." Game theory is a mathematical study of conflict and cooperation between any number of rational decision-makers, or "players." As such, it is a very useful tool for economists, as a large part of their work involves situations with multiple players working for optimal solutions.

One type of problem involves "matching," that is, the allocation of items or partners, based upon their preferences.

In this example, we look at a set of boys and girls arranging their dates. First, each player ranks the members of the opposite sex in order of their desirability.

Boys' Preferences			
Adam	**Bob**	**Charlie**	**Don**
Mary	Jane	Mary	Mary
Jane	Mary	Kate	Kate
Kate	Kate	Jane	Jane

* My father, recognizing his limitations, chose to do his lecture as a simple lesson on the "Marriage Problem," that is, the Deferred Matching Algorithm, as he taught it for many years. —*Peter Shapley*

Girls' Preferences		
Mary	**Jane**	**Kate**
Adam	Adam	Don
Bob	Charlie	Charlie
Charlie	Don	Bob
Don	Bob	Adam

Then each boy approaches the first girl on their lists.

In the first round, Mary gets three offers, and holds on to Adam, while rejecting the other two. Jane receives one offer, from Bob, so she asks him to wait. Kate receives no offers, so at the end of the day she has nobody. The girls don't commit to anyone; they just say something like "hold on while I think about it."

	Round 1	Round 2	Round 3	Round 4	Round 5
Mary	**Adam** (Charlie & Don rejected)	**Adam** (no new proposal)	**Adam** (no new proposal)	**Adam** (Bob rejected)	**Adam** (no new proposal)
Kate	No proposal	**Don** (Charlie rejected)	**Don** (no new proposal)	**Don** (no new proposal)	**Don** (Bob rejected)
Jane	**Bob**	**Bob** (no new proposal)	**Charlie** (Bob rejected)	**Charlie** (no new proposal)	**Charlie** (no new proposal)

In the second round, the two boys who aren't being held onto approach the second girls on their lists. In this case, Kate receives both proposals, holds onto Don and sends Charlie away. Since nobody proposed to Mary or Jane, they hold onto their boys from the first round.

In the third round, Charlie (the only boy not currently held by a girl), asks Jane. Since Jane ranks Charlie ahead of Bob (who she's held since the first round), she releases Bob, and holds on to Charlie.

In the fourth round, Bob asks Mary, but is rejected by her since she ranks Adam higher. In the fifth round Bob asks his last choice, Kate, but she rejects him as well, since she ranks Don higher.

At this point, all three girls have boys on hold, and the one unattached boy has been rejected by all three girls. The process is done. Adam and Mary end up together, as do Don and Kate, and Charlie and Jane. Bob ends up alone.

Since no boy proposes to any girl after she has rejected him, this algorithm will reach a stable solution in a finite number of steps. In this case it took five rounds.

Since each attached boy has been rejected by all the girls who he ranked ahead of the one he ended up with, this match is stable, since no boy could improve his matching by switching to a partner he ranked higher than the one he ended up with.

This is a simple example, but with more players, it turns out that the resulting pairs can be different if the girls do the proposing rather than the boys. But both solutions are stable.

This works with any different numbers of boys and girls. It turns out that if the boys do the proposing, the resulting pairings would be better for the boys; while if the girls do the proposing, it ends up better overall for the girls.

This problem was stated as an idealized situation, but the algorithm I created, and extensions of it, have turned out to be useful in a number of real world problems. The mathematics involved in this example, besides devising the algorithm itself, is the proof that the algorithm works, and that it results in optimal, stable solutions. Applying this to real world situations has been the work of economists.

Economic Sciences 2013

Eugene F. Fama, Lars Peter Hansen and Robert J. Shiller

"for their empirical analysis of asset prices"

The Sveriges Riksbank Prize In Economic Sciences In Memory of Alfred Nobel

Speech by Professor Per Krusell of the Royal Swedish Academy of Sciences.

Translation of the Swedish text.

Your Majesties, Your Royal Highnesses, Dear Laureates, Ladies and Gentlemen,

The prices of shares and other assets fluctuate a great deal from time to time. Take Swedish shares as an example. Today, the total value of the Stockholm stock market is about 15 times the companies' current profits. But five years ago, in 2008, the same market was valued at eight times profits, and in 2000 it was 30 times profits. What is the origin of these swings? Do share prices really reflect the true underlying ability of companies to generate profits? Or do they rather represent an irrational and sentiment-driven market that oscillates between unfounded optimism and unfounded pessimism?

These questions are of great relevance because asset prices guide central economic decisions. Household savings are turned into productive investments through financial markets, so share prices ought to signal which investments are the most productive ones. Prices should also correctly reflect differences in risks, in such a way that high-risk investments are compensated by higher average returns. Mispricing can imply significant costs for society as a whole.

In their research, Eugene Fama, Lars Peter Hansen and Robert Shiller have helped us better understand how asset prices are determined. The challenge here is to find an appropriate yardstick. To identify the "correct" asset price, we must correctly compute and discount the revenues this asset generates in the future. But without access to a crystal ball, how can we look into the future? And what weights should we place on future revenues?

In order to approach the difficult question of correct pricing, start with a simpler one: are prices predictable? In a well-functioning market, it should not be possible to foresee whether prices will rise or fall. At first, this may seem paradoxical: wouldn't it be valuable to know that the price of an asset will go up tomorrow? Not from a societal point of view. If the price could safely be predicted to go up between today and tomorrow, in a well-functioning market demand would drive up the price today until it reaches tomorrow's level. Without this market reaction to the expected price rise, today's price would be too low, and economic decisions would be misguided.

Eugene Fama's systematic studies of US share prices from the 1960s and 1970s took a short-term perspective. He found that there was virtually no price predictability at all at daily or weekly time horizons. In particular, Fama analysed the effects of new public information, such as dividend announcements. With such event studies, he demonstrated that prices react immediately, without any systematic price movements after the announcement. However, Fama also realised that some price movements ought to be predictable: those that are motivated by differences in risk. He devised a method for taking risk into account that would guide the way for all subsequent research.

In the early 1980s, Robert Shiller presented surprising findings that suggested a very different perspective on asset prices. Shiller discovered there was significant predictability over longer time horizons. Using an ingenious combination of share price and dividend data, he demonstrated that high prices relative to dividends were followed by low prices relative to dividends 3 to 7 years later—not always, but on average. Shiller's studies also indicated that the volatility of prices relative to dividends appeared excessive. His interpretation was that the asset market is not always fully rational. This hypothesis, and Shiller's subsequent work, has stimulated the emergence of a new research field, behavioral finance, which borrows from psychology to improve our understanding of asset prices.

But does longer-term predictability necessarily mean that assets are priced incorrectly? It could instead be that low prices at a given point in time correctly reflect a high assessment of risk, or a high sensitivity to this risk, at that particular point in time. In order to test this risk-based theory, however, researchers needed new statistical tools. Lars Peter Hansen's breakthrough was to develop the so-called Generalised Method of Moments, a tool that was to revolutionise not just research in finance but also empirical research in many other areas of economics. Using this method, Hansen was able to show that standard risk-based theory could not explain the movements and predictability of share prices. This finding stimulated further development of the theory, and with the help of these new ideas we now appreciate the role of risk and risk sensitivity in price determination much better.

The Laureates' contributions have also been influential outside of the research community. Their findings have been key drivers behind the emergence of new financial instruments, such as index funds, and new forms of portfolio management. Their research illustrates the fruitfulness of systematically confronting radically different theories with data. Jointly, their discoveries constitute pillars of our current understanding of asset markets. Today's intensive research—to further scrutinise price formation and lay the foundation for market reforms if needed—would not be possible without the contributions of the Laureates.

Dear Professors Fama, Hansen and Shiller,

Your empirical research has fundamentally changed our view of asset prices. Your findings have been corroborated, using newer data, for many countries, and for shares, bonds, and a range of other assets. Without your discoveries, and the methods you have developed and pursued, it would be impossible to evaluate financial markets in a scientific manner. It is an honour and a privilege to convey to you, on behalf of the Royal Swedish Academy of Sciences, our warmest congratulations. I now ask you to receive your Prize from His Majesty the King.

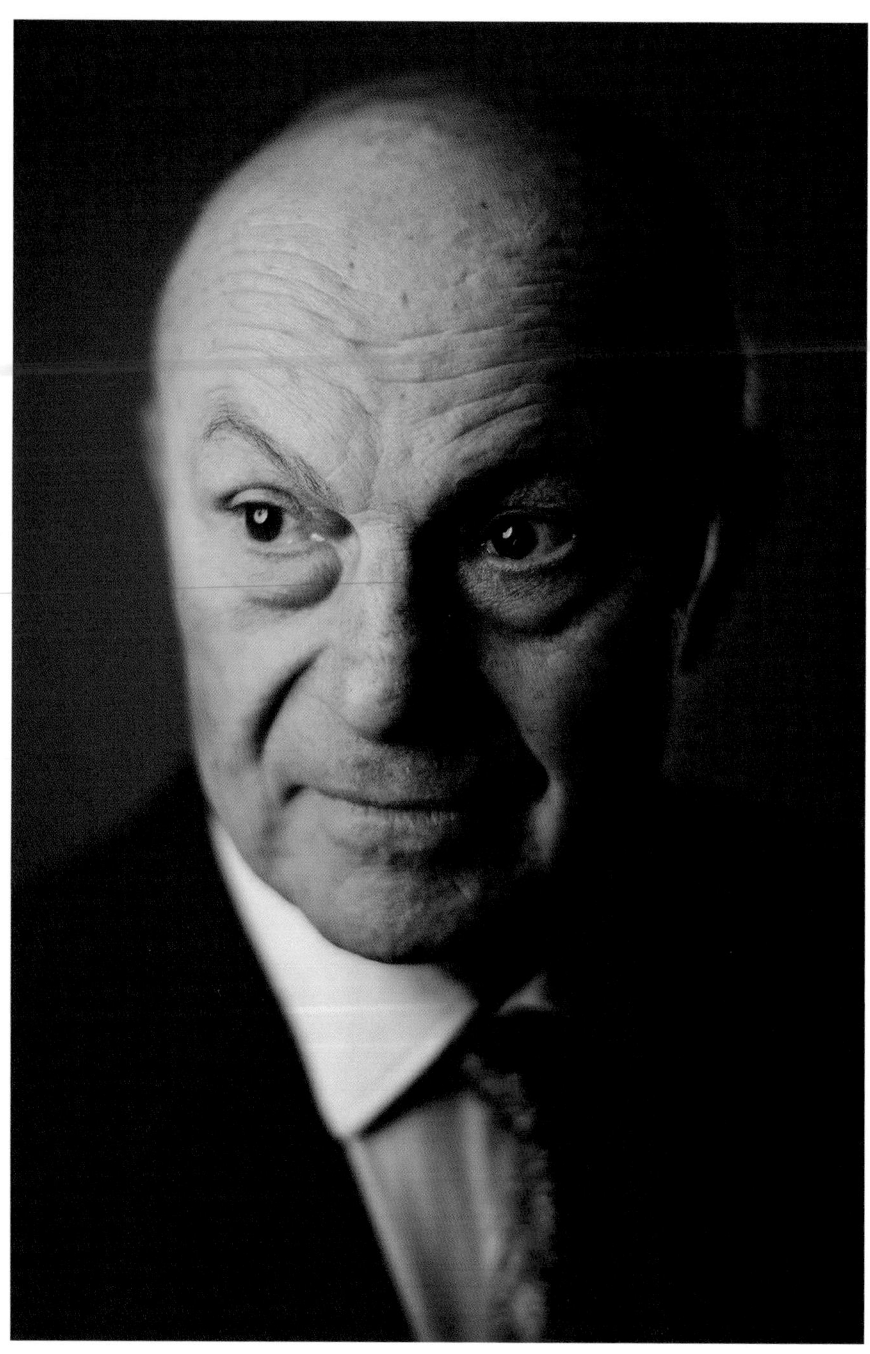

Eugene F. Fama. © Nobel Media AB. Photo: A. Mahmoud

Eugene F. Fama

My grandparents on both sides immigrated to the United States from Sicily in the early 1900s, so I am a third generation Italian-American. The second generation, my parents and aunts and uncles, were intelligent people, but they reached maturity at the start of the Great Depression, when there were few opportunities, so all worked manual jobs, when they could find them. I was the first in the lineage to go to university.

My father was a truck driver, but during the Second World War, he worked in the holds of battle ships at the Boston shipyard. The ships were lined with asbestos, so although my father never drank or smoked, he eventually died at age 70 of asbestosis, a form of lung cancer. My mother died earlier, at age 60, of cervical cancer, caused by high doses of hormones that were commonly prescribed in those days for women going through "the change of life."

I was born in Somerville, Massachusetts, a suburb of Boston, but soon thereafter my parents along with one of my father's sisters and her husband together purchased a two-flat building across the Mystic River in Medford. I doubt they had money for a down payment, but the whole neighborhood was in foreclosure, so my guess is that they just had to make the monthly payments to keep the house. I went to a Catholic grammar school (St. James) in Medford (grades 1 through 8). All the children in that school were from working class families like mine. There were 60 children in each class, but all learned to read, write, and do arithmetic, and many eventually went to college, all of which confirms recent research evidence that there is little relation between academic performance and class size or expenditures per student.

I went on to Boys Catholic High School, also known as Malden Catholic, in the city of Malden, which is next to Medford. The school had fewer than 500 students spread across four years. The teachers were Xaverian Brothers. High school sports are a big deal in the Boston area (as they are in Chicago). For some reason, which I've never understood, relatively small Catholic high schools are prominent in sports. I played basketball (poorly), ran track (second in the state meet in the high jump—not bad for a 5′8″ kid), played football (class B state champions in my junior year), and baseball (state semi-finals two years). I claim to be the inventor of the split end position in football, an innovation prompted by the beatings I took trying to block much bigger defensive tackles. I am in my high school's athletic hall of fame.

I entered Tufts University in 1956, intending to become a high school teacher and sports coach. At the end of my second year, I married my high school sweetheart, Sallyann Dimeco, now my wife of more than 55 years. Sally was a student at Girls Catholic in Malden, just across the street from Boys Catholic. Our high

FIGURE 1

FIGURE 2

school prom picture is below. We have four adult children (see picture below) and ten delightful grandchildren, all but two also adults. In an interview at the Nobel banquet, my daughter Elizabeth commented that the research success of an Economics Laureate is almost always enabled by a spouse who provides a nurturing family environment. In our family this is clearly Sally, whose family contributions dwarf mine.

At Tufts I started in Romance languages but after two years became bored with rehashing Voltaire and took an economics course. I was enthralled by the subject matter and by the prospect of escaping lifetime starvation on the wages of a high school teacher. In my last two years at Tufts, I went heavy on economics. The professors, as teachers, were as inspiring as the research stars I later profited from at the University of Chicago.

My professors at Tufts encouraged me to go to graduate school. I leaned toward a business school Ph.D. My Tufts professors (mostly Harvard economics Ph.Ds) pushed Chicago as the business school with a bent toward serious economics. I was accepted at other schools, but April 1960 came along and I didn't hear from Chicago. I called and the dean of students, Jeff Metcalf, answered. (The school was much smaller then.) They had no record of my application. But Jeff and I hit it off, and he asked about my grades. He said Chicago had a scholarship reserved for a qualified Tufts graduate. He asked if I wanted it. I accepted and, except for two great years teaching in Belgium, I have been at the University of Chicago since 1960. I wonder what path my professional life would have taken if Jeff didn't answer the phone that day. Serendipity!

During my last year at Tufts, I worked for Harry Ernst, an economics professor who also ran a stock market forecasting service. Part of my job was to invent schemes to forecast the market. The schemes always worked on the data used to design them. But Harry was a good statistician, and he insisted on out-of-sample tests. My schemes invariably failed those tests. I didn't fully appreciate the lesson in this at the time, but it came to me later, in the evolution of work on market efficiency.

During my second year at Chicago, with an end to course work and prelims in sight, I started to attend the Econometrics Workshop, at that time the hotbed for research in finance. Merton Miller had recently joined the Chicago faculty and was a regular participant, along with Harry Roberts and Lester Telser. Benoit Mandelbrot was an occasional visitor. Benoit presented in the workshop several times, and in leisurely strolls around campus, I learned lots from him about fat-tailed stable distributions and their apparent relevance in a wide range of economic and physical phenomena. Merton Miller became my mentor in finance and economics (and remained so throughout his lifetime). Harry Roberts, a statistician, instilled a philosophy for empirical work that has been my north star throughout my career.

Miller, Roberts, Telser, and Mandelbrot were intensely involved in the burgeoning work on the behavior of stock prices (facilitated by the arrival of the first reasonably powerful computers). The other focal point was MIT, with Sydney Alexander, Paul Cootner, Franco Modigliani, and Paul Samuelson. Because his co-author, Merton Miller, was now at Chicago, Franco was a frequent visitor. Like Merton, Franco was unselfish and tireless in helping people think through research ideas. Franco and Mert provided an open conduit for cross-fertilization of market research at the two universities. Both eventually became Laureates in Economic Sciences.

At the end of my second year at Chicago, it came time to write a thesis, and I went to Miller with five topics. Mert always had uncanny insight about research ideas likely to succeed. He gently stomped on four of my topics, but was excited by the fifth. From my work for Harry Ernst at Tufts, I had daily data on the 30 Dow Jones Industrial Stocks. I proposed to produce detailed evidence on (1) Mandelbrot's hypothesis that stock returns conform to non-normal (fat-tailed) stable distributions and (2) the time-series properties of returns. There was existing work on both topics, but I promised a unifying perspective and a leap in the range of data brought to bear.

Vindicating Mandelbrot, my thesis shows (in nauseating detail) that distributions of stock returns are fat-tailed: there are far more outliers than would be expected from normal distributions—a fact reconfirmed in subsequent market episodes, including the most recent. Given the accusations of ignorance on this score recently thrown our way in the popular media, it is worth emphasizing that academics in finance have been aware of the fat tails phenomenon in asset returns for 50+ years.

My thesis and the earlier work of others on the time-series properties of returns falls under what came to be called tests of market efficiency. I coined the terms "market efficiency" and "efficient markets," but they do not appear in my thesis. They first appear in "Random Walks in Stock Market Prices," paper number 16 in the series of *Selected Papers of the Graduate School of Business, University of Chicago*, reprinted in the *Financial Analysts Journal* (Fama 1965b).

The discussion above is a short history of my personal life and my early professional life. A full description of the work cited in the Economic Sciences Prize award is in the printed version of my Prize Lecture, "Two Pillars of Asset Pricing," which will soon appear in the *American Economic Review* Vol. 104, Number 6, pp. 1–20 and is also found in a slightly edited version in this volume. A more complete review of all my research in finance is in "My Life in Finance," *Annual Review of Financial Economics*, 3 (December 2011), 1–15.

VITA

February 2014

Born: February 14, 1939—Boston, Massachusetts

Marital Status: 55 years married—four children, ten grandchildren

Education

Undergraduate: Tufts University, Medford, Massachusetts; B.A., 1960.

Graduate: Graduate School of Business (now the Booth School), University of Chicago; 1960–63. MBA, 1963; Ph.D., 1964, Dissertation: *The Behavior of Stock Market Prices*.

Main Honors and Activities

The Sveriges Riksbank Prize in Economic Sciences in Memory of Alfred Nobel, 2013

Fellow, American Academy of Arts and Sciences, 1989.

Fellow of the American Finance Association, January 2001. First elected fellow.

Deutsche Bank Prize in Financial Economics, 2005, first recipient.

Morgan Stanley American Finance Association Award for Excellence in Finance, 2007, first recipient.

Onassis Prize in Finance, April 2009, first recipient.

Chaire Francqui (Belgian National Science Prize), 1982.

Doctor of Law, University of Rochester, 1987.

Doctor of Law, DePaul University, 1989.

Doctor Honoris Causa, Catholic University of Leuven, Belgium, 1995.

Doctor of Science Honoris Causa, Tufts University, 2002.

Fellow, Econometric Society.

March 2001. Membre correspondant, Acadèmie des sciences morales et politiques, section Économie, politique, statistique et finance, de l'Institut de France.

Smith-Breeden Prize (with co-author Kenneth R. French) for the best paper in the *Journal of Finance* in 1992, "The Cross-Section of Expected Stock Returns."

Fama-DFA Prize for the best paper published in 1998 in the *Journal of Financial Economics* in the areas of capital markets and asset pricing, "Market Efficiency Long-Term Returns and Behavioral Finance."

Jensen Prize (second place) for the best paper in corporate finance and organizations published in the Journal of Financial Economics in 2001. "Disappearing Dividends: Changing Firm Characteristics or Lower Propensity to Pay," (with Kenneth R. French)

Nicholas Molodovsky Award from the CFA Institute, 2006, presented for "outstanding contributions to the investment profession of such significance as to change the direction of the profession and raise it to higher standards of accomplishment."

CME Fred Arditti Innovation Award, April 24, 2007.

Jensen Prize (second place) for the best paper in corporate finance and organizations published in the Journal of Financial Economics in 2006. "Profitability, Investment, and Average Returns," (with Kenneth R. French).

Graham and Dodd Best Perspectives Award from the Financial Analysts Journal, 2012

At Tufts: Dean's List (1956–60); Society of Scholars (1957–60)—a group consisting of the top two students in each of the sophomore, junior and senior classes; Phi Beta Kappa; Omicron Chi Epsilon;

Class of 1888 Prize Scholarship (1959)—given each year to the school's outstanding student-athlete; graduated Magna Cum Laude with honors in Romance Languages.

Malden Catholic High School Athletic Hall of Fame, 1992.

Work Experience

1963–1965	Assistant Professor of Finance, University of Chicago, Graduate School of Business.
1966–1968	Associate Professor of Finance, University of Chicago, Graduate School of Business.
1968–1973	Professor of Finance, University of Chicago, Graduate School of Business.
1973–1984	Theodore O. Yntema Professor of Finance, University of Chicago, Graduate School of Business.
1975–1976	Visiting Professor, Catholic University of Leuven and European Institute for Advanced Studies in Management, Belgium.
1982–1995	Visiting Professor (Winter quarters), Anderson Graduate School of Management, University of California, Los Angeles.
1982–	Board of Directors, Dimensional Fund Advisors. Member of the Investment Strategy Committee.
1984–93	Theodore O. Yntema Distinguished Service Professor of Finance Graduate School of Business, University of Chicago.
1993–	Robert R. McCormick Distinguished Service Professor of Finance, Graduate School of Business, University of Chicago.

Professional Activities

American Economic Association, American Finance Association. Associate Editor, *Journal of Finance* (1971–73, 1977–80). Advisory Editor, *Journal of Financial Economics* (1974–). Associate Editor, *American Economic Review* (1975–77). Associate Editor, *Journal of Monetary Economics* (1984–96)

Two Pillars of Asset Pricing

Prize Lecture, December 8, 2013

by Eugene F. Fama
Booth School, University of Chicago, Chicago, IL, USA.

The Nobel Foundation asks that the Prize lecture cover the work for which the Prize is awarded. The announcement of this year's Prize cites empirical work in asset pricing. I interpret this to include work on efficient capital markets and work on developing and testing asset pricing models—the two pillars, or perhaps more descriptive, the Siamese twins of asset pricing. I start with efficient markets and then move on to asset pricing models.

EFFICIENT CAPITAL MARKETS

A. Early Work

The year 1962 was a propitious time for Ph.D. research at the University of Chicago. Computers were coming into their own, liberating econometricians from their mechanical calculators. It became possible to process large amounts of data quickly, at least by previous standards. Stock prices are among the most accessible data, and there was burgeoning interest in studying the behavior of stock returns, centered at the University of Chicago (Merton Miller, Harry Roberts, Lester Telser, and Benoit Mandelbrot as a frequent visitor) and MIT (Sidney Alexander, Paul Cootner, Franco Modigliani, and Paul Samuelson). Modigliani often visited Chicago to work with his longtime coauthor Merton Miller, so there was frequent exchange of ideas between the two schools.

It was clear from the beginning that the central question is whether asset prices reflect all available information—what I labeled the efficient markets hypothesis (Fama 1965b). The difficulty is making the hypothesis testable. We can't test whether the market does what it is supposed to do unless we specify what it is supposed to do. In other words, we need an asset pricing model, a model that specifies the characteristics of rational expected asset returns in a market equilibrium. Tests of efficiency basically test whether the properties of expected returns implied by the assumed model of market equilibrium are observed in actual returns. If the tests reject, we don't know whether the problem is an inefficient market or a bad model of market equilibrium. This is the joint hypothesis problem emphasized in Fama (1970).

A bit of notation makes the point precise. Suppose time is discreet, and P_{t+1} is the vector of payoffs at time $t + 1$ (prices plus dividends and interest payments) on the assets available at t. Suppose $f(P_{t+1} | \Theta_{tm})$ is the joint distribution of asset payoffs at $t + 1$ implied by the time t information set Θ_{tm} used in the market to set P_t, the vector of equilibrium prices for assets at time t. Finally, suppose $f(P_{t+1} | \Theta_t)$ is the distribution of payoffs implied by all information available at t, Θ_t; or more pertinently, $f(P_{t+1} | \Theta_t)$ is the distribution from which prices at $t + 1$ will be drawn. The market efficiency hypothesis that prices at t reflect all available information is,

$$f(P_{t+1} | \Theta_{tm}) = f(P_{t+1} | \Theta_t). \tag{1}$$

The market efficiency condition is more typically stated in terms of expected returns. If $E(R_{t+1} | \Theta_{tm})$ is the vector of expected returns implied by $f(P_{t+1} | \Theta_{tm})$ and the equilibrium prices P_t, and $E(R_{t+1} | \Theta_t)$ is the expected return vector implied by time t prices and $f(P_{t+1} | \Theta_t)$, the market efficiency condition is,

$$E(R_{t+1} | \Theta_{tm}) = E(R_{t+1} | \Theta_t), \tag{2}$$

The prices observed at $t + 1$ are drawn from $f(P_{t+1} | \Theta_t)$, so in this sense $f(P_{t+1} | \Theta_t)$ and $E(R_{t+1} | \Theta_t)$ are observable, but we do not observe $f(P_{t+1} | \Theta_{tm})$ and $E(R_{t+1} | \Theta_{tm})$. As a result, the market efficiency conditions (1) and (2) are not testable. To have testable propositions, we must specify how equilibrium prices at t relate to the characteristics of $f(P_{t+1} | \Theta_{tm})$. In other words, we need a model of market equilibrium—an asset pricing model, no matter how primitive—that specifies the characteristics of rational equilibrium expected returns, $E(R_{t+1} | \Theta_{tm})$.

For example, in many early tests, market efficiency is assumed to imply that returns are unpredictable based on past information. The implicit model of market equilibrium is that equilibrium expected returns are constant,

$$E(R_{t+1} | \Theta_{tm}) = E(R). \tag{3}$$

If the market is efficient so that (2) holds, then

$$E(R_{t+1} \mid \Theta_t) = E(R). \tag{4}$$

The testable implication of (4) is that a regression of R_{t+1} on variables from Θ_t, which are known at time t, should produce slopes that are indistinguishable from zero. If the test fails, we don't know whether the problem is a bad model of market equilibrium (equation (3) is the culprit) or an inefficient market that overlooks information in setting prices (equations (1) and (2) do not hold). This is the joint hypothesis problem.

The joint hypothesis problem is perhaps obvious in hindsight, and one can argue that it is implicit in Bachelier (1900), Muth (1961), Samuelson (1965), and Mandelbrot (1966). But its importance in work on market efficiency was not recognized before Fama (1970), which brought it to the forefront.

For example, many early papers focus on autocorrelations and it was common to propose that market efficiency implies that the autocorrelations of returns are indistinguishable from zero. The implicit model of market equilibrium, never acknowledged in the tests, is (3), that is, the market is trying to price stocks so that their expected returns are constant through time.

A clean statement of the joint hypothesis problem, close to that given above, is in Chapter 5 of Fama (1976b). Everybody in finance claims to have read this book, but given its sales, they must be sharing the same copy.

Market efficiency is always tested jointly with a model of market equilibrium, but the converse is also true. Common asset pricing models, like the capital asset pricing model (CAPM) of Sharpe (1964) and Lintner (1965), Merton's (1973a) intertemporal CAPM (the ICAPM), and the consumption CAPM of Lucas (1978) and Breeden (1979), implicitly or explicitly assume that all information is costlessly available to all market participants who use it correctly in their portfolio decisions—a strong form of market efficiency. Thus, tests of these asset pricing models jointly test market efficiency.

B. Event Studies

In the initial empirical work on market efficiency, the tests centered on predicting returns using past returns. Fama, Fisher, Jensen, and Roll (FFJR 1969) extend the tests to the adjustment of stock prices to announcements of corporate events. In FFJR the event is stock splits, but the long-term impact of the paper traces to the empirical approach it uses to aggregate the information about price adjustment in a large sample of events.

Like other corporate events, the sample of splits is spread over a long period (1926–1960). To abstract from general market effects that can obscure a stock's response to a split, we use a simple "market model" time series regression,

$$R_{it} = a_i + b_i R_{Mt} + e_{it}. \tag{5}$$

In this regression, R_{it} is the return on stock i for month t, R_{Mt} is the market return, and the residual e_{it} is the part of the security's return that is not a response to the market return. The month t response of the return to a split is thus embedded in e_{it}. To aggregate the responses across the stocks that experience a split, we use event time rather than calendar time. Specifically, $t = 0$ is the month when information about a split becomes available, $t = -1$ is the previous month, $t = 1$ is the following month, etc. Thus, period 0 is a different calendar month for each split. To measure the average response of returns in the months preceding and following a split, we average the residuals for the stocks in the sample for each of the 30 months preceding and following the split. To measure the cumulative response, we sequentially sum the average residuals.

The results of the split paper are striking. The cumulative average residual (Figure 1) rises in the months preceding a split. Thus, companies tend to split their stocks after good times that produce large increases in their stock prices. Once the split becomes known, however, there is no further movement in the cumulative average residual, despite the fact that about 75% of the companies that split their stocks continue to experience good times (witnessed by subsequent dividend growth rates larger than those of the market as a whole). In other words, on average, all the implications of a split for the future performance of a company are incorporated in stock prices in the months leading up to the split, with no further reaction thereafter—exactly the prediction of market efficiency.

The split paper spawned an event study industry. To this day, finance and accounting journals contain many studies of the response of stock prices to different corporate events, for example, earnings announcements, merger announcements, security issues, etc. Almost all use the simple methodology of the split paper. Like the split study, other early event studies generally confirm that the adjustment of stock prices to events is quick and complete.

Early event studies concentrate on short periods, typically days, around an event. Over short periods the assumed model for equilibrium expected returns is relatively unimportant because the change in the price of the stock in response to the event is typically much larger than short horizon expected returns. In other words, the joint hypothesis problem is relatively unimportant. More recently, researchers in behavioral finance became interested in studying price

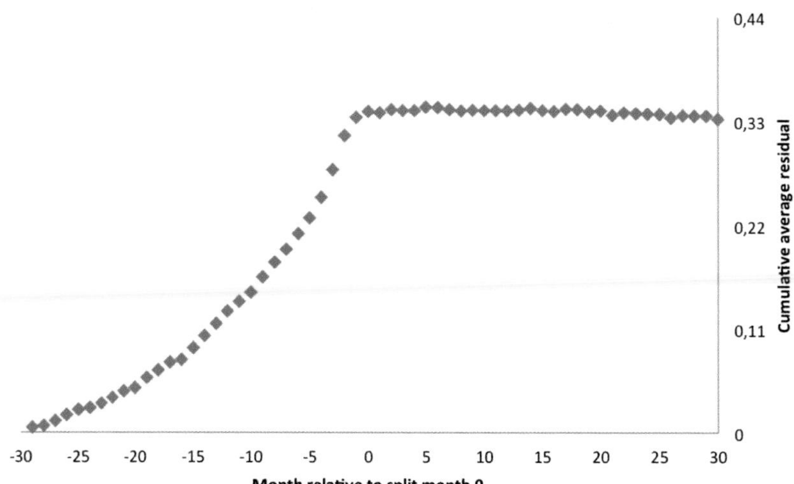

FIGURE 1. Cumulative average residuals in the months surrounding a split. Source: Fama, Fisher, Jensen, and Roll (1969).

responses for several years after an event. Over such long periods, expected returns are larger relative to the price effect of the event, and the joint hypothesis problem becomes important.

For example, the implicit model of market equilibrium in the split study is that the regression intercept and slope, a_i and b_i, in the market model regression (5) are constant through time. It is now well-known that a_i and b_i change through time. This can produce drift in long-term cumulative average regression residuals that looks like market inefficiency but is just a bad model for expected returns. These issues are discussed in Fama (1998).

C. Predictive Regressions

The early work on market efficiency focuses on stock returns. In Fama (1975), I turn to bonds to study Irving Fisher's (market efficiency) hypothesis that i_{t+1}, the time t interest rate on a short-term bond that matures at $t + 1$, should contain the equilibrium expected real return, $E(r_{t+1})$, plus the best possible forecast of the inflation rate, $E(\pi_{t+1})$,

$$i_{t+1} = E(r_{t+1}) + E(\pi_{t+1}). \tag{6}$$

The topic is not new, but my approach is novel. Earlier work uses regressions of the interest rate on lagged inflation rates,

$$i_{t+1} = a + b_1\pi_t + b_2\pi_{t-1} + \ldots + \varepsilon_{t+1}. \tag{7}$$

The idea is that the expected inflation rate (along with the expected real return) determines the interest rate, so the interest rate should be the dependent variable and the expected inflation rate should be the independent variable. Past inflation is a noisy measure of expected inflation, so equation (7) suffers from an errors-in-variables problem. More important, in an efficient market the expected inflation rate built into the interest rate surely uses more information than past inflation rates.

The insight in Fama (1975), applied by me and others in subsequent papers, is that a regression estimates the conditional expected value of the left-hand-side variable as a function of the right-hand-side variables. Thus, to extract the forecast of inflation in the interest rate (the expected value of inflation priced into the interest rate), one regresses the inflation rate for period $t + 1$ on the interest rate for $t + 1$ set at the beginning of the period,

$$\pi_{t+1} = a + bi_{t+1} + \varepsilon_{t+1}. \tag{8}$$

The expected inflation rate estimated in this way captures all the information used to set the interest rate. In hindsight, this is the obvious way to run the forecasting regression, but it was not obvious at the time.

Reversing the regression eliminates one measurement error problem, but it can introduce another, caused by variation through time in the expected real return built into the interest rate. The model of market equilibrium in Fama (1975) is that the expected real return is constant, $E(r_{t+1}) = r$. Near zero autocorrelations of real returns suggest that this proposition is a reasonable approximation, at least for the 1953–1971 period examined. Thus, at least for this period, the interest rate i_{t+1} is a direct proxy for the expected inflation rate—it is the expected inflation rate plus a constant.

The slopes in the estimates of (8) for the one-month, three-month, and six-month U.S. Treasury Bill rates and inflation rates of 1953–1971 are quite close to 1.0, and the autocorrelations of the residuals are close to zero. Thus, the bottom line from Fama (1975) is that interest rates on one-month, three-month, and six-month Treasury Bills seem to contain rational forecasts of inflation one, three, and six months ahead.

Fisher's hypothesis that expected asset returns should include compensation for expected inflation applies to all assets. Fama and Schwert (1977) test it on longer term bonds, real estate, and stock returns. The proposed model of market equilibrium has two parts. First, as in Fama (1975), the equilibrium expected real returns on bills are assumed to be constant through time, so the bill rate can again be used as the proxy for the expected inflation rate. Second, any variation in equilibrium expected real returns on other assets is assumed to be uncorrelated with expected inflation. With this model of market equilibrium, we can test Fisher's hypothesis with regressions of the nominal return on an asset, R_{t+1}, on the bill rate set at the beginning of period $t + 1$,

$$R_{t+1} = a + bi_{t+1} + \varepsilon_{t+1}. \quad (9)$$

The tests say that monthly, quarterly, and semi-annual nominal returns on longer-term bonds and real estate compensate for monthly, quarterly, and semi-annual expected inflation: that is, for these assets the slopes in the estimates of (9) are again near 1.0. Thus, we cannot reject the market efficiency proposition that bond and real estate prices incorporate the best possible forecasts of inflation and the model of market equilibrium in which expected real returns vary independently of expected inflation.

The relation between common stock returns and expected inflation, however, is perverse. The slopes in the estimates (9) for stocks are negative; expected stock returns are higher when expected inflation (proxied by the bill rate) is low and vice versa. Thus for stocks we face the joint hypothesis problem. Do the tests fail because of poor inflation forecasts (market inefficiency) or because equilibrium expected real stock returns are in fact negatively related to expected inflation (so we chose a bad model of market equilibrium)?

The simple idea about forecasting regressions in Fama (1975)—that the regression of a return on predetermined variables produces estimates of the variation in the expected value of the return conditional on the forecasting variables—has served me well. I have used it in a sequence of papers to address an old issue in the term structure literature, specifically, how well do the forward interest rates that can be extracted from prices of longer-term discount bonds forecast future one-period (spot) interest rates (Fama 1976a,c, 1984b,c, 1986, 1990a, 2005, and Fama and Bliss 1987).

To see the common insight in these term structure papers, define the term (or maturity) premium in the one-period return on a discount bond with T periods to maturity at time t as the difference between the return, RT_{t+1}, and the one-period "spot" interest rate observed at time t, S_{t+1}. Skipping the tedious details, it is easy to show that the time t forward rate for period $t + T$, $F_{t,t+T}$, contains the expected term premium, $E(RT_{t+1}) - S_{t+1}$, as well as a forecast of the spot rate for $t + T$, $E(S_{t+T})$. As a result, there is a pair of complementary regressions that use the difference between the forward rate and the current spot rate to forecast the term premium and the future change in the spot rate,

$$RT_{t+1} - S_{t+1} = a_1 + b_1(F_{t,t+T} - S_{t+1}) + e_{1,t+1} \tag{10}$$

$$S_{t+T} - S_{t+1} = a_2 + b_2(F_{t,t+T} - S_{t+1}) + e_{2,t+T} \tag{11}$$

The conclusion from this work is that the information in forward rates is primarily about expected term premiums rather than future spot rates; that is, the slope in (10) is near 1.0, and the slope in (11) is near 0.0. There is, however, some longer-term predictability of spot rates due to mean reversion of the spot rate (Fama and Bliss 1987), though not necessarily to a constant mean (Fama 2005).

In Fama (1984a), I apply the complementary regression approach to study forward foreign exchange rates as predictors of future spot rates. Again, the information in forward exchange rates seems to be about risk premiums, and there is little or no information about future spot exchange rates. The exchange rate literature has puzzled over this result for 30 years. Using the complementary regression approach, Fama and French (1987) find that futures prices for a wide range of commodities do show power to forecast spot prices—the exception to the general rule.

D. Time Varying Expected Stock Returns

As noted above, early work on market efficiency generally assumes that equilibrium expected stock returns are constant through time. This is unlikely to be true. The expected return on a stock contains compensation for bearing the risk of the return. Both the risk and the willingness of investors to bear the risk are likely to change over time, leading to a time-varying expected return. The trick is to find predetermined variables that can be used to track expected returns in forecasting regressions.

Fama and Schwert (1977) document variation in monthly, quarterly, and semi-annual expected stock returns using predetermined monthly, quarterly, and semi-annual Treasury bill rates. In later work, the popular forecasting variable on the right hand side of the regression is the dividend yield, the ratio of trailing annual dividends to the stock price at the beginning of the forecast period. The motivation, which I attribute to Ball (1978), is that a stock's price is the present value of the stream of expected future dividends, where the discount rate is (approximately) the expected stock return. Thus, a high stock price relative to dividends likely signals a lower expected return, and vice versa. The word "likely" is needed because price also depends on expected future dividends, which means the dividend yield is a noisy proxy for the expected stock return, a problem emphasized by Campbell and Shiller (1988) and others. Cochrane (2010) gives an elegant explanation of the problem in terms of complementary regressions that use the dividend yield to forecast long-term average stock returns and long-term dividend growth.

To my knowledge, the first papers that use dividend yields to track expected stock returns are Rozeff (1984) and Shiller (1984). Fama and French (1987) add an interesting wrinkle to the evidence. We find that the explanatory power of the regression, measured by the regression R^2, increases as the horizon for the return is extended in steps from a month to four years. This result may seem surprising, but it is just a consequence of the fact that dividend yields are persistent (highly autocorrelated).

For example, with persistent dividend yields, the slope in the regression of the quarterly stock return on the beginning of quarter yield will be about three times the slope in the regression of the monthly return on the beginning of month yield. Thus, the variance of the expected return estimate in the three-month regression is about nine times the variance in the one-month regression. But the variance of the residual in the three-month regression (the unexpected part of the return) is only about three times the variance of the residual in the one-month regression. As a result, R^2 is higher in the three-month regression.

Higher R^2 for longer return horizons due to the persistence of the dividend yield implies that the variance of the predictable part of returns rises faster than the variance of the unpredictable part, so in this sense longer horizon returns are more predictable. But unpredictable variation in returns also rises with the return horizon, that is, the variance of forecast errors is larger in longer-term returns, so in this more important sense, longer horizon returns are less predictable.

Efficient market types (like me) judge that predictable variation in expected returns on stocks and bonds is rational, the result of variation in risk or willingness to bear risk. In contrast, behaviorists argue that much of the predictability is due to irrational swings of prices away from fundamental values.

Fama and French (1989) address this issue. They find that the well-known variation in expected bond returns tracked by two term structure variables, (i) the default spread (the difference between the yields on long-term bonds of high and low credit risk) and (ii) the term spread (the difference between long-term and short-term yields on high grade bonds) is shared with stock returns. Likewise, dividend yields predict bond returns as well as stock returns. Moreover, default spreads and dividend yields are related to long-term business conditions, and term spreads are strongly related to short-term business cycles. The general result is that expected returns are high when business conditions are poor and low when they are strong.

The evidence that the variation in expected returns is common to stocks and bonds and related to business conditions leads Fama and French (1989) to conclude that the resulting predictability of stock and bond returns is rational. Behaviorists can disagree. Animal spirits can roam across markets in a way that is related to business conditions. No available empirical evidence resolves this issue in a way that convinces both sides.

Shiller (1981) finds that the volatility of stock prices is much higher than can be explained by the uncertain evolution of expected future dividends. This result implies that much of the volatility of stock prices comes from time-varying expected returns. The market efficiency issue is whether the variation in expected returns necessary to explain Shiller's results is beyond explanation by a model for rational expected returns. It is certainly possible to develop models for expected returns that produce this conclusion in empirical tests. But then we face the joint hypothesis problem. Do the tests fail because the market is inefficient or because we have the wrong model for rational expected returns? This and other market efficiency issues are discussed in detail in Fama (1991).

E. "Bubbles"

There is one remaining result in the literature on return predictability that warrants mention. The available evidence says that stock returns are somewhat predictable from dividend yields and interest rates, but there is no statistically reliable evidence that expected stock returns are sometimes negative. Fama and French (1987) find that predictions from dividend yields of negative returns for market portfolios of U.S stocks are never more than two standard errors below zero. Fama and Schwert (1977) find no evidence of reliable predictions of negative market returns when the forecast variable is the short-term bill rate.

These results are important. The stock market run-up to 2007 and subsequent decline is often called a "bubble." Indeed, the word "bubble," applied to many markets, is now common among academics and practitioners. A common policy prescription is that the Fed and other regulators should lean against asset market bubbles to preempt the negative effects of bursting bubbles on economic activity.

Such policy statements seem to define a "bubble" as an irrational strong price increase that implies a predictable strong decline. This also seems to be the definition implicit in most recent claims about "bubbles." But the available research provides no reliable evidence that stock market price declines are ever predictable. Thus, at least as the literature now stands, confident statements about "bubbles" and what should be done about them are based on beliefs, not reliable evidence.

"Reliable" is important in this discussion. After an event, attention tends to focus on people who predicted it. The *ex post* selection bias is obvious. To infer reliability for a particular forecaster, we need to evaluate his or her track record of forecasts of different events, and for a particular event, we must evaluate the initial predictions of all forecasters we might have chosen *ex ante*. More important, for the purposes of science and policy, we are interested in the performance of forecasting models, not the unreproducible predictions of specific individuals.

The absence of evidence that stock market price declines are predictable seems sufficient to caution that "bubble" is a treacherous term, but there is more. Figure 2 shows the December 1925 to September 2013 path of the natural log of U.S. stock market wealth, including reinvested dividends, constructed using the value-weight market portfolio of NYSE, AMEX, and NASDAQ stocks from the Center for Research in Security Prices (CRSP) of the University of Chicago. The recessions identified by the NBER are shown as shaded areas on the graph.

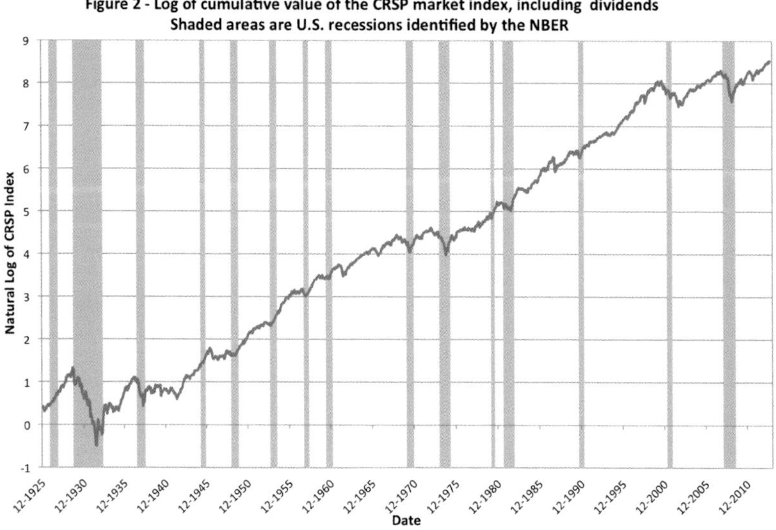

FIGURE 2. Log of cumulative value of the CRSP market index, including dividends. Shaded areas are U.S. recessions identified by the National Bureau of Economic Research (NBER).

In percent terms, and noting that these are end-of-month data, the largest five price declines in Figure 2 are (1) August 1929 to June 1932, (2) October 2007 to February 2009, (3) February 1937 to March 1938, (4) August 2000 to September 2002, and (5) August 1972 to December 1974. All these price declines are preceded by strong price increases, so these are prime "bubble" candidates.

These five periods are associated with recessions, and except for August 2000 to September 2002, the magnitude of the price decline seems to reflect the severity of the recession. The peak of the market in 1929 is the business cycle peak, but for the other four episodes, the market peak precedes the business cycle peak. Except for August 2000 to September 2002, the market low precedes the end of the recession. This pattern in stock prices also tends to occur around less severe recessions.

It thus seems that large swings in stock prices are responses to large swings in real activity, with stock prices forecasting real activity—a phenomenon studied in detail in Fama (1981, 1990b). All this is consistent with an efficient market in which the term "bubble," at least as commonly used, has no content.

One might assert from Figure 2 that major stock market swings cause recessions and market upturns bring them to an end. (One can also assert that the weatherman causes the weather—a quip stolen from John Cochrane.) At a minimum, however, (i) the absence of evidence that price declines are ever predictable, and (ii) the evidence that the prime "bubble" candidates seem to be associated with rather impressive market forecasts of real activity are sufficient to caution against use of the "bubble" word without more careful definition and empirical validation.

Common "bubble" rhetoric says that the declines in prices that terminate "bubbles" are market corrections of irrational price increases. Figure 2 shows, however, that major stock price declines are followed rather quickly by price increases that wipe out, in whole or in large part, the preceding price decline. "Bubble" stories thus face a legitimate question: which leg of a "bubble" is irrational, the up or the down? Do we see irrational optimism in the price increase corrected in the subsequent decline? Or do we see irrational pessimism in the price decline, quickly reversed? Or both? Or perhaps neither?

Finally, it is difficult to evaluate expert forecasts of "bubbles" in asset prices since we tend to hear only "success" stories identified after the fact, and for a particular "bubble," we rarely know the all-important date of an expert's first forecast that prices are irrationally high. For a bit of fun, however, we can examine two commonly cited "success" stories.

On the website for his book, *Irrational Exuberance*, Shiller says that at a December 3, 1996 lunch, he warned Fed chairman Alan Greenspan that the level of stock prices was irrationally high. Greenspan's famous "Irrational Exuberance" speech followed two days later. How good was Shiller's forecast? On December 3, 1996 the CRSP index of U.S. stock market wealth stood at 1518. It more than doubled to 3191 on September 1, 2000, and then fell. This is the basis for the inference that the original bubble prediction was correct. At its low on March 11, 2003, however, the index, at 1739, was about 15% above 1518, its value on the initial "bubble" forecast date. These index numbers include reinvested dividends, which seem relevant for investor evaluations of "bubble" forecasts. If one ignores dividends and focuses on prices alone, the CRSP price index on March 11, 2003 was also above its December 3, 1996 value (648 versus 618). In short, there is not much evidence that prices were irrationally high at the time of the 1996 forecast, unless they have been irrationally high ever since.

The second "success" story is the forecast in the mid-2000s that real estate prices were irrationally high. Many academics and practitioners made the same forecast, but an easy one to date is Case and Shiller (2003), which was probably written in late 2002 or early 2003. To give their prediction a good shot, I choose July 2003 as the date of the first forecast of a real estate "bubble." The S&P/Case Shiller 20-City Home Price Index is 142.99 in July 2003, its peak is 206.52 in July 2006, and its subsequent low is 134.07 in March 2012. Thus, the price decline from what I take to be the first forecast date is only 6.7%. The value to homeowners from housing services during the almost nine years from July 2003 to March 2012 surely exceeds 6.7% of July 2003 home values. Moreover, on the last sample date, October 2013, the real estate index, at 165.91, is 16% above its value on the initial "bubble" forecast date. Again, there is not much evidence that prices were irrationally high at the time of the initial forecast.

I single out Shiller and Case and Shiller (2003) only because their initial forecasts of these two "bubbles" are relatively easy to date. Many academics, including (alas) some of my colleagues, made the same "bubble" claims at similar times, or earlier.

F. Behavioral Finance

I conclude this section on market efficiency with a complaint voiced in my review of behavioral finance 15 years ago (Fama 1998). The behavioral finance literature is largely an attack on market efficiency. The best of the behaviorists (like my colleague Richard Thaler) base their attacks and their readings of the empirical record on findings about human behavior in psychology. Many others don't bother. They scour databases of asset returns for "anomalies" (a statistically treacherous procedure), and declare victory for behavioral finance when they find a candidate. Most important, the behavioral literature has not put forth a full blown model for prices and returns that can be tested and potentially rejected—the acid test for any model proposed as a replacement for another model.

ASSET PRICING MODELS

This year's Nobel award cites empirical research in asset pricing. Tests of market efficiency are one branch of this research. The other is tests of asset pricing models, that is, models that specify the nature of asset risks and the relation between expected return and risk. Much of my work is concerned with developing and testing asset pricing models, the flip side of the joint hypothesis problem.

A. Fama and MacBeth (1973)

The first formal model of market equilibrium is the CAPM (capital asset pricing model) of Sharpe (1964) and Lintner (1965). In this model market β, the slope in the regression of an asset's return on the market return, is the only relevant measure of an asset's risk, and the cross-section of expected asset returns depends only on the cross-section of asset βs.

In the early literature, the common approach to test this prediction was cross-section regressions of average security or portfolio returns on estimates of their βs and other variables. Black, Jensen and Scholes (1972) criticize this approach because it produces estimates of the slope for β (the premium in expected returns per unit of β) that seem too precise, given the high volatility of market returns. They rightly suspect that the problem is cross-correlation of the residuals in the regression, which leads to underestimated standard errors. They propose a complicated portfolio approach to solve this problem.

Fama and MacBeth (1973) provide a simple solution to the cross-correlation problem. Instead of regressing average asset returns on βs and other variables, one does the regression period-by-period, where the period is usually a month. The slopes in the regression are monthly portfolio returns whose average values can be used to test the CAPM predictions that the expected β premium is positive and other variables add nothing to the explanation of the cross-section of expected returns. (This is best explained in chapter 9 of Fama 1976b).

An example is helpful. Fama and French (1992) estimate month-by-month regressions of the cross-section of individual stock returns for month t, R_{it}, on estimates b_i of their βs, their (logged) market capitalizations at the beginning of month t, $MC_{i,t-1}$, and their book-to-market equity ratios, $BM_{i,t-1}$,

$$R_{it} = a_t + a_{1t}b_i + a_{2t}MC_{i,t-1} + a_{3t}BM_{i,t-1} + e_{it}. \quad (12)$$

In the CAPM the cross-section of expected returns is completely described by the cross-section of βs, so $MC_{i,t-1}$, and $BM_{i,t-1}$ should add nothing to the explanation of expected returns. The average values of the slopes a_{2t}, and a_{3t} for $MC_{i,t-1}$, and $BM_{i,t-1}$ test this prediction, and the average value of the slope a_{1t} for b_i tests the CAPM prediction that the premium for β is positive.

The key to the test is the simple insight that the month-by-month variation in the regression slopes (which is, in effect, repeated sampling of the slopes) captures all the effects of the cross-correlation of the regression residuals (and of multicollinearity of the explanatory variables). The time-series standard errors used to calculate t-statistics for the average slopes thus capture the effects of residual covariance without requiring an estimate of the residual covariance matrix. And inferences lean on the relatively robust statistical properties of t tests for sample means.

The Fama-MacBeth approach is standard in tests of asset pricing models that use cross-section regressions, but its benefits carry over to panels (time series of cross-sections) of all sorts. For example, Kenneth French and I use the approach to examine issues in corporate finance (Fama and French 1998, 2002). In applications in which the dependent variable in the regression is asset returns, autocorrelation of the period-by-period regression slopes (which are portfolio returns) is not a problem. When autocorrelation of the slopes is a problem, as is more likely in other applications, correcting the standard errors of the average slopes is straightforward.

Outside of finance, research in economics that uses panel regressions has slowly come to acknowledge that residual covariance and autocorrelation are pervasive problems. Robust regression "clustering" techniques are now available (for example, Thompson 2011). The Fama-MacBeth approach is a simple alternative.

B. The Problems of the CAPM

The evidence in Black, Jensen, and Scholes (1972) and Fama and MacBeth (1973) is generally favorable to the CAPM, or at least to Black's (1972) version of the CAPM in which there is no risk-free security. The golden age of the model is, however, brief. In the 1980s, violations, labeled anomalies, begin to surface. Banz (1981) finds that market β does not fully explain the higher average returns of small (low market capitalization) stocks. Basu (1983) finds that the positive relation between the earning-price ratio (E/P) and average return is left unexplained by β. Rosenberg, Reid, and Lanstein (1985) find a positive relation between average stock return and the book-to-market equity ratio (B/M) that is missed by the CAPM. Bhandari (1988) documents a similar result for market leverage (the ratio of debt to the market value of equity, *D/M*). As noted earlier, Ball (1978) argues that variables like size, *E/P*, *B/M*, and *D/M* are natural candidates to expose the failures of asset pricing models as explanations of expected returns since all these variables use the stock price, which, given expected dividends, is inversely related to the expected stock return.

Viewed one at a time in the papers that discovered them, the CAPM anomalies seemed like curiosity items that show that the CAPM is just a model and can't be expected to explain the entire cross-section of expected stock returns. In updated tests, Fama and French (1992) examine all the common anomalies. Apparently, seeing all the negative evidence in one place leads readers to accept our conclusion that the CAPM just doesn't work. The model is an elegantly simple and intuitively appealing *tour de force* that lays the foundations of asset pricing theory, but its major prediction that market β suffices to explain the cross-section of expected returns seems to be violated in many ways.

In terms of citations, Fama and French (1992) is high on the *Journal of Finance* all-time hit list. Its impact is somewhat surprising since there is little new in the paper, aside from a clear statement of the implications of the accumulated empirical problems of the CAPM.

C. The Three-Factor Model

An asset pricing model can only be replaced by a model that provides a better description of average returns. The three-factor model of Fama and French (1993) addresses this challenge. The model's expected return equation is,

$$E(R_{it}) - R_{Ft} = b_i[E(R_{Mt}) - R_{Ft}] + s_iE(SMB_t) + h_i\, E(HML_t). \tag{13}$$

The time-series regression used to test the model is,

$$R_{it} - R_{Ft} = a_i + b_i(R_{Mt} - R_{Ft}) + s_iSMB_t + h_iHML_t + e_{it}. \tag{14}$$

In these equations R_{it} is the return on security or portfolio i for period t, R_{Ft} is the risk-free return, R_{Mt} is the return on the value-weight (VW) market portfolio, SMB_t is the return on a diversified portfolio of small stocks minus the return on a diversified portfolio of big stocks, HML_t is the difference between the returns on diversified portfolios of high and low *B/M* stocks, and e_{it} is a zero-mean residual. The three-factor model (13) says that the sensitivities b_i, s_i, and h_i to the portfolio returns in (14) capture all variation in expected returns, so the true value of the intercept a_i in (14) is zero for all securities and portfolios i.

The three-factor model is an empirical asset pricing model. Standard asset pricing models work forward from assumptions about investor tastes and portfolio opportunities to predictions about how risk should be measured and the relation between risk and expected return. Empirical asset pricing models work backward. They take as given the patterns in average returns, and propose models to capture them. The three-factor model is designed to capture the relation between average return and size (market capitalization) and the relation between average return and price ratios like the book-to-market ratio, which were the two well-known patterns in average returns at the time of our 1993 paper.

To place the three-factor model in the rational asset pricing literature, Fama and French (1993) propose (13) as the expected return equation for a version of Merton's (1973a) ICAPM in which up to two unspecified state variables lead to special risk premiums that are not captured by the market factor. In this view, size and *B*/*M* are not themselves state variables, and *SMB* and *HML* are not portfolios that mimic state variables. Instead, in the spirit of Fama (1996), the factors are just diversified portfolios that provide different combinations of covariances with the unknown state variables. And the zero intercepts hypothesis for (14) implies that the market portfolio, the risk-free asset, *SMB* and *HML* span (can be used to generate) the relevant multifactor efficient set. In this scenario, (13) is an empirical asset pricing model that allows us to capture the expected return effects of state variables without naming them.

There is another more agnostic interpretation of the zero-intercepts hypothesis for (14). With risk-free borrowing and lending, there is one "tangency" portfolio of risky assets that is the risky component of all the mean-variance-efficient portfolios of Markowitz (1952). If the tangency portfolio can be expressed as a portfolio of the risk-free asset, the market portfolio, *SMB* and *HML*, the analysis in Huberman and Kandel (1987) implies that the intercept in (14) is zero for all assets. This view of the three-factor model covers the ICAPM interpretation of Fama and French (1993) and the behavioral stories discussed later.

Kenneth French and I have many papers that address the empirical robustness of the three-factor model and the size and *B*/*M* patterns in average returns the model is designed to explain. For example, to examine whether the size and *B*/*M* patterns in average returns observed for the post-1962 period in Fama and French (1992) are the chance result of data dredging, Davis, Fama, and French (2000) extend the tests back to 1927, and Fama and French (1998, 2012) examine international data. The results are similar to those in Fama and French (1992, 1993). Fama and French (1996, 2008) examine whether the three-factor model can explain the anomalies that cause problems for the CAPM. The three-factor model does well on the anomalies associated with size, sales growth, and various price ratios, but it is just a model and it fails to absorb other anomalies. Most prominent is the momentum in short-term returns documented by Jegadeesh and Titman (1993), which is a problem for all asset pricing models that do not add exposure to momentum as an explanatory factor, and which in my view is the biggest challenge to market efficiency.

After 1993, empirical research that uses an asset pricing model routinely includes the three-factor model among the alternatives. When the issue is the performance of a proposed new asset pricing model, victory is declared if the model comes somewhat close to explaining as much of the cross-section of average returns as the three-factor model. Research on the performance of managed portfolios (for example, mutual funds) routinely uses the intercepts ("alphas") produced by (14), often augmented with a momentum factor (for example, Carhart 1997, and more recently Kosowski et al. 2006 or Fama and French 2010).

A long time passed before the implications of the work on market efficiency for portfolio choice had an impact on investment practice. Even today, active managers (who propose to invest in undervalued securities) attract far more funds than passive managers (who buy market portfolios or whole segments of the market). This is puzzling, given the high fees of active managers and four decades of evidence (from Jensen 1968 to Fama and French 2010) that active management is a bad deal for investors.

In contrast, the work on the empirical problems in the CAPM model for expected returns, culminating in Fama and French (1992, 1993), had an immediate impact on investment practice. It quickly became common to characterize professionally managed portfolios in terms of size and value (high B/M) or growth (low B/M) tilts. And it quickly became common to use the regression slopes from the three-factor model to characterize the tilts and to use the intercept to measure abnormal average returns (alpha).

There is longstanding controversy about the source of the size and especially the value premium in average returns. As noted above, Fama and French (1993, 1996) propose the three-factor model as a multifactor version of Merton's (1973a) ICAPM. The high volatility of the SMB and HML returns is consistent with this view. The open question is: what are the underlying state variables that lead to variation in expected returns missed by the CAPM market β? There is a literature that proposes answers to this question, but the evidence so far is unconvincing.

The chief competitor to our ICAPM risk story for the value premium is the overreaction hypothesis of DeBondt and Thaler (1987) and Lakonishok, Shleifer, and Vishny (1994). They postulate that market prices overreact to the recent good times of growth stocks and the bad times of value stocks. Subsequent price corrections produce the value premium (high average returns of value stocks relative to growth stocks). The weakness of this view is the presumption that investors never learn about their behavioral biases, which is necessary to explain the persistence of the value premium. Moreover, Fama and French (1995) find that the high average returns of value stocks and the low average returns of growth stocks persist for at least five years after stocks are allocated to value and growth portfolios, which seems rather long to be attributed to correction of irrational prices.

Asset pricing models typically assume that portfolio decisions depend only on properties of the return distributions of assets and portfolios. Another possibility, suggested by Fama and French (2007) and related to the stories in Daniel and Titman (1997) and Barberis and Shleifer (2003), is that tastes for other characteristics of assets play a role. ("Socially responsible investing" is an example.) Perhaps many investors get utility from holding growth (low B/M) stocks, which tend to be profitable fast-growing firms, and they are averse to value stocks, which tend to be relatively unprofitable with few growth opportunities. If such tastes persist, they can have persistent effects on asset prices and expected returns, as long as they don't lead to arbitrage opportunities. This is a behavioral story, but it is not about irrational behavior. In economics, we take tastes as given and make no judgments about them.

To what extent is the value premium in expected stock returns due to ICAPM state variable risks, investor overreaction, or tastes for assets as consumption goods? We don't know. An agnostic view of the three-factor model that doesn't require a choice among stories is that the model uses empirical regularities observed in many markets to find portfolios that together span the mean-variance-efficient set of Markowitz (1952). The analysis in Huberman and Kandel (1987) then implies that the model can be used to describe expected returns on all assets.

CONCLUSIONS

In my view, finance is the most successful branch of economics in terms of rich theory, extensive empirical tests, and penetration of the theory and evidence into other areas of economics and real-world applications. Markowitz' (1952, 1959) portfolio model is widely used by professional portfolio managers. The portfolio model is the foundation of the CAPM of Sharpe (1964) and Lintner (1965), and it gets a multifactor extension in Merton (1973a). The CAPM is one of the most extensively tested models in economics, it is well-known to students in areas of economics other than finance, and it is widely used by practitioners.

The options pricing model of Black and Scholes (1973) and Merton (1973b) is a must for students in all areas of economics, and it is the foundation for a huge derivatives industry. However one judges market efficiency, it has motivated a massive body of empirical work that has enhanced our understanding of markets, and like it or not, professional money managers have to address its challenges. Its sibling, rational expectations, first exposited by Muth (1961), has had a similar run in macroeconomics. The three-factor model of Fama and French (1993) is arguably the most successful asset pricing model in empirical tests to date, it can't be avoided in tests of competing asset pricing models, and it is a handy tool that has shaped the thinking of practitioners. Can any other branch of economics claim similar academic and applied impact?

Acknowledgments

I am grateful for the comments of George Constantinides, Douglas Diamond, Anil Kashyap, Richard Leftwich, Juhani Linnainmaa, Tobias Moskowitz, Lubos Pastor, Pietro Veronesi, G. William Schwert, Amir Sufi, and Richard Thaler. Special thanks to John Cochrane and my longtime coauthor, Kenneth R. French. I am a consultant to, board member of, and shareholder in Dimensional Fund Advisors.

Literature Cited

Bachelier, Louis. 1900. Theorie de la Speculation. (doctoral dissertation in mathematics) University of Paris

Ball, Ray. 1978. "Anomalies in Relationships Between Securities' Yields and Yield-Surrogates." *Journal of Financial Economics* 6:103–26.

Banz, Rolf W. 1981. "The Relationship Between Return and Market Value of Common Stocks." *Journal of Financial Economics* 9:3–18.

Barberis, Nicholas, and Andrei Shleifer. 2003. "Style Investing." *Journal of Financial Economics* 68:161–99.

Basu, Sanjoy. 1983. "The Relationship Between Earnings Yield, Market Value, and Return for NYSE Common Stocks: Further Evidence." *Journal of Financial Economics* 12:129–56.

Bhandari, Laxmi C. 1988. "Debt/Equity Ratio and Expected Common Stock Returns: Empirical Evidence." *Journal of Finance* 43:507–28.

Black, Fischer. 1972. "Capital Market Equilibrium with Restricted Borrowing." *Journal of Business* 45:444–54.

Black, Fischer, and Michael C. Jensen, Myron S. Scholes. 1972. "The Capital Asset Pricing Model: Some Empirical Tests." In *Studies in the Theory of Capital Markets*, edited by Michael C. Jensen, 79–121. New York: Praeger.

Black, Fischer, and Myron S. Scholes. 1973. "The Pricing of Options and Corporate Liabilities." *Journal of Political Economy* 81: 638–54.

Breeden, Douglas T. 1979. "An Intertemporal Asset Pricing Model with Stochastic Consumption and Investment Opportunities." *Journal of Financial Economics* 7:265–96.

Campbell, John Y., and Robert J. Shiller. 1988. "The Dividend-Price Ratio and Expectations of Future Dividends and Discount Factors." *Review of Financial Studies* 1: 195–27.

Carhart, Mark M. 1997. "On Persistence in Mutual Fund Performance." *Journal of Finance* 52:57–82.

Case, Karl E., and Robert J. Shiller. 2003. "Is There a Bubble in the Housing Market?" *Brookings Paper on Economic Activity* No. 2: 299–342.

Cochrane, John H. 2010. "Presidential Address: Discount Rates." *Journal of Finance* 66: 1047–1108.

Daniel, Kent, and Sheridan Titman. 1997. "Evidence on the Characteristics of Cross Sectional Variation in Stock Returns." *Journal of Finance* 52:1–33.

Davis, James L., and Eugene F. Fama, Kenneth R. French. 2000. "Characteristics, Covariances, and Average Returns: 1929–1997." *Journal of Finance* 55:389–06.

DeBondt, Werner F.M., and Richard H. Thaler. 1987. "Further Evidence on Investor Overreaction and Stock Market Seasonality." *Journal of Finance* 42:557–81.

Fama, Eugene F. 1965a. "The Behavior of Stock Market Prices." *Journal of Business* 38:34–105.

Fama, Eugene F. 1965b. "Random Walks in Stock Market Prices." *Financial Analysts Journal* September/October: 55–59.

Fama, Eugene F. 1970. "Efficient Capital Markets: A Review of Theory and Empirical Work." *Journal of Finance* 25:383–17.

Fama, Eugene F. 1975. "Short-Term Interest Rates as Predictors of Inflation." *American Economic Review* 65:269–82.

Fama, Eugene F. 1976a. "Forward Rates as Predictors of Future Spot Rates." *Journal of Financial Economics* 3:361–77.

Fama, Eugene F. 1976b. *Foundations of Finance*. New York: Basic Books.

Fama, Eugene F. 1976c. "Inflation Uncertainty and Expected Returns on Treasury Bills." *Journal of Political Economy* 84: 427–48.

Fama, Eugene F. 1981. "Stock Returns, Real Activity, Inflation, and Money." *American Economic Review* 71: 545–65.

Fama, Eugene F. 1984a. "Forward and Spot Exchange Rates." *Journal of Monetary Economics* 14:319–38.

Fama, Eugene F. 1984b. "The Information in the Term Structure." *Journal of Financial Economics* 13:509–28.

Fama, Eugene F. 1984c. "Term Premiums in Bond Returns." *Journal of Financial Economics* 13:529–46.

Fama, Eugene F. 1986. "Term Premiums and Default Premiums in Money Markets." *Journal of Financial Economics* 17:175–96.

Fama, Eugene F. 1990a. "Term Structure Forecasts of Interest Rates, Inflation, and Real Returns." *Journal of Monetary Economics* 25:59–76.

Fama, Eugene F. 1990b. "Stock Returns, Expected Returns, and Real Activity." *Journal of Finance* 45:1089–1108.

Fama, Eugene F. 1991. "Efficient Markets II." *Journal of Finance* 46:1575–1617.

Fama, Eugene F. 1996. "Multifactor Portfolio Efficiency and Multifactor Asset Pricing." *Journal of Financial and Quantitative Analysis* 31: 441–65.

Fama, Eugene F. 1998. "Market Efficiency, Long-Term Returns, and Behavioral Finance." *Journal of Financial Economics* 49: 283–06.

Fama, Eugene F., and Kenneth R. French. 2002. "Testing Tradeoff and Pecking Order Predictions about Dividends and Debt." *Review of Financial Studies* 15: 1–33.

Fama, Eugene F. 2005. "The Behavior of Interest Rates." *Review of Financial Studies* 19:359–79.

Fama, Eugene F. 2011. "My Life in Finance." *Annual Review of Financial Economics* 3: 1–15.

Fama, Eugene F., and Robert R. Bliss. 1987. "The Information in Long-Maturity Forward Rates." *American Economic Review* 77:680–92.

Fama, Eugene F., and Lawrence Fisher, Michael C. Jensen, Richard Roll. 1969. "The Adjustment of Stock Prices to New Information." *International Economic Review* 10: 1–21.

Fama, Eugene F., and Kenneth R. French. 1987. "Commodity Futures Prices: Some Evidence on Forecast Power Premiums and the Theory of Storage." *Journal of Business* 60: 55–73.

Fama, Eugene F., and Kenneth R. French. 1989. "Business Conditions and Expected Returns on Stocks and Bonds." *Journal of Financial Economics* 25: 23–49.

Fama, Eugene F. and Kenneth R. French. 1992. "The Cross-Section of Expected Stock Returns." *Journal of Finance* 47:427–65.

Fama, Eugene F., and Kenneth R. French. 1993. "Common Risk Factors in the Returns on Stocks and Bonds." *Journal of Financial Economics* 33:3–56.

Fama, Eugene F., and Kenneth R. French. 1995. "Size and Book-to-Market Factors in earnings and Returns." *Journal of Finance* 50:131–56.

Fama, Eugene F., and Kenneth R. French. 1996. "Multifactor Explanations of Asset Pricing Anomalies." *Journal of Finance* 51: 55–84.

Fama, Eugene F., and Kenneth R. French. 1998. "Value Versus Growth: The International Evidence." *Journal of Finance* 53: 1975–1999.

Fama, Eugene F., and Kenneth R. French. 2007. "Disagreement, Tastes, and Asset Prices." *Journal of Financial Economics* 83:667–89.

Fama, Eugene F., and Kenneth R. French. 2008. "Dissecting Anomalies." *Journal of Finance* 63:1653–1678.

Fama, Eugene F., and Kenneth R. French. 2010. "Luck Versus Skill in the Cross-Section of Mutual Fund Returns." *Journal of Finance* 65: 1915–1947.

Fama, Eugene F., and Kenneth R. French. 2012. "Size, Value, and Momentum in International Stock Returns." *Journal of Financial Economics* 105: 457–72.

Fama, Eugen F., and James D. MacBeth. 1973. "Risk, Return, and Equilibrium: Empirical Tests." *Journal of Political Economy* 81:607–36.

Fama, Eugene F., and G. William Schwert. 1979. "Inflation, Interest and Relative Prices." *Journal of Business* 52:183–09.

Fama, Eugene F., and G. William Schwert. 1977. "Asset Returns and Inflation." *Journal of Financial Economics* 5:115–46.

Huberman, Gur, and Shmuel Kandel. 1987. "Mean-Variance Spanning." *Journal of Finance* 42: 873–88.

Jegadeesh, Narasimhan, and Sheridan Titman. 1993. "Returns to Buying Winners and Selling Losers: Implications for Stock Market Efficiency." *Journal of Finance* 48:65–91.

Jensen, Michael C. 1968. "The Performance of Mutual Funds in the Period 1945–1964." *Journal of Finance* 23:2033–2058.

Kosowski, Robert, and Allan Timmermann, Russ Wermers, Hal White. 2006. "Can Mutual Fund "Stars" Really Pick Stocks? New Evidence from a Bootstrap Analysis." *Journal of Finance* 61:2551–2595.

Lakonishok, Josef, and Andrei Shleifer, Robert W. Vishny. 1994. "Contrarian Investment, Extrapolation, and Risk." *Journal of Finance* 49:1541–1578.

Lintner, John. 1965. "The Valuation of Risk Assets and the Selection of Risky Investments in Stock Portfolios and Capital Budgets." *Review of Economics and Statistics* 47:13–37.

Lucas Jr., Robert E. 1978. "Asset Prices in an Exchange Economy." *Econometrica* 46:1429–1446.

Mandelbrot, Benoit. 1966. "Forecasts of Future Prices, Unbiased Markets, and Martingale Models." *Journal of Business* (Special Supplement, January). 39:242–55.

Markowitz, Harry. 1952. "Portfolio Selection." *Journal of Finance* 7:77–99.

Markowitz, Harry. 1959. *Portfolio Selection: Efficient Diversification of Investments*. Cowles Foundation Monograph No. 16. New York: John Wiley & Sons, Inc.

Merton, Robert C. 1973a. "An Intertemporal Capital Asset Pricing Model." *Econometrica* 41:867–87.

Merton, Robert C. 1973b. "Theory of Rational Options Pricing." *Bell Journal of Economics and Management Science* 4:141–83.

Muth, John F. 1961. "Rational Expectations and the Theory of Price Movements." *Econometrica* 29: 315–35.

Rosenberg, Barr, and Kenneth Reid, Ronald Lanstein. 1985. "Persuasive Evidence of Market Inefficiency." *Journal of Portfolio Management* 11:9–17.

Rozeff, Michael S. 1984. "Dividend Yields and Equity Risk Premiums." *Journal of Portfolio Management* 68–75.

Samuelson, Paul A. 1965. "Proof That Properly Anticipated Prices Fluctuate Randomly." *Industrial Management Review* 6:41–49.

Sharpe, William F. 1964. "Capital Asset Prices: A Theory of Market Equilibrium Under Conditions of Risk." *Journal of Finance* 19:425–42.

Shiller, Robert J. 1981. "Do Stock Prices Move Too Much to be Justified by Subsequent Changes in Dividends?" *American Economic Review* 71: 421–36.

Shiller, Robert J. 1984. "Stock Prices and Social Dynamics." *Brookings Papers on Economic Activity* 2: 457–98.

Thompson, Samuel B. 2011. "Simple Formulas for Standard Errors that Cluster by Both Firm and Time." *Journal of Financial Economics* 99: 1–10.

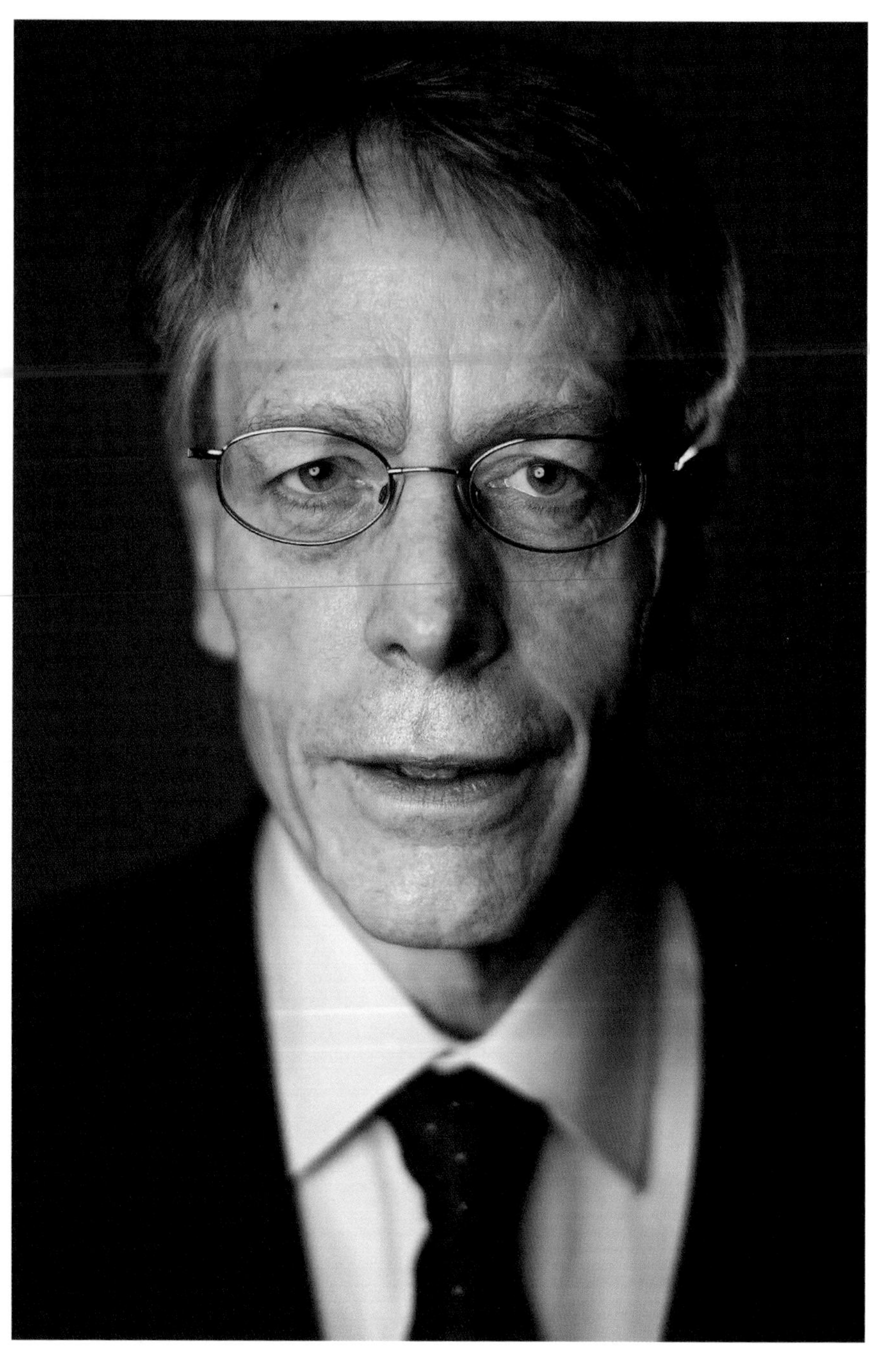

Lars Peter Hansen. Photo: A. Mahmoud

Lars Peter Hansen

My name sounds very Nordic. Seven of my great-great-grandparents were born in Denmark and two more in Sweden. My first name comes from my Swedish great-great-grandfather, Lars Toolson, whose son also had the first name Lars. My middle name is from my great-grandfather Peter Hansen, who was born in Denmark. Fifteen of my sixteen great-great-grandparents, emigrating from Denmark, England, Sweden and Wales in the mid-nineteenth century, settled in Cache Valley, Utah.

My maternal grandfather George Rees was a country doctor who was accustomed to making house calls and often took payment in kind. Given his profession, he was one of the first owners of a car, a Ford Model A. My mother recently reminded us of that car: her first trip to Yellowstone National Park was made while riding in the rumble seat of that car, eighty years earlier. My grandfather attended the University of Chicago 70 years before I first worked there; he enrolled in a joint program between Rush Medical College and the university in 1911. During this time, my grandmother Veda Rees supported his medical training by working at Marshall Field's, an iconic department store in downtown Chicago.

My paternal grandfather, Willard Hansen, was a proud farmer, committed to helping his sons launch their own successful farming ventures. When my father, R. Gaurth Hansen, told my grandfather Willard that he wanted to continue his studies beyond a four-year degree, my grandfather said, "If so, then be sure to study something useful, and become a doctor or a veterinarian." My father was very close to his mother, Syble Toolson Hansen, and she quietly urged him to follow his academic and intellectual interests. Rather than a career in farming or animal care, my father became a biochemist and an expert in nutrition.

According to my maternal grandparents, my mother, Anna Lou Rees Hansen, knew my father from infancy. As the story goes, her father took her along when he made house calls to my grandmother Hansen and her infant son Gaurth. My mother grew up having the responsibility of taking important phone messages from patients who needed her father's care from a very young age. Later, my mother and father were classmates in a one-room schoolhouse in Smithfield. Both of my parents went to college at Utah State University, my dad for three years before going on mission for the Mormon Church and my mother for four years and graduating in 1942. It was indeed a close-knit community in which everyone knew each other; both of my grandfathers served as mayor of the town of Smithfield, Utah.

My father received his bachelor's degree from the University of Wisconsin, eventually leaving with a Ph.D. in 1948. His academic contributions included enzyme analysis of galactose metabolism in micro-organisms and animals, and painstakingly interviewing patients for family histories to seek clues to genetic transmission of galactosemia. In addition to applying his training to conducting nutrition surveys and consulting for the U.S. Department of Agriculture and the U.S. Public Health Service, he played a pivotal role in consolidating biochemistry at Michigan State University. I learned much about academic organization and management from dinner time conversations about my father's administrative adventures.

The third of three sons, I was born in Urbana, Illinois. My oldest brother, Roger, is seven years my senior and has spent most of his professional career as a water resource engineer with the Bureau of Reclamation. My second brother, Ted, is five years my senior and is a geneticist and immunologist who just recently retired from Washington University in St. Louis. Ted took an active interest in my intellectual and athletic development at an early age. My athletic exploits ended after my second year in high school, but Ted's interest in my studies had a long-lasting impact. Roger and I became closer later in life, when he came to Utah State University during my last years in college after serving in the Coast Guard.

In grade school, I developed a speech impediment, suffering from severe stuttering, especially in public. I still remember losing an election for class president in grade school in part because I had trouble speaking to the school. My reaction was to avoid public speaking for many years. Of course, as an academic one cannot really avoid speaking, so I have improved by practicing.

When I was almost 16, my parents moved back to Utah when my father was given the opportunity to become first Academic Vice President and later Provost of Utah State University. The university is in Logan, Utah, in Cache Valley and near Smithfield where they were born, so this was a return home for them. Although the move to Logan made it possible for me to get to know my grandparents better, it was a difficult adjustment for me. I led an undistinguished academic career at Logan High School. Once I brought home double check marks under "does not respect authority." In part, this reflected my independent thinking, but I was not an easy student for some of my teachers. My parents were patient with me, hoping I would eventually turn things around. My parents arranged for time off from school in order to work part time in a chemistry lab.

Once I entered Utah State University in 1970, I began to really apply myself. To my parents' surprise, I was able to pay my way through my undergraduate education. I worked various jobs, including one in an animal science lab, a political polling venture, and working my parents' "hobby farm" of about eighty acres in Cache Valley. Our crops included barley, oats, and alfalfa, all requiring manual labor to redirect water from mountain streams to the crops. Academically, I pursued interests in social science, majoring in political science, along with mathematics. Many faculty members took an interest in me, and three stand out. Michael Windham helped me better understand and appreciate the field of mathematics. Doug Alder, who taught an honors European history class, gave me some advice that caught me by surprise. He told me, "Lars, do not just follow the course of others but find your unique talents and aim to do something different." The idea that I even might have unique talents had not occurred to me. By the end of my sophomore year, I decided to try combining my interests in mathematics and political science with the field of economics. A third professor, Bartell Jensen, helped me design an accelerated economics curriculum allowing me to take essential undergraduate classes in economics during my junior year, and some graduate classes by the time I was a senior. The fast pace helped me prepare for a Ph.D. program in a short period of time. Obtaining some distinction in mathematics and political science with my college degree, along with an accelerated curriculum in economics, enabled me to proceed to the University of Minnesota for a Ph.D.

At Minnesota, I was lucky in two ways. First, I was allowed to augment my economics classes with those from the graduate mathematics department. I pursued an eclectic mix of analysis, probability theory, and statistics classes that has served me well. Second, at Minnesota I met my intellectual mentors Chris Sims and Tom Sargent, when they were young scholars. Both had launched their stellar academic careers and were becoming recognized as major contributors to macroeconomics and econometrics. While Tom and Chris have different research perspectives, there was also much complementarity between their approaches. My training and experience at the University of Minnesota in the 1970s helped to shape my research and nurtured my interest in economic dynamics and time series econometrics. I learned to think of macroeconomic models as restrictions on stochastic processes, random processes that evolve over time.

Influenced by some lectures by Chris, I also began working on large sample approximation arguments; some of this research grew into my paper on Generalized Method of Moments (GMM) estimation. I found Tom's willingness to engage me in joint research while I was still a graduate student very stimulating, and this grew into a long-standing collaboration. Tom and I have written many papers on such topics as rational expectations econometrics, present-value budget balance and robustness in decision-making.

Leaving graduate school, Carnegie Mellon University was an ideal first job for me. The faculty there in the late 1970s was skewed demographically: there were few senior faculty, and the younger faculty members were given much responsibility for the Ph.D. program and for running research workshops. Looking back on those years, I see what a valuable environment it was. I had the opportunity to share ideas with many young scholars who went on to distinguished careers.

Carnegie was where I first learned about asset pricing theory and began to explore with co-authors how to study empirical implications of these models in novel ways. I learned much from my collaborations: Bob Hodrick helped me explore international finance, Scott Richard worked with me on testable implications of asset pricing models, and Marty Eichenbaum collaborated on preference parameter estimation for dynamic macroeconomic models. My work with Ken Singleton was particularly valuable, developing novel ways to study the consumption-based capital asset pricing models. Working on these papers helped me to better motivate and reinforce the development of GMM estimation.

I visited the University of Chicago in the fall of 1981, and have been there ever since. The research environment at the University of Chicago is uniquely rewarding. It has historically been a highly interactive environment in which economics is taken very seriously. When I arrived, I had Gary Becker, Jim Heckman and Bob Lucas as senior colleagues. Each went on to win Nobel prizes and each set incredible examples of scholarship along the way.

After arriving, José Scheinkman and I shared many students and collaborated on papers. I gained great insight from our interactions and was sorry when he left later for Princeton. José and I had complementary perspectives on the field of finance. Even after he left, José and I continued our collaborations and have recently been working on methods for characterizing the term structure of risk prices. Surprisingly to me, the eminent labor economist Sherwin Rosen was another great colleague, proving to have a substantive interest in economic time series. I always enjoyed our interactions. Jim Heckman and I have had many conversations over the years on an extremely wide variety of topics related to economics. Jim served as a continual reminder that the best econometrics is grounded in economic analysis and empirical evidence. I can easily expand the list of influential colleagues. At Chicago, criticism can be intense but also very valuable.

The nearby business school has strong intellectual roots in financial economics, proving to be a valuable place to exchange ideas. Scholars there, like John Cochrane and later John Heaton, share my appreciation for economic dynamics and time series econometrics as fundamental ingredients in the study of asset valuation. In 2007, I was asked to join the Statistics Department at the University, further broadening my interactions on campus. My interdisciplinary research interests have been bolstered greatly by these connections across campus and diverse interactions as I explored productive connections between macroeconomics, finance and statistics.

With my father as an example, I have served the department in various capacities, including as its department chair and in helping to launch the Milton Friedman Institute, which eventually became the Becker Friedman Institute for Research in Economics. Opportunities at other universities occasionally presented themselves, but I always decided to stay.

I have also had the opportunity to advise many excellent students. Starting with Ravi Jagannathan at Carnegie Mellon, I've advised sixty students and served on committees for many more. These former students now hold a wide range of posts in academia, the private sector, and government, with an equally wide range of accomplishments and interests. I greatly benefited and learned from my interactions with them while they were students; it has been rewarding to watch their careers flourish over the years.

Shortly after moving to Chicago, I met my future wife Grace Tsiang, a graduate student in economics at the time. I asked her out in part because she understood my unique sense of humor. We were married in 1984. It is impossible to explain adequately her influence on my life in a short space; she has been a continual source of support and encouragement. With her Chicago price-theoretic training, she has often pushed me hard to write better and think more broadly. She challenges me to explain why my seemingly abstract approaches to economic analysis deliver important practical insights. It has been a joy to watch how Grace has played a lead role in building the undergraduate program, the most popular major at the University of Chicago. Grace has helped many students discover their personal path to success by helping to design a curriculum to suit their personal interests, goals, and strengths. This example has helped me in my own student advising.

Grace's influence in my life is far-reaching. We introduced Grace's parents to the scenery and wildlife of Yellowstone and Grand Teton National Parks on a summer driving tour. While we were walking by Old Faithful, we passed other tourists on the narrow wooden walkways who recognized my father-in-law. A young couple from Taiwan had seen news stories there in which Grace's father, Sho-Chieh Tsiang, discussed his economic policy recommendations. While I was initially surprised, in retrospect I should not have been. Grace's father, along with Ta-Chung Liu, both Cornell University economists, were key economic advisors to the Taiwanese government in advance and during the "Taiwan Miracle," a time period of rapid economic growth. This set quite an example for how to use economic analysis in the policy sphere.

My parents' interest in farming and projects influenced how I spent time away from the office. Shortly after Grace and I were married, we acquired a log cabin in the countryside where we could relax and our son Peter and our energetic dog Rufus could run around endlessly on the weekends. The log cabin was on ten acres of wooded land near Harvard, Illinois, and provided many opportunities for outdoor projects. My father helped us build a garden, and our property included two ponds stocked with fish that provided food and habitat for wood ducks, blue herons, and snapping turtles. Near the end of the century, with considerable reluctance, Grace and I sold the property; we decided to spend future vacations in the mountains and national parks of western Wyoming, hiking, skiing and participating in other outdoor activities. While time away from Chicago includes fun activities with the family, it also serves as a valuable opportunity to regroup, recharge, and rethink whatever problems occupy my mind at the time. I have made progress on many research projects by having these blocks of time to think and write.

We have lived in Hyde Park all of our time together in Chicago. Hyde Park is a local community in Chicago that includes the University of Chicago and home for many of its faculty. Over the years we have enjoyed many interactions with others in this community, getting to know other families—many with ties to the University of Chicago. Our son Peter was born in 1992 in Hyde Park. It has been rewarding to watch him grow and thrive. The three of us have traveled all over the world and have I enjoyed these trips and our long conversations together. Peter will graduate as a mathematics major at the University of Chicago in the spring of 2014. Grace, Peter and I will march in the academic procession to honor the occasion.

Over the years, I have received some recognition for my professional accomplishments. I remember my dad, the biochemist, attending the ceremony when I was inducted into the National Academy of Sciences. He was proud, but was also still coming to grips with the notion that social sciences—including economics—should be part of the National Academy. I tried to convey that the scientific method can be applied even when it is difficult to verify models with testing and experimentation. I still jokingly refer to the social sciences as the truly "hard" sciences for exactly this reason when talking to biological and physical scientists about the issue. My two brothers, a sister-in-law and my mother-in-law joined our family in Madrid when I was recognized by the BBVA Foundation in 2010. In 2012, Utah State University gave me an honorary Doctor of Science degree. My mother, a USU alum, and many other family members were able to come to the ceremony—making this a very special event. Although my father was no longer living, this was all the more gratifying because my father received this same degree in 1991. I tend to shy away from the spotlight, but sharing these honors with family has always meant a lot to me.

Looking ahead, I will continue to investigate a variety of research related to the implications of uncertainty—both as a modeler of dynamic economies and as an econometrician. The real consequences of uncertainty are important for a variety of questions in economics with policy relevance. I look forward to advising more students and learning from them. I hope I can encourage young scholars to advance research in fields to which I have contributed.

Uncertainty Outside and Inside Economic Models*

Prize Lecture, December 8, 2013

by Lars Peter Hansen
University of Chicago, Chicago, IL, USA.

> We must infer what the future situation would have been without our interference, and what change will be wrought in it by our action. Fortunately or unfortunately, none of these processes is infallible, or indeed ever accurate and complete. Knight (1921: 201–202)

1 INTRODUCTION

Asset pricing theory has long recognized that financial markets compensate investors who are exposed to some components of uncertainty. This is where macroeconomics comes into play. The economy-wide shocks, the primary concern of macroeconomists, by their nature are not diversifiable. Exposures to these shocks cannot be averaged out with exposures to other shocks. Thus, returns on assets that depend on these macroeconomic shocks reflect "risk" premia and are a linchpin connecting macroeconomic uncertainty to financial markets. A risk premium reflects both the price of risk and the degree of exposure to risk. I will be particularly interested in how the exposures to macroeconomic impulses are priced by decentralized security markets.

* I thank Manuel Arellano, Amy Boonstra, Philip Barrett, Xiaohong Chen, John Cochrane, Maryam Farboodi, Eric Ghysels, Itzhak Gilboa, Massimo Marinacci, Nan Li, Monika Piazzesi, Eric Renault, Scott Richard, Larry Samuelson, Enrique Sentana, José Scheinkman, Martin Schneider, Stephen Stigler, Harald Uhlig, Amir Yaron an anonymous referee and especially Jaroslav Borovička, James Heckman, Thomas Sargent and Grace Tsiang for helpful comments.

How do we model the dynamic evolution of the macroeconomy? Following the tradition initiated by Slutsky (1927, 1937) and Frisch (1933), I believe it is best captured by stochastic processes with restrictions; exogenous shocks repeatedly perturb a dynamic equilibrium through the model's endogenous transmission mechanisms. Bachelier (1900), one of the developers of Brownian motion, recognized the value of modeling financial prices as responses to shocks.[1] It took economists fifty years to discover and appreciate his insights. (It was Savage who alerted Samuelson to this important line of research in the early 1950s.) Prior to that, scholars such as Yule (1927), Slutsky (1927, 1937) and Frisch (1933) had explored how linear models with shocks and propagation mechanisms provide attractive ways of explaining approximate cyclical behavior in macro time series. Similarities in the mathematical underpinnings of these two perspectives opened the door to connecting macroeconomics and finance.

Using random processes in our models allows economists to capture the variability of time series data, but it also poses challenges to model builders. As model builders, we must understand the uncertainty from two different perspectives. Consider first that of the econometrician, standing outside an economic model, who must assess its congruence with reality, inclusive of its random perturbations. An econometrician's role is to choose among different parameters that together describe a family of possible models to best mimic measured real world time series and to test the implications of these models. I refer to this as *outside uncertainty*. Second, agents inside our model, be it consumers, entrepreneurs, or policy makers, must also confront uncertainty as they make decisions. I refer to this as *inside uncertainty*, as it pertains to the decision-makers within the model. What do these agents know? From what information can they learn? With how much confidence do they forecast the future? The modeler's choice regarding insiders' perspectives on an uncertain future can have significant consequences for each model's equilibrium outcomes.

Stochastic equilibrium models predict risk prices, the market compensations that investors receive for being exposed to macroeconomic shocks. A challenge for econometric analyses is to ascertain if their predictions are consistent with data. These models reveal asset pricing implications via stochastic discount factors. The discount factors are stochastic to allow for exposures to alternative

---

[1] See Davis and Etheridge (2006) for a translation and commentary and Dimson and Mussavian (2000) for an historical discussion of the link between Bachelier's contribution and subsequent research on efficient markets.

macroeconomic random outcomes to be discounted differently. Moreover, the compounding of stochastic discount factors shows how market compensations change with the investment horizon. Stochastic discount factors thus provide a convenient vehicle for depicting the empirical implications of the alternative models. I will initially describe the methods and outcomes from an econometrician *outside* the model.

Stochastic discount factors are defined with respect to a probability distribution relevant to investors inside the model. Lucas (1972) and others imposed rational expectations as an equilibrium concept, making the probability distribution relevant to investors inside the model coincide with the probability distribution implied by the solution to the model. It is an elegant response for how to model agents *inside* the model, but its application to the study of asset pricing models has resulted in empirical puzzles as revealed by formal econometric methods that I will describe. These and other asset pricing anomalies have motivated scholars to speculate about investor beliefs and how they respond to or cope with uncertainty. In particular, the anomalies lead me and others to explore specific alternatives to the rational expectations hypothesis.

In this essay I will consider alternatives motivated in part by a decision theory that allows for distinctions between three alternative sources of uncertainty: i) risk conditioned on a model, ii) ambiguity about which is the correct model among a family of alternatives, and iii) potential misspecification of a model or a family of possible models. These issues are pertinent to outside econometricians, but they also may be relevant to inside investors. I will elaborate on how the distinctions between uncertainty components open the door to the investigation of market compensations with components other than more narrowly defined risk prices. Motivated by empirical evidence, I am particularly interested in uncertainty pricing components that fluctuate over time.

Why is it fruitful to consider model misspecification? In economics and as in other disciplines, models are intended to be revealing simplifications, and thus deliberately are not exact characterizations of reality; it is therefore specious to criticize economic models merely for being wrong. The important criticisms are whether our models are wrong in having missed something essential to the questions under consideration. Part of a meaningful quantitative analysis is to look at models and try to figure out their deficiencies and the ways in which they can be improved. A more subtle challenge for statistical methods is to explore systematically potential modeling errors in order to assess the quality of the model predictions. This kind of uncertainty about the adequacy of a model or model family is not only relevant for econometricians outside the model but potentially also for agents inside the models.

This essay proceeds as follows. In Section 2, I review the development of time series econometric modeling, including the initiation of rational expectations econometrics. In Section 3, I review my contributions to the econometric study of partially specified models, adapting to the study asset pricing and macroeconomic uncertainty. I describe methods and approaches to the study of fully specified models based on asset pricing considerations in Section 4. In Section 5, I explore the consequences for asset pricing models when investor beliefs are not in full accord with an underlying model, which can result in investor behavior that resembles extreme risk aversion. In Section 6, I review perspectives on model ambiguity which draw on work by decision theorists and statisticians to revisit the framework that I sketch in Section 5. I draw some conclusions in Section 7.

2 RATIONAL EXPECTATIONS ECONOMETRICS

Rational expectations econometrics explores structural stochastic models of macroeconomic time series with the ambition to be a usable tool for policy analysis. It emerged in response to a rich history of modeling and statistical advances. Yule (1927) and Slutsky (1927, 1937) provided early characterizations of how time series models can generate interesting cyclical behavior by propagating shocks. Yule (1927) showed that a second-order autoregression could reproduce intriguing patterns in the time series. He fit this model to sunspot data, known to be approximately but not exactly periodic. The model was built using independent and identically distributed (iid) shocks as building blocks. The model produced a damped periodic response to random impulses. Similarly, Slutsky (1927, 1937) constructed models that were moving-averages of iid shocks and showed how such processes could be arbitrarily close to exact periodic sequences.[2] He also demonstrated how moving-average type models could account for British business cycle data.

Frisch (1933), who shared the first Sveriges Riksbank Prize in Economics with Tinbergen, pushed this agenda further by exploring how to capture dynamic economic phenomenon through probability models with explicit economic underpinnings. Frisch discussed propagation from initial conditions and described an important role for random impulses building in part on the work of Yule (1927) and Slutsky (1927, 1937). In effect, Frisch (1933) introduced

[2] I cite two versions of Slutsky's paper. The first one was published in Russian. The second one was published in English a decade later with a more comprehensive set of results. English translations of the first paper were circulated well in advance of 1937.

impulse response functions to economics as a device to understand the intertemporal impact of shocks on economic variables. Haavelmo (1944) took an additional step by providing foundations for the use of statistical methods to assess formally the stochastic models. This literature set the foundation for a modern time series econometrics that uses economics to interpret evidence in a mathematically formal way. It featured important interactions among economics, mathematics and statistics and placed a premium on formal model building.[3] Haavelmo (1944) confronts uncertainty as an econometrician *outside* the model that is to be estimated and tested.

Investment and other decisions are in part based on people's views of the future. Once economic decision makers are included into formal dynamic economic models, their expectations come into play and become an important ingredient to the model. This challenge was well appreciated by economists such as Pigou, Keynes and Hicks, and their suggestions have had durable impact on model building. Thus, the time series econometrics research agenda had to take a stand on how people inside the model made forecasts. Alternative approaches were suggested including static expectations, adaptive expectations or appeals to data on beliefs; but these approaches left open how to proceed when using dynamic economic models to assess hypothetical policy interventions.

A productive approach to this modeling challenge has been to add the hypothesis of *rational expectations*. This hypothesis appeals to long histories of data to motivate the modeling expectations. The Law of Large Numbers gives an approximation whereby parameters that are invariant over time are revealed by data, and this revelation gives a model builder a way to formalize the expectations of economic investors inside our models.[4] This approach to completing the specification of a stochastic equilibrium model was initiated within macroeco-

---

[3] Frisch, in particular, nurtured this ambitious research agenda by his central role in the foundational years of the Econometric Society. His ambition is reflected in the 1933 mission statement he wrote for the journal *Econometrica*: ". . . Experience has shown that each of these three viewpoints, that of statistics, economic theory, and mathematics, is a necessary, but not by itself a sufficient, condition for a real understanding of the quantitative relations in modern economic life. It is the unification of all three that is powerful. And it is this unification that constitutes econometrics." Frisch (1933b).

[4] More than three hundred years ago, Jacob Bernoulli proved a result that implied a Law of Large Numbers. He was motivated in part by social problems for which probabilities had to be estimated empirically, in contrast to typical gambling problems. Bernoulli's result initiated an enduring discussion of both the relevance of his simple model specification and of the approximation he established. See Stigler (2014) for an interesting retrospective on Bernoulli's contribution.

nomics by Muth (1961) and Lucas (1972). Following Lucas (1972) in particular, rational expectations became an integral part of an equilibrium for a stochastic economic model.

The aim of structural econometrics is to provide a framework for policy analysis and the study of counterfactuals. This vision is described in Marschak (1953) and articulated formally in the work of Hurwicz (1962). While there are a multitude of interesting implications of the rational expectations hypothesis, perhaps the most important one is its role in policy analysis. It gives a way to explore policy experiments or hypothetical changes that are not predicated on systematically fooling people. See Sargent and Wallace (1975) and Lucas (1976) for a discussion.[5]

From an econometric standpoint, rational expectations introduced important cross-equation restrictions. These recognize that parameters governing the dynamic evolution of exogenous impulses to the model must also be present in decision rules and equilibrium relations. These restrictions reflect how decision-makers within the model are forward-looking. For instance, an investment choice today depends on the beliefs about how profitable such investments will be in the future. Investors forecast the future, and the rational expectations hypothesis predicts how they do this. The resulting cross-equation restrictions add a new dimension to econometric analysis; but these restrictions are built on the premise that investors have figured much out about how the future will evolve. See Sargent (1973), Wallis (1980) and my first published paper, Hansen and Sargent (1980), for characterizations of these restrictions.[6] To implement this approach to rational expectations econometrics, a researcher is compelled to specify correctly the information sets of economic actors.[7] When building actual stochastic models, however, it is often not clear what information should be presumed on the part of economic agents, how they should use it, and how much confidence they have in that use.

The introduction of random shocks as impulses to a dynamic economic model in conjunction with the assumption of rational expectations is an example of uncertainty *inside* a model. Under a rational expectations equilibrium, an

[5] To be clear, rational expectations offers an approach for comparing distinct stochastic equilibria but not the transitions from one to another. For an interesting extension that allows for clustering of observations near alternative *self-confirming equilibria* in conjunction with escapes from such clusters see Sargent (1999).

[6] While this was my first publication of a full length paper, this was not my first publication. My first was a note published in *Economic Letters*.

[7] See Sims (2012) for a discussion of the successes and limitations of implementing the Haavelmo (1944) agenda to the study of monetary policy under rational expectations.

investor inside the model knows the model-implied stochastic evolution for the state variables relevant for decision making and hence the likely consequences of the impulses. An econometrician also confronts uncertainty *outside* a model because of his or her lack of knowledge of parameters or maybe even a lack of confidence with the full model specification. There is an asymmetry between the inside and the outside perspectives found in rational expectations econometrics that I will turn to later. But first, I will discuss an alternative approach to imposing rational expectations in econometric analyses.

3 ROBUST ECONOMETRICS UNDER RATIONAL EXPECTATIONS

My econometrics paper, Hansen (1982b), builds on a long tradition in econometrics of "doing something without having to do everything." This entails the study of partially specified models—that is, models in which only a subset of economic relations are formally delineated. I added to this literature by analyzing such estimation problems in greater generality, giving researchers more flexibility in modeling the underlying time series while incorporating some explicit economic structure. I studied formally a family of Generalized Method of Moments (GMM) estimators, and I adapted these methods to applications that study linkages between financial markets and the macroeconomy.[8] By allowing for partial specification, these methods gain a form of robustness. They are immune to mistakes in how one might fill out the complete specification of the underlying economic model.

The approach is best thought of as providing initial steps in building a time series econometric model without specifying the full econometric model. Consider a research program that studies the linkages between the macroeconomy and financial markets. One possibility is to construct a fully specified model of

---

[8] My exposure to using GMM estimators as a vehicle to represent a broad family of estimators originally came from Christopher Sims' lectures. As a graduate student I became interested in central limit approximations that allow for econometric error terms to possess general types of temporal dependence by using central limit approximations of the type demonstrated by Gordin (1969). I subsequently established formally large sample properties for GMM estimators in such circumstances. Interestingly, *Econometrica* chose not to publish many of the formal proofs for results in my paper. Instead they were published thirty years later by the *Journal of Econometrics*, see Hansen (2012). Included in my original submission and in the published proofs is a Uniform Law of Large Numbers for stationary ergodic processes. See Hansen (2001) and Ghysels and Hall (2002) for further elaborations and discussion about the connection between GMM and related statistics literatures. See Arellano (2003) for a discussion of applications to panel data.

the macroeconomy including the linkages with financial markets that are presumed to exist. This is a lot to ask in early stages of model development. Of course, an eventual aim is to produce a full model of stochastic equilibrium.

The econometric tools that I developed are well suited to study a rich family of asset pricing models, among other things. Previously, Ross (1978) and Harrison and Kreps (1979) produced mathematical characterizations of asset pricing in frictionless asset pricing markets implied by the absence of arbitrage. Their work provides a general way to capture how financial markets value risky payoffs. My own research, and that with collaborators, built on this conceptual approach, but with an important reframing. Our explicit consideration of stochastic discounting, left implicit in the Ross (1978) and Harrison and Kreps (1979) framework, opened the door to new ways to conduct empirical studies of asset pricing models using GMM and related econometric methods. I now describe these methods.

3.1 A GMM Approach to Empirical Asset Pricing

A productive starting point in empirical asset pricing is

$$E\left[\left(\frac{S_{t+\ell}}{S_t}\right)Y_{t+\ell}|\mathcal{F}_t\right]=Q_t \tag{1}$$

where $S > 0$ is a stochastic discount factor (SDF) process. In formula (1), $Y_{t+\ell}$ is a vector of payoffs on assets at time $t + \ell$, and Q_t is a vector of corresponding asset prices. The event collection (sigma algebra), $\mathcal{F}_t$, captures information available to an investor at date t. The discount factor process is stochastic in order to adjust market values for risk. Each realized state is discounted differently and this differential discounting reflects investor compensation for risk exposure. Rational expectations is imposed by presuming that the conditional expectation operator is consistent with the probability law that governs the actual data generation. With this approach a researcher does not specify formally that probability law and instead "lets the data speak."

Relations of type (1) are premised on investment decisions made in optimal ways and are fundamental ingredients in stochastic economic models. The specification of a SDF process encapsulates some economics. It is constructed from the intertemporal marginal rates of substitution of marginal investors. Investors consider the choice of consuming today or investing to support opportunities to consume in the future. There are a variety of investment opportunities with differential exposure to risk. Investors' risk aversion enters the SDF and influences the nature of the investment that is undertaken. While I have used the language of financial markets, this same formulation applies to investments in physical and human capital. In a model of a stochastic equilibrium, this type of relation holds when evaluated at equilibrium outcomes. Relation (1) by itself is typically not sufficient to determine fully a stochastic equilibrium, so focusing on this relation alone leads us to a partially specified model. Additional modeling ingredients are required to complete the specification. The presumption is that whatever those details might be, the observed time series come from a stochastic equilibrium that is consistent with an equation of the form (1).

Implications of relation (1), including the role of SDFs and the impact of conditioning information used by investors, were explored systematically in Hansen and Richard (1987). But the origins of this empirically tractable formulation traces back to Rubinstein (1976), Lucas (1978) and Grossman and Shiller (1981), and the conceptual underpinnings to Ross (1978) and Harrison and Kreps (1979).[9] To implement formula (1) as it stands, we need to specify the information set of economic agents correctly. The Law of Iterated Expectations allows us to understate the information available to economic agents.[10] For instance let $\widehat{\mathcal{F}}_t \subset \mathcal{F}_t$ denote a smaller information set used by an external analyst. By averaging over the finer information set $\mathcal{F}_t$ conditioned on the coarser information set $\widehat{\mathcal{F}}_t$, I obtain

$$E\left[\left(\frac{S_{t+\ell}}{S_t}\right)(Y_{t+\ell})' - (Q_t)' \mid \widehat{\mathcal{F}}_t\right] = 0. \tag{2}$$

I now slip in conditioning information through the "back door" by constructing a conformable matrix Z_t with entries in the reduced information set (that are $\widehat{\mathcal{F}}_t$ measurable). Then

$$E\left[\left(\frac{S_{t+\ell}}{S_t}\right)(Y_{t+\ell})' Z_t - (Q_t)' Z_t \mid \widehat{\mathcal{F}}_t\right] = 0.$$

[9] The concept of a SDF was first introduced in Hansen and Richard (1987). Stochastic discount factors are closely connected to the "risk-neutral" probabilities used in valuing derivative claims. This connection is evident by dividing the one-period SDF by its conditional mean and using the resulting random variable to define a new one-period conditional probability distribution, the risk neutral distribution.

[10] In his study of interest rates, Shiller (1972) in his PhD dissertation suggested omitted information as a source of an "error term" for an econometrician. In Hansen and Sargent (1980), we built on this insight by contrasting implications for a "Shiller error-term" as a disturbance term to processes that are unobserved to an econometrician and enter structural relations. In Hansen and Sargent (1991) we show how to allow for omitted information in linear or log-linear time series models using quasi-likelihood methods.

Under an asset pricing interpretation, $(Y_{t+\ell})'Z_t$ is a synthetic payoff vector with a corresponding price vector $(Q_t)'Z_t$. Finally, we may form the unconditional expectation by averaging over the coarser conditioning information set $\widehat{\mathcal{F}}_t$:

$$E\left[\left(\frac{S_{t+\ell}}{S_t}\right)(Y_{t+\ell})' - (Q_t)' \mid \widehat{\mathcal{F}}_t\right] = 0. \tag{3}$$

This becomes an estimation problem once we parameterize the SDF in terms of observables and unknown parameters to be estimated.

Hansen and Singleton (1982) is an initial example of this approach.[11] In that work we consider the case in which the SDF process can be constructed from observables along with some unknown parameters. Economics comes into play in justifying the construction of the SDF process and sometimes in the construction of returns to investment. From an econometric perspective, time series versions of Laws of Large Numbers and Central Limit Theorems give us approximate ways to estimate parameters and test restrictions as in Hansen (1982b).

In Hansen (1982b), I also studied statistical efficiency for a class of GMM estimators given a particular choice of Z in a manner that extends an approach due to Sargan (1958, 1959).[12] When (3) has more equations than unknown parameters, multiple GMM estimators are the outcome of using (at least implicitly) alternative linear combinations of these equations equal to the number of parameters. Since there are many possible ways to embark on this construction, there is a family of GMM estimators. This family of estimators has an attainable efficiency bound derived and reported in Hansen (1982b).[13] When the number

[11] An earlier application of GMM inference is found in my work Hansen and Hodrick (1980). In that paper we studied the empirical relationship between the logarithm of a future spot exchange and the logarithm of the current forward rate and other possible predictors. We applied ordinary least squares in our work, but with corrected standard errors. Others were tempted to (and in fact did) apply generalized least squares (GLS) to "correct for" serial correlation, but applied in this setting GLS is statistically inconsistent. The counterpart to the moment conditions studied here are the least squares orthogonality conditions. The contract interval played the role of ℓ in this least squares analysis and was typically larger than one. In subsequent work, Hansen and Hodrick (1983), we used a SDF formulation to motivate further empirical characterizations, which led us to confront over-identification. See also Bilson (1981) and Fama (1984) who featured a cross-currency analysis.

[12] See Arellano (2002) for a nice discussion relating GMM estimation to the earlier work of Sargan.

[13] See Hansen (2007b) for a pedagogical discussion of GMM estimation including discussions of large sample statistical efficiency and tests.

of equations exceeds the number of free parameters, there is also a direct way to test equations not used formally in estimation. While nesting estimators into a general GMM framework has great pedagogical value, I was particularly interested in applying a GMM approach to problems requiring new estimators as in many of the applications to financial economics and elsewhere.[14]

Notice that the model, as written down in equation (3), is only partially specified. Typically we cannot invert this relation, or even its conditional counterpart, to deduce a full time series evolution for economic aggregates and financial variables.[15] Other relations would have to be included in order to obtain a full solution to the problem.

3.2 Further Econometric Challenges

I now digress temporarily and discuss some econometric extensions that I and others contributed to.

3.2.1 Semiparametric Efficiency

Since the model is only partially specified, the estimation challenge leads directly to what is formally called a semiparametric problem. Implicitly the remainder of the model can be posed in a nonparametric manner. This gives rise to a problem with a finite-dimensional parameter vector of interest and an infinite-dimensional "nuisance" parameter vector representing the remainder of the model. This opens the door to the study of semiparametric efficiency of a large class of estimators as will be evident from the discussion that follows. In typical GMM problems, the actual introduction of the nuisance parameters can be sidestepped.

Relation (2) conditions on the information set of economic agents. We have great flexibility in choosing the matrix process Z. The entries of Z_t should be in the $\widehat{\mathcal{F}}_t$ information set, but this still leaves many options when building a Z process. This flexibility gives rise to an infinite class of estimators. In Hansen (1982b), I studied statistical efficiency given a particular choice of Z. This

---

[14] Other econometricians have subsequently found value in unifying the treatment of GMM estimators into a broader type of extremum estimators. This, however, misses some of the special features of statistical efficiency within a GMM framework and does not address the issue of how to construct meaningful estimators from economic models.

[15] For those reluctant to work with partially specified models, Lucas (1978) showed how to close a special case of this model by considering an endowment economy. But from an empirical standpoint, it is often not necessary to take the endowment nature of the economy literally. The consumption from the endowment economy may be conceived of as the equilibrium outcome of a model with production and preserves the same pricing relations.

approach, however, understates the class of possible GMM estimators in a potentially important way. Hansen (1985) shows how to construct an efficiency bound for the much larger (infinite dimensional) class of GMM estimators. This efficiency bound is a greatest lower bound on the asymptotic efficiency of the implied GMM estimators. Not surprisingly, it is more challenging to attain this bound in practice. For some related but special (linear) time series problems, Hansen and Singleton (1996) and West et al. (2009) discuss implementation strategies.

There is a more extensive literature exploring these and closely related questions in an iid (independent and identically distributed) data setting, including Chamberlain (1987), who looks at an even larger set of estimators. By connecting to an extensive statistics literature on semiparametric efficiency, he shows that this larger set does not improve the statistical efficiency relative to the GMM efficiency bound. Robinson (1987), Newey (1990), and Newey (1993) suggest ways to construct estimators that attain this efficiency bound for some important special cases.[16] Finally, given the rich array of moment restrictions, there are opportunities for more flexible parameterizations of, say, a SDF process. Suppose the conditional moment restrictions contain a finite-dimensional parameter vector of interest along with an infinite-dimensional (nonparametric) component. Chamberlain (1992) constructs a corresponding efficiency bound and Ai and Chen (2003) extend this analysis and estimation for such problems. While these richer efficiency results have not been shown in the time series environment I consider, I suspect that they can indeed be extended.

3.2.2 Model Misspecification

The approaches to GMM estimation that I have described so far presume a given parameterization of a SDF process. For instance, the analysis of GMM efficiency in Hansen (1982b) and Hansen (1985) and related literature presumes that the model is correctly specified for one value of the unknown (to the econometrician) parameter. Alternatively, we may seek to find the best choice of a parameter value even if the pricing restrictions are only *approximatively* correct. In our paper, Hansen and Jagannathan (1997), we suggest a modification of GMM estimation in which appropriately scaled pricing errors are minimized. We propose this as a way to make model comparisons in economically meaningful ways. Recently, Gosh et al. (2012) adopt an alternative formulation of model

[16] Relatedly, Zhang and Gijbels (2003), Kitamura et al. (2004) and Antoine et al. (2007) studied methods based on restricting nonparametric estimates of conditional density functions to attain Chamberlain (1987)'s efficiency bound in an estimation environment with independent and identically distributed data generation.

misspecification extending the approach of Stutzer (1995) described later. This remains an interesting and important line of investigation that parallels the discussion of model misspecification in other areas of statistics and econometrics. I will return to this topic later in this essay.

3.2.3 Nonparametric Characterization

A complementary approach to building and testing new parametric models is to treat the SDF process as unobserved by the econometrician. It is still possible to deduce empirical characterizations of such processes implied by asset market data. This analysis provides insights into modeling challenges by showing what properties a valid SDF process must possess.

It turns out that there are potentially many valid stochastic discount factors over a payoff horizon ℓ:

$$s \equiv \frac{S_{t+\ell}}{S_t}$$

that will satisfy either (2) or the unconditional counterpart (3). For simplicity, focus on (3).[17] With this in mind, let

$$y' = (Y_{t+\ell})' Z_t$$
$$q' = (Q_t)' Z_t$$

where for notational simplicity, I omit the time subscripts on the left-hand side of this equation. In what follows I will assume some form of a Law of Large Numbers so that we can estimate such entities. See Hansen and Richard (1987) for a discussion of such issues. Rewriting (3) with this simpler notation:

$$E[sy' - q'] = 0. \tag{4}$$

This equation typically implies many solutions for a positive $s > 0$. In our previous discussion of parametric models, we excluded many solutions by adopting a parametric representation in terms of observables and an unknown parameter vector. In practice this often led to a finding that there were *no* solutions, that is no values of s solving (4), within the parametric family assumed for s. Using Hansen (1982b), this finding was formalized as a test of the pricing restrictions. The finding alone left open the question: rejecting the parametric restrictions

[17] For conditional counterparts to some of the results I summarize see Gallant et al. (1990) and Cochrane and Hansen (1992).

for what alternative? Thus a complementary approach is to characterize properties of the family of s's that do satisfy (4). These solutions might well violate the parametric restriction.

The interesting challenge is how to characterize the family of SDFs that solve (4) in useful ways. Here I follow a general approach that is essentially the same as that in Almeida and Garcia (2013). I choose this approach both because of its flexibilty and because it includes many interesting special cases used in empirical analysis. Consider a family of convex functions ϕ defined on the positive real numbers:[18]

$$\phi(r) = \frac{1}{\theta(1+\theta)}\left[(r)^{1+\theta} - 1\right] \tag{5}$$

for alternative choices of the parameter θ. The specification $\theta = 1$ is commonly used in empirical practice, in which case ϕ is quadratic. We shall look for lower bounds on the

$$E\left[\phi\left(\frac{s}{Es}\right)\right]$$

by solving the convex optimization problem:[19]

$$\lambda = \inf_{s>0} E\left[\phi\left(\frac{s}{Es}\right)\right] \text{ subject to } E\left[sy' - q'\right] = 0. \tag{6}$$

By design we know that

$$E\left[\phi\left(\frac{s}{Es}\right)\right] \geq \lambda.$$

Notice that $E\left[\phi\left(\frac{s}{Es}\right)\right]$ hence λ are nonnegative by Jensen's Inequality because ϕ is convex and $\phi(1) = 0$. When $\theta = 1$,

---

[18] This functional form is familiar from economists' use of power utility (in which case we use $-\phi$ to obtain a concave function), from statisticians' use of F-divergence measures between two probability densities, the Box-Cox transformation, and the applications in the work of Cressie and Read (1984).

[19] Notice that the expectation is also an affine transformation of the moment generating function for log s.

$$\sqrt{2E\left[\phi\left(\frac{s}{Es}\right)\right]}$$

is the ratio of the standard deviation of s to its mean and $\sqrt{2\lambda}$ is the greatest lower bound on this ratio.

From the work of Ross (1978) and Harrison and Kreps (1979), arbitrage considerations imply the economically interesting restriction $s > 0$ with probability one. To guarantee a solution to optimization problem (6), however, it is sometimes convenient to include s's that are zero with positive probability. Since the aim is to produce bounds, this augmentation can be justified for mathematical and computational convenience. Although this problem optimizes over an infinite-dimensional family of random variables s, the dual problem that optimizes over the Lagrange multipliers associated with the pricing constraint (4) is often quite tractable. See Hansen et al. (1995) for further discussion.

Inputs into this calculation are contained in the pair (y, q) and a hypothetical mean Es. If we have time series data on the price of a unit payoff at date $t + \ell$, Es can be inferred by averaging the date t prices over time. If not, by changing Es we can trace out a frontier of solutions. An initial example of this is found in Hansen and Jagannathan (1991) where we constructed mean-standard deviation tradeoffs for SDFs by setting $\theta = 1$.[20,21]

While a quadratic specification of ϕ ($\theta = 1$) has been the most common one used in empirical practice, other approaches have been suggested. For instance, Snow (1991) considers larger moments by setting θ to integer values greater than one. Alternatively, setting $\theta = 0$ yields

$$E\left[\phi\left(\frac{s}{Es}\right)\right] = \frac{E\left[s\left(\log s - \log Es\right)\right]}{Es},$$

[20] This literature was initiated by a discussion in Shiller (1982) and my comment on that discussion in Hansen (1982a). Shiller argued why a volatility bound on the SDF is of interest, and he constructed an initial bound. In my comment, I showed how to sharpen the volatility bound, but without exploiting that $s > 0$. Neither Shiller nor I explored mean-standard deviation tradeoffs that are central in Hansen and Jagannathan (1991). In effect, I constructed one point on the frontier characterized in Hansen and Jagannathan (1991).

[21] When θ is one, the function φ continues to be well defined and convex for negative real numbers. As noted in Hansen and Jagannathan (1991), if the negative choices of s are allowed in the optimization problem (which weakens the bound), there are quasi-analytical formulas for the minimization problems with simple links to Sharpe ratios commonly used in empirical finance.

which Stutzer (1995) featured this in his analysis. When $\theta = -1$,

$$E\left[\phi\left(\frac{s}{Es}\right)\right] = -E\log s + \log Es$$

and use of this specification of ϕ gives rise to a bound that has been studied in several papers including Bansal and Lehmann (1997), Alvarez and Jermann (2005), Backus et al. (2011), and Backus et al. (2014). These varying convex functions give alternative ways to characterize properties of SDFs that work through bounding their stochastic behaviour.[22] He and Modest (1995) and Luttmer (1996) further extended this work by allowing for the pricing equalities to be replaced by pricing inequalities. These inequalities emerge when transaction costs render purchasing and selling prices distinct.[23]

3.3 The Changing Price of Uncertainty

Empirical puzzles are only well defined within the context of a model. Hansen and Singleton (1982, 1983) and others documented empirical shortcomings of macroeconomic models with power utility versions of investor preferences. The one-period SDF of such a representative consumer is:

$$\frac{S_{t+1}}{S_t} = \exp(-\delta)\left(\frac{C_{t+1}}{C_t}\right)^{-\rho} \tag{7}$$

where C_t is consumption, δ is the subjective rate of discount and $\frac{1}{\rho}$ is the intertemporal elasticity of substitution. Hansen and Singleton and others were the bearers of bad news: the model didn't match the data even after taking account of statistical inferential challenges.[24]

[22] The continuous-time limit for the conditional counterpart results in one-half times the local variance for all choices of ϕ for Brownian information structures.

[23] There has been some work on formal inferential methods associated with these methods. For instance, see Burnside (1994), Hansen et al. (1995), Peñaranda and Sentana (2011) and Chernozhukov et al. (2013).

[24] Many scholars make reference to the "equity premium puzzle." Singleton and I showed how to provide statistically rigorous characterizations of this and other empirical anomalies. The puzzling implications coming from this literature are broader than the expected return differential between an aggregate stock portfolio and bonds and extend to differential returns across a wide variety of securities. See, for instance, Fama and French (1992) for empirical evidence on expected return differences, and see Cochrane (2008) and the discussion by Hansen (2008) for an exchange about the equity premium and related puzzles.

This empirical work nurtured a rich literature exploring alternative preferences and markets with frictions. Microeconomic evidence was brought to bear that targeted financial market participants when constructing the SDFs. These considerations and the resulting modeling extensions led naturally to alternative specifications on SDFs and suggestions for how they might be measured.

The nonparametric methods leading to bounds also added clarity to the empirical evidence. SDFs encode compensations for exposure to uncertainty because they discount alternative stochastic cash flows according to their sensitivity to underlying macroeconomic shocks. Thus, empirical evidence about SDFs sheds light on the "risk prices" that investors need as compensations for being exposed to aggregate risk. Using these nonparametric methods, the empirical literature has found that the risk price channel is a fertile source for explaining observed variations in securities prices and asset returns. SDFs are highly variable (Hansen and Jagannathan (1991)). The unconditional variability in SDFs could come from two sources: on-average conditional variability or variation in conditional means. As argued by Cochrane and Hansen (1992), it is really the former. Conditional variability in SDFs implies that market-based compensations for exposure to uncertainty are varying over time in important ways. Sometimes this observation about time variation gets bundled into the observation about time-varying risk premia. Risk premia, however, depend both on the compensation for being exposed to risk (the price of risk) and on how big that exposure is to risk (the quantity of risk). Price variability, exposure variability or a combination of the two could be the source of fluctuations in risk premia. Deducing the probabilistic structure of SDFs from market data thus enables us to isolate the price effect. In summary, this empirical and theoretical literature gave compelling reasons to explore sources of risk price variation not previously captured, and provided empirical direction to efforts to improve investor preferences and market structures within these models.

Campbell and Cochrane (1999) provided an influential specification of investor preferences motivated in part by this empirical evidence. Consistent with the view that time variation in uncertainty prices is vital for understanding financial market returns, they constructed a model in which SDFs are larger in magnitude in bad economic times than good. This paper is prominent in the asset pricing literature precisely because it links the time series behavior of risk prices to the behavior of the macroeconomy (specifically aggregate consumption), and it suggests one preference-based mechanism for achieving this variation. Under the structural interpretation provided by the model, the implied risk aversion is very large in bad economic times and modest in good times as measured by the history of consumption growth. This work successfully avoided the need for large risk aversion in all states of the world, but it did not avoid the need for large risk aversion in some states. The statistician in me is intrigued by the possibility that observed incidents of large risk aversion might be proxying for investor doubts regarding the correctness of models. I will have more to say about that later.

4 ECONOMIC SHOCKS AND PRICING IMPLICATIONS

While the empirical methods in asset pricing that I described do not require that an econometrician identify the fundamental macroeconomic shocks pertinent to investors, this shortcut limits the range of questions that can be addressed. Without accounting for shocks, we can make only an incomplete assessment of the consequences for valuation of macroeconomic uncertainty. To understand fully the pricing channel, we need to know how the SDF process itself depends on fundamental shocks. This dependence determines the equilibrium compensations to investors that are exposed to shocks. We may think of this as valuation accounting at the juncture between the Frisch (1933) vision of using shock and impulses in stochastic equilibrium models and the Bachelier (1900) vision of asset values that respond to the normal increments of a Brownian motion process. Why? Because the asset holders exposed to the random impulses affecting the macroeconomy require compensation, and the equilibrating forces affecting borrowers and lenders interacting in financial markets determine those compensatory premia.

In what follows, I illustrate two advantages to a more complete specification of the information available to investors that are reflected in my work.

4.1 Pricing Shock Exposure over Alternative Horizons

First, I explore more fully how a SDF encodes risk compensation over alternative investment horizons. I suggest a way to answer this question by describing valuation counterparts to the impulse characterizations advocated by Frisch (1933) and used extensively in quantitative macroeconomics since Sims (1980) proposed a multivariate and empirical counterpart for these characterizations. Recall that an impulse response function shows how alternative shocks tomorrow influence future values of macroeconomic variables. These shocks also represent alternative exposures to macroeconomic risk. The market-based compensations for these exposures may differ depending on the horizon over which a cash flow is realized. Many fully specified macroeconomic models proliferate shocks, including random changes in volatility, as a device for matching time series. While the additional shocks play a central role in fitting time series, eventually we must seek better answers to what lies within the black box of candidate impulses. Understanding their role within the models is central to opening this black box in search of the answers. Empirical macroeconomists' challenges for identifying shocks for the macroeconomy also have important consequences for financial markets and the role they play in the transmission of these shocks. Not all types of candidate shocks are important for valuation.

I now discuss how we may distinguish which shock exposures command the largest market compensation and the impact of these exposures over alternative payoff horizons. I decompose the risk premia into *risk prices* and *risk exposures* using sensitivity analyses on underlying asset returns. To be specific, let X be an underlying Markov process and W a vector of shocks that are random impulses to the economic model. The state vector X_t depends on current and past shocks. I take as given a solved stochastic equilibrium model and reveal its implications for valuation. Suppose that there is an implied stochastic factor process S that evolves as:

$$\log S_{t+1} - \log S_t = \psi_s (X_t, W_{t+1}). \tag{8}$$

Typically economic models imply that this process will tend to decay over time because of the role that S plays as a discount factor. For instance, for the yield on a long-term discount bond to be positive,

$$\lim_{t\to\infty} \frac{1}{t} \log E\left[\frac{S_t}{S_o} | X_o = x \right] < 0.$$

Specific models provide more structure to the function ψ_s relating the stochastic decay rate of S to the current state and next period shock. In this sense, (8) is a reduced form-relation. Similarly, consider a one-period, positive cash-flow G that satisfies:

$$\log G_{t+1} - \log G_t = \psi_g (X_t, W_{t+1}). \tag{9}$$

The process G could be aggregate consumption, or it could be a measure of aggregate corporate earnings or some other process. The logarithm of the expected one-period return of a security with this payoff is:

$$\upsilon_t = \log E\left[\frac{G_{t+1}}{G_t} | \mathcal{F}_t \right] - \log E\left[\frac{S_{t+1} G_{t+1}}{S_t G_t} | \mathcal{F}_t \right]. \tag{10}$$

So-called risk return tradeoffs emerge as we change the exposure of the cash flow to different components of the shock vector W_{t+1}.

Since cash flow growth $\frac{G_{t+1}}{G_t}$ depends on the components of W_{t+1} as a source of risk, *exposure* is altered by changing how the cash flow depends on the underlying shocks. When I refer to *risk prices*, formally I mean the sensitivity of the logarithm of the expected return given on the left-hand side of (10) to change in cash-flow risk. I compute *risk prices* from measuring how v_t changes as we alter the cash flow, and compute *risk exposures* from examining the corresponding changes in the logarithm of the expected cash-flow growth: $\log E\left[\frac{G_{t+1}}{G_t} | \mathcal{F}_t\right]$ (the first-term on the right-hand side of (10)).

These calculations are made operational by formally introducing changes in the cash-flows and computing their consequences for expected returns. When the changes are scaled appropriately, the outcomes of both the price and exposure calculations are elasticities familiar from price theory. To operationalize the term *changes*, I must impose some additional structure that allows a researcher to compute a derivative of some type. Thus I must be formal about changes in $\frac{G_{t+1}}{G_t}$ as a function of W_{t+1}. One way to achieve this formality is to take a continuous-time limit when the underlying information structure is that implied by an underlying Brownian motion as in the models of financial markets as originally envisioned by Bachelier (1900). This reproduces a common notion of a risk price used in financial economics. Another possibility is to introduce a perturbation parameter that alters locally the shock exposure, but maintains the discrete-time formulation.

These one-period or local measures have multi-period counterparts obtained by modeling the impact of small changes in the components of W_{t+1} on cash flows in future time periods, say $\frac{G_{t+\tau}}{G_t}$, for $\tau \geq 1$. Proceeding in this way, we obtain a valuation counterpart to impulse response functions featured by Frisch (1933) and by much of the quantitative macroeconomics literature. They inform us which exposures require the largest compensations and how these compensations change with the investment horizon. I have elaborated on this topic in my Fisher-Schultz Lecture paper (Hansen (2011)), and I will defer to that and related papers for more specificity and justification.[25] My economic interpretation of these calculations presumes a full specification of investor information as is commonly the case when analyzing impulse response functions.

4.2 A Recursive Utility Model of Investor Preferences

Next I consider investor preferences that are particularly sensitive to the assumed available information. These preferences are constructed recursively

[25] See Hansen et al. (2008), Hansen and Scheinkman (2009), Borovička et al. (2011), Hansen and Scheinkman (2012) and Borovička and Hansen (2014).

using continuation values for prospective consumption processes, and they are featured prominently in the macro-asset pricing literature. With these preferences the investor cares about intertemporal composition of risk as in Kreps and Porteus (1978) with these preferences. As a consequence, general revisions of the recursive utility model make investor preferences potentially sensitive to the details of the information available in the future. As I will explain, this feature of investor preferences makes it harder to implement a "do something without doing everything" approach to econometric estimation and testing.

The more general recursive utility specification nests the power utility model commonly used in macroeconomics as a special case. Interest in a more general specification was motivated in part by some of the statistical evidence that I described previously. Stochastic equilibrium models appealing to recursive utility featured in the asset pricing literature were initially advocated by Epstein and Zin (1989) and Weil (1990). They provide researchers with a parameter to alter risk preferences in addition to the usual power utility parameter known to determine the intertemporal elasticity of substitution. The one-period SDF measured using the intertemporal marginal rate of substitution is:

$$\frac{S_{t+1}}{S_t} = \exp(-\delta)\left(\frac{C_{t+1}}{C_t}\right)^{-\rho}\left[\frac{V_{t+1}}{\mathcal{R}_t(V_{t+1})}\right]^{\rho-\gamma} \tag{11}$$

where C_t is equilibrium consumption, δ is the subjective rate of discount, $\frac{1}{\rho}$ is the elasticity of intertemporal substitution familiar from power utility models, V_t is the forward-looking continuation value of the prospective consumption process, and $\mathcal{R}_t(V_{t+1})$ is the risk adjusted continuation value:

$$\mathcal{R}_t(V_{t+1}) = \left(E\left[(V_{t+1})^{1-\gamma} \mid \mathcal{F}_t\right]\right)^{\frac{1}{1-\gamma}}.$$

The parameter γ governs the magnitude of the risk adjustment. The presence of the forward-looking continuation values in the stochastic discount factor process adds to the empirical challenge in using these preferences in an economic model. When $\rho = \gamma$, the forward-looking component drops out from the SDFs and the preferences become the commonly used power utility model as is evident by comparing (7) and (11). Multi-period SDFs are the corresponding products of single period discount factors.

The empirical literature has focused on what seems to be large values for the parameter γ that adjusts for the continuation value risk. Since continuation values reflect all current prospective future consumption, increasing γ enhances the aversion of the decision maker to consumption risk. Applied researchers have only been too happy to explore this channel. A fully solved out stochastic equilibrium model represents C and V as part of the model solution. For instance log C might have an evolution with the same form as log G as specified in (9) along a balanced stochastic growth trajectory. Representing S as in (8) presumes a solution for V_t or more conveniently $\frac{V_t}{C_t}$ as a function of X_t along with a risk adjusted counterpart to V_t and these require a full specification of investor information.

For early macro-finance applications highlighting the computation of continuation values in equilibrium models, see Hansen et al. (1999) and Tallarini (2000). The subsequent work of Bansal and Yaron (2004) showed how these preferences in conjunction with forward looking beliefs about stochastic growth and volatility have a potentially important impact on even one-period (in discrete time) or instantaneous (in continuous time) risk prices through the forward-looking channel. Hansen (2011) and Borovička et al. (2011) show that the prices of growth rate shocks are large for all payoff horizons with recursive utility and when γ is much larger than ρ. By contrast, for power utility models with large values of $\rho = \gamma$, the growth rate shock prices start off small and only eventually become large as the payoff horizon increases. The analyses in Hansen et al. (2008) and Restoy and Weil (2011) also presume that one solves for the continuation values of consumption plans or their equivalent. This general approach to the use of recursive utility for investor preferences makes explicit use of the information available to investors and hence does not allow for the robustness that I discussed in section 3.[26]

Sometimes there is a way around this sensitivity to the information structure when conducting an econometric analysis. The empirical approach of Epstein and Zin (1991) assumes that an aggregate equity return measures the return on an aggregate wealth portfolio. In this case the continuation value relative to a risk-adjusted counterpart that appears in formula (11) is revealed by the return on the wealth portfolio for alternative choices of the preference parameters. Thus there is no need for an econometrician to compute continuation values provided that data are available on the wealth portfolio return. Epstein and Zin (1991) applied GMM methods to estimate preference parameters and test model restrictions by altering appropriately the approach in Hansen and

[26] Similarly, many models with heterogenous consumers/investors and incomplete markets imply pricing relation (1) for marginal agents defined as those who participate in the market over the relevant investment period. Such models require either microeconomic data and/or equilibria solutions computed using numerical methods.

Singleton (1982). Given that the one-period SDF can be constructed from consumption and return data, the full investor information set does not have to be used in the econometric implementation.[27] Campbell (1993) and Campbell and Vuolteenaho (2004) explored a related approach using a log-linear approximation, but this research allowed for market segmentation. Full participation in financial markets is not required because the econometric specification that is used to study the risk-return relation avoids having to use aggregate consumption. Like Epstein and Zin (1991), this approach features the return on the wealth portfolio as measured by an aggregate equity return, but now prospective beliefs about that return also contribute to the (approximate) SDF.

4.3 A Continuing Role for GMM-based Testing

Even when fully specified stochastic equilibria are formulated and used as the basis for estimation, there remains the important task of assessing the performance of the pricing implications remains. SDFs constructed from fully specified and estimated stochastic equilibrium models can be constructed *ex post* and used in testing the pricing implications for a variety of security returns. These tests can be implemented formally using direct extensions of the methods that I described in section 3. Thus the SDF specification remains an interesting way to explore empirical implications, and GMM-style statistical tests of pricing restrictions remain an attractive and viable way to analyze models.

In the remainder of this essay I will speculate on the merits of one productive approach to addressing empirical challenges based in part on promising recent research.

5 MISSPECIFIED BELIEFS

So far I have focused primarily on uncertainty *outside the model* by exploring econometric challenges, while letting risk averse agents inside the model have rational expectations. Recall that rational expectations uses the model to construct beliefs about the future.[28] I now consider the consequences of altering

---

[27] In contrast to recursive utility models with $\rho \neq \gamma$, often GMM-type methods can be applied to habit persistence models of the type analyzed by Sundaresan (1989), Constantinides (1990) and Heaton (1995) without having to specify the full set of information available to investors.

[28] A subtle distinction exists between two efforts to implement rational expectations in econometric models. When the rational expectations hypothesis is imposed in a fully specified stochastic equilibrium model, this imposition is part of an internally consistent

beliefs inside the model for two reasons. First, investor beliefs may differ from those implied by the model even if other components of the model are correctly specified. For instance, when historical evidence is weak, there is scope for beliefs that are different from those revealed by infinite histories of data. Second, if some of the model ingredients are not correct but only approximations, then the use of model-based beliefs based on an appeal to rational expectations is less compelling. Instead there is a rationale for the actors inside the model to adjust their beliefs in face of potential misspecification.

For reasons of tractability and pedagogical simplicity, throughout this and the next section I use a baseline probability model to represent conditional expectations, but not necessarily the beliefs of the people inside the model. Presuming that economic actors use the baseline model with full confidence would give rise to a rational expectations formulation, but I will explore departures from this approach. I present a tractable way to analyze how varying beliefs will alter this baseline probability model. Also, I will continue my focus on the channel by which SDFs affect asset values. A SDF and the associated risk prices, however, are only well-defined relative to a baseline model. Alterations in beliefs affect SDFs in ways that can imitate risk aversion. They also can provide an additional source of fluctuations in asset values.

My aim in this section is to study whether statistically *small* changes in beliefs can imitate what appears to be a *large* amount of risk aversion. While I feature the role of statistical discipline, explicit considerations of both learning and market discipline also come into play when there are heterogeneous consumers. For many environments there may well be an intriguing interplay between these model ingredients, but I find it revealing to narrow my focus. As is evident from recent work by Blume and Easley (2006), Kogan et al. (2011) and Borovička (2013), distorted beliefs can sometimes survive in the long run. Presumably when statistical evidence for discriminating among models is weak, the impact of market selection, whereby there is a competitive advantage of confidently

---

model specification a model. A model builder may impose these restrictions prior to looking at the data. The expectations become "rational" once the model is fit to data, assuming that the model is correctly specified. I used GMM and related methods to examine only a portion of the implications of a fully specified, fully solved model. In such applications, an empirical economist is not able to use a model solution to deduce the beliefs of economic actors. Instead these methods presume that the beliefs of the economic actors are consistent with historical data as revealed by the Law of Large Numbers. This approach presumes that part of the model is correctly specified, and the data are used as part of the implementation of the rational expectations restrictions.

knowing the correct model, will at the very least be sluggish. In both this and the next section, I am revisiting a theme considered by Hansen (2007a).

5.1 Martingale Models of Belief Perturbations

Consider again the asset pricing formula but now under an altered or perturbed belief relative to a baseline probability model:

$$\tilde{E}\left[\left(\frac{\tilde{S}_{t+\ell}}{\tilde{S}_t}\right)Y_{t+\ell} \mid \mathcal{F}_t\right] = Q_t \tag{12}$$

where the $\tilde{E}$ is used to denote the perturbed expectation operator and $\tilde{S}$ is the SDF derived under the altered expectations. Mathematically, it is most convenient to represent beliefs in an intertemporal environment using a strictly positive (with probability one) stochastic process M with a unit expectation for all $t \geq 0$. Specifically, construct the altered conditional expectations via the formula:

$$\tilde{E}\left[B_\tau \mid \mathcal{F}_t\right] = E\left[\left(\frac{M_\tau}{M_t}\right)B_\tau \mid \mathcal{F}_t\right]$$

for any bounded random variable B_τ in the date $\tau \geq t$ information set $\mathcal{F}_\tau$. The martingale restriction imposed on M is necessary for the conditional expectations for different calendar dates to be consistent.[29]

Using a positive martingale M to represent perturbed expectations we rewrite (12) as:

$$E\left[\left(\frac{M_{t+\ell}\tilde{S}_{t+\ell}}{M_t\tilde{S}_t}\right)Y_{t+\ell} \mid \mathcal{F}_t\right] = Q_t$$

which matches our original pricing formula (1) provided that

$$S = M\tilde{S}. \tag{13}$$

---

[29] The date zero expectation of random variable B_t that is in the $\mathcal{F}_t$ information set may be computed in multiple ways

$$\tilde{E}\left[B_t \mid \mathcal{F}_0\right] = E\left[\left(\frac{M_\tau}{M_0}\right)B_t \mid \mathcal{F}_0\right] = E\left[\left(\frac{M_t}{M_0}\right)B_t \mid \mathcal{F}_0\right]$$

for any $\tau \geq t$. For this equality to hold for all bounded random variables B_t in the date t information set, $E(M_\tau \mid \mathcal{F}_t) = M_t$. This verifies that M is a martingale relative to $\{\mathcal{F}_t : t \geq 0\}$.

This factorization emerges because of the two different probability distributions that are in play. One comes from the baseline model and another is that used by investors. The martingale M makes the adjustment in the probabilities. Risk prices relative to the $\tilde{\cdot}$ distribution are distinct from those relative to the baseline model. This distinction is captured by (13).

Investor models of risk aversion are reflected in the specification of $\tilde{S}$. For instance, example (7) implies an $\tilde{S}$ based on consumption growth.[30] The martingale M would then capture the belief distortions including perhaps some of the preferred labels in the writings of others such as "animal spirits," "over-confidence," "pessimism," *etc.* Without allowing for belief distortions, many empirical investigations resort to what I think of as "large values of risk aversion." We can see, however, from factorization (13) that once we entertain belief distortions it becomes challenging to disentangle risk considerations from belief distortions.

My preference as a model builder and assessor is to add specific structure to these belief distortions. I do not find it appealing to let M be freely specified. My discussion that follows suggests a way to use some tools from statistics to guide such an investigation. They help us to understand if statistically small belief distortions in conjunction with seemingly more reasonable (at least to me) specifications of risk aversion can explain empirical evidence from asset markets.

5.2 Statistical Discrepancy

I find it insightful to quantify the statistical magnitude of a candidate belief distortion by following in part the analysis in Anderson et al. (2003). Initially, I consider a specific alternative probability distribution modeled using a positive martingale M with unit expectation and I ask if this belief distortion could be detected easily from data. Heuristically when the martingale M is close to one, the probability distortion is small. From a statistical perspective we may think of M as a relative likelihood process of a perturbed model *vis a vis* a baseline probability model. Notice that M_t depends on information in $\mathcal{F}_t$, and can be viewed as a "data-based" date t relatively likelihood. The ratio $\frac{M_t+1}{M_t}$ has conditional

[30] When $\rho \neq \gamma$ in (11), continuation values come into play; and they would have to be computed using the distorted probability distribution. Thus M would also play a role in the construction of $\tilde{S}$. This would also be true in models with investor preferences that displayed "habit persistence" that is internalized when selecting investment plans. Chabi-Yo et al. (2008) nest some belief distortions inside a larger class of models with state-dependent preferences and obtain representations in which belief distortions also have an indirect impact on SDFs.

expectation equal to unity, and this term reflects how new data that arrive between dates t and $t + 1$ are incorporated into the relative likelihood.

A variety of statistical criteria measure how close M is to unity. Let me motivate one such model by bounding probabilities of mistakes. Notice that for a given threshold η,

$$\log M_t - \eta \geq 0$$

implies that

$$\left[M_t \exp(-\eta)\right]^{\alpha} \geq 1 \tag{14}$$

for positive values of α. Only α's that satisfy $0 < \alpha < 1$ interest me because only these α's provide meaningful bounds. From (14) and Markov's Inequality,

$$Pr\left\{\log M_t \geq \eta | \mathcal{F}_0\right\} \leq \exp(-\eta\alpha) E\left[(M_t)^{\alpha} | \mathcal{F}_0\right]. \tag{15}$$

The left-hand side gives the probability that a log-likelihood formed with a history of length t exceeds a specified threshold η. Given inequality (15),

$$\frac{1}{t} \log Pr\left\{\log M_t \geq \eta | \mathcal{F}_0\right\} \leq -\frac{\eta\alpha}{t} + \frac{1}{t} \log E\left[(M_t)^{\alpha} | \mathcal{F}_0\right]. \tag{16}$$

The right-hand side of (16) gives a bound for the log-likelihood ratio to exceed a given threshold η for any $0 < \alpha < 1$. The first term on the right-hand side converges to zero as t gets large but often the second term does not and indeed may have a finite limit that is negative. Thus the negative of the limit bounds the decay rate in the probabilities as they converge to zero. When this happens we have an example of what is called a large deviation approximation. More data generated under the benchmark model makes it easier to rule out an alternative model. The decay rate bound underlies a measure of what is called Chernoff (1952) entropy. Dynamic extensions of Chernoff entropy are given by first taking limits as t gets arbitrarily large and then optimizing by the choice of α:

$$\kappa(M) = -\inf_{0<\alpha<1} \limsup_{t\to\infty} \frac{1}{t} \log E\left[(M_t)^{\alpha} | \mathcal{F}_0\right].$$

Newman and Stuck (1979) characterize Markov solutions to the limit used in the optimization problem. Minimizing over α improves the sharpness of the bound. If the minimized value is zero, the probability distortion vanishes and investors eventually settle on the benchmark model as being correct.

A straightforward derivation shows that even when we change the roles of the benchmark model and the alternative model, the counterpart to $\kappa(M)$ remains the same.[31] Why is Chernoff entropy interesting? When this common decay rate is small, even long histories of data are not very informative about model differences.[32] Elsewhere I have explored the connection between this Chernoff measure and Sharpe ratios commonly used in empirical finance, see Anderson et al. (2003) and Hansen (2007a).[33] The Chernoff calculations are often straightforward when both models (the benchmark and perturbed models) are Markovian. In general, however, it can be a challenge to use this measure in practice without imposing considerable *a priori* structure on the alternative models.

In what follows, I will explore discrepancy measures that are similar to this Chernoff measure but are arguably more tractable to implement. What I describe builds directly on my discussion of GMM methods and extensions. Armed with factorization (13), approaches that I suggested for the study of SDFs can be adapted to the study of belief distortions. I elaborate in the discussion that follows.

5.3 Ignored Belief Distortions

Let me return to GMM estimation and model misspecification. Recall that the justification for GMM estimation is typically deduced under the premise that the underlying model is correctly specified. The possibility of permanent belief distortions, say distortions for which $\kappa(M) > 0$, add structure to the model misspecification. But this is not enough structure to identify fully the belief distortion unless an econometrician uses sufficient asset payoffs and prices to reveal the SDF. Producing bounds with this extra structure can still proceed along the lines of those discussed in Section 3.2.3 with some modifications. I sketch below one such approach.

---

[31] With this symmetry and other convenient properties of $\kappa(M)$, we can interpret the measure as a metric over (equivalence classes of) martingales.

[32] Bayesian and max-min decision theory for model selection both equate decay rates in type I and type II error rates.

[33] The link is most evident when a one-period (in discrete time) or local (in continuous time) measure of statistical discrimination is used in conjunction with a conditional normal distribution, instead of the large t measure described here.

Suppose the investors in the model are allowed to have distorted beliefs, and part of the estimation is to deduce the magnitude of the distortions. How big would these distortions need to be in a statistical sense in order to satisfy the pricing restrictions? What follows makes some progress in addressing this question. To elaborate, consider again the basic pricing relation with distorted beliefs written as unconditional expectation:

$$E\left[\left(\frac{M_{t+\ell}\tilde{S}_{t+\ell}}{M_t\tilde{S}_t}\right)(Y_{t+\ell})'Z_t - (Q_t)'Z_t\right] = 0.$$

As with our discussion of the study of SDFs without parametric restrictions, we allow for a multiplicity of possible martingales and impose bounds on expectations of convex functions of the ratio $\frac{M_{t+\ell}}{M_t}$.

To deduce restrictions on M, for notational simplicity I drop the t subscripts and write the pricing relation as:

$$\begin{aligned} E(m\tilde{s}y' - q') &= 0 \\ E(m-1) &= 0. \end{aligned} \tag{17}$$

To bound properties of m solve

$$\inf_{m>0} E[\phi(m)] \tag{18}$$

subject to (17) where ϕ is given by equation (5). This formulation nests many of the so-called F-divergence measures for probability distributions including the well known Kullback-Leibler divergence ($\theta = -1, 0$). A Chernoff-type measure can be imputed by computing the bound for $-1 < \theta < 0$ and optimizing after an appropriate rescaling of the objective by $\theta(1 + \theta)$. As in the previous analysis of Section 3.2.3, there may be many solutions to the equations given in (17). While the minimization problem selects one of these, I am interested in this optimization problem to see how small the objective can be in a statistical sense. If the infimum of the objective is small, then statistically small changes in distributions suffice to satisfy the pricing restrictions. Such departures allow for "behavior biases" that are close statistically to the benchmark probabilities used in generating the data.

I have just sketched an *unconditional* approach to this calculation by allowing conditioning information to be used through the "back door" with the specification of Z but representing the objective and constraints in terms of unconditional expectations. It is mathematically straightforward to study a conditional counterpart, but the statistical implementation is more challenging. Application of the Law of Iterated Expectations still permits an econometrician to condition on less information than investors, so there continues to be scope for robustness in the implementation. By omitting information, however, the bounds are weakened.

By design, this approach allows for the SDF to be misspecified, but in a way captured by distorted beliefs. If the SDF $\tilde{S}$ depends on unknown parameters, say subjective discount rates, intertemporal elasticities of substitution or risk aversion parameters, then the parameter estimation can be included as part of the minimization problem. Parameter estimation takes on a rather different role in this framework than in GMM estimation. The large sample limits of the resulting parameter estimators will depend on the choice of θ unless (as assumed in much of existing econometrics literature) there are no distortions in beliefs.[34] Instead of featuring these methods as a way to get parameter estimators, they have potential value in helping applied econometricians infer how large probability distortions in investor beliefs would have to be from the vantage point of statistical measures of discrepancy. Such calculations would be interesting precursors or complements to a more structured analysis of asset pricing with distorted beliefs.[35] They could be an initial part of an empirical investigation and not the ending point as in other work using bounds in econometrics.

Martingales are present in SDF processes, even without resort to belief distortions. Alvarez and Jermann (2005), Hansen and Scheinkman (2009), Hansen

[34] Extensions of a GMM approach have been suggested based on an empirical likelihood approach following Qin and Lawless (1994) and Owen (2001) ($\theta = -1$), a relative-entropy approach of Kitamura and Stutzer (1997) ($\theta = 0$), a quadratic discrepancy approach of Antoine et al. (2007) ($\theta = 1$) and other related methods. Interestingly, the quadratic ($\theta = 1$) version of these methods coincides with a "continuously updating" GMM estimator of Hansen et al. (1996). Empirical likelihood methods and their generalizations estimate a discrete data distribution given the moment conditions such as pricing restrictions. From the perspective of parametric efficiency, Newey and Smith (2004) show these methods provide second-order asymptotic refinements to what is often a "second-best" efficiency problem. Recall that the statistical efficiency problem studied in Hansen (1982b) took the unconditional moment conditions as given and did not seek to exploit the flexibility in their construction giving rise to a second-best problem. Perhaps more importantly, these methods sometimes have improvements in finite sample performance but also can be more costly to implement. The rationales for such methods typically abstract from belief distortions of the type featured here and typically focus on the case of iid data generation.

[35] Although Gosh et al. (2012) do not feature belief distortions, with minor modification and reinterpretation their approach fits into this framework with $\theta = 0$.

(2011) and Bakshi and Chabi-Yo (2012) all characterize the role of martingale components to SDF's and their impact on asset pricing over long investment horizons. Alvarez and Jermann (2005), Bakshi and Chabi-Yo (2012) and Borovička et al. (2014a) suggest empirical methods that bound this martingale component using a very similar approach to that described here. Since there are multiple sources for martingale components to SDF's, adding more structure to what determines other sources of long-term pricing can play an essential role in quantifying the martingale component attributable to belief distortions.

In summary, factorization (13) gives an abstract characterization of the challenge faced by an econometrician outside the model trying to disentangle the effects of altered beliefs from the effects of risk aversion on the part of investors inside the model. There are a variety of ways in which beliefs could be perturbed. Many papers invoke "animal spirits" to explain lots of empirical phenomenon in isolation. However, these appeals alone do not yield the formal modeling inputs needed to build usable and testable stochastic models. Adding more structure is critical to scientific advancement if we are to develop models that are rich enough to engage in the type of policy analysis envisioned by Marschak (1953), Hurwicz (1962) and Lucas (1976). What follows uses decision theory to motivate some particular constructions of the martingale M.[36]

Next I explore one strategy for adding structure to the martingale alterations to beliefs that I introduced in this section.

6 UNCERTAINTY AND DECISION THEORY

Uncertainty often takes a "back seat" in economic analyses using rational expectations models with risk averse agents. While researchers have used large and sometimes state dependent risk aversion to make the consequences of exposure to risk more pronounced, I find it appealing to explore uncertainty in a conceptually broader context. I will draw on insights from decision theory to suggest ways to enhance the scope of uncertainty in dynamic economic modeling. Decision theorists, economists and statisticians have wrestled with uncertainty for a very long time. For instance, prominent economists such as Keynes (1921) and Knight (1921) questioned our ability to formulate uncertainty in terms of

[36] An alternative way to relax rational expectations is to presume that agents solve their optimization problems using the expectations measured from survey data. See Piazzesi and Schneider (2013) for a recent example of this approach in which they fit expectations to time series data to produce the needed model inputs.

precise probabilities. Indeed Knight (1921) posed a direct challenge to time series econometrics:

> We live in a world full of contradiction and paradox, a fact of which perhaps the most fundamental illustration is this: that the existence of a problem of knowledge depends on the future being different than the past, while the possibility of the solution of the problem depends on the future being like the past.

While Knight's comment goes to the heart of the problem, I believe the most productive response is not to abandon models but to exercise caution in how we use them. How might we make this more formal? I think we should use model misspecification as a source of uncertainty. One approach that has been used in econometric model-building is to let approximation errors be a source for random disturbances to econometric relations. It is typically not apparent, however, where the explicit structure comes from when specifying such errors; nor is it evident that substantively interesting misspecifications are captured by this approach. Moreover, this approach is typically adopted for an outside modeler but not for economic actors inside the model. I suspect that investors or entrepreneurs inside the models we build also struggle to forecast the future.

My co-authors and I, along with many others, are reconsidering the concept of uncertainty and exploring operational ways to broaden its meaning. Let me begin by laying out some constructs that I find to be helpful in such a discussion. When confronted with multiple models, I find it revealing to pose the resulting uncertainty as a two-stage lottery. For the purposes of my discussion, there is no reason to distinguish unknown models from unknown parameters of a given model. I will view each parameter configuration as a distinct model. Thus a model, inclusive of its parameter values, assigns probabilities to all events or outcomes within the model's domain. The probabilities are often expressed by shocks with known distributions and outcomes are functions of these shocks. This assignment of probabilities is what I will call *risk*. By contrast there may be many such potential models. Consider a two-stage lottery where in stage one we select a model and in stage two we draw an outcome using the model probabilities. Call stage one model ambiguity and stage two risk that is internal to a model.

To confront model ambiguity, we may assign *subjective* probabilities across models (including the unknown parameters). This gives us a way of averaging model implications. This approach takes a two-stage lottery and *reduces it* to a single lottery through subjective averaging. The probabilities assigned by each of a family of models are averaged using the subjective probabilities. In a dynamic setting in which information arrives over time, we update these probabilities using Bayes' Rule. de Finetti (1937) and Savage (1954) advocate this use of subjective probability. It leads to an elegant and often tractable way to proceed. While both de Finetti (1937) and Savage (1954) gave elegant defenses for the use of subjective probability, in fact they both expressed some skepticism or caution in applications. For example, de Finetti (as quoted by Dempster (1975) based on personal correspondence) wrote:[37]

> Subjectivists should feel obligated to recognize that any opinion (so much more the initial one) is only vaguely acceptable . . . So it is important not only to know the exact answer for an exactly specified initial problem, but what happens changing in a reasonable neighborhood the assumed initial opinion.

Segal (1990) suggested an alternative approach to decision theory that avoids reducing a two-stage lottery into a single lottery. Preserving the two-stage structure opens the door to decision making in which the behavioral responses for risk (stage two) are distinct from those for what I will call *ambiguity* (stage one). The interplay between uncertainty and dynamics adds an additional degree of complexity into this discussion, but let me abstract from that complexity temporarily. Typically there is a recursive counterpart to this construction that incorporates dynamics and respects the abstraction that I have just described. It is the first stage of this lottery that will be the focus of much of the following discussion.

6.1 Robust Prior Analysis and Ambiguity Aversion

One possible source of *ambiguity*, in contrast to risk, is in how to assign subjective probabilities across the array of models. Modern decision theory gives alternative ways to confront this ambiguity from the first stage in ways that are tractable. Given my desire to use formal mathematical models, it is important to have conceptually appealing and tractable ways to represent preferences in environments with uncertainty. Such tools are provided by decision theory. Some of the literature features axiomatic development that explores the question of what is a "rational" response to uncertainty.

The de Finetti quote suggests the need for a prior sensitivity analysis. When there is a reference to a decision problem, an analysis with multiple priors can

---

[37] Similarly, Savage (1954) wrote: "No matter how neat modern operational definitions of personal probability may look, it is usually possible to determine the personal probabilities of events only very crudely." See Berger (1984) for further discussion.

deduce bounds on the expected utility consequences of alternative decisions, and more generally a mapping from alternative priors into alternative expected outcomes. Building on discussions in Walley (1991) and Berger (1994), there are multiple reasons to consider a family of priors. This family could represent the views of alternative members of an audience, but they could also capture the *ambiguity* to a single decision maker struggling with which prior should be used. Ambiguity aversion as conceived by Gilboa and Schmeidler (1989) and others confronts this latter situation by minimizing the expected utility for each alternative decision rule. *Max-min* utility gives a higher rank to a decision rule with the larger expected utility outcome of this minimization.[38]

Max-min utility has an extension whereby the minimization over a set of priors is replaced by a minimization over priors subject to penalization. The penalization limits the scope of the prior sensitivity analysis. The penalty is measured relative to a benchmark prior used as a point of reference. A discrepancy measure for probability distributions, for instance some of the ones I discussed previously, enforce the penalization. See Maccheroni et al. (2006) for a general analysis and Hansen and Sargent (2007) for implications using the relative entropy measure that I already mentioned. Their approach leads to what is called *variational preferences.*

For either form of ambiguity aversion, with some additional regularity conditions, a version of the Min-Max Theorem rationalizes a worst-case prior. The chosen decision rule under ambiguity aversion is also the optimal decision rule if this worst-case prior were instead the single prior of the decision maker. Dynamic counterparts to this approach do indeed imply a martingale distortion when compared to a benchmark prior that is among the set of priors that are entertained by a decision maker. Given a benchmark prior and a dynamic formulation, this worst-case outcome implies a positive martingale distortion of the type that I featured in Section 5. In equilibrium valuation, this positive martingale represents the consequences of ambiguity aversion on the part of investors inside the model. This martingale distortion emerges endogenously as a way to confront multiple priors that is ambiguity averse or robust. In sufficiently simple environments, the decision maker may in effect learn the model that generates the data in which case the martingale may converge to unity.

There is an alternative promising approach to ambiguity aversion. A decision theoretic model that captures this aversion can be embedded in the analysis of Segal (1990) and Davis and Pate-Cornell (1994), but the application to

[38] See Epstein and Schneider (2003) for a dynamic extension that preserves a recursive structure to decision making.

ambiguity aversion has been developed more fully in Klibanoff et al. (2005) and elsewhere. It is known as a *smooth ambiguity* model of decision making. Roughly speaking, distinct preference parameters dictate behavior responses to two different sources of uncertainty. In addition to aversion to risk given a model captured by one concave function, there is a distinct utility adjustment for ambiguity aversion that emerges when weighting alternative models using a Bayesian prior. While this approach does not in general imply a martingale distortion for valuation, as we note in Hansen and Sargent (2007), such a distortion will emerge with an exponential ambiguity adjustment. This exponential adjustment can be motivated in two ways, either as a penalization over a family of priors as in variational preferences or as a smooth ambiguity behavioral response to a single prior.

6.2 Unknown Models and Ambiguity Aversion

I now consider an approach with an even more direct link to the analysis in Section 5. An important initiator of statistical decision theory, Wald (1939), explored methods that did not presume *a priori* weights could be assigned across models. Wald (1939)'s initial work generated rather substantial literatures in statistics, control theory and economics. I am interested in such an approach as a structured way to perform an analysis of robustness. The alternative models represented as martingales may be viewed as ways in which the benchmark probability model can be misspecified. To explore robustness, I start with a family of probability models represented as martingales against a benchmark model. Discrepancy measures are most conveniently expressed in terms of convex functions of the martingales as in Section 5. Formally the ambiguity is over models, or potential misspecifications of a benchmark model.

What about learning? Suppose that the family of positive martingales with unit expectations is a convex set. For any such martingale M in this set and some $0 < \omega < 1$, construct the mixture $\omega M + (1 - \omega)$ is a positive martingale with unit expectations. Notice that

$$\frac{\omega M_{t+\tau} + (1-\omega)1}{\omega M_t + (1-\omega)1} = \frac{\omega M_t \left(\frac{M_{t+\tau}}{M_t}\right) + (1-\omega)1}{\omega M_t + (1-\omega)1}.$$

The left-hand side is used to represent the conditional expectations operator between dates $t + \tau$ and t. If we interpret ω as the prior assigned to model M and $(1 - \omega)$ as the prior assigned to a benchmark model, then the right-hand side reveals the outcome of Bayes' rule conditioning on date t information where Mt is a date t likelihood ratio between the two original models. Since all convex combinations are considered, we thus allow all priors including point priors. Here I have considered mixtures of the two models, but the basic logic extends to a setting with more general *a priori* averages across models.

Expected utility minimization over a family of martingales provides a tractable way to account for this form of ambiguity aversion, as in max-min utility. Alternatively the minimization can be subject to penalization as in variational preferences. Provided that we can apply the Min-Max Theorem, we may again produce a (constrained or penalized) worst-case martingale distortion. The ambiguity averse decision maker behaves as if he or she is optimizing using the worst-case martingale as the actual probability specification. This same martingale shows up in first-order conditions for optimization and hence in equilibrium pricing relationships. With this *as if* approach I can construct a distorted probability starting from a concern about model misspecification. The focus on a worst-case distortion is the outcome of a concern for robustness to model misspecification.

Of course there is no "free lunch" for such an analysis. We must limit the family of martingales to obtain interesting outcomes. The idea of conducting a sensitivity analysis would seem to have broad appeal, but of course the "devil is in the details." Research from control theory as reflected in Basar and Bernhard (1995) and Petersen et al. (2000), Hansen and Sargent (2001) and Hansen et al. (2006) and others has used discrepancies based on discounted versions of relative entropy measured by $E[M_t \log M_t | \mathcal{F}_0]$. For a given date t this measure is the expected log-likelihood ratio under the M probability model and lends itself to tractable formulas for implementation.[39] Another insightful formulation is given by Chen and Epstein (2002), which targets misspecification of transition densities in continuous time. Either of these approaches requires additional parameters that restrict the search over alternative models. The statistical discrepancy measures described in Section 5 provide one way to guide this choice.[40]

As Hansen and Sargent (2007) emphasize, it is possible to combine this multiple models approach with a multiple priors approach. This allows simultaneously for multiple benchmark models and potential misspecification. In addition there is ambiguity in how to weight the alternative models.

[39] See Strzalecki (2011) for an axiomatic analysis of associated preferences.

[40] See Anderson et al. (2003) for an example of this approach.

6.3 What Might We Achieve?

For the purposes of this essay, the important outcome of this discussion is the ability to use ambiguity aversion or a concern about model misspecification as a way to generate what looks like distorted beliefs. In an application, Chamberlain (2000) studied individual portfolio problems from the vantage point of an econometrician (who could be placed inside a model) using max-min utility and featuring calculations of the endogenously determined worst-case models under plausible classes of priors. These worst-case models give candidates for the distorted beliefs mentioned in the previous section. A worst-case martingale belief distortion is part of the equilibrium calculation in the macroeconomic model of Ilut and Schneider (2014). These authors study simultaneously production and pricing using a recursive max-min formulation of the type advocated by Epstein and Schneider (2003) and introduce ambiguity shocks as an exogenous source of fluctuations.

Ambiguity aversion with unknown models provides an alternative to assuming large values of risk aversion parameters. This is evident from the control theoretic link between what is called risk sensitivity and robustness, noted in a variety of contexts including Jacobson (1973), Whittle (1981) and James (1992). Hansen and Sargent (1995) and Hansen et al. (2006) suggest a recursive formulation of risk sensitivity and link it to recursive utility as developed in the economics literature. While the control theory literature features the equivalent interpretations for decision rules, Hansen et al. (1999), Anderson et al. (2003), Maenhout (2004) and Hansen (2011) consider its impact on security market prices. This link formally relies on the use of relative entropy as a measure of discrepancy for martingales, but more generally I expect that ambiguity aversion often will have similar empirical implications to (possibly extreme) risk aversion for models of asset pricing. Formal axiomatic analyses can isolate behaviorally distinct implications. For this reason I will not overextend my claims of the observational similarity between risk and ambiguity. Axiomatic distinctions, however, are not necessarily present in actual empirical evidence.

The discussion so far produces an ambiguity component to prices in asset markets in addition to the familiar risk prices. There is no endogenous rationale for market compensations fluctuating over time. While exogenously specified stochastic volatility commonly used in asset pricing models also delivers fluctuations, this is a rather superficial success that leaves open the question of what the underlying source is for the implied fluctuations. The calculations in Hansen (2007a) and Hansen and Sargent (2010) suggest an alternative mechanism. Investors concerned with the misspecification of multiple models view these models differently in good versus bad times. For instance, persistence in economic growth is welcome in good times but not in bad times. Given ambiguity about how to weight models and aversion to that ambiguity, investors' worst-case models shift over time leading to changes in ambiguity price components.

Introducing uncertainty about models even with a unique prior will amplify risk prices, although for local risk prices this impact is sometimes small (see Hansen and Sargent (2010) for a discussion). Introducing ambiguity aversion or a concern about model misspecification will lead to a different perspective on both the source and magnitude of the market compensations for exposure to uncertainty. Moreover, by entertaining multiple models and priors over those models there is additional scope for variation in the market compensations as investors may fear different models depending on the state of the economy.[41]

A framework for potential model misspecification also gives a structured way to capture "over-confidence." Consider an environment with multiple agents. Some express full commitment to a benchmark model. Others realize the model is flawed and explore the consequences of model misspecification. If indeed the benchmark model is misspecified, then agents of the first type are over-confident in the model specification. Such an approach offers a novel way to capture this form of heterogeneity in preferences.

What is missing in my discussion of model misspecification is a prescription for constructing benchmark models and/or benchmark priors. Benchmarks are important for two reasons in this analysis. They are used as a reference point for robustness and as a reference point for computing ambiguity prices. I like the transparency of simpler models especially when they have basis in empirical work, and I view the ambition to construct the perfect model to be unattainable.

7 CONCLUSION

I take this opportunity to make four concluding observations.

1. The first part of my essay explored formal econometric methods that are applicable to a researcher outside the model when actors inside the model possess rational expectations. I showed how to connect GMM estimation methods with SDF formulations of stochastic discount factors

[41] See Collin-Dufresne et al. (2013) for a Bayesian formulation with parameter learning that generates interesting variation in risk prices. Given that recursive utility and a preference for robustness to model misspecification have similar and sometimes identical implications for asset pricing in other settings, it would be of interest to see if this similarity carries over to the parameter learning environments considered by these authors.

to estimate and assess asset pricing models with connections to the macroeconomy. I also described how to use SDF formulations to assess the empirical implications of asset pricing models more generally. I then shifted to a discussion of investor behavior inside the model, perhaps even motivated by my own experiences as an applied econometrician. More generally these investors may behave as if they have distorted beliefs. I suggested statistical challenges and concerns about model misspecification as a rationale for these distorted beliefs.

2. I have identified ways that a researcher might alter beliefs for the actors within a model, but I make no claim that this is the only interesting way to structure such distortions. Providing structure, however, is a prerequisite to formal assessment of the resulting models. I have also suggested statistical measures that extend the rational expectations appeal to the Law of Large Numbers for guiding the types of belief distortions that are reasonable to consider. This same statistical assessment should be a valuable input into other dynamic models within which economic agents have heterogeneous beliefs.
3. How best to design econometric analysis in which econometricians and agents formally acknowledge this misspecificaton is surely a fertile avenue for future research. Moreover, there remains the challenge of how best to incorporate ambiguity aversion or concerns about model misspecification into a Marschak (1953), Hurwicz (1962) and Lucas (1972) style study of counterfactuals and policy interventions.
4. Uncertainty, generally conceived, is not often embraced in public discussions of economic policy. When uncertainty includes incomplete knowledge of dynamic responses, we might well be led away from arguments that "complicated problems require complicated solutions." When complexity, even formulated probabilistically, is not fully understood by policy makers, perhaps it is the simpler policies that are more prudent. This could well apply to the design of monetary policy, environmental policy and financial market oversight. Enriching our toolkit to address formally such challenges will improve the guidance that economists give when applying models to policy analysis.

REFERENCES

Ai, Chunrong and Xiaohong Chen. 2003. Efficient Estimation of Models with Conditional Moment Restrictions Containing Unknown Functions. *Econometrica* **71** (6):1795–1843.

Almeida, Caio and Rene Garcia. 2013. Robust Economic Implications of Nonlinear Pricing Kernels. Tech. rep., Social Science Research Network. http://ssrn.com/abstract=1107997.

Alvarez, Fernando and Urban J. Jermann. 2005. Using Asset Prices to Measure the Persistence of the Marginal Utility of Wealth. *Econometrica* **73** (6):1977–2016.

Anderson, Evan W., Lars Peter Hansen, and Thomas J. Sargent. 2003. A Quartet of Semigroups for Model Specification, Robustness, Prices of Risk, and Model Detection. *Journal of the European Economic Association* **1** (1):68–123.

Antoine, Bertille, Helene Bonnal, and Eric Renault. 2007. On the Efficient Use of Informational Content of Estimating Equations: Implied Probabilities and Euclidean Empirical Likelihood. *Journal of Econometrics* **138**:461–487.

Arellano, Manuel. 2002. Sargan's Instrumental Variables Estimation and the Generalized Method of Moments. *Journal of Business and Economic Statistics* **20** (4):450–459.

———. 2003. *Panel Data Econometrics*. Advanced Texts in Econometrics. Oxford University Press.

Bachelier, Louis. 1900. Theorie de la Speculation. *Annales Scientifiques de l' Ecole Normale Superieure* **17**:21–86.

Backus, David, Mikhail Chernov, and Ian Martin. 2011. Disasters Implied by Equity Index Options. *The Journal of Finance* **66** (6):1969–2012.

Backus, David K., Mikhail Chernov, and Stanley E. Zin. 2014. Sources of Entropy in Representative Agent Models. *Journal of Finance* **69** (1):51–99.

Bakshi, Gurdip and Fousseni Chabi-Yo. 2012. Variance Bounds on the Permanent and Transitory Components of Stochastic Discount Factors. *Journal of Financial Economics* **105** (1): 191–208.

Bansal, Ravi and Bruce N. Lehmann. 1997. Growth-Optimal Portfolio Restrictions on Asset Pricing Models. *Macroeconomic Dynamics* **1** (02):333–354.

Bansal, Ravi and Amir Yaron. 2004. Risks for the Long Run: A Potential Resolution of Asset Pricing Puzzles. *Journal of Finance* **59** (4):1481–1509.

Basar, Tamer and Pierre Bernhard. 1995. *H^∞-Optimal Control and Related Minimax Design Problems: A Dynamic Game Approach*. Birkhauser.

Berger, James O. 1984. The Robust Bayesian Viewpoint. In *Robustness of Bayesian Analysis*, edited by Joseph B. Kadane, 63–144. North-Holland.

———. 1994. An Overview of Robust Bayesian Analysis (with discussion). *Test* **3** (1):5–124.

Bilson, John F. O. 1981. The "Speculative Efficiency" Hypothesis. *The Journal of Business* **54** (3):435–451.

Blume, Lawrence and David Easley. 2006. If You're so Smart, why Aren't You Rich? Belief Selection in Complete and Incomplete Markets. *Econometrica* **74** (4):929–966.

Borovička, Jaroslav. 2013. Survival and Long-Run Dynamics with Heterogeneous Beliefs Under Recursive Preferences. Tech. rep., New York University.

Borovička, Jaroslav and Lars Peter Hansen. 2014. Examining Macroeconomic Models Through the Lens of Asset Pricing. *Journal of Econometrics* forthcoming.

Borovička, Jaroslav, Lars Peter Hansen, Mark Hendricks, and José A. Scheinkman. 2011. Risk Price Dynamics. *Journal of Financial Econometrics* **9**:3–65.

Borovička, Jaroslav, Lars Peter Hansen, and José A. Scheinkman. 2014a. Misspecified Recovery. SSRN Working Paper.

———, 2014b. Shock Elasticities and Impulse Response Functions. *Mathematics and Financial Economics* Forthcoming.

Burnside, Craig. 1994. Hansen-Jagannathan Bounds as Classical Tests of Asset-Pricing Models. *Journal of Business and Economic Statistics* **12** (1):57–79.

Campbell, John Y. 1993. Intertemporal Asset Pricing Without Consumption Data. *The American Economic Review* **83** (3):487–512.

Campbell, John Y. and John Cochrane. 1999. Force of Habit: A Consumption-Based Explanation of Aggregate Stock Market Behavior. *Journal of Political Economy* **107** (2):205–251.

Campbell, John Y and Thomo Vuolteenaho. 2004. Bad Beta, Good Beta. *American Economic Review* **94** (5):1249–1275.

Chabi-Yo, Fousseni, Rene Garcia, and Eric Renault. 2008. State Dependence Can Explain the Risk Aversion Puzzle. *Review of Financial Studies* **21** (2):973–1011.

Chamberlain, Gary. 1987. Asymptotic Efficiency in Estimation with Conditional Moment Restrictions. *Journal of Econometrics* **34** (3):305–334.

———. 1992. Efficiency Bounds for Semiparametric Regression. *Econometrica* **60** (3):567–96.

———. 2000. Econometric Applications of Maxmin Expected Utility. *Journal of Applied Econometrics* **15** (6):625–644.

Chen, Zengjing and Larry Epstein. 2002. Ambiguity, Risk, and Asset Returns in Continuous Time. *Econometrica* **70** (4):1403–1443.

Chernoff, Herman. 1952. A Measure of Asymptotic Efficiency for Tests of a Hypothesis Based on the Sum of Observations. *The Annals of Mathematical Statistics* **23** (4):493–507.

Chernozhukov, Victor, Emre Kocatulum, and Konrad Menzel. 2013. Inference on Sets in Finance. Unpublished, MIT, DRW Trading Group and NYU.

Cochrane, John. 2008. *Financial Markets and the Real Economy*, 237–322. Elsevier.

Cochrane, John H. and Lars Peter Hansen. 1992. Asset Pricing Explorations for Macroeconomics. *NBER Macroeconomics Annual* **7**:115–165.

Collin-Dufresne, Pierre, Michael Johannes, and Lars A. Lochstoer. 2013. Parameter Learning in General Equilibrium: The Asset Pricing Implications. Tech. rep., Columbia University, 3022 Broadway, New York, NY 10027.

Constantinides, George M. 1990. Habit Formation: A Resolution of the Equity Premium Puzzle. *Journal of Political Economy* **98** (3):519–543.

Cressie, Noel and Timothy R. C. Read. 1984. Multinomial Goodness-of-Fit Tests. *Journal of the Royal Statistical Society. Series B (Methodological)* **46** (3):440–464.

Davis, Donald B. and M.-Elisabeth Pate-Cornell. 1994. A Challenge to the Compound Lottery Axiom: A Two-Stage Normative Structure and Comparison to Other Theories. *Theory and Decision* **37** (3):267–309.

Davis, Mark and Alison Etheridge. 2006. *Louis Bachelier's Theory of Speculation: The Origins of Modern Finance*. Princeton University Press.

Dempster, A.P. 1975. A Subjectivist Look at Robustness. *Bulletin of the International Statistical Institute* **46**:349–374.

Dimson, Elroy and Massoud Mussavian. 2000. Market Efficiency. In *The Current State of Business Disciplines*, vol. **3**, 959–970. Spellbound Publications.

Epstein, Larry and Stanley E. Zin. 1989. Substitution, Risk Aversion and the Temporal Behavior of Consumption and Asset Returns: A Theoretical Framework. *Econometrica* **57** (4):937–969.

Epstein, Larry G. and Martin Schneider. 2003. Recursive Multiple-Priors. *Journal of Economic Theory* **113** (1):1–31.

Epstein, Larry G and Stanley E Zin. 1991. Substitution, Risk Aversion, and the Temporal Behavior of Consumption and Asset Returns: An Empirical Analysis. *Journal of Political Economy* **99** (2):263–86.

Fama, Eugene F. 1984. Forward and Spot Exchange Rates. *Journal of Monetary Economics* **14** (3):319–338.

Fama, Eugene F and Kenneth R. French. 1992. The Cross-Section of Expected Returns. *Journal of Finance* **47** (2):427–465.

de Finetti, Bruno. 1937. La Prevision: Ses Lois Logiques, ses Sources Subjectives. *Annales de l'Institute Henri Poincaré* **7**:1–68.

Frisch, Ragnar. 1933. Propagation Problems and Impulse Problems in Dynamic Economics. In *Economic Essays in Honour of Gustav Cassel*, 171–205. Allen and Unwin.

Frisch, Ragnar. 1933b. Editor's note. *Econometrica* **1** (1): 1–4.

Gallant, A. Ronald, Lars Peter Hansen, and George Tauchen. 1990. Using Conditional Moments of Asset Payoffs to Infer the Volatility of Intertemporal Marginal Rates of Substitution. *Journal of Econometrics* **45**:141–179.

Ghysels, Eric and Alastair Hall. 2002. Interview with Lars Peter Hansen. *Journal of Business and Economic Statistics Twentieth Anniversary Issue on the Generalized Method of Moments* **20** (4):442–447.

Gilboa, Itzhak and David Schmeidler. 1989. Maxmin Expected Utility with Non-Unique Prior. *Journal of Mathematical Economics* **18** (2):141–153.

Gordin, Mikhail I. 1969. The Central Limit Theorem for Stationary Processes. *Soviet Mathematics Doklady* **10**:1174–1176.

Gosh, Anisha, Christian Julliard, and Alex Taylor. 2012. What is the Consumption-CAPM Missing? An Information-Theoretic Framework for the Analysis of Asset Pricing Models. Working paper, Tepper School of Business, Carnegie Mellon University.

Grossman, Sanford J. and Robert J. Shiller. 1981. The Determinants of the Variability of Stock Market Prices. *The American Economic Review* **71** (2):222–227.

Haavelmo, Trygve. 1944. The Probability Approach in Econometrics. *Econometrica* **12** supplement:1–115.

Hansen, Lars Peter. 1982a. Consumption, Asset Markets, and Macroeconomic Fluctuations: A Comment. *Carnegie-Rochester Conference Series on Public Policy* **17**:239–250.

——. 1982b. Large Sample Properties of Generalized Method of Moments Estimators. *Econometrica* **50** (4):1029–1054.

——. 1985. A Method for Calculating Bounds on the Asymptotic Covariance Matrices of Generalized Method of Moments Estimators. *Journal of Econometrics* **30** (1):203–238.

——. 2001. Generalized Method of Moments Estimation: A Time Series Perspective (published title Method of Moments). In *International Encyclopedia of the Social and Behavior Sciences*, edited by S.E. Fienberg and J.B. Kadane. Pergamon: Oxford. http://www.larspeterhansen.org/generalized-method-of-moments-estimation-32.html.

——. 2007a. Beliefs, Doubts and Learning: Valuing Macroeconomic Risk. *American Economic Review* **97** (2):1–30.

——. 2007b. Generalized Method of Moments Estimation. In *The New Palgrave Dictionary of Economics*, edited by Steven N. Durlauf and Lawrence E. Blume. Palgrave Macmillan.

——. 2008. *Discussion of: Financial Markets and the Real Economy, by J. Cochrane*, 326–329. Elsevier.

——. 2011. Dynamic Valuation Decomposition Within Stochastic Economies. *Econometrica* **80** (3):911–967. Fisher-Schultz Lecture at the European Meetings of the Econometric Society.

——. 2012. Proofs for Large Sample Properties of Generalized Method of Moments Estimators. *Journal of Econometrics* **170** (2):325–330.

Hansen, Lars Peter and Robert J. Hodrick. 1980. Forward Exchange Rates as Optimal Predictors of Future Spot Rates: An Econometric Analysis. *Journal of Political Economy* **88** (5):829–853.

——. 1983. Risk Averse Speculation in the Forward Foreign Exchange Market: An Econometric Analysis of Linear Models. In *Exchange Rates and International Macroeconomics*, NBER Chapters, 113–152. National Bureau of Economic Research, Inc.

Hansen, Lars Peter, C.A. Helt, and D. Peled. 1978. A note on first degree stochastic dominance *Economics Letters* **1** (4): 315–319.

Hansen, Lars Peter and Ravi Jagannathan. 1991. Implications of Security Market Data for Models of Dynamic Economies. *Journal of Political Economy* **99** (2):225–262.

——. 1997. Assessing Specification Errors in Stochastic Discount Factor Models. *The Journal of Finance* **52** (2):557–590.

Hansen, Lars Peter and Scott F. Richard. 1987. The Role of Conditioning Information in Deducing Testable Restrictions Implied by Dynamic Asset Pricing Models. *Econometrica* **50** (3):587–613.

Hansen, Lars Peter and Thomas Sargent. 2010. Fragile Beliefs and the Price of Uncertainty. *Quantitative Economics* **1** (1):129–162.

Hansen, Lars Peter and Thomas J. Sargent. 1980. Formulating and Estimating Dynamic Linear Rational Expectations Models. *Journal of Economic Dynamics and Control* **2**:7–46.

———. 1991. Exact Liner Rational Expectations Models: Specification and Estimation. In *Rational Expectations Econometrics: Specification and Estimation*, edited by Lars Peter Hansen and Thomas J. Sargent, 45–76. Westview Press.

———. 1995. Discounted Linear Exponential Quadratic Gaussian Control. *IEEE Transactions on Automatic Control* **40** (5):968–971.

———. 2001. Robust Control and Model Uncertainty. *The American Economic Review* **91** (2):60–66.

———. 2007. Recursive Robust Estimation and Control Without Commitment. *Journal of Economic Theory* **136** (1):1–27.

Hansen, Lars Peter and Jose Scheinkman. 2009. Long-Term Risk: An Operator Approach. *Econometrica* **77** (1):117–234.

———. 2012. Pricing Growth-Rate Risk. *Finance and Stochastics* **16** (1):1–15.

Hansen, Lars Peter and Kenneth J. Singleton. 1982. Generalized Instrumental Variables Estimation of Nonlinear Rational Expectations Models. *Econometrica* **50** (5):1269–1286.

———. 1983. Stochastic Consumption, Risk Aversion, and the Temporal Behavior of Asset Returns. *Journal of Political Economy* **91** (2):249–265.

———. 1996. Efficient Estimation of Linear Asset-Pricing Models with Moving Average Errors. *Journal of Business and Economic Statistics* **14** (1):53–68.

Hansen, Lars Peter, John Heaton, and Erzo G. J. Luttmer. 1995. Econometric Evaluation of Asset Pricing Models. *The Review of Financial Studies* **8** (2):237–274.

Hansen, Lars Peter, John Heaton, and Amir Yaron. 1996. Finite-Sample Properties of Some Alternative GMM Estimators. *Journal of Business and Economic Statistics* **14** (3):262–280.

Hansen, Lars Peter, Thomas J. Sargent, and Jr. Tallarini, Thomas D. 1999. Robust Permanent Income and Pricing. *The Review of Economic Studies* **66** (4):873–907.

Hansen, Lars Peter, Thomas J. Sargent, Gauhar A. Turmuhambetova, and Noah Williams. 2006. Robust Control and Model Misspecification. *Journal of Economic Theory* **128** (1):45–90.

Hansen, Lars Peter, John C. Heaton, and Nan Li. 2008. Consumption Strikes Back?: Measuring Long Run Risk. *Journal of Political Economy* **116** (2):260–302.

Harrison, J. Michael and David M. Kreps. 1979. Martingales and Arbitrage in Multiperiod Securities Markets. *Journal of Economic Theory* **20** (3):381–408.

He, Hua and David M. Modest. 1995. Market Frictions and Consumption-Based Asset Pricing. *Journal of Political Economy* **103** (1):94–117.

Heaton, John C. 1995. An Empirical Investigation of Asset Pricing with Temporally Dependent Preference Specifications. *Econometrica* **63** (3):681–717.

Hurwicz, Leonid. 1962. On the Structural Form of Interdependent Systems. *Logic, Methodology and Philosophy of Science: Proceedings of the 1960 International Congress* 232–239.

Ilut, Cosmin and Martin Schneider. 2014. Ambiguous Business Cycles. *American Economic Review* forthcoming.

Jacobson, David H. 1973. Optimal Stochastic Linear Systems with Exponential Performance Criteria and Their Relation to Deterministic Differential Games. *IEEE Transactions for Automatic Control* AC-18 (2):1124–131.

James, Matthew R. 1992. Asymptotic Analysis of Nonlinear Stochastic Risk-Sensitive Control and Differential Games. *Mathematics of Control, Signals and Systems* **5** (4):401–417.

Keynes, John Maynard. 1921. *A Treatise on Probability*. London: Macmillan.

Kitamura, Yuichi and Michael Stutzer. 1997. An Information-Theoretic Alternative to Generalized Method of Moments Estimation. *Econometrica* **65** (4):861–874.

Kitamura, Yuichi, Gautam Tripathi, and Hyungtaik Ahn. 2004. Empirical Likelihood-Based Inference in Conditional Moment Restriction Models. *Econometrica* **72** (6):1667–1714.

Klibanoff, Peter, Massimo Marinacci, and Sujoy Mukerji. 2005. A Smooth Model of Decision Making Under Uncertainty. *Econometrica* **73** (6):1849–1892.

Knight, Frank H. 1921. *Risk, Uncertainty, and Profit*. Houghton Mifflin.

Kogan, Leonid, Stephen A. Ross, Jiang Wang, and Mark M. Westerfield. 2011. Market Selection. Tech. rep., Massachusetts Institute of Technology.

Kreps, David M. and Evan L. Porteus. 1978. Temporal Resolution of Uncertainty and Dynamic Choice. *Econometrica* **46** (1):185–200.

Lucas, Robert E. 1972. Econometric Testing of the Natural Rate Hypothesis. In *The Econometrics of Price Determination*, edited by O. Eckstein, 50–59. Board of Governors of the Federal Reserve Board.

——. 1976. Econometric Policy Evaluation: A Critique. *Carnegie-Rochester Conference Series on Public Policy* **1** (0):19–46.

——. 1978. Asset Prices in an Exchange Economy. *Econometrica* **46** (6):1429–1445.

Luttmer, Erzo G. J. 1996. Asset Pricing in Economies with Frictions. *Econometrica* **64** (6):1439–1467.

Maccheroni, Fabio, Massimo Marinacci, and Aldo Rustinchini. 2006. Ambiguity Aversion, Robustness, and the Variational Representation of Preferences. *Econometrica* **74** (6):1147–1498.

Maenhout, Pascal J. 2004. Robust Portfolio Rules and Asset Pricing. *Review of Financial Studies* **17**:951–983.

Marschak, Jacob. 1953. Economic Measurements for Policy and Prediction. In *Studies in Econometric Method*, edited by Tjalling Charles Koopmans and William C. Hood, 1–26. John Wiley and Sons.

Muth, John H. 1961. Rational Expectations and the Theory of Price Movements. *Econometrica* **29** (3):315–335.

Newey, Whitney K. and Richard J. Smith. 2004. Higher Order Properties of GMM and Generalized Empirical Likelihood Estimators. *Econometrica* **72** (1):219–255.

Newey, W.K. 1990. Efficient Instrumental Variables Estimation of Nonlinear Models. *Econometrica* **58** (4):809–837.

———. 1993. Efficient Estimation of Models with Conditional Moment Restrictions. In *Handbook of Statistics*, vol. **11**, edited by G.S. Maddala, C.R. Rao, and H.D. Vinod, 809–837. Amsterdam: North-Holland.

Newman, C. M. and B. W. Stuck. 1979. Chernoff Bounds for Discriminating Between Two Markov Processes. *Stochastics* **2** (1–4):139–153.

Owen, Art B. 2001. *Empirical Likelihood*, vol. **92** of *CRC Monographs on Statistics and Applied Probability*. Chapman and Hall.

Peñaranda, Francisco and Enrique Sentana. 2011. Inferences about Portfolio and Stochastic Discount Factor Mean Variance Frontiers. Working Paper, UPF and CEMFI.

Petersen, I.R., M.R. James, and P. Dupuis. 2000. Minimax Optimal Control of Stochastic Uncertain Systems with Relative Entropy Constraints. *Automatic Control, IEEE Transactions on* **45** (3):398–412.

Piazzesi, Monika and Martin Schneider. 2013. Inflation and the Price of Real Assets. Unpublished, Stanford University.

Qin, Jin and Jerry Lawless. 1994. Empirical Likelihood and General Estimating Equations. *The Annals of Statistics* **22** (1):300–325.

Restoy, Fernando and Philippe Weil. 2011. Approximate Equilibrium Asset Prices. *Review of Finance* **15** (1):1–28.

Robinson, P. M. 1987. Asymptotically Efficient Estimation in the Presence of Heteroskedasticity of Unknown Form. *Econometrica* **55** (4):875–891.

Ross, Stephen A. 1978. A Simple Approach to the Valuation of Risky Streams. *The Journal of Business* **51** (3):453–75.

Rubinstein, Mark. 1976. The Valuation of Uncertain Income Streams and the Pricing of Options. *The Bell Journal of Economics* **7**:407–425.

Sargan, J. D. 1958. The Estimation of Economic Relationships Using Instrumental Variables. *Econometrica* **26** (3):393–415.

———. 1959. The Estimation of Relationships with Autocorrelated Residuals by the Use of Instrumental Variables. *Journal of the Royal Statistical Society. Series B (Methodological)* **21** (1):91–105.

Sargent, Thomas J. 1973. Rational Expectations, the Real Rate of Interest, and the Natural Rate of Unemployment. *Brookings Papers in Economic Activity* **4** (2):429–480.

———. 1999. *The Conquest of American Inflation*. Princeton, New Jersey: Princeton University Press.

Sargent, Thomas J. and Neil Wallace. 1975. "Rational" Expectations, the Optimal Monetary Instrument, and the Optimal Money Supply Rule. *Journal of Political Economy* **83** (2):241–254.

Savage, Leonard J. 1954. *The Foundations of Statistics*. Wiley Publications in Statistics.

———. 1961. The Foundations of Statistics Reconsidered. In *Proceedings of the Fourth Berkeley Symposium on Mathematical Statistics and Probability*, edited by Jerzy Neyman, 575–586.

Segal, Uzi. 1990. Two-Stage Lotteries Without the Reduction Axiom. *Econometrica* **58** (2):349–377.

Shiller, Robert. 1972. *Rational Expectations and the Structure of Interest Rates*. Ph.D. thesis, M.I.T.

———. 1982. Consumption, Asset Markets and Macroeconomic Fluctuations. *Carnegie Rochester Conference Series on Public Policy* **17**:203–238.

Sims, Christopher A. 1980. Macroeconomics and Reality. *Econometrica* **48** (1):1–48.

———. 2012. Statistical Modeling of Monetary Policy and Its Effects. *The American Economic Review* **102** (4):1187–1205.

Slutsky, Eugen. 1927. The Summation of Random Causes as the Source of Cyclic Processes. In *Problems of Economic Conditions*, vol. **3**. Moscow: The Conjuncture Institute.

———. 1937. The Summation of Random Causes as the Source of Cyclic Processes. *Econometrica* **5** (2):105–146.

Snow, Karl N. 1991. Diagnosing Asset Pricing Models Using the Distribution of Asset Returns. *The Journal of Finance* **46** (3):955–983.

Stigler, Stephen. 2014. Soft Questions, Hard Answers: Jacob Bernoulli's Probability in Historical Context. *International Statistical Review* forthcoming.

Strzalecki, Tomasz. 2011. Axiomatic Foundations of Multiplier Preferences. *Econometrica* **79**:47–73.

Stutzer, Michael. 1995. A Bayesian Approach to Diagnosis of Asset Pricing Models. *Journal of Econometrics* **68** (2):367–397.

Sundaresan, Suresh M. 1989. Intertemporally Dependent Preferences and the Volatility of Consumption and Wealth. *The Review of Financial Studies* **2** (1):73–89.

Tallarini, Thomas D. 2000. Risk-Sensitive Real Business Cycles. *Journal of Monetary Economics* **45** (3):507–532.

Wald, Abraham. 1939. Contributions to the Theory of Statistical Estimation and Testing Hypotheses. *The Annals of Mathematical Statistics* **10** (4):299–326.

Walley, Peter. 1991. *Statistical Reasoning with Imprecise Probabilities*. CRC Monographs on Statistics and Applied Probability. Chapman and Hall.

Wallis, Kenneth F. 1980. Econometric Implications of the Rational Expectations Hypothesis. *Econometrica* **48** (1):49–73.

Weil, Philippe. 1990. Nonexpected Utility in Macroeconomics. *The Quarterly Journal of Economics* **105** (1):29–42.

West, Kenneth, Ka fu Wong, and Stanislav Anatolyev. 2009. Instrumental Variables Estimation of Heteroskedastic Linear Models Using All Lags of Instruments. *Econometric Reviews* **28** (5):441–467.

Whittle, Peter. 1981. Risk Sensitive Linear Quadratic Gaussian Control. *Advances in Applied Probability* **13** (4):764–777.

Yule, G. Udny. 1927. On a Method of Investigating Periodicities in Disturbed Series, with Special Reference to Wolfer's Sunspot Numbers. *Philosophical Transactions of the Royal Society of London. Series A, Containing Papers of a Mathematical or Physical Character* 226:267–298.

Zhang, Jian and Irene Gijbels. 2003. Sieve Empirical Likelihood and Extensions of the Generalized Least Squares. *Scandinavian Journal of Statistics* **30** (1):1–24.

Robert J. Shiller. © Nobel Media AB. Photo: A. Mahmoud

Robert J. Shiller

In reflecting on my own life history on the occasion of the Nobel Prize, I find myself wondering about some traits of my research, about the kind of colleagues I have chosen to associate with in research, and why I even went into economics. I have used this occasion to think about the true origins of these inclinations and life directions.

I began my professional career in economics as an econometrician, producing a Ph.D. dissertation focusing on the econometrics of rational expectations models, Bayesian statistics and distributed lag estimation. Throughout my career I continued to be an applied econometrician, interested in the interface between theory and data, with an abiding appreciation of the importance of models and their careful testing.

However, as years have gone by, I have developed a research style that finds opportunities in avoiding so much specialization in any one field as narrow as econometrics. I increasingly tended to think that, for me, these econometric methods are best augmented with other approaches, if I am really to be useful in adding to an understanding that allows for better economic policy and practice. In doing so, I believe that some aspects of my research have evolved so as to be described by some as going down the wrong road. I have been more willing than most to entertain inventions or ideas that may seem eccentric. I have also tended to be relatively eclectic, borrowing more from other social sciences, violating economics profession norms. I have been more eager to go out and collect data (as for example by doing questionnaire surveys) that many people might dismiss as uninteresting, and happier to do mundane or low-brow research for little more reason than that it interests me and no one else seems to be doing it. I have also apparently tilted from most of my academic colleagues in choosing to devote some of my time to journalism, writing scholarly-trade books instead of purely scholarly books, and writing regular newspaper columns I believe that the experience of doing such diverse work has made me a better researcher even from a purely scholarly point of view, though I have to admit that others, with a different inspiration, may thrive more on specialization.

The aspect of my research that was stressed by the Scientific Background for the Nobel Prize, my econometric work in asset pricing, was a bit eccentric by some standards. When it was first published, and for at least a decade, I encountered considerable hostile criticism from some quarters. In fact, after I won the Nobel Prize, I received a postcard from a colleague who recalled talking with me at the AEA Convention in 1982, when I told him I wished I had never written a paper that now is cited as a centerpiece of my work. Over the years, the pain of the rejection I felt by many in my profession has faded, but it seems that as a young economist it was quite uncomfortable to be attacked for work that was seen as so out of line with professional conventions. Others in the academic world have had similar experience when their research seems to offend the norm, only to be recognized later.

In thinking about my early life, I can see some of the experiences and inclinations that preceded my career as a researcher who pursued somewhat unusual directions. In writing my life history I will work to create an understanding of formative life experiences and inborn personality traits that contributed in significant ways to my life course.

FAMILY HISTORY

All four of my grandparents, Jurgis Šileris, Amelia Mileriutė, Vincas Radzvilas and Rozalia Šerytė came separately to America 1906–10 from Lithuania. They joined the Lithuanian-American community and within that they met and married here.

Two of these last names are Lithuanian spellings of German names, and my Grandfather had a decision to make on how to spell his name in America. Everyone agreed the name was German, and he lived in the town Gaurė in part of Lithuania that was substantially German in origin, and close to the Prussian border and the city of Königsberg (now Kaliningrad), but he had no known family history to link to Germany and he spoke only minimal German. He chose to spell his name George Shiller in America, while his brother coming around the same time chose Michael Schiller. The others became Amelia Miller, Rosalia Serys, and Vincent/William Radzvill.

We remain in contact with our Lithuanian relatives after more than one hundred years because both my grandmothers corresponded for the rest of their lives by mail with their families back home, and established a connection from them to me. My second cousin Nijolė Krotkutė in Lithuania has reported to me research on our family history, through the Radzvill branch, to Lithuania in the 14th century. After the Nobel ceremony in December 2013, we went to Lithuania and were regaled at a celebration with a dozen of our relatives from there, who concluded by seating me in the center of a circle of them, singing to me old Lithuanian folksongs. But, still, after more than a century of separation, Lithuania now seems largely foreign to me, and our sense of identity contains no more than a glimmer of our memories of this past.

I think instead that the individual migration to America (as to other destination cities or areas around the world) selects for people with independent spirit, who invest in a new culture, and who may also convey this culture to their progeny. My grandfather Shiller, reacting to the Russo-Japanese war in 1904, left to avoid conscription into the Russian army, which he considered an occupying army. My grandmother Miller came in part to avoid an arranged marriage to a man she loathed. My grandfather Vincent Radzvill came to attend college at the Cleveland Institute of Art. My grandmother Rosalia Serys came by herself via London, just to make a good life for herself. They all became part of a new Lithuanian-American culture that produced me.

ELEMENTARY SCHOOL

In my first few years of elementary school at the Edison School in Detroit, I did poorly. I remember worrying that I might fail the second grade and be held back. Perhaps I had a touch of attention deficit-hyperactivity disorder (my wife is convinced that I still do) but I grew up before this was regularly diagnosed. My second-grade teacher, Mrs. Ashdown, would say to me "Bobby, if you get up from your seat one more time I am going to tie you down." It wasn't just independence of spirit; I was very restless and talkative, uncontrollably so, which earned me a very low grade in "citizenship."

Whatever it was, I was very distractible, but also could be highly focused if something caught my attention, particularly written material. My mother used to tell a story about when she had taken a book from the library entitled *Care of the Feet* because of a minor foot problem she then had. She never had time to read the book, but I as a child found it and read the whole thing and told her all about it.

Even today, I am easily distracted by reading material, and will pick up articles on virtually any factual material if I have the time. Fortunately, some of my traits were discovered by my elementary school science teacher, Mr. Keener, who took an interest in me as well as my brother John and helped both of us form strong identities with scientists.

As a psychologist, my wife Ginny argues that attentional differences are important, and don't simply represent "deficits" but also can underlie creativity. She is amused at my interest in giving interviews to reporters; perhaps she is right that the desire to talk that got me in trouble in elementary school is well-channeled in expounding on my viewpoints with the media.

GENERAL INTEREST IN SCIENCE

As a child, I was fascinated by any branch of physical or biological science. Even today, I find great excitement in discovering the complexity and variability of the world we live in, getting a glimpse into the deeper reality that we mostly ignore in our everyday human activities. I want to know diverse facts about such things as galaxies or molecules or proteins or insect species.

I have an impulse to want to know the little details, which are usually of no significance to non-specialists. I own a dissection microscope, and if there is an insect in the house I sometimes catch it and look at it under the microscope. I find myself marveling at these tiny things, finding them most impressive when one really sees them, and I enjoy wondering about how they came to be. I have felt the greatest admiration for true scientists, leaving me often wondering why other people seem to have so much admiration for actors and singers, who sometimes seem to know little about the real workings of the world.

In some sense science became a sort of religion to me. I do not remember how or when I first discovered Albert Einstein's article "Religion and Science" that he first published in *The New York Times Magazine* in 1930, long before I was born. Perhaps my father told me about it. But at some point I found it and it became an inspiration. Einstein described his own visceral spiritual longings and said in his life they were transformed into a quest to discover the true laws of nature. He concluded: "I maintain that the cosmic religious feeling is the strongest and noblest motive for scientific research . . . in this materialistic age of ours the serious scientific workers are the only profoundly religious people."

FAMILY IMPULSES TO ENTREPRENEURSHIP

My father Benjamin Shiller had an exceptionally entrepreneurial attitude, even for America. This attitude was revealed in many little things he did that I recall.

My father's greatest achievement in his life was the founding of his firm The Sahara Corporation, which manufactured fluidized-sand industrial ovens according to a patent he obtained on his invention. The event ended badly, with difficulties getting the business established and with interruption by his disabling heart attack in 1973, when he was 62 years old.

Watching him must have colored my thinking. I have always thought that my own profession should pay more attention to invention. Journals should publish ideas about how things could be done differently, and not just ideas about manipulating the usual government policy tools, or about which bad practices should be made illegal. There should be more articles offering trial-balloon ideas about how economic institutions and methods could be set on a completely different framework, even if the ideas are not fully developed.

But there isn't enough of a tradition for such thinking in academia, certainly not in economics, which seems overly focused on quantification of the behavior of the world as it has existed in the past. Undeniably, it is difficult to keep the right balance between innovation and development of established ideas. Management schools and law schools sometimes seem more attuned to practical economic inventions, though they tend often to fail to appreciate economic theory.

HIGH SCHOOL AND COLLEGE

While I was just beginning high school at Southfield High School near Detroit in 1960, my brother John, who is four years older than I, came home on a holiday from college with his assigned textbook, *Economics* by Paul Samuelson. Samuelson, at M.I.T., was later to win the 1970 Nobel Prize in Economic Sciences. I managed to read much of the book on that holiday, and this launched my interest in economics. I felt that economics, as Samuelson practiced it at least, really is a science. I was intrigued that economic models can actually explain many important things that happen in our lives.

I went off to college from Southfield High first to Kalamazoo College, a small liberal arts college in Michigan. I had a good freshman year there, but I wanted to try also the big university, and so I transferred for fall 1964 into the University of Michigan, where my brother John had also been a student.

I started writing there for the *Michigan Daily*, the student newspaper, and that surely was an important experience for me. I found the fact-finding that a newspaper writer does appealing. The experience of writing for a broad newspaper readership may seem completely different from the work of a scientist, but it did not to me. I saw a parallel in both roles as getting to the real facts. I was not writing grass for general readers, and I imagined my actual readers, however few, were as sophisticated as real scientists. The main point of a newspaper seemed to me to be that there was great value to there being a place for certain kinds of inquiry, about topics of immediate importance, helping us to tie events already in our mind into our broader world view.

A couple of faculty members at Michigan had significant influences on me while I was an undergraduate there. Kenneth Boulding, in the economics department, advocated what he called "general systems," meaning an approach to research that is respectful of the interconnections between the various sciences. I have held the conviction ever since that these interconnections are vitally important. He also conveyed a moral imperative for economists to work to make a better world.

Though I had only one lecture from George Katona, in the Michigan psychology department, he was the first person to impress me about the importance of psychology for economics. He was perhaps the real beginning of behavioral economics for me. I kept his ideas in the back of my mind for years, but they then seemed to belong to the psychology department. I felt then that I had to make a choice between economics and psychology, one or the other, but could not have both.

As I approached the end of my undergraduate career, I agonized about what career choice to make. In fact, I took so many long walks mulling over choices that I was eventually diagnosed with a stress fracture of a metatarsal, which the doctor told me then, was typical of soldiers on long forced marches.

The two most prominent alternatives, beyond economics, were physics and medicine. I was very attracted to medicine, but I did not think the life of a typical doctor would be attractive to me; having appointments booked back to back seemed onerous. Perhaps my hyperactive nature made me prefer the relatively unstructured life of an academic. However, I could have gone into either field, and it may be just a matter of chance that it ended up to be economics, the chance event of my thinking at the time in my life when I needed to make a decision.

GRADUATE SCHOOL

From Michigan I went directly in 1967 to enter the Ph.D. in economics program at Massachusetts Institute of Technology. There I met Theodore Keeler and Jeremy Siegel, fellow graduate students, who have remained friends for life. We went our separate ways geographically after receiving our Ph.D.s, but have remained close.

At MIT, I felt honored to have the man I so admired in high school, Paul Samuelson, as a teacher. I felt that there was something different about him, when compared with many other academics, for he approached economics as a real scientist. Some of this feeling may have been superficial. He, more than any other economics professor I had ever had, would make frequent analogies to principles of the physical sciences. But I think that there indeed was something fundamentally different about him too, for he approached economics with the kind of creativity and respect for evidence that befits a real scientist. Samuelson was important to me also because of his warmth to his students. He called me up on some occasions long afterwards.

My dissertation adviser and first coauthor was Franco Modigliani, who later also won the Nobel Prize, in 1985. I was attracted to him as an adviser because he combined an interest in economic theory with a really lively interest in the real world. He had a sense of reality that appealed to my own inclinations, and my sense of what science should be about. He attracted others with the same inclinations at the time, notably my fellow graduate student Mario Draghi, now head of the European Central Bank.

I didn't fully share all of Franco's interests, however. At the time I was a graduate student, Franco was working with Albert Ando at the University of Pennsylvania on a gigantic simulation model of the U.S. economy called the MIT-Penn-SSRC Model. I felt that that model was too ambitious and too cumbersome, and felt skeptical about its likely effectiveness as a forecaster. It turns out that a lot of other people were skeptical too, and this skepticism seems to have led to the rational expectations revolution, which focused on one aspect of such models, their representation of expectations.

While I was first attracted to the field of econometrics in graduate school, I decided later not to make econometrics as my narrow field of specialization. I came to think that for me, I needed to stay focused on the real economic questions, not just on methodology. Econometrics remains of course very important, and I have continued to follow the field and to publish and do some work using new econometric methods, such as the index numbers, but I long ago decided that I wanted to my own driving more on the big elusive questions that cannot be addressed entirely with statistical methods.

MARRIAGE AND FAMILY

I met Ginny, now my wife of 37 years, in 1974 at an M.I.T. folk-dancing party. This happened while I was back in Cambridge, Mass. visiting the National Bureau of Economic Research and Harvard University and then M.I.T. I found a kindred spirit in her, and I am sure that whatever successes I have had are attributable to our good marriage, her intellectual companionship, and her willingness to allow me considerable time to spend on my research while she shouldered domestic responsibilities.

In our early marriage, while she got a Ph.D. in clinical psychology from the University of Delaware, we lived in Newark, Delaware, and I commuted to my job at the University of Pennsylvania. While at Delaware, Ginny regularly brought home books and articles about many fields of psychology, and I continued with my habit of picking up interesting reading material. I also went to parties with psychology faculty and graduate students, and thus picked up ideas that I wasn't exposed to within the field of economics.

More recently, when I have engaged in more popular writing, Ginny has consistently provided a sounding board for my ideas. She steers me away from ideas that may be too eccentric, and helps me frame ideas in ways which make them more attractive and accessible for popular audiences.

We had two sons together, and they followed in my footsteps of not being top-notch students at early ages. However, I am proud to say that our older son Benjamin Shiller is now an assistant professor of economics at Brandeis University in Waltham, Massachusetts, with a specialty in information economics and industrial organization. Our younger son Derek Shiller is currently in the philosophy Ph.D. program at Princeton University, and also a lecturer at the University of Nebraska in Omaha. He is interested in epistemology, meta-philosophy, and Bayesian inference, interests that in some important ways parallel my own interests. While Ginny largely works as a practitioner, she has an academic appointment at the Yale Child Study Center and has written and lectured throughout her career.

ACADEMIC CAREER, COLLEAGUES AND CO-AUTHORS

My first academic position after my Ph.D. was at the University of Minnesota in 1972–74. I had close colleagues, Thomas Sargent and Christopher Sims, who themselves won the Nobel Prize together in 2011. I was a great admirer of their work, and found interaction with them stimulating. But I gave up my faith in strict rational expectations models more definitively than they did, or sooner. My tendency towards skepticism began to divide us a bit. Eventually I just didn't believe that these rational expectations models, or their finance counterparts, efficient markets models, could possibly be basically right, except in certain special cases. Maybe I overreacted against these models, but the good result was that I began to get much more interested in other social sciences, and learned a great deal.

Irving Fisher (1867–1947), who taught at Yale for his entire career, was never my colleague, as our lives overlapped only by a year and I never met him. Yet his example has always stimulated my imagination, and I have pursued somewhat similar ideas in a similar style. Both he and I developed a theory of index numbers. We both advocated inflation-indexed bonds, and we also both tried to launch new securities. Both he and I were ready to propose inventions, in his case including an analogue computer for solving economic equilibrium, a new map projection, and a new folding chair. Fisher and I both wrote books for a broader public and also wrote regular newspaper columns. I think some of these similarities represent a common belief that one needs to take risks in research, risks of appearing undignified or even unprofessional to some who judge on superficial qualities, but that one must work to be sure these activities are sincere and based on the best interpretation of scientific method.

My actual colleague at Yale, James Tobin (1918–2002), who was awarded the 1981 Sveriges Riksbank Prize in economics, also was an inspiration; he shared my respect for fact-oriented economic science, as well as a commitment to moral causes. He overlapped with me at Yale for 20 years.

The skepticism I had developed in graduate school about large-scale econometric models led me to do some work with Ray Fair at Yale, comparing modeling techniques. We concluded that at least one large-scale simulation model, his FairModel, does indeed seem to carry useful information about the future beyond that of other simpler statistical models and judgmental forecasts. So, my skepticism about these large-scale models, like the one my advisor Modigliani had worked on and that I had been doubtful of, was reduced substantially.

I met Richard Thaler when he was at Cornell University and I gave a talk there in 1982. He and I took a walk around campus then, and talked about the scientific method and where economics was going. This was the beginning of a long collaboration with him, specifically to organize seminars on behavioral economics, starting at the National Bureau of Economic Research in 1991 and ever since. He and I have together watched the economics profession become less isolated from other social sciences as the years go by. Our behavioral economics community has now expanded dramatically beyond just our colleagues in psychology: it now includes other social sciences as well, and biological sciences—most significantly, in recent years, neuroscience.

I wrote over a dozen scholarly papers with my Yale graduate student John Campbell, now a professor of economics at Harvard, on expectations models in finance. John has a precise mind and the energy to complete the ideas that come to him. He has been a major influence on all my work. He brought my initial results on the excess volatility in financial markets into much clearer focus, so that the results could be seen to survive formidable criticism.

Karl Case, who eventually co-developed with me the home price indices that are still produced today, also worked with me on understanding the bubble in home prices that preceded the recent financial crisis. Our 2003 Brookings Paper had an analysis that showed some of the dangers ahead.

I have also worked extensively with George Akerlof, who won the Nobel Prize in Economic Sciences in 2001, on a 2009 book *Animal Spirits* about the foundations of macroeconomics. This book is a statement about ultimate causes of macroeconomic fluctuations, pushing macroeconomics back to its inevitable origins in human behavior. We are working on yet another book together, for we find a lot that is similar, or complementary, in our patterns of thinking. We work well together, augmenting each other's imaginations, often indulging even more in speculative thinking together than we would alone, but our joint interaction also provides some discipline to our thinking.

My latest co-authors are my Yale student advisee Oliver Bunn, now at Barclays Bank, and others on the research team at Barclays, who have helped lend another new dimension to my work with their different experience and focus.

In all, I calculated that I have written joint work with 46 co-authors in my career. The 46 count includes 14 co-authors I had on a single project, who were finance specialists who collaborated on *The Squam Lake Report: Fixing the Financial System*, 2010. Long lists of co-authors for a single work are not common in economics as they are in the physical sciences, and my other co-authored papers were usually the product of close collaboration with only one co-author.

I have had a similarly large number of research assistants, both graduate students and undergraduates, and dissertation and senior-essay advisees. I have enjoyed my relation with all of them.

Throughout my career I have been able to find others who complement my own thinking in many ways, and my own research under my own name reflects their contributions. One of the greatest joys of academic research is discovering this meeting of minds with all of these people. It is something like the joy I remember singing hymns with a community in church, or singing folk song duets with my fiancée Ginny forty years ago.

On that note, it is most important to mention that, after having had Ginny's indirect input on my research and writing for so many years in our long marriage, I have finally written an economics article with my wife Ginny, entitled "Economists as Worldly Philosophers," that is an appeal to economists to take a broad view and to incorporate evidence from other disciplines into their work. This reflects attitudes that were consolidated by our marriage 37 years ago, that follows from discussions she and I had from the very beginning of our relationship, and that in some sense continue to define our marriage today.

MY ENTREPRENEURSHIP AND OTHER FORAYS INTO THE REAL WORLD

My father's memory was probably the influence for me to be an entrepreneur. Not many economics professors start companies. There was something from my father that gave me the impulse to venture into the business world, to go outside the ivory tower. My drive to be an entrepreneur didn't really come from the desire to become wealthy, but more from the desire to have a genuine impact on the world.

I consider part of my entrepreneurship to be books with inventions in them, which include my 1993 book *Macro Markets*, my 2003 book *New Financial Order*, my 2008 book *Subprime Solution*, and my 2012 book *Finance and the Good Society*. These books contained specific, though incompletely worked out, proposals for the creation of new financial markets and institutions and different types of regulations of financial markets, as well as a broad vision for the future of our society in the financial capitalism that is sweeping the world.

Then too I became directly involved in establishing companies that would pursue some of these ideas, picking and choosing among them for some that we might realistically get started with the help of a team of people. I continued to work full time at Yale University, which tolerates, even encourages, such activities as long as time devoted to them is limited.

In 1991 Case Shiller Weiss, Inc. (CSW) was launched with my colleague Karl Case and my former student at Yale, Allan Weiss, to produce an array of home price indices. That company was a success, for it led to the production of the Case-Shiller home price indices as well as an automated valuation model (AVM) for home prices that our team developed, and which we called CASA. We were the first company to have automated home valuation available to the general public on the Internet. We sold CSW in 2002 to Fiserv, Inc., and in 2013 it was resold to CoreLogic, Inc.

When we first sold CSW we kept a patent that Allan and I wrote, for *MacroShares*, paired long and short securities tied to an index. We used that to launch a new company MacroMarkets LLC, named after my book *Macro Markets*. We hired Samuel Masucci to be CEO of MacroMarkets and this new company licensed the production of our home price indices to Standard & Poor's in 2006, creating the S&P/Case-Shiller Home Price Indices. At the same time, our company worked with the Chicago Mercantile Exchange to launch home price futures in 2006 on each of ten U.S. cities and on the U.S. as a whole. MacroMarkets LLC is no longer active, and unfortunately did not manage to establish the MacroShares we hoped would importantly change the economy. I was quite disappointed that my dream of establishing new markets that might benefit many people did not succeed better, but the experience has only strengthened my belief that such new markets will become important eventually.

Another line of work outside of traditional economics that I have consistently done over the years has been questionnaire survey work about economic attitudes and opinions. I did a questionnaire survey of individual and institutional investors within days of the biggest one-day stock market crash ever, on October 19, 1987, asking people why they sold that day. Starting in 1989, and to this day with the help of the Yale School of Management, I have been doing regular surveys of stock market participants' attitudes. With my colleague Yoshiro Tsutsui, we extended these surveys to Japan. Starting in 1988, working with Karl Case, I began regular surveys of home buyers, inquiring why they bought when they did. In 1990 I began working with Maxim Boycko in Russia and Vladimir Korobov in Ukraine, comparing attitudes to free markets across countries. Many of the questions on these surveys are open-ended, with space for write-in answers, which I think help me to understand what people were really thinking at economic turning points.

These surveys are motivated by sociological and cultural-anthropological literature, which I think are underappreciated by most economists. It pays to be a good listener (without taking answers at face value) when trying to understand human behavior. I particularly enjoy listening to a large sample of people. If we don't listen to their views at important historical junctures, we will later never be able to understand the events.

Undertaking such surveys is difficult, requires an organization, and is in a way entrepreneurial. Indeed, one of my colleagues at MacroMarkets, Terry Loebs, I think partly out of our collaboration, has just started a new survey research company called Pulsenomics

After having first begun to write for newspapers in college, I have in recent years returned to writing newspaper columns, with regular columns at newspapers that are members of Project Syndicate since 2003 and at *The New York Times* as a regular *Economic View* columnist since 2007. Still today, I do not regard these columns as simply popularizations of economics, but as part of a dialogue that informs academic research as well. Academic economics needs this kind of research. Economics is less of an exact science than are the traditional sciences, for it is more in need of approximations and has less control of circumstances, and must keep up with continuing fundamental changes in our economic world. Hence a broad looking-around at what is going on currently is especially important for economics.

LOOKING BACK ON A LONG CAREER IN ECONOMICS

I suspect that most people with a scientific proclivity sense a sort of personal tragedy that the best one can do with one's interests is to specialize quite a bit. One cannot understand it all, cannot work through it all, so one will never know the final answers to all of one's deepest questions. Economics became my specialty. But I have discovered after many years that the tragedy is not really so severe, as I find myself interacting with people in more and more branches of social and even physical and biological sciences, and with kindred spirits in management and business and legal professions as well, as we try to find the truth. For me the sense of tragedy has faded with all the rewarding experiences and friendships with people of diverse intellectual positions I have had in the course of my career.

Having been devoted to the field of economics now nearly a half century, I think that I certainly made a good decision to go into economics. As I have detailed here, my temperament was suited for such career, and to pursue the research directions I chose. Even if economics lacks some of the exact science qualities that had been my original interest as an adolescent, the field seems to offer interesting challenges to those who admire the essence of a scientific method. I haven't been disappointed by the field.

My various co-authors were chosen by me (or me by them, sometimes with the help of matchmakers) to help look for evidence of the truth behind theories. I have not found it difficult within the economics profession to find congenial colleagues who can share in this quest to genuinely advance our understanding.

Working with other people, colleagues and students, has been rewarding as well because with them I have found more and more that our work has a moral basis, in finding ways to improve lives and our society.

Speculative Asset Prices[1]

Prize Lecture, December 8, 2013

by Robert J. Shiller[2]
Yale University, New Haven, CT, U.S.A.

I will start this lecture with some general thoughts on the determinants of long-term asset prices such as stock prices or home prices: what, ultimately, drives these prices to change as they do from time to time and how can we interpret these changes? I will consider the discourse in the profession about the role of rationality in the formation of these prices and the growing trend towards behavioral finance and, more broadly, behavioral economics, the growing acceptance of the importance of alternative psychological, sociological, and epidemiological factors as affecting prices. I will focus on the statistical methods that allow us to learn about the sources of price volatility in the stock market and the housing market, and evidence that has led to the behavioral finance revolution in financial thought in recent decades.

The broader purpose here is to appreciate the promise of financial technology. There is a great deal of popular skepticism about financial institutions afoot these days, after the financial and economic crisis that has dragged on ever since the severest days in 2008. I want to consider the possibilities for the future of finance in general terms, rather than focusing on current stopgap measures to

---

[1] This is a substantial revision (February 1, 2014) of the lecture I gave for the Sveriges Riksbank Prize in Economic Sciences in Memory of Alfred Nobel, on December 8, 2013, www.nobelprize.org/mediaplayer/index.php?id=1996.

[2] Sterling Professor of Economics, Yale University, New Haven CT 06511 (e-mail robert.shiller@yale.edu). I am grateful to Nicholas C. Barberis, John Y. Campbell, Peter J. Dougherty, and Bengt Holmstrom for help on interpretation of the literature and comments on drafts of this lecture.

deal opportunistically with symptoms of our current economic crisis. The talk about the rationality of markets is a precursor to this talk of financial technology, for it underpins our notions of what is possible with technology.

I will conclude that the markets have already been "human-factors-engineered" to function remarkably well, and that as our understanding of the kind of psychology that leads to bubbles and related problems is improved, we can further innovate to improve the functioning of these markets.

1. PRICE VOLATILITY, RATIONAL EXPECTATIONS, AND BUBBLES

The history of thought in financial markets has shown a surprising lack of consensus about a very fundamental question: what ultimately causes all those fluctuations in the price of speculative assets like corporate stocks, commodities, or real estate? One might think that so basic a question would have long ago been confidently answered. But the answer to this question is not so easily found.[3]

At the same time, there has been an equally widespread acceptance in other quarters of the idea that markets are substantially driven by psychology. Indeed, since 1991 Richard Thaler and I have been directors of the National Bureau of Economic Research program in behavioral economics, which has featured hundreds of papers that seem mostly at odds with a general sense of rationality in the markets.[4]

The term "speculative bubble" is often used and applied carelessly. The word "bubble" first became popular at the time of the Mississippi Bubble in European stock markets that came to an end in the 1720, a time often mentioned as one of craziness, but whether that was best described as a time of wild irrationality still remains controversial, see Garber (2000) and Goetzmann *et al.* (2013). I would say that a speculative bubble is a peculiar kind of fad or social epidemic that is regularly seen in speculative markets; not a wild orgy of delusions but a natural consequence of the principles of social psychology coupled with imperfect news media and information channels. In the second edition of my book *Irrational Exuberance* I offered a definition of bubble that I thought represents the term's best use:

> A situation in which news of price increases spurs investor
> enthusiasm which spreads by psychological contagion from person
> to person, in the process amplifying stories that might justify the

---

[3] There is a similarly disconcerting lack of consensus in the economics profession over what drives fluctuations from quarter to quarter in aggregate economic activity, as measured by gross domestic product, see Shiller (1987), Akerlof and Shiller (2009).

[4] http://www.econ.yale.edu/~shiller/behfin/index.htm

> price increase and bringing in a larger and larger class of investors, who, despite doubts about the real value of the investment, are drawn to it partly through envy of others' successes and partly through a gambler's excitement.

My definition puts the epidemic nature, the emotions of investors, and the nature of the news and information media at center of the definition of the bubble. Bubbles are not, in my mind, about craziness of investors. They are rather about how investors are buffeted *en masse* from one superficially plausible theory about conventional valuation to another. One thinks of how a good debater can take either side of many disputes, and, if the debater on the other side has weak skills, can substantially convince the audience of either side. College debate teams demonstrate this phenomenon regularly, and they do it by suppressing certain facts and amplifying and embellishing others. In the case of bubbles, the sides are changed from time to time by the feedback of price changes—at the proliferation caused by price increases of reminders of basic facts that a debater might use to defend the bubble—and the news media are even better at presenting cases than are typical college debaters.

Investing ideas can spread like epidemics. Economists traditionally have not shown much interest in epidemiology, sociology, social psychology, or communications and journalism, and it takes some effort for them to consider such alien academic traditions.

There is a troublesome split between efficient markets enthusiasts (who believe that market prices incorporate accurately all public information and so doubt that bubbles even exist) and those who believe in behavioral finance (who tend to believe that bubbles and other such contradictions to efficient markets can be understood only with reference to other social sciences such as psychology). I suspect that some of the apparent split is illusory, from the problem that there is not a widely accepted definition of the term "bubble." The metaphor might suggest that speculative bubbles always burst suddenly and irrevocably, as soap bubbles seem to do, without exception. That would be silly, for history does not generally support the catastrophic burst notion. Though the abrupt ends of stock market booms in 1929, 2000 and 2007 might seem consonant with such a metaphor, these booms were reflated again before long (1933–37, 2003–2007, and 2009–present respectively).

I think that the eventuality of a sudden irrevocable burst is not essential to the general term speculative bubble as the term is used appropriately. The metaphor may be misleading: It suggests more drama than there in fact is, imparting a sense of uniqueness to current events, which might help explain the popularity of the term by news reporters vying for the attention of readers. Just as reporters like to stir people up by reporting that an index has hit another record high (disregarding the fact that record highs occur quite often, especially since reporters hardly ever correct for inflation) so too they like to suggest the possibility of a collapse in the offing that will be remembered many years later.

I sometimes wish we had a different metaphor. One might consider substituting the term "wind trade," Dutch *Windhandel* a term that was used during the Tulipmania, the famous boom and burst in tulip prices in the early 1600s, sharing the reference to thin air, but not encapsulating it in a fragile bubble.

Curiously, in his Nobel Lecture in Medicine during the 2013 Nobel Week in Stockholm, James E. Rothman (2013) brought in soap bubbles too, for their analogy to the cell vesicles that his Nobel Prize research was about. He showed a movie of two soap bubbles being physically pressed together, and, surprisingly to most of us, they did not burst but merged into a single larger bubble. That's analogous to what cell vesicles can do, he said. It led me to wonder if we could say that the stock market bubble and the housing bubble of the early 2000s somehow merged into a larger bubble that created the financial crisis that burst around 2008. Imaginative thinking is fun, and maybe even inspirational, but we cannot let the bubble metaphor, or any simple metaphor, guide our models beyond the very beginnings, for any metaphor will surprise if we carried it to its absurd conclusions.

A. Efficient Markets Theory

From the very beginning, in his 1964 Ph.D. dissertation, written under the supervision of Merton Miller and Harry Roberts, Eugene Fama found that stock prices are not very forecastable. He found then that the average correlation coefficient between successive days' log price changes over the thirty Dow Jones Industrial Average stocks between 1957 and 1962 was only 0.03, which he described as "probably unimportant for both the statistician and the investor."[5] The same year saw the appearance of Paul Cootner's *The Random Character of Stock Market Prices*, which reached similar conclusions about market efficiency.

The "efficient markets theory," widely attributed to Fama and the academic work that he stimulated, maintains that prices have a rational basis in terms of fundamentals like the optimal forecast of earnings, or assessments of the standard deviation of risk factors facing corporations. As the theory went, because they are rationally determined, they are changed from day to day primarily by genuine news, which is by its very nature essentially unforecastable. There

[5] Fama (1964), Table 10 and p. 70.

was an efficient markets revolution in finance, propelled by Fama's work. I was part of the movement then, less than a decade later, with my Ph.D. dissertation (1972) about the efficiency of the long-term bond market.

B. Alternative Views and Forecastability of Returns

These conclusions came against a backdrop of public interest then in speculative bubbles encouraged by the strong bull market in the United States: real stock prices more than quadrupled in the 16 years from 1948 to 1964. John Kenneth Galbraith's best-selling 1954 book *The Great Crash, 1929*, described in literary terms the follies of the boom of the 1920s and subsequent collapse and concluded that "the chances for a recurrence of a speculative orgy are rather good"[6]

His book was followed up by another popular book, Charles Poor Kindleberger's *Manias, Panics, and Crashes*, 1978, which used a similar method of recounting of human events laced with descriptions of human foolishness. Neither of them made much use of academic research in psychology or sociology, writing many years before the behavioral finance revolution, and so they came across to some as insubstantial. While both Galbraith and Kindleberger were respected academics, and the stories in their books were often compelling, many felt that their works did not have the scientific credibility of the careful data analysis that was widely taken to support market efficiency, though then again, they were provocative.

Ultimately, the question in reconciling the apparently conflicting views comes down to that of constructing the right statistical tests. It turns out that the apparently impressive evidence for market efficiency was not unimpeachable.

2. EXPECTED PRESENT VALUE MODELS AND EXCESS VOLATILITY

The simplest version of the efficient markets model—which maintains that stock price movements can be interpreted entirely as reflecting information about future payouts of dividends, and that hence that there is never a good time or bad time to enter the market—has, ever since the efficient markets revolution began, maintained a powerful hold on scholarly imaginations as a worthy approximation to more complex models. This form sets price equal to the expectation, conditional on publicly available information at the time of the present value of future dividends discounted at a constant rate through time:

[6] Galbraith 1954 p. 194.

$$P_t = E_t \sum_{k=0}^{\infty} \frac{D_{t+k}}{(1+r)^{k+1}} \quad (1)$$

One way to test this efficient markets model is to regress the return between t and $t + 1$, $t = 1, \ldots, n$ onto information variables known at time t, I_t, $t = 1, \ldots, n$. Often, these tests can be described approximately as tests of the "random walk hypothesis," that price changes are purely random and unforecastable. One accepts the efficient markets model if the coefficients of the information variables used to forecast future returns or price changes are not significantly different from zero. Moreover, even if the model is rejected, if the proportion of variance in returns that is predicted is small, one concludes that the model is a good approximation to reality.

These tests, and various analogues of them, are the kinds of tests of market efficiency that abounded in the literature. But the power of such tests of perpetual unforecastability of returns against an alternative that represents the world as driven entirely by temporary fads and fashions—with no fundamental reason for any change in prices—can be very low, since plausible such alternatives also imply that only a tiny fraction of month-to-month returns is forecastable. Shiller (1984, 1989), Summers (1986).

Many tests of market efficiency use daily observations of prices, and because the observations come so frequently, there may be many hundreds of observations, even if the span of the data is only a few decades. There is a tendency for many people to think that hundreds of observations must be a lot of data, but it is not necessarily a lot of data from the standpoint of distinguishing an efficient markets model from a relevant alternative.

We might, for example, be trying to distinguish using price time series data a random walk from a continuous-time first-order autoregressive process.[7] In the former, whether prices are too high or too low has no ability to predict future changes. In the latter, when prices are too high relative to the mean they should tend eventually to fall (a sort of bursting of the bubble, though not a sudden catastrophic one). But, tests may have very little power to distinguish the two models, if the autoregressive parameter is close enough to one, even with a large number of observations, even with millions of minute to minute observations. With a fixed span of data increasing the frequency of observation, even to the limit of continuous observation, does not bring power to one, Shiller and Perron (1985), Phillips and Perron (1988).

---

[7] In continuous time, we are speaking of distinguishing a Wiener process from an Ornstein-Uhlenbeck process.

The *Scientific Background* for the 2013 Nobel Prize in Economics (Economic Sciences Prize Committee of the Royal Swedish Academy of Sciences 2013) emphasized the results of this year's laureates as confirming that there is better forecastability (in terms of R squared) of speculative asset returns for longer time horizons. This accords with longstanding advice that investors should be patient, that they cannot expect to see solid returns over short time intervals. But this is just the opposite of what one would expect in weather forecasting, where experts can forecast tomorrow's temperature fairly well but can hardly forecast a year from tomorrow's temperature.

It is easy to see why short-term forecastability of price changes in investable assets should in some sense be unlikely: if investment returns were substantially forecastable from day to day, it would be too easy to get rich in a year or so by trading on these forecasts, and we know it cannot be easy to make a lot of money trading. This notion was formalized in a continuous-time framework by Sims (1990), who defined "instantaneous unpredictability" of a speculative asset price by the requirement that the R squared of the prediction from time t to time $t + s$ goes to zero as s goes to zero. He showed under certain regularity conditions that if prices are not instantaneously unpredictable then simple rapid-trading schemes could achieve unbounded profits, which of course cannot match reality.

Taking these primal reasons to doubt that returns are forecastable over short horizons into account, the low R squared in many tests of short-run market efficiency is neither surprising nor interesting. The tests tell us only the obvious, and do not tell us about the rationality of markets beyond that people are not missing easy opportunities to get rich very fast.

I proposed that an alternative class of tests, based on the estimated volatility of returns, tests for "excess volatility" would have more power against the important alternatives to efficient markets theory, first for the bond market, rejecting the expectations model of the term structure of interest rates with U.S. and U.K. data (Shiller 1979) and then rejecting the simplest efficient markets model for the U.S. stock market (1981a).[8] Independent work by Kenneth Singleton (1980) used a variance bounds test to reject the expectations model of the term structure of interest rates with U.S. data, and Stephen LeRoy and Richard Porter (1981) rejected the simple efficient markets theory for the U.S. stock market. Variance bounds tests were also used to test consumption-discount-based efficient markets models, (Shiller 1982, Lars Hansen and Ravi Jagannathan 1991).

---

[8] The volatility tests were partly inspired by work Jeremy Siegel did (1977) which involved calculation of ex-post rational price series.

Efficient markets models also imply bounds on the covariance between asset prices (Beltratti and Shiller 1993).

These tests may be more powerful than regression tests of the basic efficient markets notions against important alternatives. It is true that under the conventional assumptions of the regression model the usual t-test for the coefficient of a forecasting variable in a regression with excess return as the dependent variable has well-known optimality properties. But testing market efficiency by regressing excess returns on information variables makes no use of the terminal condition that requires that all movements in prices need to be justified by information about subsequent movements in fundamentals. I showed (1981) that if we broaden the maintained hypothesis for this condition, then a regression test is not optimal. In fact, under certain extreme assumptions about data alignment, a simple variance ratio test, instead of a regression test, may be uniformly most powerful.[9]

Another kind of test of market efficiency is the event study, which is an analysis of the effects of a specified event (such as a stock split) on the price of an asset in the days before and after the event, taking many different examples of a kind of event and showing the average price performance. It is analogous to a regression test, of a panel of time series of daily returns of many stocks on a dummy variable representing the day of a certain kind of event and on dummies representing the days after the event became public. The test of market efficiency is a test for significance of the coefficients of the dummies corresponding to days after the event. The first event study in the academic literature has been taken to be Dolley (1933), but, as the *Scientific Background* for the 2013 Nobel Prize in Economics notes, it was not until the impressive 1969 paper by Eugene Fama, Lawrence Fisher, Michael Jensen and Richard Roll that it was shown that, conditioning on an event, one tends to see a lack of any consistent and important further price response after the event is public knowledge. Dolley in his 1933 article was immersed in all the details of stock splits, and of course did not mention efficient markets theory. Fama, Fisher, Jensen and Roll instead showed evidence for this newly developed and expanded theory, evidence that could be seen visually impressively in a plot of stock returns before and after the event.

---

[9] John Cochrane, in his review of my volatility tests (1991), stressed a sense in which there is an equivalence of volatility tests and regression tests. But this is about the equivalence of null hypotheses, not equivalence of test power. Cochrane later followed this up with a paper (2008) recognizing the importance of the terminal condition; see also Lewellen and Campbell and Yogo (2006).

But again, the efficient markets tests, which are essentially the same as regression tests, do not have the power to tell us whether there are also bubbles affecting prices, or even whether the major component of stock price movements comes from bubbles.

The variance bounds test rejections of market efficiency could not be dismissed as correct but unimportant, as were the inefficiencies that the efficient markets literature had discovered, for they suggested that most of the variability of the aggregate stock market was not explainable as related to information about future fundamentals.

Critics of the variance bounds tests became abundant, and I endeavored at first to answer some of them, answering Terry Marsh and Robert Merton (1986) in Shiller (1986) and answering Allan Kleidon (1986) in Shiller (1988). But the volume of the literature expanded beyond my abilities to respond, and significantly changed its direction as well. Sometimes the disagreements got abstract and seemed to raise deep issues about epistemology or the philosophy of logic. I must leave it to a broader professional consensus what is the outcome of this debate.

I collected my papers on the subject and summarized the literatures in my book *Market Volatility*, 1989, at which point I largely abandoned my econometric work on excess volatility. Others continued the line of work, and much more has happened since.

A. Visual Portrayals of Excess Volatility and of the Stock Market as Forecaster

Just as event studies visually convinced many readers of some merits of efficient markets theory by showing event study plots of stock prices before and after an event, so too other simple plots seem to have been convincing in a different way that stock market are really not so efficient.

Figure 1 is an updated version of one that I showed in my 1981 paper, a third of a century ago, of the real level of the stock market since 1871, as well as the behavior through time of the actual present value of future real dividends discounted at a constant rate. The real stock price series is one published by Standard & Poor's, called the S&P Composite (after 1957 the S&P 500) deflated by the U.S. consumer price index.

The earlier version of this plot turned out to be the centerpiece of that paper, judging from the attention that others gave to it. Sometimes a simple plot seems to be more disturbing than a formal analysis. Looking at the data is like seeing a photojournalist's account of a historical event rather than reading a chronology: it is more immediate and invites intuitive comparisons.

To produce this figure, the present value of dividends for each date in 1871–2013 was computed from the actual subsequent real dividends using a constant real discount rate $r = 7.6\%$ per annum, equal to the historical average real return on the market since 1871. For this figure, we can make use of the actual dividends, as published by Standard & Poor's since 1926 (and extended back to 1871 by Alfred Cowles 1939 as I described in my book (1989)). We did not know dividends after 1979 when I published the original version of this figure, and we do not know at this writing of dividends after 2013.

For this lecture, in 2013 as I did in 1981, I made some simple assumptions about the as-yet-unseen future dividends, beyond 2013. This time I used a conventional dividend discount model, the Gordon Model, using the most recent 2013 S&P 500 real dividend as a base for forecasts of dividends after 2013 showing two alternative assumptions about dividends after 2013. In one, I assumed that real dividends will grow forever from the last observed dividend, in 2013, at the same average growth rate as over the most recent ten years, 5.1% per year, which gives a 2013 value of 1292 for P^*. In another, the calculations are the same but the growth rate of dividends after 2013 are taken as the geometric average growth rate over the last thirty years, 2.5% a year. This gives a 2013 value of 669 for P*. Both of these may be contrasted with real market values of the S&P 500 index over the year 2013 ranging from 1494 to 1802.[10]

Should we take the latest ten years real dividend growth as a guide to the future, rather than the last 30 years or some other interval? The ten-year data are more recent, but ten years is a short time historically speaking, and the years 2003 to 2013 were unusual, starting with the aftermath of the 2001 recession, and encompassing the biggest financial crisis and government stimulus packages since the Great Depression. Reasonable people will certainly find reasons to differ. Worse than that, there is no objective way to forecast dividends out for decades, which is why I showed both here, as a crude indication of uncertainty today about future dividends and why it is hard to imagine that the market somehow "knows" the correct optimal forecast.

The point of showing the two different P* series is that, clearly, there is substantial uncertainty about the present value of dividends after 2013, but there is

---

[10] Jeremy Siegel (2005), (2008) has made the point that since the dividend payout rate for earnings has been trending down since World War II, dividend growth should be higher in the future than it was. If companies reinvest earnings rather than pay them out, they should have more dividends to pay in the future. The validity of this theory is not without doubters. Arnott and Asness (2003) point out that perhaps lower dividend payouts may reflect managers' decision in the face of evidence that they have that earnings growth will be lower.

not so much variability from year to year, as seen today, about the present value of subsequent dividends for earlier years. For earlier years, say before 1980, 2013 is so far in the future and is discounted so heavily that over a wide range of possible 2013 dividend values there is not much difference in P*.

The striking fact is that by either assumption the present value of dividends (on the log scale used in the figure) looks pretty much like a steady exponential growth line, while the stock market oscillates a great deal around it. I asked in 1981: if, as efficient markets theory asserts, the actual price is the optimal forecast as of any date of the present value as of that date, why is the stock market so volatile?

Different people have different reactions to this figure, but a common reaction is that the efficient markets model $P_t = E_t\left(P_t^*\right)$ looks implausible here. Why is price jumping around so much if the value it is tracking is just such a simple trend? It is not that P_t should always look smoother through time than P_t^*, for it is consistent with the model that there can be sudden shifts in price when there is important new information about subtle changes in trend. But it would seem that important new information should be something that occurs only rarely, given the smooth nature of dividends.

To see the problem for efficient markets here, imagine that the series labeled P_t^* is not price but air temperature, and that P_t is a weather forecaster's forecast of the temperature for that day *t*. We might be inclined to label this weather

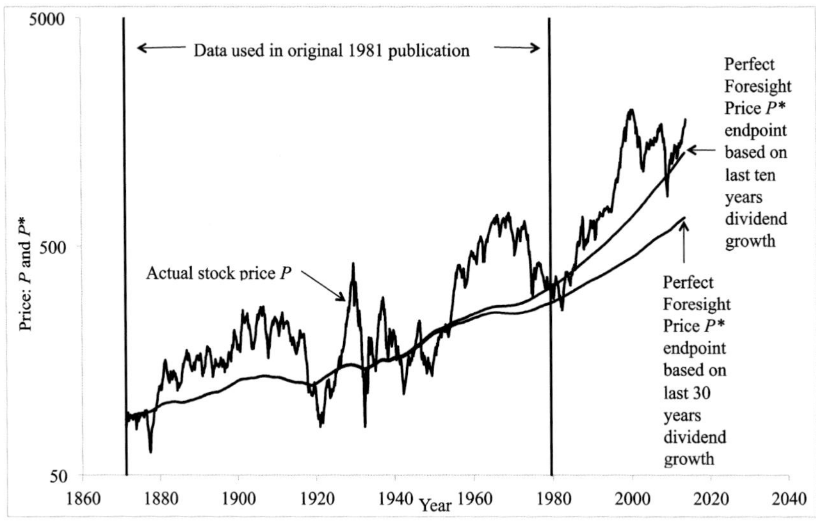

FIGURE 1. Real Standard & Poor's Composite Stock Price Index along with Present values with constant discount rate of subsequent real dividends accruing to the index 1871–1913. The two present values differ in their assumption about dividend growth after 2013.

forecaster as insane. Even though in the stock market there isn't immediate feedback to the forecaster about forecast errors, still a forecaster should avoid adjusting forecasts up and down frequently, unless there is actual new information, and clearly there wasn't, not information about something that actually happened in stock market history.

One very basic thing that is learned from this figure is that the model that people essentially know the future, a model that is often suggested as an approximation, is wildly wrong in all periods. Sometimes people have suggested that the low stock prices seen in the Great Depression of the 1930s were justified because people rationally saw the damage to future real dividends caused by the Depression. But, in fact, at the worst of the stock market depression, in 1932, subsequent dividends just weren't low enough for long enough to depress P^*_{1932} by much at all. Nothing has ever deflected real dividends for very long from a long-run growth trend of a couple percent a year.

In my original paper (1981), I detrended the data (as is shown in a reproduction of that plot in the *Scientific Background* (2013) shown on the Nobel Foundation website), thinking that it is reasonable to assume that people know the trend. Under that assumption, the efficient markets model implies that the variance around trend should be less for P than for P^*, which is plainly not the case in Figure 1. But, there was a lot of negative reaction by critics of my paper to the assumption that the trend is essentially known.

Generally, these criticisms held that there was always some reason to think that the path of dividends might eventually depart markedly from its historical growth path, and that investors were evaluating constant new information about that possibility, and that they were rational to do so even if the dividend growth path never deviated far for long from a trend. This assumes that all the fluctuations are because of genuine information about those "black swan" outlier events that might have happened in more than a century but just didn't happen. Some of the criticism had to do with the possibility that the dividend series might have a unit root, and so that the apparent smooth trend was just a chance outcome that might not be continued into the future.[11]

The uncertainty about the present value of dividends after 2013 as shown in Figure 1 does highlight an important problem. At every point in history there must have been some such uncertainty about future dividends. There are always

[11] Unit root problems pose potentially serious problems for financial econometrics, see Torous (2004), Campbell, and Yogo (2006), Cochrane (2007). Campbell and I (1988) proposed log-differencing to recast excess volatility tests in more robust terms, West (1988) showed another elegant approach, which strengthened the evidence for excess volatility.

factors that creative minds can bring up that would suggest a higher or lower rate of growth of dividends in the future.

For example, can we tell an efficient markets story why the stock market was so low in the Great Depression? The present value of actual future dividends was not particularly low in the Depression, but maybe people thought that they would be low, given the extant theories of the time. Or maybe they thought that the government would eventually nationalize the stock market without compensation. One might say that it would not be manifestly irrational, not crazy, to believe such stories. But, why, then, do these stories come and go through time, causing the fluctuations in the market?

B. Variations on the Present Value Model

Of course, as we have noted, the basic notion of efficient markets does not necessarily require that discount rates are constant or that returns are not forecastable. A more general form of efficient markets would allow discount rates to depend on the time-varying one-period rate of interest:

$$P_t = E_t\left(P_t^{*r}\right) = E_t \sum_{k=0}^{\infty} \prod_{j=0}^{k} \frac{1}{(1 + r_{t+j} + \varphi)} D_{t+k} \tag{2}$$

Or, in a model proposed by LeRoy (1973) and Lucas (1978), it could depend on consumption, using the marginal rate of substitution between consumption in successive periods as a discount rate:

$$P_t = E_t\left(P_t^{*C}\right) = E_t \sum_{k=0}^{\infty} \prod_{j=0}^{k} M_{t+j} D_{t+k} \tag{3}$$

where M_t = marginal rate of substitution in consumption between t and $t + 1$, which is, assuming constant relative risk aversion A, $\rho(C_t / C_{t+1})^A$ and C_t is real per capita consumption at time t.

Figure 2 shows the actual stock price in the U.S. and the perfect foresight stock price corresponding to each of the three measures.[12] Once again, the figure reveals that there is little correspondence between any of these measures

[12] The parameter φ was estimated to make the average $r_t + \varphi$ equal the average real return on the stock market 1871-2013. The parameter A was set at four and ρ at one. The one-year interest rate is pieced together from various sources as described in Shiller (1989, 2005) and real per capita consumption is from the U.S. National Income and Product Accounts.

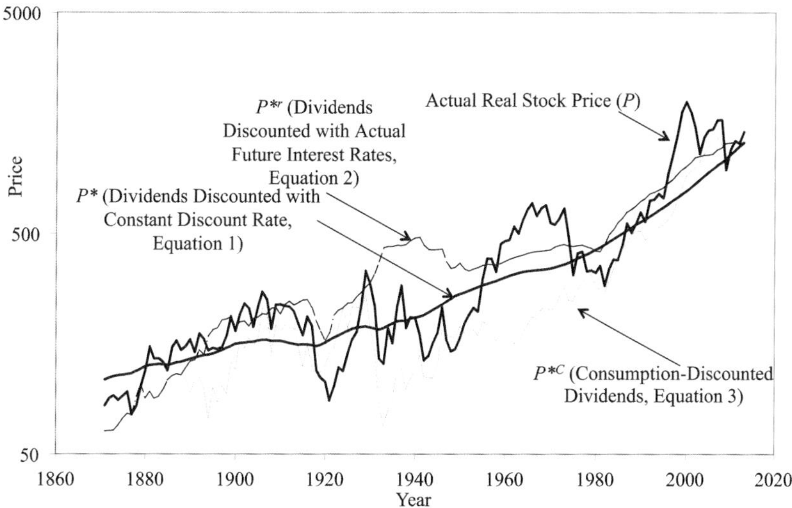

FIGURE 2. Real Standard & Poor's Composite Stock Price Index along with three present values of subsequent real dividends accruing to the index, 1871–2013. All three present values assume real dividend growth 2003–13 will continue forever after 2013. The three present values differ from each other only in the assumed time series of discount rates.

of ex-post rational price and actual stock price. People did not behave, in setting stock prices, as if they knew the future of these variables and reacted rationally to this knowledge. Moreover, if we assume that they did not actually have knowledge of the future, then one is led to wonder why the actual stock prices varied through time as much or more than the perfect foresight prices did.

There are continuing attempts to modify the consumption-based model to improve its fit, Campbell and Cochrane (1999) and Lars Hansen, in his Nobel Lecture (2013) but not yet any model that could be set alongside Figure 2 here as an inspiring vindication of efficient markets theory.

John Campbell and John Ammer (1993) did a variation decomposition of unexpected excess returns using time series methods and U.S. postwar data. The decomposition is based on the log linearization of the present value relation used in Campbell and Shiller (1988). The time $t+1$ innovation $E_{t+1} - E_t$ in the excess return over the risk free rate e_{t+1} can be shown, with a terminal stationarity condition, as a tautology, to be the sum of three innovations:

$$e_{t+1} - E_t e_{t+1} = \left(E_{t+1} - E_t\right)\left\{\sum_{j=0}^{\infty}\rho^j \Delta d_{t+1+j} - \sum_{j=0}^{\infty}\rho^j r_{t+1+j} - \sum_{j=1}^{\infty}\rho^j e_{t+1+j}\right\}$$

Using this decomposition and a vector-autoregressive model in difference form, with post World War II stock market returns, Campbell and Ammer found that excess returns innovations have a standard deviation that is two or three times greater than the standard deviation of innovations in future dividend growth. Aggregate stock market fluctuations have therefore been dominated by fluctuations in predicted future returns, not by news about future dividends paid to investors.[13]

C. Interpretations of Return Predictability

Sociologists have a possible interpretation of these results, an interpretation that reflects a body of thought that goes back over a hundred years. The market fluctuates as the sweep of history produces different mindsets at different points of time, different zeitgeists. Emile Durkheim (1893) spoke of the "collective consciousness" that represents the shared beliefs, attitudes and moral judgments that characterize a time. Maurice Halbwachs (1925) spoke of the "collective memory," the set of facts that are widely remembered at any point of time, but that are forgotten eventually if word of mouth and active news media do not perpetuate their memory. News media tend to slant their stories towards ideas of current interest, rather than useful facts that readers no longer find interesting.[14] Surely simple forgetting of past experiences affects popular judgments. How many people today could give any account of the financial panic of 1907, or of the housing boom of the late 1940s? One could stop anyone on the street in those times and get a ready account, now blank ignorance from almost everyone. When a bubble is building, the suppression of some facts and embellishment of other facts (just as with winning college debaters) occurs naturally through the decay of collective memory, when media and popular talk are no longer reinforcing memories of them, and because of the amplification of other facts through the stories generated by market events.

It is hardly plausible that speculative prices make effective use of all information about probabilities of future dividends. It is far more plausible that the aggregate stock market price changes reflect inconstant perceptions, changes which Keynes referred to with the term "animal spirits," changes that infect the thinking even of the most of the so-called "smart money" in the market. Keynes

---

[13] These results have been criticized by Goyal and Welch (2003), (2008), Chen and Zhao (2009) and Chen, Da, and Zhao (2013), and rebutted by Campbell, Polk, and Vuolteenaho (2010) and Engsted, Pedersen, and Tanggaard (2012).

[14] See Shiller (2000) and Mullainathan and Shleifer (2005).

anticipated this in his 1921 *Treatise on Probability*, which asserted that probabilities are not precisely measurable in the sense that decision theory supposes; that there are always ambiguities. He said that because of this fundamental ambiguity, in financial transactions there is inevitably an "element of caprice."[15] Critical decisions are made on impulse rather than calculation. One may have done calculations of probabilities, but one usually does not fully believe one's own calculations, and proceeds on gut feeling.

In an early behavioral finance paper of mine, that I wrote thirty years ago, "Stock Prices and Social Dynamics" (1984), I proposed yet another expected present value model for consideration as a model of stock prices, though it is one that we cannot plot back to 1871 as we did with the three expected present models shown and plotted above, because it depends on a time-varying factor that is not objectively quantifiable, at least for now. I have been attempting to measure a stock market factor like this with survey techniques, of individual and institutional investors, but only since 1989. There are other surveys of investor sentiment as well, but the results are hardly definitive. My surveys of individual and institutional investors starting in 1989[16] as well as my surveys with Karl E. Case of homebuyers starting in 1988[17] are being continued by the Yale School of Management.

Thirty years ago I called this as yet unmeasured factor the demand for stocks by ordinary investors, but today let us call it animal spirits, A_t. A_t represents the demand for stocks per share at time t by everyone who is not smart money, people not really paying attention, not systematic, not engaged in research, buffeted by casually-encountered information. They are certainly the majority of investors. Suppose, to take this model to an extreme, that their opinions reflect nothing more than changing fashions and fads and idle talk and overreaction to irrelevant news stories. A_t is likely to be sluggish through time (usually people don't all change their naïve opinions *en masse* on a dime).

The core idea here was that there are also smart money investors, who are not subject to illusion, but have to be wary of investing in the stock market not only because future dividends are not known with certainty, but also because these ordinary investors are somewhat unpredictable and their erratic

[15] Keynes (1921) p. 23.

[16] http://som.yale.edu/faculty-research/our-centers-initiatives/international-center-finance/data/stock-market-confidence. Greenwood and Shleifer (2013) examine the relation to stock price data of investor sentiment indices from six different survey sources including mine.

[17] Case and Shiller (1988, 2004), Case, Shiller, and Thompson (2012).

behavior could cause price changes that might produce losses in the market for the smart money if they invest too much in it. For these investors, information is constantly coming in about the likely future values of A_t and, as with all genuinely new information, this new information is uncorrelated and unpredictable through time. I supposed the demand per share for stocks by the smart money equals their rationally expected excess return on the stock market over and above an alternative riskless return r which I take for simplicity to be constant through time, the difference divided by a constant risk factor φ. The two demands, the demand of the ordinary investors plus the demand of the smart money, must add up to one for the markets to clear. Solving the resulting rational expectations model forward leaves us with our fourth present value model:[18]

$$P_t = E_t\left(P_t^{*A}\right) = E_t \sum_{k=0}^{\infty} \frac{1}{(1+r+\varphi)^{k+1}} \left(D_{t+k} + \varphi A_{t+k}\right) \tag{4}$$

If $\varphi = 0$, smart money dominates and this collapses to equation (1) above. As φ goes to infinity, smart money drops out, it collapses to $P_t = A_t$, and ordinary investors completely determine the price. It is the intermediate case that is interesting. In this intermediate case, price may have low predictability from day to day or month to month, consistent with efficient markets theory, even if animal spirits dominate the broad movements in P_t. The price is responding to news about animal spirits, not just news about future dividends. Event study tests, described above, testing market reaction over time to news about and subsequently reality of such events as stock splits, may come out as beautifully supporting efficient markets, for much of the effect of the event on both dividends and animal spirits will be incorporated into price as soon as the event becomes news to the smart money, not when the event actually happens.

There is another important argument widely used for efficient markets, the argument that a model like (4) with an intermediate φ cannot represent a stable equilibrium because the smart money would get richer and richer and eventually take over the market, and φ would go to zero. In fact this will not generally happen, for there is a natural recycling of investor abilities. The smart money people usually do not start out with a lot of money and it takes them many years to acquire significant wealth, meanwhile they get old and retire, or they rationally lose interest in doing the work to pursue their advantage after they have acquired sufficient wealth to live comfortably on. The market will be efficient enough that advantages to beating the market are sufficiently small and

---

[18] This is equation (3) in that paper, with slight changes in notation.

uncertain and slow to repay one's efforts, so most smart people will devote their time to more personally meaningful things—like managing a company, getting a Ph.D. in finance, or some other more enjoyable activity—leaving the market substantially to ordinary investors. Genuinely smart money investors cannot in their normal life cycle amass enough success experience to prove to ordinary investors that they can manage their money effectively: it takes too many years and there is too much fundamental uncertainty for them to be able to do that assuredly. By the time they prove themselves they may have lost the will or ability to continue (Shleifer and Vishny 1997).

D. Individual Stocks

These conclusions about the aggregate stock market, however, do not carry over fully to individual stocks. Paul Samuelson has asserted that:

> "[The market is] micro efficient but macro inefficient. That is, individual stock price variations are dominated by actual new information about subsequent dividends, but aggregate stock market variations are dominated by bubbles."[19]

Tuomo Vuolteenaho (2002), using methodology analogous to that of Campbell and Ammer, concluded that for individual stocks the variance of expected return news is approximately one half of the variance of cash-flow news. For market-adjusted individual stock log returns (log return minus cross-sectional average log return) the variance of the expected return news is only one fifth of the variance of cash-flow news. Thus, bubbles and their bursts cannot have more than a minor impact on the returns of individual stocks, and most of the variation in their returns comes from news about the future payouts the firms will make.

In a 2005 paper I did with Jeeman Jung, which looked at long-span data sets of stocks which had survived without significant capital changes for over half a century, we reached similar conclusions. To give a visual impression how well the

---

[19] Samuelson went on to say "Modern markets show considerable *micro* efficiency (for the reason that the minority who spot aberrations from micro efficiency can make money from those occurrences and, in doing so, tend to wipe out any persistent inefficienes). In no contradiction to the previous sentence, I had hypothesiszed considerable *macro* inefficiency, in the sense of long waves in the time series of aggregate indexes of security prices below and above various definitions of fundamental values." From a private letter from Paul Samuelson to John Campbell and Robert Shiller.

efficient markets theory works for individual firms, we felt that we could display how successfully dividend growth could be predicted from the dividend-price ratio. Simple efficient markets suggests that firms with relatively low dividend price ratios should eventually, in future years, show higher dividend increases as a fraction of today's price. To make such a visual diagram in such simple terms, we sought out long-lived firms (though such a procedure risks a selection bias)

We found all firms on the CRSP tape that remained alive and for which there was uninterrupted data from 1926 to 1976. There were only 49 such firms, giving us 2499 firm-year observations 1926–76. Each point on the scatter in Figure 3 shows $\sum_{k=0}^{24} \frac{D_{t+k} / P_t}{(1+r)^k}$, the present value of future changes in dividends for the next twenty-five years (measured in dollars, and discounted by the historical average stock market return) divided by current dollar price, against $\frac{D_{t-1}}{P_t}$, the current dividend divided by current price. Efficient markets with constant discount rate, equation (1), imply—if there is not a problem with our truncation of the present value at 25 years—that a regression line through these points should have a slope of minus one and a constant term equal to the constant discount rate. In words, if markets are efficient then a high dividend price yield for a particular stock today occurs only if people have a real reason to expect dividends to decline, and so demand to be compensated today for that future loss if they are to hold the stock today. Similarly, low dividend yield stocks must be those for

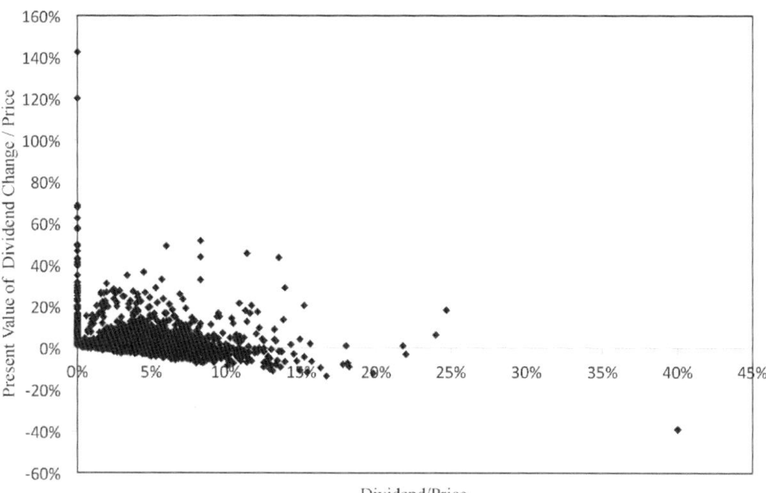

FIGURE 3. Present value of future changes in dividends plotted against the dividend price ratio for 49 U.S. individual stocks, 1926–1976, from Jung and Shiller (2005).

which there is genuine evidence that dividends will rise in the future, eventually compensating today's investors for the low dividend return they are receiving.

The estimated slope of a line fitted through this scatter is –0.5, far from the ideal −1.0 but negative as expected. The dividend-price ratio predicts subsequent dividend changes in the right direction for these firms. Zero-dividend firms (which one can see strung out along the vertical axis) tended to have appropriately high subsequent dividend growth relative to price. The right-most observation, which corresponds to the firm Schlumberger in 1931, a firm that had tried to maintain its dividend despite falling fortunes in the Great Depression, had a dividend payment that was 40% of its current price. People in the market then apparently figured out that the firm could not continue to pay such a dividend, that it would not be followed by another significant dividend for a very long time, and reflected that knowledge in the approximately 40% dividend-price ratio. In individual firms there is sometimes a lot of action in the ratios, and the action in fact often reflects real knowledge about future cash flows. That is an example of the kind of idiosyncratic knowledge about individual firms that makes the efficient markets model a useful approximation of reality for individual firms.[20]

E. Real Estate Prices

The market for real estate is larger in valuation than that of the entire stock market. According to the Financial Accounts of the United States, in 2013 the value of real estate owned by households and nonprofit organizations was $21.6 trillion, while their holdings of corporate equity shares, whether directly or indirectly, had a market value of on only $20.3 trillion.[21]

And yet, when I first joined with Karl Case to do joint work on real estate prices in the 1980s, we found that hardly any scholarly research had been done on the efficiency of real estate markets. The state of knowledge about these markets was abysmal. Under the influence of a widely-held presumption at that time that all markets must be efficient, many economists, at least in their popular pronouncements, seemed to assume that real estate markets must be efficient too.

---

[20] Ang and Bekaert (2007) conclude that the dividend yield's ability to predict dividends is not robust over sample periods or countries, but do not include individual stock data in their study.

[21] U.S. Federal Reserve Board, Z.1, Financial Accounts of the United States, Table B.100 Balance Sheet of Households and Nonprofit Organizations and Table B.100.e Balance Sheet of Households and Nonprofit Organizations with Equity Detail, December 9, 2013.

This presumption appeared to us as quite possibly wrong, based on anecdotal evidence suggesting that real estate prices are not at all well approximated by a random walk as is the case for stocks, but often tend to go in the same direction, whether up or down, again and again for years and years.

Case and I decided to try to test the efficiency of this market for single family homes, but quickly discovered the importance of a stumbling block that had inhibited research: individual homes sell extremely infrequently, with interval between sales for individual homes measured not in seconds as with stocks but in years or decades. One cannot do any of the most popular tests of efficiency with such data. No runs tests or event studies would ever be possible with individual homes, and so tests of market efficiency would have to be based on indices.

There were some home price indices of sorts available then, but they had serious problems. There was a median sales price of existing homes, published by the National Association of Realtors, but it often appeared to jump around erratically. It was just the median price of whatever homes were selling now, was not controlled for anything, and it appeared that different kinds of homes sold in different months. It had a very strong seasonality, which we suspected arose because people who sold in the summer, in phase with the academic year and the job market, typically had bigger or higher-quality homes which had higher prices.

There was also at that time a "Price of New Homes Sold," also called "Constant Quality Index," produced by the U.S. Department of Census, that was a more sophisticated hedonic index, holding constant such things as square feet of floor space and number of bedrooms, but again it was obviously not trustworthy for testing market efficiency through time since it was based on different homes every quarter, whatever and wherever homes had just been built that quarter.

So Case and I constructed our own "repeat sales" home price index based on an inspiration of his (Case 1986) and then on a method we devised that inferred price changes only from the change in prices of individual existing homes (Case and Shiller 1987, 1989, 1990). We showed how a quarterly index could be computed even if homes sell much less frequently than quarterly. We discovered that Case's inspiration was largely anticipated by Baily, Muth and Nourse (1963), but we had a number of improvements, taking better account of heteroscedasticity. Later, I made the index arithmetic and value weighted, as are the most prominent stock price indices (Shiller 1991). With my former student Allan Weiss we founded Case Shiller Weiss, Inc. in 1991 and we were the first to produce repeat sales indices in real time for regular publication. Our indices are now produced by CoreLogic, Inc., and the major indices are managed by Standard & Poor's Corporation.

A plot of our quarterly national index corrected for CPI inflation is shown in Figure 4, along with the Census Constant Quality Index, also converted to real terms.

Simply producing these data and looking at a plot, as shown in Figure 4, yields some surprises. First of all, the home price data are generally *extremely* smooth through time, except for a small amount of seasonality. Home prices do indeed go through years of price increases and then years of price decreases. So, the random walk model of home price behavior is just not even close to being true for home prices (Case and Shiller 1988). Home prices might seem to be described as in accordance with model (4) above with the parameter φ extremely large, so that the smart money, who might go in and out of the market quickly in response to news, is hardly a factor.

Secondly, while it was not apparent when we first computed these indices, it is clear from these data from today's vantage point that there was a huge boom in home prices after 2000 that was not very visible from the Census Constant Quality Index. Why is the boom and bust in home prices after 2000 so much more prominent in our repeat sales index? New homes are built where it is possible and profitable to build them, typically outside congested urban areas where price swings may be most pronounced, and so their level through time may be

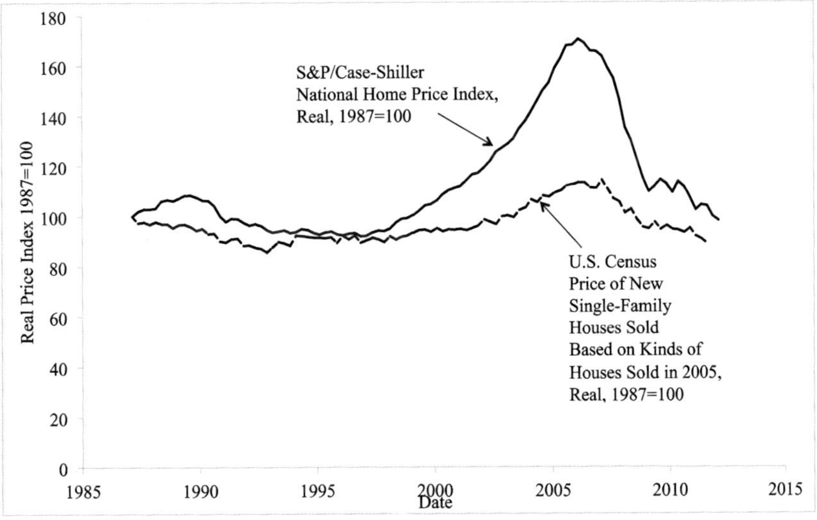

FIGURE 4. Two indices of U.S. home prices divided by the consumer price index (CPI-U), both then scaled to 1987 = 100, monthly 1987–2013.

more nearly determined by simple construction costs. Thus, our data collection revealed not only market inefficiencies, but much bigger price swings as well.

The inefficiency that we documented in single family home prices must be related to market conditions, and so efficiency must be improvable with changes in market institutions. The inefficiency of the market for single family homes relative to that of the stock market must be partly traced to the relatively much higher cost of trading in that market. It is much more costly for professional traders to trade in and out of the market for single family homes to profit from predictable price movements. It is difficult to do short sales of overpriced individual homes. Buying and selling individual homes may not work well for professionals also because of high carrying costs, low rental income, moral hazard of the renters who have relatively little incentive to care for the property, and difficulty keeping up with all the local factors that might change the demand for individual houses, so that remote institutional investors would risk being picked off as ignorant losers. Some institutional investors are in the news recently thinking they can survive and make money in this market. We will see if they succeed.

We thought that the market efficiency could be improved if an index of home prices could be made tradable. Working with Standard & Poor's, and with the people in our company MacroMarkets LLC, we helped the Chicago Mercantile Exchange with plans to set up futures markets based on our indices for ten U.S. cities. These markets were launched in 2006, and are still trading today, albeit with nothing close to the volume of trade that we hoped to see in these markets.[22] We hoped that the creation of these new markets would change the nature of prices in real estate markets, with price discovery that made the price of homes behave more like the random walk that efficient markets theory suggests.

Real estate markets remain wildly inefficient all over the world. We can only look forward to the day when liquid markets support more trade that might permit something rather closer to the efficient markets that theorists have expected.

To achieve such improvements in efficiency, in real estate markets, in stock markets, or in any speculative markets, it is most helpful to understand the

---

[22] The market maker John Dolan has a website with up-to-date information about this market, http://homepricefutures.com. Our firm MacroMarkets LLC led by Allan Weiss and Sam Masucci also created paired long and short securities, MacroShares, with ticker symbols UMM (for up major metro) and DMM (for down major metro) based on the S&P/Case-Shiller Ten-City Index that traded on the New York Stock Exchange from August to December 2010.

causes of market inefficiency, and that requires serious study from the broad perspective afforded by an array of other sciences outside of economics.

3. BEHAVIORAL FINANCE AND BEHAVIORAL ECONOMICS

The behavioral economics revolution, which brings psychology and other social sciences into economics, saw its first beginnings in the 1980s, but did not attract public attention until the 1990s. Richard Thaler and I started our behavioral economics workshops at the National Bureau of Economic Research in 1991, and there behavioral finance played the dominant role.[23] There are a number of surveys of the behavioral finance literature, notably Baker and Wurgler (2011), Barberis (2003), Shefrin (2008), Shiller (2003) and Shleifer (2000).

The behavioral finance revolution seemed to take its beginnings from the evidence of market inefficiency that was by then starting to look significant. Once we acknowledge that the efficient markets theory has no special claim to priority for price determination, we can look more sympathetically to other factors to understand market fluctuations. The anomalies literature points indeed to some oddball factors as playing a role. Benos and Jochec (2013) showed that patriotism affects stock prices, in that U.S. stocks with the words "America(n)" or "USA" in their names earn an abnormal return of 6% a year during wartime. Saunders (1993) found that the weather in New York affects stock prices. If such silly things as these affect stock prices, it should be no surprise if more plausible but half-baked theories (about the central bank, fiscal policy, energy prices, the future of capitalism, and on and on) would also affect market prices.

Most stock market investors do not pay much attention to fundamental indicators of value. We might argue that their inattention is in some sense rational, since there is a cost to collecting information. Christopher Sims has devised a model of rational inattention (2003). But, it is hard to believe that their inattention is systematic and thoughtful. The dominance of mutual funds that charge fees but consistently underperform the market is itself a puzzle for efficient markets theory (Gruber 1996).

A. Early History of Behavioral Finance

Behavioral finance until the 1980s was mostly relegated to the community of investment analysts who did not generally attract notice in academia, and who did not generally draw on research from the social sciences. There were however

[23] See http://www.econ.yale.edu/~shiller/behfin/index.htm

some gems from this period. Notable among these analysts were Benjamin Graham and David Dodd, who, in the 1940 edition of their book *Security Analysis*, based their investing method on their observations of "ignorance, of human greed, of mob psychology, of trading costs, of weighting of the dice by insiders and manipulators."[24]

Keynes gave a view of speculative markets that was ahead of its time. In his 1936 book *The General Theory of Employment, Interest and Money*. Keynes described speculative markets as akin to a newspaper competition he saw offered by a local newspaper to its readers. His metaphor is widely referred to as Keynes' "beauty contest" theory of the stock market. Each reader was invited to submit from a page with one hundred photos of pretty faces a list of the six that he or she thought prettiest. The winner would be the one whose list most closely corresponded to the most popular faces among all the lists of six that readers sent in. Of course, to win this contest a rational person would not pick the faces that personally seem prettiest. Instead one should pick the six faces that one thinks others will think prettiest. Even better, one should pick the faces one thinks that others think that others think prettiest, or one should pick the faces one thinks that others think that others think that others think prettiest. The same is true with stock market investing. Keynes thought that "there are some, I believe, who practice the fourth, fifth and higher degrees,"[25] further degrees of removal from reality than was embodied in equation (4) above. That is how speculative markets function, Keynes said. Active participants are trying to buy into their predictions of the conventional valuation of assets in the near future, not the true value.

A key Keynesian idea is that the valuation of long-term speculative assets is substantially a matter of convention, just as it is with judgments of facial beauty. Whatever price people generally have come to accept as the conventional value, and that is embedded in the collective consciousness, will stick as the true value for a long time, even if the actual returns fail for some time to live up to expectations. If an asset's returns are carefully tabulated and disappoint for long enough, people will eventually learn to change their views, but it may take the better part of a lifetime. And many assets, such as owner-occupied homes, do not have unambiguously measured returns, and a mistaken "conventional valuation" based on a faulty popular theory can persist indefinitely. The presumed investment advantages of, say, living in an expensive land-intensive single family home near

[24] Graham and Dodd (2002), p. 276.

[25] Keynes General Theory (1936), Chapter 12 p. 156 (Harbinger 1965 edition).

a big city rather than renting a cheaper and more convenient apartment in a high-rise there may just not exist, and most people will never figure that out.

Conventional valuation can be a very subtle phenomenon at any point of time, reflecting popular theories of the time that are perceived by many, who have never studied the theories, as reflecting professional wisdom. In a beauty contest, people have even less incentive to consider the validity of this wisdom, since they view it as substantially entrenched in others' thinking. I am reminded, for example, of Modigliani and Cohn's (1979) study showing that inflation-induced biases in conventional accounting practices caused a massive understatement of earnings, a study which allowed them to call roughly, within a few years, the historic bottom of the stock market in 1982. The absence of immediate reaction to their study was just the kind of thing one might expect to see in a beauty contest world, since no one expected anyone else to react much to their paper.

B. The Blossoming of Behavioral Finance after 1980

The idea that speculative prices are somehow uniquely authoritative, as the best possible judgment of true value, still has its popular appeal even today. But, it has lost its unique claim on the attention of economic theorists. Theoretical models of speculative markets that are analogous to Keynes' beauty contest theory, that stress the expectation of reselling to other people who may have optimistic beliefs, have been offered by Harrison and Kreps (1978), Morris (1996), Scheinkman and Xiong (2003), Wu and Guo (2004), Hong Scheinkman and Xiong (2006), Allen Morris and Shin (2006), and Hong and Sraer (2011). In addition, there are also models that represent bubbles as related to leverage cycles tied in with heterogeneous beliefs: Fostel and Geanakoplos (2008), Geanakoplos (2009), Cao (2010), and He and Xiong (2012). Noise trader models (Kyle 1985, De Long *et al.* 1990) and Campbell and Kyle (1993) have begun to replace models with all rational agents.

Moreover, there are models of financial markets that replace the assumption of rational expected-utility-maximizing agents with alternative models of human behavior, such as Prospect Theory (Kahneman and Tversky 1979). Prospect theory, which is a theory of human choice in the face of risk that is based on experimental evidence in the psychology laboratory, is not a theory of rationality in the traditional sense, for it recognizes violations of the basic axioms of rational behavior (Savage, 1954).The human behavior prospect theory describes is vulnerable to the arbitrariness of psychological framing; insignificant changes in context or suggestion can produce profound differences in human behavior.

Barberis, Huang and Santos showed (2001) that prospect theory with investors who derive direct utility from fluctuations in the value of their wealth can help explain the excess volatility of stock market. returns. A “house money effect” can help make bubbles grow even bigger—an analogy to gamblers at casinos who, after they have won some money, become very risk tolerant with that money because they frame it as somebody else’s money that they can afford to lose. Investors’ “narrow framing” (Barberis, Huang and Thaler 2006) and the disposition to sell winners and hold losers (Shefrin and Statman 1985) can explain other evidence against efficient markets.

The field of psychology offers many other principles of human behavior that have been shown to be relevant for evaluating the efficient markets theory. For example, there is evidence that a general human tendency towards overconfidence causes investors to trade too much (Odean, 2000) and CEOs to squander internally generated funds on pet projects (Malmendier and Tate, 2005). There is a tendency for investors to be overly distracted by news stories (Barber and Odean, 2008) and to overreact to cash dividends (Shefrin and Statman, 1984).

Financial theory has also advanced to allow us a better understanding of the effects of the ambiguity regarding probabilities, the fundamental difficulties in placing numerical values for probabilities, that Keynes spoke of, Bewley (2002), Bracha and Brown (2013).

Psychologists have documented a tendency for people to anchor their opinions in ambiguous situations on arbitrary signals that are psychologically salient even if they are obviously irrelevant (Tversky and Kahneman 1974).

Neuroscience has begun to understand how the human brain handles ambiguity. Hsu et al. (2005) and Huettel et al. (2006) use functional magnetic imaging to study brain reactions to situations with clear versus ambiguous probabilities, Huettel et al. concluded that “decision making under ambiguity does not represent a special, more complex case of risky decision making, instead, these two forms of uncertainty are supported by distinct mechanisms.”[26] The rapid progress we are now seeing in neuroscience will likely yield new insights into the ambiguity, animal spirits and caprice that Keynes and others since him have stressed.

4. IMPLICATIONS FOR FINANCIAL INNOVATION

The financial institutions that we have today are the product of centuries of experience with the volatility of speculative asset prices, with the important

[26] Huettel et al. (2006), p. 765.

information discovery that these market prices can reveal, as well as the potential for erratic behavior in these markets. The reliability of these markets in revealing genuine information about fundamentals is not terrific, but it is certainly not negligible either, and the reliability might be improved through time with better financial institutions. Efficient markets should be considered a goal, not an established fact. The financial institutions that we have are the results of experimentation designing around this experience; the institutions we will have in the future depend on our continuing experimentation and redesign.

Like mechanical engineering, financial engineering should pay attention to human factors, to make devices that serve people well with full consideration of human talents and foibles. As this experience accumulates with each successive financial crisis and each improvement in information technology, financial innovation can make these institutions work better for humankind.

For example, the very invention centuries ago of stock markets has created an atmosphere for investing that—while it regularly produces the excesses of bubbles—creates an incentive for people to launch exciting new enterprises, to keep up to date on relevant information, and to protect themselves if they want from the inevitable risks of those very bubbles.

As David Moss (2002) has chronicled, a general limited liability statute covering all stock market investors was not such an obviously good idea when the world's first such law was passed in New York in 1811, but it turned out to be of fundamental importance for investors' psychology. By clearly forbidding suing shareholders for a company's sins, it limited the downside risk of investing to psychologically manageable proportions (no more worries that any one of your investments could explode and land you in debtors' prison), and it permitted portfolio diversification to proceed without exhaustive investigation of each company's management.[27] The stock market became an exciting place, like a gambling casino, but tied to business reality rather than mere amusement, and it was a place where investors could diversify and limit their risks. It therefore was highly effective in attracting capital for enterprise.

More recently, people have been experimenting with other details of the stock markets, such as insider trader rules, risk retention rules, capital requirements, and other factors. These interact with human psychology in ways that can improve market functioning but whose effects cannot be accurately foretold from any received theory.

---

[27] Moss (1984) documents much discussion and experimentation with liability rules in the early 19th century, as with "double liability" that limits shareholders' liability to twice their initial investment, or liability that ends when the shares are sold.

Much of my work has been involved in considering how both financial theory and human factors need to be considered in designing new financial structures. I have written a number of books devoted to this: *Who's Minding the Store?* (1992), *Macro Markets* (1993), *New Financial Order* (2003), *Subprime Solution* (2008) and *Finance and the Good Society* (2012). Most of the ideas I have expressed in those books are calls for experimentation, not finished ideas. The ideas I discussed are mostly as yet untested, and their final forms, if and when they ever do get implemented—perhaps in the distant future, and with far better information technology—are hard to see in advance.

The ideas in these books, and associated articles, are diverse, go in many directions, and have to be judged as beginnings of ideas. They may look awkward just as the earliest designs of aircraft did; their later incarnations may look less so.

The overarching theme of this work of mine is that we need to *democratize* and *humanize* finance in light of research on human behavior and the functioning of markets (Shiller 2011). Democratizing finance means making financial institutions work better for real people, dealing with the risks that are most important to them individually, and providing opportunities for inspiration and personal development. Humanizing finance means making financial institutions interact well with actual human behavior, taking account of how people really think and act.

Lionel Robbins, with his 1932 book *An Essay on the Nature and Significance of Economic Science* has had the honor of inventing the most common definition today of economic science, of the unifying core idea that defines this science. He wrote then:

> The economist studies the disposal of scarce means. He is interested in the way different degrees of scarcity of different goods give rise to different ratios of valuation of them, and he is interested in the way in which changes in conditions of scarcity, whether coming from changes in ends or changes in means—from the demand side or the supply side—affect these ratios.[28]

The importance of prices in allocating scarce resources is an idea whose beginnings go back at least to Adam Smith in the 18th century, with his "invisible hand," and there was a certain wisdom in Robbin's framing of the entire field of economics around this idea. This wisdom still today is not fully apparent to the untrained public. Most people do not appreciate that all of our economic activities and all of our pleasures and satisfactions, and those of subsequent

[28] Robbins 1932 p. 15.

generations, are ultimately guided by prices of scarce resources as formed in the markets.

There is a problem, however, with the interpretation of economics that Robbins so persuasively gave. For his definition appeared to cast the economic problem exclusively as about scarcity of production resources, like energy and food, rather than also about scarcity of human intellectual and psychological resources. He casts the problem as man against nature, when in fact much of the economic problem is dealing with man against himself.[29]

Long-term asset prices as they are observed today—prices of stocks, bonds, real estate, and commodities, and prices of derivative products such as futures, swaps and options, and of other institutions like long-term insurance—are especially significant for economics, and especially problematic, since the scarcity that these prices represent is one that is never really objective and directly revealed today. Their levels are influenced by expectations of the distant, and generally nebulous, future. The market prices of speculative assets at any given time reflect, as is commonly asserted, both tastes and technology of that time. But they also reflect expected tastes and technology of the future, the likelihood of discovery of new resources or the technology to develop them. They also reflect sociology and social psychology, and anticipated future changes in these, in government policy such as taxation, and in other primary forces—such as changes in the inequality of incomes and likely social and governmental reactions to these, the potential threat of wars and other catastrophes, and the likely use of and policy towards the assets in such times.

Fischer Black, in his 1984 presidential address before the American Finance Association, offered a new definition of market efficiency: He redefined an "efficient market" as "one in which price is within a factor of 2 of value, i. e., the price is more than half of value and less than twice value . . . By this definition, I think almost all markets are efficient almost all of the time."[30]

And yet, even assuming he is somehow right, the existing efficient markets theory remains the fundamental framework from which much economic policy decisions, and decisions to innovate or not, are made. No one would seriously propose the elimination of stock markets even if we all accepted Fischer Black's impression as fact. So, why should we not consider other risk markets, markets that have not come into being yet just through accidents of history and timing of associated technological breakthroughs?

---

[29] See for example Mullainathan and Shafir (2013).

[30] Black (1986). p. 533.

Institutions can be redesigned so that they reframe people's thinking, to the longer term and to things that are better subjects for their attention, by making markets for risks that are better tied to fundamentals people should be thinking about. Institutions that change framing might sometimes qualify as institutions providing a "nudge" as Richard Thaler and Cass Sunstein (2009) have put it, suggesting the right direction for people without being coercive. They base their thinking on a philosophy they call "libertarian paternalism" emphasizing the government's providing incentives for appropriate behavior without coercion. Though our groundings in behavioral economics are similar, I wouldn't stress that term, perhaps because it seems to suggest a top-down structure for society, with government at the top. The development of financial capitalism seems to be, or can be, a matter of the voluntary organization of most of society, integrating the activities of people in all walks of life in fulfillment of their diverse purposes. A vision for a better financial capitalism should not be top-down at all.

Some recent examples of financial innovation, examples of new experiments, can help clarify how innovation might help in an imperfect financial world. Consider first the social policy bonds proposed by Ronnie Horesh (1999), which have taken recently taken actual form by the social impact bonds first issued with the help of the nonprofit Social Finance Ltd in 2010 in the United Kingdom. These redirect speculative impulses into solving social problems over a meaningful horizon that is chosen by the issuer to be neither too short nor too long to allow effective solutions.

Consider also the new crowdfunding initiatives, to create websites that allow large numbers of dispersed people each to share information and each to invest a small amount of money directly into new enterprises, without the usual financial intermediaries, which have sprouted in many places around the world, with web sites like kiva.org or kickstarter.com. They are poised after the U.S. Jumpstart Our Business Startups (JOBS) Act of 2012 to transform venture capital. Such innovations can and certainly will cause some runaway bubbles and abuse of ignorant investors. But they could on the other hand, if designed and regulated right, create a new way of arousing animal spirits and focusing informed attention onto venture investments. Crowdfunding may be more effective in funding ideas that are hard to prove, whose payoff is not immediate, that have a subtle social, environmental or inspirational purpose beyond mere profits, and that only a small percentage of the population is equipped to understand.

Consider also the new benefit corporations that are now offered in twenty U.S. states. They are amalgams of for-profit and non-profit corporations, fundamentally changing the mental framing that investors are likely to have of their investments in them, and encouraging both investors' excitement and more idealistic thinking about these investments.[31] The participation nonprofit business form that I advocated (2012), which makes nonprofits psychologically more similar to equity-financed business, would, if it is ever implemented, increase philanthropy and make it more effective.

These are only the beginning of the financial innovations that we might expect to see in our future, helped along by our improved understanding of behavioral finance, of mathematical economics, and steadily improving information technology. In particular, it would seem that great benefit can be derived by expanding the scope of our financial markets, to allow trading of risks that really matter.

We might benefit from the expansion of trading to include trading of other indices that have only recently come to be measured but that reflect real and important risks. I have already alluded to the futures market for single family homes that was started at the Chicago Mercantile Exchange in 2006, and if that market becomes more successful it will eventually provide price discovery for a value of great personal importance to individuals, and might lead to a cash market for real estate that is not so woefully inefficient. The home futures market, if it became more successful, would facilitate the creation of many more risk management products, such as home equity insurance (Shiller and Weiss 1998) or mortgages with preplanned workouts (Shiller 2012, Shiller, Wojakowski et al. 2013).

Had there been a well-developed real estate market before the financial crisis of 2008 it would plausibly have *reduced* the severity of the financial crisis, because it would have allowed, even encouraged, people to hedge their real estate risks. The severity of that crisis was substantially due to the leveraged undiversified positions people were taking in the housing market, causing over fifteen million U.S. households to become underwater on their mortgages, and thus reducing their spending. There is no contradiction at all in saying that there are bubbles in the housing market, yet saying that we ought to create better and more liquid markets for housing.

Even further, I along with others have argued that a market for claims on the flow of gross domestic product or other large macroeconomic aggregates should be developed, to help countries share their risks, Shiller (1993, 2003, 2008), Athanasoulis and Shiller (2000, 2001), Kamstra and Shiller (2009), or markets for other significant economic variables like occupational incomes to share their livelihood risks (Shiller 1993, Shiller and Schneider 1998, Shiller 2003).

[31] See http://benefitcorp.net/

Had the government debts of European countries taken the form of GDP shares, then most likely we would not have had the severe European sovereign debt crisis that started in 2009, for the countries would not have as big a short-run refinancing problem and would find their government obligations cushioned by declining obligations due to declining GDP. Had people sought protection for their own welfare by hedging themselves in occupational income markets, many of them would have suffered less in this crisis.

Examples of innovations that might reframe into better and longer-term thinking about fundamentals include the "perpetual futures" that I have proposed (1993)[32], or the application the concept of index participations developed by the American Stock Exchange in 1989 to flow indexes[33], or the long-term MacroShares my colleagues and I once have striven to launch based on various indices[34], or the markets for individual future dividend dates on stock price indices that Michael Brennan (1999) argued might "focus investor attention on the fundamentals that determine the value of the index rather than simply on the future resale value of the index."[35]

The development of inflation-indexed bonds, which have gradually grown in importance over the last half century worldwide, are an important past success, but as yet an incomplete one. Such markets, and other indexing institutions, might be enhanced by further deliberate changes in psychological framing. If inflation-indexed units of account, which create an easier way in our language to refer to indexed quantities, were created and widely used, they would help people around their money illusion which inhibits intelligent design of contracts around the real outcomes that really matter. I have been advocating the proliferation of these units of account where they first began in Chile (2002), and in the United States (2003), and the United Kingdom (2009).[36] Their widespread use might have helped prevent the real estate bubble that preceded the

---

[32] These are defined in Shiller (1993) in terms of a daily settlement formula involving both the change in settle price and another index representing a cash flow.

[33] See Shiller (1993) p. 40.

[34] In 2006 our firm MacroMarkets LLC launched paired long and short twenty-year oil MacroShares on the American Stock Exchange, with ticker symbols UCR for Up-Crude and DCR for Down-Crude. The securities traded from November 2006 to June 2008, and at one point reached US$1.6 billion in total value, but were not ultimately a success.

[35] Brennan (1999) p. 12. Since 2008, dividend futures markets for stock price indices have appeared on a number of European and Asian exchanges, though it is not clear that these new markets have had much of the desired effect of reframing investors' thinking.

[36] Chile created its *Unidad de Fomento* (UF) in 1967, still in use there today, http://valoruf.cl/

current financial woes, a bubble that was likely helped along by the widely-held impression that single family homes have historically shown high real capital gains when in fact over the last century the gains overall have been only nominal and hence illusory (Shiller 2005).

We want such innovations, if not exactly the ones I and others have been advocating to date, because their predecessor innovations, the financial institutions we already have today, have brought such prosperity, despite the occasional big disruptions caused by bubbles and financial crises. There is no economic system other than financial capitalism that has brought the level of prosperity that we see in much of the world today, and there is every reason to believe that further expansion of this system will yield even more prosperity.

The patterns of behavior that have been observed in speculative asset prices are consistent with a view of market efficiency as a half-truth today and at the same time with a view that there are behavioral complexities in these markets that need to be met with properly engineered financial innovations and financial regulations.

Changes in our financial institutions that take the form of creative reinventions in the kinds of risks traded, that change the psychological framing of the things traded, that change our social relations with business partners and adversaries, can make financial markets less vulnerable to excesses and crashes and more effective in helping us achieve our ultimate goals.

REFERENCES

Akerlof, George A., and Robert J. Shiller. 2009. *Animal Spirits: How Human Psychology Drives the Economy and Why this Matters for Global Capitalism*, Princeton: Princeton University Press.

Allen, Franklin, Stephen Morris, Hyun Song Shin. 2006. "Beauty Contests, Bubbles and Iterated Expectations in Financial Markets." *Review of Financial Studies*, 19:719–52.

Ang, Andrew, and Geert Bekaert. 2007. "Stock Return Predictability: Is It there?" *Review of Financial Studies*, 20:651–757.

Arnott, Robert D., and Clifford S. Asness. 2003. "Surprise! Higher Dividends = Higher Earnings Growth." *Financial Analysts Journal*, 59(1):70–87.

Athanasoulis, Stefano, and Robert J. Shiller. 2000. "The Significance of the Market Portfolio," *Review of Financial Studies*, 13:2, 301–329.

———. 2001."World Income Components: Measuring and Exploiting Risk Sharing Opportunities," *American Economic Review*, 91(4):1031–54.

Bailey, Martin J., Richard F. Muth and Hugh O. Nourse. 1963. "A Regression Method for Real Estate Price Index Construction." *Journal of the American Statistical Association*, 58:933042.

Baker, Malcolm, and Jeffrey Wurgler, "Behavioral Corporate Finance: An Updated Survey." NBER Working Paper No. 17333.

Barber, Brad, and Terrance Odean. 2008. "All that Glitters: The Effect of Attention on the Buying Behavior of Individual and Institutional Investors." *Review of Financial Studies*, 21(2):785–818.

Barberis, Nicholas. 2003. "A Survey of Behavioral Finance." Elsevier: *Handbook of the Economics of Finance*.

Barberis, Nicholas, Robin Greenwood, Lawrence Jin, and Andrei Shleifer. 2013. "X-CAPM: An Extrapolative Capital Asset Pricing Model." Working paper, Yale University.

Barberis, Nicholas, Andrei Shleifer and Robert Vishny. 1998. "A Model of Investor Sentiment." *Journal of Financial Economics*, 49(3):307–43.

Barberis, Nicholas, Ming Huang and Tano Santos. 2001. "Prospect Theory and Asset Prices." *Quarterly Journal of Economics*, 116(1):1–53.

Barberis, Nicholas, Ming Huang and Richard H. Thaler. 2006. "Individual Preferences, Monetary Gambles, and Stock Market Participation: A Case for Narrow Framing." *American Economic Review*, 96(4):1069:1090.

Beltratti, Andrea, and Robert J. Shiller. 1993. "Actual and Warranted Movements in Asset Prices." *Oxford Economic Papers*, 45:387–402.

Benos, Evangelos, and Marek Jochec. 2013. "Patriotic Name Bias and Stock Returns." *Journal of Financial Markets*, 16(3):550–70.

Bewley, Truman. 2002. "Knightian Decision Theory. Part I" *Decisions in Economics and Finance*, 25(2):79–110.

Black, Fischer. 1986. "Noise." *Journal of Finance*, 41:529–43.

Bracha, Anat, and Donald J. Brown. 2013. "(IR)Rational Exuberance: Optimism, Ambiguity and Risk." New Haven: Cowles Foundation Discussion Paper No. 1898.

Brennan, Michael. 1999. "Stripping the S&P 500 Index." *Financial Analysts Journal*, 54(1):12–22.

Brunnermeier, Markus, Alp Simsek and Wei Xiong. 2013. "A Welfare Criterion for Models with Distorted Beliefs." Unpublished paper, Princeton University.

Buiter, Willem. 1987. "Efficient 'Myopic" Asset Pricing in General Equilibrium: A Potential Pitfall in Excess Volatility Tests." *Economics Letters*, 25(2):143–8.

Bunn, Oliver, and Robert J. Shiller. 2013. "Changing Times, Changing Values: A Historical Analysis of Sectors within the U.S. Stock Market." unpublished paper, Yale University.

Campbell, John Y. 1991. "A Variance Decomposition for Stock Returns." *Economic Journal*, 101:57–179.

Campbell, John Y. and John Ammer. 1993. "What Moves the Stock and Bond Markets? A Variance Decomposition for Long-Term Asset Returns." *Journal of Finance*, 48:3–37.

Campbell, John Y., and John Cochrane. 1999. "By Force of Habit: A Consumption-Based Explanation of Aggregate Stock Market Behavior." *Journal of Political Economy*, 107:205–51.

Campbell, John Y. and Albert S. Kyle. 1993. "Smart Money, Noise Trading, and Stock Market Behavior." *Review of Economic Studies*, 60(1):1–34.

Campbell, John Y., Christopher Polk and Tuomo Vuolteenaho. 2010. "Growth or Glamor? Fundamentals and Systemtic Risk in Stock Returns." *Review of Financial Studies*, 23:305–44.

Campbell, John Y., and Robert J. Shiller. 1987. "Cointegration and Tests of Present Value Models." Journal of Political Economy, 95:1062–1088.

——— and ———. 1996. "The Dividend-Price Ratio and Expectations of Future Dividends and Discount Factors," with J.Y. Campbell, *Review of Financial Studies*, 1:3, 195–228, fall 1988.

——— and ———. 1989. "The Dividend Ratio Model and Small Sample Bias: A Monte Carlo Study." *Economics Letters*, 29:325–31.

——— and ———. 1988. "Interpreting Cointegrated Models," with J.Y. Campbell, *Journal of Economic Dynamics and Control*, Special Issue, ed. M. Aoki, "Economic Time Series Models with Random Walk and Other Nonstationary Components," 12:505–522.

———, and ———. 1988. "Stock Prices, Earnings and Expected Dividends." *Journal of Finance*, 43:3, 661–76.

———, and Luis Viceira. 2002. *Strategic Asset Allocation*. New York: Oxford University Press.

———, and Tuomo Vuolteenaho. 2004. "Bad Beta, Good Beta." *American Economic Review*, 94:1249–75.

Campbell, John Y. and Luis Viceira. 2002. *Strategic Asset Allocation*, New York: Oxford University Press.

Campbell, John Y., and Motohiro Yogo. 2006. "Efficient Tests of Stock Return Predictability." 81(1):27–60.

Case, Karl E. 1986. "The market for Single Family Homes in Boston." *New England Economic Review*, May/June, 38–48.

Case, Karl E., and Robert J. Shiller. 1988. "The Behavior of Home Buyers in Boom and Post-Boom Markets." *New England Economic Review*, Nov/Dec pp. 29–46.

——— and ———. 1989. "The Efficiency of the Market for Single Family Homes." *American Economic Review*, 79:1, 125–37.

——— and ———. 1990. "Forecasting Prices and Excess Returns in the Housing Market." *AREUEA Journal*, 18(3): 253–73.

———, and ———. 2004. Is There a Real Estate Bubble?" *Brookings Papers on Economic Activity*, 2004-I.

——— and ———. 1987. "Prices of Single-Family Homes Since 1970: New Indexes for Four Cities," with Karl E. Case, *New England Economic Review*, pp. 46–56.

Case, Karl E., Robert J. Shiller and Anne Kinsella Thompson. 2012. "What Have They Been Thinking? Home Buyer Behavior in Hot and Cold Markets." Brookings Papers on Economic Activity, 2012–II.

Case, Karl E., Robert J. Shiller, and Allan N. Weiss. 1993. "Index-Based Futures and Options Trading in Real Estate." *Journal of Portfolio Management*, Winter.

Chen, Long, and Xinlei Zhao. 2009. "Return Decomposition." *Review of Financial Studies*, 22(12):5212–49.

———. 2013. "What Drives Stock Price Movements?" *Review of Financial Studies*, 26(4):841–76.

Chen, Long, Zhi Da and Richard Priestly. 2012. "Dividend Smoothing and Predictability." *Management Science*, 58(10):

Cochrane, John H. 2001. *Asset Pricing*. Princeton NJ: Princeton University Press.

———. 2007. "The Dog that Did Not Bark: A Defense of Return Predictability." *Review of Financial Studies*, 21(4):1533–1575.

———. 1992. "Explaining the Variance of Price-Dividend Ratios." *Review of Financial Studies*, 5:243–280.

———. 1991. "Volatility Tests and Efficient Markets Theory: A Review Essay." *Journal of Monetary Economics*, 27:463–85.

Cootner, Paul. 1964. *The Random Character of Stock Market Prices*. MIT Press.

Cutler, David, James Poterba, and Lawrence Summers. 1990. "Speculative Dynamics and the Role of Feedback Traders." *American Economic Review Papers and Proceedings*, 80:63–68.

Cutler, David M, James M. Poterba, and Lawrence H. Summers. 1989. "What Moves Stock Prices?" *The Journal of Portfolio Management*, 15(3):4–12.

Debondt, Werner F. M., and Richard H. Thaler. 1985. "Does the Stock Market Overreact?" *Journal of Finance*, 40:557–81.

De Long, J. Bradford, Andrei Shleifer, Lawrence Summers, and Robert Waldmann. 1990. "Noise Trader Risk in Financial Markets." *Journal of Political Economy*, 98(4):703–38.

Dolley, James C. 1933. "Common Stock Split-Ups—Motives and Effects." *Harvard Business Review*, 12(1):70–81.

Durkheim, Émile. 1893. *De la division du travail social*. Paris: Alcan.

Economic Sciences Prize Committee of the Royal Swedish Academy of Sciences. 2013. *Scientific Background on the Sveriges Riksbank Prize in Economic Sciences in Memory of Alfred Nobel. 2013*. http://www.nobelprize.org/nobel_prizes/economic-sciences/laureates/2013/advanced-economicsciences2013.pdf

Engsted, Tom, Thomas Q. Pedersen and Carsten Tanggaard. 2012. "Pitfalls in VAR Based Return Decompositions: A Clarification." *Journal of Banking and Finance*, 36(5):1255–65.

Fabozzi, Frank, Robert Shiller and Radu Tunaru. 2009. "Hedging Real Estate Risk." *Journal of Portfolio Management*, 35(5):92–103

Fama, Eugene, 1965 "Random Walks in Stock Market Prices." *Financial Analysts Journal*, Sept/Oct. pp. 55–59.

Fama, Eugene. 1964. *The Distribution of the Daily Differences of the Logarithms of Stock Prices*. Ph.D. Dissertation, University of Chicago. Reprinted in *The Journal of Business* as "The Behavior of Stock Market Prices," 38(1):34–105.

———. 1970. "Efficient Capital Markets: A Review of Theory and Empirical Work." *Journal of Finance*, 25, 383-417.

———. 1971. "Risk, Return, and Equilibrium." *Journal of Political Economy*, 79:1.

———. 2013. "Two Pillars of Asset Pricing." Prize Lecture for 2013 Nobel Prize in Economic Sciences, http://www.nobelprize.org/mediaplayer/index.php?id=1994

Fama, Eugene F., Lawrence Fisher, Michael Jensen and Richard Roll. 1969. "The Adjustment of Stock Prices to New Information." *International Economic Review*, 10:1–21.

Fama, Eugene, and Kenneth R. French. 1988. "Permanent and Temporary Components of Stock Prices." *Journal of Political Economy*, 96:2.

Flavin, Marjorie. 1983. "Excess Volatility in the Financial Markets: A Reassessment of the Empirical Evidence." *Journal of Political Economy*, 96:246–73.

Fostel, Ana, and John Geanakoplos. 2008. "Leverage Cycles in an Anxious Economy." *American Economic Review*, 93:1211–1244.

Garber, Peter M. 2000. *Famous First Bubbles: The Fundamentals of Early Manias*. Cambridge, MA: MIT Press.

Geanakoplos, John. 2009. "The Leverage Cycle." *NBER Macroeconomics Annual 24*, 1–65.

Galbraith, John Kenneth. 1954. *The Great Crash, 1929*. Boston: Houghton Mifflin.

Gibson, George. 1889. *The Stock Markets of London, Paris and New York*. New York: G.P. Putnam's Sons.

Goetzmann, William N., and K. Geert Rouwenhorst, editors, *The Origins of Value: The Financial Innovations that Created Modern Capital Markets*. Oxford: Oxford University Press.

Goetzmann, William N., Catherine Labio, K. Geert Rouwenhorst and Timothy G. Young, editors. 2013. *The Great Mirror of Folly: Finance, Culture and the Crash of 1720*. New Haven: Yale University Press.

Goyal, Amit, and Ivo Welch. 2008. "A Comprehensive Look at the Empirical Performance of Equity Premium Prediction." *Review of Financial Studies*, 21:1455–508.

——— and ———. 2003. "Predicting the Equity Premium with Dividend Ratios." *Management Science*, 49:639–54.

Graham, David, and David Dodd. 2002. *Security Analysis: The Classic 1940 Edition*. McGraw Hill.

Greenwood, Robin, and Andrei Sheifer. 2013. "Expectations of Returns and Expected Returns." NBER Working Paper No 18686, January.

Grossman, Sanford, and Robert J. Shiller, 1981. "The Determinants of the Variability of Stock Market Prices." *American Economic Review*, 71:222 27.

Gruber, Martin J. 1996. "Another Puzzle: The Growth in Actively Managed Funds." *Journal of Finance*, 51:783–810.

Halbwachs, Maurice. 1925. "Les Cadres Sociaux de la Mémoire," in *Les Travaux de L'Année Sociologique*, Paris: Alcan.

Hansen, Lars Peter. 1991. "Implications of Security Market Data for Models of Dynamic Economies." *Journal of Political Economy*, 99:2.

———. 2013. "Uncertainty Outside and Inside Economics Models." Prize Lecture for 2013 Nobel Prize in Economic Science Sciences, http://www.nobelprize.org/media-player/index.php?id=1994

Hansen, Lars Peter, and Kenneth J. Singleton. 1983. "Stochastic Consumption, Risk-Aversion, and the Temporal Behavior of Asset Returns." *Journal of Political Economy*, 91(6):929–56.

Harrison, Michael, and David Kreps. 1978. "Speculative Investor Behavior in a Stock Market with Heterogeneous Expectations." *Quarterly Journal of Economics*, 92:323–36.

Horesh, Ronnie. 2000. "Injecting Incentives into the Solution of Social Problems: Social Policy Bonds." *Economic Affairs*, 20(3):2.

Hansen, Lars Peter, and Kenneth J. Singleton. 1983. "Stochastic Consumption, Risk Aversion, and the Temporal Behavior of Asset Returns." *Journal of Political Economy* 91:2.

——, and Ravi Jagannathan. 1991. "Implications of Security Market Data for Models of Dynamic Economies." *Journal of Political Economy*, 99(2):225–92.

Holden, Karen C., and Pamela J. Smock. 1991. "The Economic Costs of Marital Dissolution: Why Do Women Bear a Disproportionate Cost?" *Annual Review of Sociology*, 17:51–78. http://www.jstor.org/stable/208333.

Hong, Harrison, Jose Scheinkman and Wei Xiong. 2006. "Asset Float and Speculative Bubbles." *Journal of Finance*, 61:1073–1117.

——, and David Sraer. 2011. "Quiet Bubbles." Working Paper, Princeton University.

Hsu, Ming, Meghana Batt, Ralph Adolphs, Daniel Tranel and Colin F. Camerer. 2005. "Neural Systems Responding to Degrees of Uncertainty in Human Decision-Making." *Science*, 310:1680–1683.

Huettel, Scott A., C. Jill Stowe, Evan M. Gordon, Brent T. Warner and Michael L. Platt. 2006. "Neural Signatures of economic Preferences for Risk and Ambiguity. *Neuron*, 49(5):765–775.

Janis, Irving. 1982. *Groupthink: Psychological Studies of Policy Decisions and Fiascoes*, Boston: Houghton Mifflin.

Jung, Jeeman, and Robert Shiller. 2005. "Samuelson's Dictum and the Stock Market." *Economic Inquiry*, Vol. 43, Issue 2, pp. 221–228.

Kahneman, Daniel, Jack Knetsch, and Richard Thaler, "Fairness as a Constraint on Profit Seeking: Entitlements in the Market." *American Economic Review*, 76(4): 1986.

Kahneman, Daniel, and Amos Tversky. 2000. *Choices, Values and Frames*. Cambridge: Cambridge University Press.

——. 1979. Prospect Theory: An Analysis of Decision under Uncertainty." *Econometrica*, 47:236–91.

Kamstra, Mark, and Robert J. Shiller. 2009. "The Case for Trills: Giving the People and Their Pension Funds a Stake in the Wealth of the Nation." New Haven: Cowles Foundation, Working Paper No. 1717.

Keynes, John Maynard. 1936. *The General Theory of Employment Interest and Money*. London: MacMillan.

——. 1921. *A Treatise on Probability*. London: Macmillan.

Kindleberger, Charles Poor. 1978. *Manias, Panics and Crashes: A History of Financial Crises*. New York: Macmillan.

Kleidon, Allan W. 1986. "Variance Bounds Tests and Stock Price Valuation Models." *Journal of Political Economy*, 94:953–1001.

Koopmans, Tjalling. 1951. "Efficient Allocation of Resources." *Econometrica*, 19(4):455–65.

Kruskal, William, and Frederick Mosteller. 1980. "Representative Sampling, IV: The History of the Concept in Statistics, 1895–1939." *International Statistical Review / Revue Internationale de Statistique*, Vol. 48, No. 2 pp. 169–195.

Kübler, Felix, and Karl Schmedders. 2012. "Financial Innovation and Asset Price Volatility." *American Economic Review*, 102(3):147–51.

Kyle, Albert. 1985. "Continuous Auctions and Insider Trading." *Econometrica*, 53(6):1315–1335.

LeRoy, Stephen F. 1973. "Risk Aversion and the Martingale Property of Stock Prices." *International Economic Review*, 14(2):436–66.

LeRoy, Stephen F., and Richard D. Porter. 1987. "Stock Price Volatility: Tests Based on Implied Variance Bounds." *Econometrica*, 49:97–113.

Lewellen, Jonathan. 2004. "Predicting Returns with Financial Ratios." *Journal of Financial Economics*, 74(2):209–35.

Lucas, Robert E. 1978. "Asset Prices in an Exchange Economy." *Econometrica*, 46(6):1429–45.

Malmendier, Ulrike, and Geoffrey Tate. 2005. "CEO Overconfidence and Corporate Investment." *Journal of Finance*, 60(6):2661–2700.

Marsh, Terry A., and Robert C. Merton. 1986. "Dividend Variability and Variance Bound Tests for the Rationality of Stock Market Prices." *American Economic Review*, 76:483–98.

Modigliani, Franco, and Richard Cohn. 1979. "Inflation, Rational Valuation and the Market." *Financial Analysts Journal*, 35(2):24–44.

Morris, Stephen. 1996. "Speculative Investor Behavior and Learning." *Quarterly Journal of Economics*, 62:1327–47.

Moss, David A. 2002. *When All Else Fails: the Government as Ultimate Risk Manager*. Cambridge: Harvard University Press.

Mullainathan, Sendhil, and Eldar Shafir. 2013. *Scarcity*. Princeton: Princeton University Press.

Mullainathan, Sendhil, and Andre Shleifer. 2005. "The Market for News." *American Economic Review*, 95(4):1031.

Odean, Terrance. 2000. "Do Investors Trade too Much?" in Hersh Shefrin, Editor, *Behavioral Finance*, Northampton, MA: Edward Elgar.

Phillips, Peter C. B., and Pierre Perron. 1988. "Testing for a Unit Root in Time Series Regression." *Biometrika*, 75(2):335–46.

Poterba, James M., and Lawrence H. Summers. 1988. "Mean Reversion in Stock Prices: Evidence and Implications." *Journal of Financial Economics*, 22:26–59.

Robbins, Lionel. 1932. *An Essay on the Nature and Significance of Economic Science*. London: MacMillan.

Rothman, James E. 2013. "The Principle of Membrane Fusion in the Cell." Prize Lecture, 2013 Nobel Prize in Medicine, http://www.nobelprize.org/mediaplayer/index.php?id=1975

Saunders, Edward M. 1993. "Stock Prices and the Weather." *American Economic Review*, 83(5):1337–1245.

Savage, Leonard J. 1954. *Foundations of Statistics*. New York: Wiley.

Scheinkman, Jose, and Wei Xiong. 2003. "Overconfidence and Speculative Bubbles." *Journal of Political Economy*, 111:1133–1219.

Shefrin, Hersh M. 2008. *A Behavioral Approach to Asset Pricing*. North Holland: Elsevier.

Shefrin, Hersh M., and Meir Statman. 1984. "Explaining Investor Preference for Cash Dividends." *Journal of Financial Economics*, 13(2):253–82.

Shefrin, Hersh M., and Meir Statman. 1985. "The Disposition to Sell Losers too Early and Ride Losers too Long: Theory and Evidence." *Journal of Finance*, 40(3):777–90.

Shiller, Robert J. 1991. "Arithmetic Repeat Sales Price Estimators." *Journal of Housing Economics*, 1:110–26.

———. 2009. *Baskets: A Proposal to Launch Indexed Units of Account in the UK during the Current Financial Crisis*. Policy Exchange, London.

———. 1982. "Consumption, Asset Markets and Macroeconomic Fluctuations." *Carnegie Rochester Conference Series on Public Policy*, 17:203 38.

———. 1987. "Conventional Valuation and the Term Structure of Interest Rates," in *Macroeconomics and Finance: Essays in Honor of Franco Modigliani*, ed. R. Dornbusch, S. Fischer and J. Bossons, pp. 63–88. Cambridge, MA, M.I.T. Press.

———. 2011. "Democratizing and Humanizing Finance." In Randall S. Kroszner and Robert J. Shiller, *Reforming U.S. Financial Markets: Reflections Before and Beyond Dodd-Frank* (Alvin Hansen Symposium on Public Policy at Harvard University). Cambridge MA: MIT Press.

———. 1981a. "Do Stock Prices Move Too Much to be Justified by Subsequent Changes in Dividends?" *American Economic Review*, 71:3,421–36

———. 2003. "From Efficient Markets Theory to Behavioral Finance." *Journal of Economic Perspectives*, 17(1): 83–104.

———. 2002. "Indexed Units of Account: Theory and Analysis of Historical Experience," in Fernando Lefort and Klaus Schmidt-Hebbel, *Indexation, Inflation, and Monetary Policy*. Central Bank of Chile, Santiago Chile, 2002.

———. 2005. *Irrational Exuberance*, Princeton: Princeton University Press, 2nd Edition.

———. 1993. *Macro Markets: Creating Institutions for Managing Society's Largest Economic Risks*. New York: Oxford University Press, 1993.

———. 1986. "The Marsh-Merton Model of Managers' Smoothing of Dividends." *American Economic Review*, 76:3, 499–503.

———. 2003. *The New Financial Order: Risk in the 21st Century*. Princeton: Princeton University Press.

———. 1988. "Portfolio Insurance and Other Investor Fashions as Factors in the 1987 Stock Market Crash," in NBER Macroeconomics Annual, ed. S. Fischer.

———. 1997. "Public Resistance to Indexation: A Puzzle," *Brookings Papers on Economic Activity*, 1997-I, 159–211.

———. 1972. *Rational Expectations and the Term Structure of Interest Rates*. Unpublished Ph.D. dissertation, Massachusetts Institute of Technology.

———. 1992 *The Report of the Twentieth Century Fund Task Force on Market Speculation and Corporate Governance*. New York: Twentieth Century Fund.

———. 1984."Stock Prices and Social Dynamics." *Brookings Papers on Economic Activity*, pp. 457 98, 2.

———. 2008. *Subprime Solution: : How Today's Global Financial Crisis Happened and What to Do about It*, Princeton: Princeton University Press.

———. 1987. "Ultimate Sources of Aggregate Variability." *American Economic Review, Papers and Proceedings*, 77:2, 87–92.

———. 1981b. "The Use of Volatility Measures in Assessing Market Efficiency." *Journal of Finance*, 36:291 304.

———. 1979. "The Volatility of Long-Term Interest Rates and Expectations Models of the Term Structure." *Journal of Political Economy*, 87:6.

———. 1992. *Who's Minding the Store? The Report of the Twentieth Century Fund Task Force on Market Speculation and Corporate Governance*. New York: The Twentieth Century Fund.

———. 2014. "Why Is Housing Finance Still Stuck in such a Primitive Stage?" Forthcoming, *American Economic Review*, May.

Shiller, Robert J., and Andrea Beltratti. 1992. "Stock Prices and Bond Yields: Can Their Comovements Be Explained in Terms of Present Value Models?" *Journal of Monetary Economics*, Vol. 30.

Shiller, Robert J., and Pierre Perron. 1985. "Testing the Random Walk Hypothesis: Power versus Frequency of Observation." *Economics Letters*, 18:381–86.

Shiller, Robert, and John Pound. 1989. "Survey Evidence on the Diffusion of Interest and Information Among Investors." *Journal of Economic Behavior and Organization*, 12:47–66.

Shiller, Robert J., and Ryan Schneider. 1998. "Labor Income Indices Designed for Use in Contracts Promoting Income Risk Management." *Review of Income and Wealth*, 44(2):163–82

Shiller, Robert J., and Jeremy J. Siegel. 1977. "The Gibson Paradox and Historical Movements in Real Long Term Interest Rates." *Journal of Political Economy*, 85:5, 891–98.

Shiller, Robert J., and Allan N. Weiss. 1999. "Evaluating Real Estate Valuation Systems." *Journal of Real Estate Finance and Economics*, 18:2,147–61.

———. 1999. "Home Equity Insurance." *Journal of Real Estate Finance and Economics*, 19:1, 21–47.

Shiller, Robert, Rafal Wojakowski, M. Shahid Ebrahim, and Mark B. Shackleton, 2013. "Mitigating Financial Fragility with Continuous Workout Mortgages." *Journal of Economic Behavior and Organization*, 85:269–85.

Shleifer, Andrei. 2000. *Inefficient Markets: A Survey of Behavioral Finance*. New York: Oxford University Press.

Shleifer, Andrei, and Robert Vishny. 1997. "Limits to Arbitrage." *Journal of Finance*, 52(1):35–55.

Siegel, Jeremy J. 2005. *The Future for Investors: The Tried and True Beats the Bold and New*. New York: Crown Business.

———. 2008. *Stocks for the Long Run*. 4th Edition. New York: McGraw Hill.

Sims, Christopher A. 2003. "Implications of Rational Inattention." *Journal of Monetary Economics*, 50:665–90.

———. 1990. "Martingale-Like Behavior of Prices and Interest Rates." Discussion Paper No. 205, Center for Economic Research, Department of Economics, University of Minnesota.

Singleton, Kenneth J. 1980. "Expectations Models of the Term Structure and Implied Variance Bounds." *Journal of Political Economy*, 88:1159–1176.

Smith, Edgar Lawrence. 1924. *Common Stocks as Long-Term Investments*. New York: Macmillan.

Summers, Lawrence H. 1986. "Does the Stock Market Rationally Reflect Fundamental Values." *Econometrica*, 41:591–601.

Thaler, Richard H., and Cass R. Sunstein. 2009. *Nudge: Improving Decisions about Health, Wealth and Happiness*. New Haven: Yale University Press.

Torous, Walter, Rossen Valkanov, and Shu Yan. 2004. "On Predicting Stock Returns with Nearly Integrated Explanatory Variables." *Journal of Business*, 77:937–66.

Tversky, Amos, and Daniel Kahneman. 1974. "Judgment under Uncertainty: Heuristics and Biases." *Science*, 185:1124–31.

Viceira, Luis. 2002. "Optimal Portfolio Choice for Long-Horizon Investors with Non-tradable Labor Income." *Journal of Finance*, 56(2):433–70.

Vuolteenaho, Tuomo. 2002. "What Drives Firm-Level Stock Returns? *Journal of Finance*, 57(1): 233–264.

West, Kenneth D. 1988. "Dividend Innovations and Stock Price Volatility." *Econometrica*, 56:37–61.

Wu, Ho-Mou, and Wen-Chung Guo. 2004. "Asset Price Volatility and Trading Volume with Rational Beliefs." *Economic Theory*, 23:795–829.

Economic Sciences 2014

Jean Tirole

"for his analysis of market power and regulation"

The Sveriges Riksbank Prize In Economic Sciences In Memory of Alfred Nobel

Speech by Professor Tore Ellingsen of the Royal Swedish Academy of Sciences.

Your Majesties, Your Royal Highnesses, Dear Laureates, Ladies and Gentlemen,

"Someone who is very strong has to be very nice also."

This is what Swedish children's author Astrid Lindgren says about the title character in her 1947 book *Do You Know Pippi Longstocking?* Pippi has caught two thieves and made them cry, but as a farewell present she gives them each a gold coin to buy food.

Astrid Lindgren was hopeful and visionary, but not naïve. She saw that not all those with power are good or even responsible. In her 1954 book *Mio, my Son*, the evil Sir Kato has a heart of stone – and only a sword that has been forged for thousands of years can penetrate a heart of stone.

What, then, is the magic sword that can cut through stone? This sword is a law that creates prosperity and justice.

At one time, the law of the strong prevailed – the ruler's word was law. But eventually, in country after country, the decrees and whims of the sovereign have given way to parliamentary laws and voluntary contracts. The sword is ours to lift together. When political power is open to democratic competition, we act together to monitor and replace governments. Our common sword performs its magic feats without spilling a drop of blood.

But what about economic power? Who monitors and replaces the owner of a company? Often, the answer is that no sword is needed. Even a baker with a heart of stone sells good bread at reasonable prices, because if the bread tastes bad or is too expensive, the baker will have no customers.

But in markets without room for more than one or a few companies, customers have nowhere else to go. There a sword is needed. Most countries have public authorities that regulate transport, postal and telecom companies, water companies, power grids and banks. They also have authorities that monitor large companies – even in the bakery trade – to make sure they do not abuse their power. They must not prevent new bakeries, with better recipes, from entering the marketplace.

How shall we encourage powerful companies to act in the best interest of society? A good regulatory system should balance many objectives. On the one hand, we want to reward good performance – on the other hand, we do not want to spend tax money unnecessarily. On the one hand, we want to tax excess profits – on the other hand, we do not want to wipe out profits that will enable a company to survive. On the one hand we want well-run, productive companies to grow large – on the other hand, we do not want old companies that were yesterday's best to stand in the way of new companies that will be tomorrow's best.

For generations, we have pondered these issues and failed to resolve them.

Jean Tirole realised that we needed new tools to find the answers. With the help of game theory, he has shown how we can understand behaviour in markets with a few players – how the decisions of companies depend on their opportunities to improve efficiency, their information and their opportunities to sign binding contracts.

He has shown how we should curb natural monopolies when the regulator has less information than the company. He has shown how regulators themselves can become players and how rules should constrain them as well. He has shown how competition laws should reflect the peculiarities of each individual industry – from banking to telecommunications, search engines and social networking services.

Dear Professor Tirole,

Once upon a time, we sought a magic sword that would cut through any stone. Then, one day a new blacksmith arrived. He forged many swords, each of them stronger and more flexible than any we had seen before, and he showed us which sword cut which sort of stone. Finally, on each sword, he engraved Voltaire's commandment: *Un grand pouvoir impose une lourde responsabilité* (With great power comes great responsibility).

You are that blacksmith.

It is an honour and a privilege for me to convey to you, on behalf of the Royal Swedish Academy of Sciences, our warmest congratulations. May I now ask you to please step forward and receive your prize from the hands of His Majesty the King.

Jean Tirole. Photo: A. Mahmoud

Jean Tirole

MY EDUCATIONAL BACKGROUND

I was born and raised in Troyes, a town located east of Paris and north of Burgundy. Troyes was the capital of Champagne in the middle ages; its fairs hosted trade between Northern Italian cities and Flanders among others; Troyes has accordingly preserved a rich cultural heritage. My father, who passed away in 1992, was an obstetrician/gynecologist; my mother, who still lives in Troyes, taught French, Latin and Greek in high school. My parents as well of some of my teachers taught me the value of knowledge. I have two sisters, Marie-Claude and Laurence. My youth was a pretty uneventful and happy one.

I left Troyes after my baccalaureate to carry out preparatory studies at the Lycée Henri Poincaré in Nancy (1971–1973). I then entered the *Ecole Polytechnique* (1973–1976), followed by the *Ecole des Ponts et Chaussées* (1976–1978), a "doctorat de troisieme cycle" (a degree intermediate between a Master degree and a PhD, which has since disappeared) in decision mathematics from *Université Paris-Dauphine* (1976–1978), and finally a PhD in economics from MIT (1978–1981).

In high school, I was particularly interested in mathematics and social sciences (history and psychology in particular). I kept a strong interest in sciences at the *Ecole Polytechnique*, especially in mathematics with professors such as Laurent Schwartz, a Field medalist for his theory of distributions. Economics was not an obvious choice of study given my family background and the rather weak economic culture in France. As a matter of fact, I was rather unknowledgeable about the topic. I attended my first course in economics at *Ecole Polytechnique* at the age of 21. I was fascinated by the issues and liked how it combines rigorous analysis and social sciences. I started thinking about becoming an economist.

In 1976 I joined the engineering "corps of roads and bridges" (*Corps des Ponts et Chaussées*), an applied corps of civil servants dating back to 1716 and that most members enter after the *Ecole Polytechnique*, and accordingly studied at the *Ecole des Ponts et Chaussées*, a school created in 1747. The corps has been very generous with me, supporting me while I studied for a PhD in the US and thereafter in my career in France. I am still a member of the corps, and I'm obviously grateful for its letting me accomplish my passion for research.

This choice of the *Corps des Ponts* may seem an odd choice for someone about to become an economist; yet, the corps has a long tradition of excellence in economics since Jules Dupuit, who in 1844 discovered—as he was studying public infrastructures and railroads—the notion of consumer surplus (the difference between the price consumers as a whole are willing to pay—the "willingness to pay," a measure of which can be derived from the demand curve—and the actual price they do pay) and the principles underlying market segmentation (through non-linear pricing and by offering a range of different qualities). This tradition of excellence was continued by François Divisia and René Roy, and many others since. Co-authors of mine who originate from that corps include Roger Guesnerie (whom I met during classes he gave at the *Ecole Polytechnique*, at the *Ecole des Ponts* and who was my adviser in Paris; he just retired from the economics chair at the *Collège de France*), Roland Bénabou (Princeton) and Bernard Caillaud (*Paris Sciences Economiques*). *Corps des Ponts* members have included five Presidents of the Econometric Society, the most prestigious international society for economics. The 70 former Presidents of this society (founded in 1930) include Irving Fisher, Schumpeter, Keynes, Arrow, Samuelson, and many Nobel Prize winners. *Corps des Ponts* "engineer-economists" outside the academic sphere have also always been very active in the public debate.

WHY ECONOMICS?

Research in economics offers a twofold opportunity: addressing demanding, intellectually absorbing theoretical problems and contributing to decision-making in the public and private sectors. On the latter point, economics is a positive discipline (in so far as it seeks to document and analyze individual and collective behavior), but it is also, and ultimately, normative: Its goal is to "make the world a better place" by recommending economic policy measures. This strong normative content is, in my opinion, an important factor behind its appeal.

My engineering degrees (which in the French tradition were fairly mathematics-oriented) may not have been the most direct route to economics, but they were not as distant as might be thought.

My research deals both with methodological aspects and with applications to different areas of economic life. Applied economic theory offers some analogies with engineering sciences. The starting point is a concrete problem, either already identified or gleaned from observing reality or listening to decision-makers, public or private. Then follows a detour through abstraction. The essence of the problem is extracted in order to focus on its key aspects. In this simplification process lies much of the difficulty of the exercise; for tractability, the researcher cannot take everything into consideration. (S)he must select what is important and sort out what is anecdotal (i.e., its omission has little chance of changing the analysis). The experience of the researcher and discussions with practitioners are very useful at this stage, although ultimately a study of the robustness to underlying assumptions is highly desirable. Then, the model can be tested: econometrically if past data are available, and in the lab or in the field as well. One cannot underestimate the interaction between theory and empirics: empirical work needs theory, both to guide it and to make it useful for policy. Theory needs empirical work to strengthen the confidence in policy recommendations and also to suggest key omitted ingredients.

THE PhD YEARS

In 1978, I traveled across the Atlantic to undertake a PhD in Economics at the Massachusetts Institute of Technology (MIT), graduating in 1981. MIT had a relatively low profile in the field of economics until the arrival of Paul Samuelson in 1940, but in the 1960s it became the best economics department in the world. The intellectual vibrancy, the professors' dedication to teaching, and passion for an economic discipline which is both rigorous and application-orientated are all part of the culture of MIT. Ever since then, I have been deeply convinced that the field can advance only through mutual respect across fields and across research styles.

An anecdote here: being a civil servant, I was given two years to obtain my PhD and return to France. This was of course highly unrealistic. I rushed to pass waivers in the first-year core courses and (like my classmate Drew Fudenberg) to pass my generals at the end of the first year. Having been raised in an exam-intensive environment, I succeeded in doing so at the detriment of understanding economics. Indeed, after a core macroeconomics waiver, Rudi Dornbusch wondered how I succeeded in passing, understanding so little to the field; he wisely advised me to attend the course nonetheless (without taking the final exam), which I did. During this year of PhD coursework, my four fields of specialization were theory, public finance, econometrics and international economics. I then started a thesis under the supervision of Eric Maskin, a 29 year-old MIT professor. At the end of my second year at MIT, I received a letter saying

FIGURE 1. With my PhD advisor Eric Maskin at the 2007 Nobel concert (Eric won the prize that year).

that I was allowed to stay in the US for a third year. This pressure-free third year turned out to be a fantastic opportunity, as I could devote the time to deepening my understanding of economics, take courses in fields I was completely unknowledgeable about, and start on new research projects.

At that time, Eric Maskin initiated MIT PhD students to game theory and information theory. Outside of regular class time, he very generously spent many hours every week in tutorials with fellow Maskin-advisee Drew Fudenberg and me. You can imagine how overjoyed Drew and I, like all former Maskin students, were when Eric deservedly received the Nobel Prize in 2007.

As I explain in the Nobel lecture, I was also very lucky to discover at MIT, thanks to Drew Fudenberg, industrial organization and regulation, fields I was not aware of prior to starting my PhD. I never took these fields for credit, but I sat in classes given by Paul Joskow and Dick Schmalensee and started writing papers with Drew on game theory and industrial economics (later, we also wrote a PhD-level textbook for doctoral students called "Game Theory").

My thesis, as is often the case now, covered a range of topics: investigating the possibility of bubbles in financial assets (a bubble exists when the value of a financial asset exceeds the "fundamental" of the asset, in other words the discounted value of dividends, interest and rents it will yield today and in the future). Drew Fudenberg and I conducted a first analysis of sequential bargaining under asymmetric information and the resulting inefficiencies ("sequential bargaining" describes a situation where two or more parties bid until one accepts the offer of the other. The study analyzed the dynamics of concessions and the length of the bargaining process before an agreement is reached, when the parties do not have the same information). Finally, the thesis covered research (also in collaboration with Drew Fudenberg) on pre-emptive strategies through the accumulation of productive capacity in oligopolistic markets. None of these subjects were directly within the scope of Eric Maskin's research topics but, like all great teachers, he never pushed his students to follow and refine his work, but rather encouraged and supported their own initiatives.

While Eric Maskin was instrumental in my development as an economist, I interacted with a number of professors other than my thesis advisor, as well as several talented fellow PhD students. Equally important was the opportunity to take a number of specialization courses (macroeconomics, public economics, international economics, etc.) in fields not directly related to my thesis. In economics, research fields change quickly and multidisciplinary knowledge is often essential to bring fresh thinking.

From 1980 to 1983, I also often spent time at Stanford, especially during the summer. While MIT and Harvard were the best departments for general economics, Stanford University and Northwestern University, whose researchers also often visited Stanford, were at the cutting edge of the revolution of game theory and information economics, ahead of their rivals on the east coast (with of course a few exceptions, such as Eric Maskin).

THE POST-PhD YEARS: RESEARCH & TEACHING, AND AN IMPORTANT ENCOUNTER

After my PhD in 1981, I did not go on the job market and went back to France to work as a researcher at the *Ecole Nationale des Ponts et Chaussées (ENPC)*. At the time, a small economics research centre, CERAS, was being established with, notably, Serge Kolm as Director, Roger Guesnerie working there part time and Bernard Caillaud (with whom I have since often collaborated) as student.

In 1982 I began my work on the regulation of network industries and public procurement with Jean-Jacques Laffont, whom I had met in Rio in 1980 during an Econometric Society conference. Jean-Jacques Laffont, who had resisted the call of major American universities and was starting to establish a school of economics in Toulouse, regularly came to the ENPC to work on this subject. A student of Ken Arrow at Harvard (like Eric Maskin, with whom he had already done very innovative work), he had already contributed fundamental papers on information theory and public choice theory.

We thus began to talk about structural reform in sectors such as telecoms, electricity, postal services and the railways. The performance of incumbent operators in most countries across the globe was unsatisfactory, and economists and decision-makers were reflecting on potential reforms which could make companies more accountable for their costs, and on reforms that would facilitate competition in non-bottleneck segments. Jean-Jacques Laffont and I felt that the new theories of information and industrial economics could add an important perspective on this type of reforms and their limits.

In the fall of 1982, I received an offer to teach as an associate professor at MIT, which I accepted. Having just met my future wife Nathalie (we got married in 1984), who had to finish her master degree in law at the University of Paris in 1983–1984, I started to teach at MIT in September 1984.

1984–1991: Back to MIT, the Consolidation Years

The MIT years were seven years of research and teaching in a perfect environment: a reasonable teaching workload focused mainly on doctoral courses, no administrative work, and above all an exceptional intellectual environment. The economics department had a very collective and congenial atmosphere. The tone was set by professors such as Paul Samuelson, Bob Solow, Franco Modigliani, all Nobel Prize winners, who showed humility, refused to set themselves above others and emphasized the ability of the younger faculty to identify promising areas for recruitment.

FIGURE 2. My official MIT professor picture (1987).

Beyond the obvious intellectual attraction, I learned at MIT about mechanisms for good governance in a department and university, which later helped me think about potential reforms in the French university system.

MIT has always treated me very nicely. When in 1992 I decided to stay in Toulouse, I was invited to be a visiting professor for six weeks per year (four of them during July, when I teach a minicourse for PhD students). This year will be the 24th year of this yearly arrangement, from which I have benefited a lot. I always return there with much pleasure, even though older mentors such as Paul Samuelson and Bob Solow and many of my collaborators or people I discussed most with during my faculty years there have moved to other academic or non-academic institutions, retired or passed away: Olivier Blanchard, Peter Diamond, Rudi Dornbusch, Stan Fischer, Drew Fudenberg, Oliver Hart, Jerry Hausman, Paul Joskow, Eric Maskin, Dick Schmalensee, to mention only a few senior faculty, and many others as well. The key point is that a top department is more than its members; it is a culture. When I return, I am struck by the observation that the spirit, the creativity of research and the devotion to students has remained intact despite a substantial turnover.

1991: A pivotal sabbatical year, the Jean-Jacques Laffont effect

In 1991 I took out a sabbatical year in Toulouse to finish a book, "A Theory of Incentives in Regulation and Procurement," with Jean-Jacques Laffont. In the 1980s we had discussed his plans to make the University of Toulouse 1 Capitole one of the best European universities in the field of economics, in particular thanks to the creation of an Institute for Industrial Economics (IDEI) which would be financed largely by partners from the public and private sector. The IDEI was established in 1990. Jean-Jacques Laffont and the group of friends who helped him in this initial phase had already managed to bring in a handful of leading researchers to Toulouse and wanted to use IDEI to provide a few more resources to develop a top-level European department. Jean-Jacques Laffont was the director of IDEI until 2002 (Jacques Cremer, Patrick Rey and Hervé Ossard have directed it since) and I have been IDEI's scientific director since its creation.

In 1992, my wife Nathalie and I decided to stay in Toulouse. Our daughter Naïs was born in Boston in 1989; our two other children, Margot (1992) and Romain (1996), would be Toulousains. I returned to the Corps des Ponts, working at the University, and later developed a secondary affiliation with the Ecole des Hautes Etudes en Sciences Sociales (1995) and became a member of the *Académie des Sciences Morales et Politiques* (2011).

My motivation for moving to Toulouse was not to work with Jean-Jacques Laffont, since we were already working closely together despite being separated by the Atlantic Ocean. Rather, I was attracted by the collective ambition and the desire to improve the university environment in France (on a small scale of course). I had total trust in Jean-Jacques Laffont, who apart from his well-known intellectual capacity (he would have been a serious candidate for the Nobel Prize), had remarkable human qualities as well as being a highly competent manager, which is quite unusual in the research world.

The project has been successful and many talented researchers have since joined the group. In the mid-1990s an economics doctoral program was created (entirely in English to attract the best students, both French and foreign—who learn French during their thesis) with a second year of doctorate courses added (a year of courses after the former advanced studies diploma, the DEA, now called M2); this second year, which exists in leading US PhD programs, was uncommon in Europe; and because it has no legal existence in France, we have been financing it on our own funds. It provides students with greater autonomy to write their thesis and a stronger foundation for research.

After my return to Europe, and even though my academic activities always take precedence, I also got more involved in policy-making over the years, through various economic committees such as the French Council of Economic Advisors (*Conseil d'Analyse Economique*), a non-partisan body that issues reports and opinions related to current policy issues, of which I have been a member since 1999, or other committees dealing with higher education and research. In the academic world, I have been long associated with the Econometric Society and the European Economic Association, which I presided over in 1998 and 2001, respectively.

MEETING THE INSTITUTION-BUILDING CHALLENGE

In 2004 Jean-Jacques Laffont died of cancer in Toulouse. A terribly sad time. At his funeral, Eric Maskin spoke about his friend Jean-Jacques through a short description of a scrabble game played at the Laffont family's summer house in Lacanau in the early 80s. Within two minutes, the scrabble game described many of Jean-Jacques' expressions that were familiar to all his friends; it ended in Jean-Jacques' winning with the word "magnifique."

Chances were that the group would disband after such a blow, as Jean-Jacques Laffont had played such an important role in the ex-nihilo construction of the Toulouse economics department and Toulouse had no strong tradition in economics before him. The best tribute to him is that the group did not

FIGURE 3. Helsinki, December 1993: Inaugural Yrjö Jahnsson Award of the European Economic Association, jointly with Jean-Jacques Laffont.

break apart and actually worked entrepreneurially to further his organizational project.

In 2006, we won a national competition to create 13 centers of excellence across all fields in France. This provided some financial resources and most importantly enabled us to create a private foundation, the Fondation Jean-Jacques Laffont/Toulouse School of Economics (TSE), which I directed until 2009 (at which stage vice-director Christian Gollier took over) and have been chairing its board since. This foundation has received, in roughly equal shares, public and private money. It enjoys the flexibility of private management, while being overseen by the French General Accounting Office (*Cour des Comptes*). Its board is almost entirely external (13 directors out of 15) and its scientific council fully external: two substantial departures from internally governed French higher education institutions. With the help of the university (Toulouse 1 Capitole) in which we are located, we were thereby able to introduce a number of other policies that may seem trite viewed from abroad, but have been innovative in the French landscape: for instance, creation of tenure tracks for junior faculty (who since the mid-1990s have never been recruited internally); new recruiting processes; creation of a "grande école" within the university system . . . Like other research-intensive departments in Europe, we also very much benefited from the creation of the European Research Council (ERC) in 2007. The ERC's goal is to help Europe compete for international talent in an environment in which academic careers often lack attractiveness. It now plays a major role in keeping talented researchers in (or bringing them back to) Europe.

I have long been interested in other social sciences and done research at the border of, in particular, political science (independent agencies, party organization and electoral strategies), sociology (stereotypes and collective reputations, real and formal authority, cliques and collusion, modes of communication, leadership and influence) and psychology (longstanding research agenda with Roland Bénabou related to the psychological aspects of incentives on the one hand, and to motivated beliefs and identity on the other hand). I was therefore very happy when, in 2011, our project to create an "Institute of Advanced Study in Toulouse (IAST)" was selected by an international jury and funded within the program "Investissements d'Avenir." At the date of its writing, this institute, directed by Paul Seabright, is still a start-up, but has got off to a very promising start. It successfully brings together political scientists, lawyers, psychologists, sociologists, anthropologists, biologists, economists and historians in a fruitful cross-disciplinary exchange.

The history of the Toulouse economics group is that of a team. I must say that this collective institution-building work has been very rewarding and I am grateful to my colleagues—too many to cite here—for what they have contributed.

WITH GRATEFULNESS

This Prize is so much the outcome of a collective effort that it is impossible to acknowledge all those who contributed to it in their own ways: my wife and family for their unfaltering support; my teachers, colleagues and students for making me a better economist (they still are); the staff at TSE and MIT for their cheerful and very professional help (for instance my assistants Pierrette Vaissade, Emily Gallagher and Marie-Pierre Boe); and all those who have, often anonymously, helped us build our department in Toulouse.

A researcher's main motivation is the pleasure of discovery, as described by the French mathematician Henri Poincaré: "Thought is only a flash in the middle of a long night. But this flash means everything." But like everyone else, the researcher is not indifferent to peer recognition. I have received many more honors than I deserve, but I am definitely grateful for all of them. Some were particularly emotional as well as highly honorific: my first honorary degree in 1989 (8 years after my PhD) at the Université Libre de Bruxelles, a very risky choice but an incredible show of trust from ULB, and the one honor that my father was able to witness; the ceremony for CNRS gold medal in 2007 (the second awarded to an economist after Allais in 1978), to which numerous friends came and at which Eric Maskin, on his way back from receiving the Nobel Prize in Stockholm, delivered a hilarious speech explaining to the crowd in the Sorbonne's Grand Amphitheatre that I actually was an impostor; and many other very memorable moments as well . . .

But there is of course nothing quite comparable to the Nobel experience. After the phone call from Stockholm and my calling Nathalie and my mother, students and faculty flocked to the building and gave me an incredible reception. Zillions of friends as well as strangers sent warm congratulations, many of them very touching; to the point that, under the general overload, the server broke down and a number of messages were lost.

There is something magic about such moments, as everyone, from the closely related to the more distant, rightfully shares the excitement. The following two months were a series of kind gestures of friendship, culminating with a concert given in my honor by Tugan Sokhiev and the Capitole National Orchestra in the evening of December 4, the day before my leaving for Stockholm. The Nobel week was, needless to say, very special. Sharing these moments with my family and friends was wonderful. Colleagues who had contributed to my receiving the

FIGURE 4. A rather emotional moment.

FIGURE 5. Tirole family: Naïs, Romain, Margot, Nathalie and Jean.

Prize came to Stockholm, even though some of them could not even attend the ceremony and banquet due to the limited number of slots. Many others could not come, but shared the moment nonetheless.

IN CONCLUSION

Research is largely a question of motivation and passion. The intellectual environment is absolutely vital, not only for learning and updating knowledge, but also for motivation. During my career I have been extremely fortunate to "find myself at the right place at the right time" and also to benefit from working with exceptional colleagues and students of the highest caliber, from whom I have learned very much and who often became dear friends. I may just have been very lucky, but I never regretted my early choice of a career as a researcher. As I said in my Banquet speech, wisdom now forces me to return as soon as possible to my previous activities, to the colleagues to whom I am indebted for the Prize, in short to the wonderful life of a researcher.

Market Failures and Public Policy*

Prize Lecture, December 8, 2014

by Jean Tirole
Toulouse School of Economics, France.

1. INTRODUCTION

Economists have long extolled the virtues of markets. Unfettered competition protects consumers from the political influence of lobbies and forces producers to deliver products and services at cost. Alas, competition is rarely perfect, markets fail, and market power—the firms' ability to raise price substantially above cost or to offer low quality[1]—must be kept in check.

Industrial organization studies the exercise and control of market power. To this purpose, it builds models that capture the essence of the situation. The predictions of the model can then be tested econometrically and possibly in the lab or the field. In the end, the reasonableness of, and robustness to modeling assumptions and the quality of empirical fit determine how confident economists are in making recommendations to public decision-makers for intervention, and to companies for the design of their business model.

* This lecture is dedicated to the memory of Jean-Jacques Laffont. It is of course unlike any lecture I had ever given. It is filled with emotion, intellectual indebtedness and very fond memories. The lecture is also very unfair to the community of researchers who have developed industrial organization economics in its modern form. The lecture indeed is in no way a survey, even on its very limited subset of topics, and does not attempt to recognize contributions. Its purpose rather is to use examples drawn from my own research to illustrate the approach and use of theoretical industrial organization. This should however not obscure the fact that modern industrial organization is the outcome of a collective undertaking by a (still vibrant) community of talented researchers.

Industrial organization has a long tradition: first theoretical, with the work of French "engineer-economists" Antoine Augustin Cournot (1838) and Jules Dupuit (1844); then policy-oriented with the enactment of the Sherman Act (1890) and subsequent legislation; then descriptive with the studies of the Harvard school ("Structure-Conduct-Performance") comforting and refining the antitrust drive; and finally skeptical with the Chicago school. The Chicago school correctly pointed out the lack of underlying theoretical doctrine and went on to cast doubt on the whole edifice. However, it did not develop an alternative antitrust doctrine, perhaps because it was broadly suspicious of regulation.

By the late seventies and early eighties, the antitrust and regulation doctrine was in shambles and had to be rebuilt. The modern intellectual corpus that then emerged has been very much a collective effort, involving not only me, but also my closest collaborators on the topic[2] and the many scholars whose own work and discussions with me have deeply influenced my thinking. My being under the spotlight owes more to their contribution than to my own talent. But I claim credit for having been in the right places at the right times and in having learned from fabulous colleagues and students, in the area for which the prize was awarded and in other fields as well.

With sometimes a bit of luck, as when my MIT fellow classmate and fellow Eric Maskin advisee, Drew Fudenberg told me about an interesting field (I actually did not know what "industrial organization" meant . . .). Having already taken my generals, I then sat in fascinating lectures given by Paul Joskow and Dick Schmalensee, and started fruitful collaboration with Drew.

A stroke of good fortune indeed, as the required tools, game theory and information economics, were witnessing a series of breakthroughs.

On the policy front, there was widespread recognition that old-style public utility regulation, which by and large insured public utilities against poor cost performance, led to inflated cost and poor customer satisfaction, and so reforms were called for.

To crown it all, institutional change favored the use of economic reasoning. Where disputes were settled and regulations designed opaquely in the minister's office, transparent processes run by independent agencies were put in place. For instance, competition authorities and regulatory agencies sprang up in Europe, which used economic reasoning.

This most fortunate conjunction of circumstances led to a new paradigm. As was emphasized in the committee's scientific background report, this paradigm is rich and complex. First, counting the number of firms or their market shares provides only a rough indication as to whether the market is competitive.

Second, industries have their specificities. Competition in IT, payment cards, innovation, railroads or cement is different.

Economists accordingly have advocated a case-by-case or "rule of reason" approach to antitrust, away from rigid "per se" rules (which mechanically either allow or prohibit certain behaviors, ranging from price-fixing agreements to resale price maintenance). The economists' pragmatic message however comes with a double social responsibility. First, economists must offer a rigorous analysis of how markets work, taking into account both the specificities of particular industries and what regulators do and do not know;[3] this latter point calls for "information light" policies, that is, policies that do not require information that is unlikely to be available to regulators.

Second, economists must participate in the policy debate. The financial crisis, whose main ingredients could be found in academic journals, is a case in point. But of course, the responsibility here goes both ways. Policymakers and the media must also be willing to listen to economists.

2. RESTRAINING MARKET POWER TO THE BENEFIT OF CONSUMERS

Regulators affect industries in multiple ways:

- Sectoral regulators in telecoms, electricity, railroads or postal services regulate incumbent operators' rate of return and monitor the conditions under which they give rivals access to the bottlenecks that they control.
- Antitrust authorities allow or invalidate horizontal as well as vertical mergers and agreements, and decide whether certain behaviors and contractual covenants constitute an abuse of a dominant position.
- Patent and trademark offices and courts grant, uphold or reject a patent, and determine its scope, its breadth, whether the grantee can seek injunctions and so forth.

Ultimately, these various forms of regulation have in common that regulators face a trade-off between lowering the price for the users, thereby ensuring wider diffusion, and granting a fair return to the firm.

Consider for example the foreclosure doctrine in its modern form.[4] In Figure 1, an upstream firm U has a unique access to an "essential facility," "infrastructure" or "bottleneck input," some input that cannot be reproduced or bypassed by others at a low cost: a railroad tracks and stations network, a power transmission grid, a key patent[5] . . .

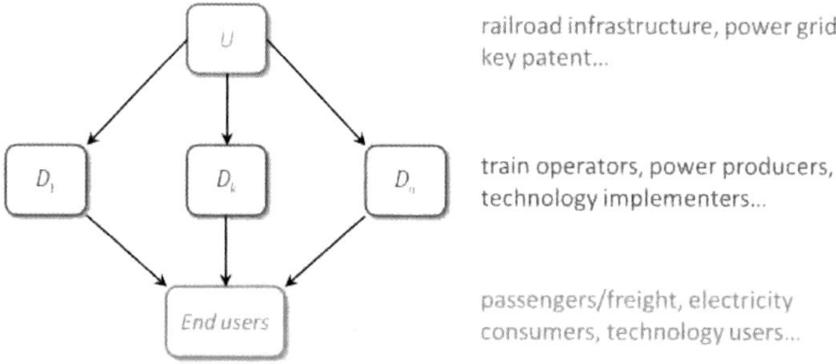

FIGURE 1.

The competition-policy issue is whether the upstream firm should give "equal" or "fair" access to all downstream suppliers (alternative train operators, power producers, technology implementers, $D_1, \ldots, D_n$ in the figure) or whether it should be allowed to "foreclose" access to the bottleneck to all downstream firms but one or a couple of affiliated entities or allies. Such fair access, so goes the argument, allows downstream firms to compete for the end users on a level playing field. Yet, as we will see, what constitutes "fair access" and "enabling of downstream competition" requires some thinking.

Provided that *bilateral negotiations* between the upstream supplier and individual downstream firms are not precluded, downstream competition dissipates the profit that can be extracted from end-users. To see this intuitively, suppose that downstream competitors sell a homogeneous product with demand curve $Q = D(p)$ or $p = P(Q)$, that production upstream and downstream is costless, and that downstream firms transform 1 unit of input into 1 unit of output. The question is whether, by controlling the bottleneck, the upstream firm is able to capture the monopoly profit $\pi_m = \max\{QP(Q)\} = Q^m P(Q^m)$, where Q^m and P^m are the monopoly quantity and price respectively.

Let U and D_i negotiate a quantity q_i to be delivered by U and then put on the market by D_i. Suppose that D_i anticipates that the other downstream firms will bring $Q_{-i} = q_1 + \ldots + q_{i-1} + q_{i+1} + \ldots + q_n$ to the market. Then the quantity q_i that maximizes the sum of U and D_i's profits[6] is the best Cournot reaction $R^C(Q_{-i})$ to Q_{-i}:

$$q_i = R^C(Q_{-i}) = \arg\max \{q_i P(q_i + Q_{-i})\}$$

In this example, the outcome of bilateral, private negotiations is therefore the *Cournot equilibrium* with n firms. The upstream firm behaves opportunistically and does not internalize the negative externality on other downstream firms when negotiating an increase in supply with downstream firm D_i.

Because the upstream profit is capped by the downstream profit, equal to the Cournot industry profit, fair access jeopardizes the ability of the upstream firm to profit from the essential facility: the upstream bottleneck owner is victim of its inability to commit not to flood the downstream market. The more competitive the downstream industry (the larger n is), the more the profit is destroyed and the more eager the upstream firm is to regain its market power (the upstream monopolist makes zero profit in the limit of large n, and this even if it enjoys full bargaining power—i.e., appropriates the joint surplus—in bilateral negotiations). The more general message is clear: under unfettered bilateral negotiations, downstream competition erodes the upstream firm's market power.

In practice therefore, the upstream firm often favors its downstream subsidiary (D_1 in Figure 2) in a myriad of ways, for example by refusing to deal with rivals or to grant them a license, by charging prohibitive access prices, or by making its technology incompatible with the rivals'. If not vertically integrated, it may enter a "sweet deal" with a downstream firm to the same effect. In short, the upstream firm uses exclusivity to restore its market power. For example, a biotech company with a patent on a new drug will grant exclusive rights for the product approval, production and marketing stage to a single pharmaceutical company, either in-house (Sanofi for Genzyme) or external.

A well-meaning antitrust authority might want to promote competition by requiring that the upstream firm give equal treatment to all downstream firms. This policy requires some transparency in contracting, i.e., all contracts must be made public. The equal access requirement will, however, involuntarily lead to

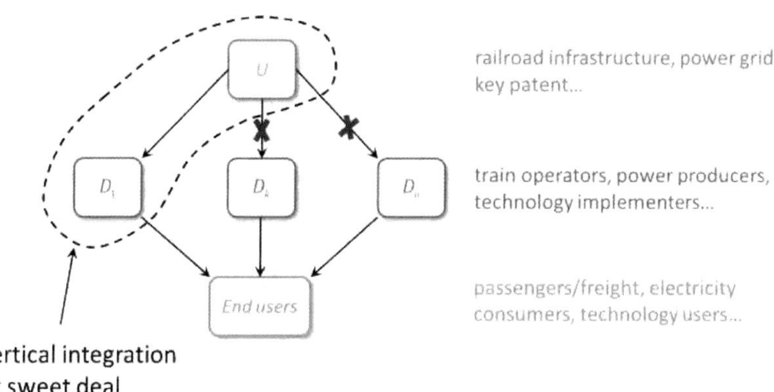

FIGURE 2.

monopoly pricing! The upstream firm can do so for example by offering Q^m/n against payment π^m/n to all downstream firms. Alternatively, it can offer to give free access to the bottleneck resource to whoever will make lump-sum payment π^m; at most one downstream firm would accept the deal, as entry by a second firm would destroy downstream profit and not allow it to recoup the lump-sum payment to the bottleneck owner.[7] Thus, "equal treatment" by no means guarantees low prices for end-users; if anything, it helps the upstream firm to secure its monopoly profit.

Summing up, whether the antitrust authority tolerates such exclusionary behavior or not, it de facto regulates the rate of return on the upstream infrastructure. Should the authority clamp down on exclusionary behaviors? The (common sense) answer summarized in Figure 3 hinges on the answer to the following question: Does the bottleneck result from an investment, an innovation? Or is it associated with political connections, wrong market design or sheer luck? Simply, is there an investment worth of a reward or not? For instance,

- the beneficiary of a highway, harbor or airport concession deserves its monopoly power if the monopoly position was acquired through a competitive, well-designed auction, but not if it was acquired free of charge or through a biased auction design.
- An inventor should be allowed to exploit the innovation himself or grant an exclusive license if the innovation is major, but not if the innovation lacks novelty or is obvious, but nonetheless is protected by intellectual property law.
- A public utility should earn a reasonable profit on investment, but not benefit from lucky cost and demand conditions. For example, it should not be able to benefit from a fall in the market price of a key input, while being able to renegotiate the regulatory contract if that price shoots up.

Market power is

	deserved	undeserved
concession	competitive, well-designed auction	unpaid-for legal monopoly
intellectual property	major innovation	obvious, not novel innovation
utility regulation	investment/effort	lucky cost and demand conditions

FIGURE 3.

The same reasoning underlies much of antitrust doctrine, which, following Schumpeter, does not view monopoly power as illegal, but frowns upon the further acquisition of market power through merger or abuse of a dominant position.[8]

To be certain, finer information may be needed to assess the substantive merit of market power. Software markets are often dominated at any given point of time by a large firm benefiting from network externalities among users. Such network externalities may result from chance (users have just coordinated on the platform) or may have been created through investment. Similarly, it is often not obvious whether a utility's profit comes from its cost-reducing or demand-expanding effort or sheer luck. This brings me to the issue of regulatory information.

Handling a firm's informational superiority

Regulators face a double asymmetry of information, called adverse selection and moral hazard respectively.

- First, regulated firms have superior knowledge about their environment: their technology, the cost of their inputs, the demand for their products and services.
- Second, they take actions that affect cost and demand: human resource management, strategic choices of plant capacity, R&D and brand image, quality control, risk management and so forth.

In its simplest version, the firm's cost function can be written as:

$$C = f(\beta, e, \boldsymbol{q}) + \varepsilon,$$

where β is an efficiency parameter known only to the firm, e (possibly multidimensional) is a cost-reducing effort, $\boldsymbol{q} = (q_1, \ldots, q_n)$ is the vector of outputs, and ε stands for exogenous uncertainty about the final realization of the cost. The effort e is also unobserved by the regulator and is costly to the firm.

Unsurprisingly, authorities that neglect the asymmetry of information fail to deliver effective, cost-efficient regulation.[9] There are two broad principles here.

The first is obvious. Authorities should attempt to reduce the asymmetry of information: by collecting data of course; but also by benchmarking the firm's performance to that of similar firms operating in different markets; and finally by auctioning off the monopoly rights (as firms reveal information about industry cost when competing with each other).

The second principle is that one size does not fit all: one should let the regulated firm make use of its information. Before we get to this, imagine that you are in charge of dealing with a contractor. Two familiar contracts will probably come to your mind:

- you can offer to fully reimburse the contractor's cost, plus some set payment over this cost; such a contract is called a "cost plus" contract if the taxpayer foots the bill or a "rate-of-return" contract if the cost and reward are derived from revenue from the users;
- or you can fix the total payment and tell the firm that this payment will cover its return as well as its cost, whatever the latter turns out to be; such a contract is called a "fixed price" or "price cap" contract.

The two contracts differ in the strength of incentives provided to the contractor: The cost-plus contract shelters the firm from fluctuations in its cost performance, while the fixed price contract makes the firm fully accountable for its cost performance. For example, in the case of a non-marketed good, the *net* return t for the firm is:

$$t = a - bC,$$

with $b = 0$ for a cost-plus contract,[10] $= 1$ for a fixed-price contract, and between 0 and 1 more generally. The slope b is called the "power of the incentive scheme" or "cost-sharing parameter."

The fixed price contract obviously elicits more cost-reducing effort from the firm. It however has the drawback of leaving substantial profit to the firm in lucky circumstances in which costs turn out to be particularly low or demand high, independently of any effort made by the firm. In the example above, the fixed fee a must be set sufficiently high so as to induce the firm to produce if its cost is high.

Returning to the "one size does not fit all" idea, one can show that regulated firms should be confronted with a menu of options; to oversimplify, this menu might take the form of a choice between a fixed-price and a cost-plus contract. The firm then self-selects: an efficient firm will opt for being accountable for its cost, while an inefficient firm will opt for the protection of cost-plus.[11]

Raising the power of incentives has been key to remedy the dismal cost performance of traditional regulation. However, theory and practice indicate some caveats regarding high-powered incentives:[12]

First, making the firm accountable for its cost performance also provides the firm with an incentive to skimp quality; so powerful incentives must go together with a more thorough monitoring of quality.

Second, the observation that powerful incentives generate both high effort and high profit (or rent) implies that regulators cannot have their cake and eat it too. The firm will be rewarded both for its effort to reduce cost (as it should) and for lucky circumstances (as it should not: this is an undeserved rent); but asymmetric information means that there is no way to tell the two apart. While regulators, under the pressure of public opinion, may be tempted to take back this rent ex post, such policy reversal destroys the firm's incentive to reduce cost.[13] A wider knowledge of this principle would have prevented some wishful thinking when powerful incentives were introduced.

Thus, powerful incentives require commitment; this commitment in turn requires an independent regulatory agency, protected from the pressure of public opinion.

Third, the possibility of high rents increases the benefit for the firm of capturing its regulator. So, if you cannot guarantee the regulator's independence from industry (and if you do not have enough competition), don't go for powerful incentives.

Be careful when tinkering with the price structure

The essence of regulation is often to ensure that undeserved market power does not translate into high overall prices. Traditionally, though, regulators have gone way beyond price-*level* regulation; they also have tampered with the ratio of prices, that is, with the price *structure*. There, too, they face a substantial informational handicap. Moreover the need for intervention is much less obvious than in the case of the price level: While it is clear that a monopoly has incentives to charge high prices, it is a priori less clear that it is biased in its choice of letting Bob rather than Anna bear the brunt of market power.

In 1956, Marcel Boiteux, building on earlier work by Franck Ramsey, asked: how should the fixed infrastructure cost of a regulated firm be covered by markups on the various goods sold by the firm? This fixed cost is presumably large, as the motivation for regulating the firm is its monopoly power, protected by the reluctance of entrants to duplicate the fixed cost. Boiteux showed that regulated firms should exhibit a price structure similar to that of ordinary, unregulated ones: in equation (1), the price p_i in segment i should be low if the segment is cheap to serve (the cost c_i is low), and has a high elasticity of demand η_i (that is, if a price increase implies a substantial reduction in demand).[14] As the fixed production cost to be covered through markups increases, these markups also increase (i.e., θ increases). Thus, regulated prices should be "business-oriented," similar to, but overall lower than those set by an unregulated monopoly (for whom the coefficient θ would be equal to 1.

$$\frac{p_i - c_i}{p_i} = \frac{\theta}{\eta_i} \tag{1}$$

Furthermore, and under some conditions,[15] the regulatory problem decomposes: the trade-off between rents and cost-reducing effort should be addressed through the cost—or profit—sharing rule, and pricing should obey the Ramsey-Boiteux principle. This dichotomous result has practical implications, as we will see shortly.

Yet regulators used to force regulated firms to set an economically very inefficient price structure. Typically, utilities charged low prices on inelastic segments such as monthly subscription fees to be connected to the power or telephone network, and high prices on elastic consumption (e.g., long distance phone calls). They also charged high prices to business and low prices to residential consumers, while the former had more bypass opportunities. One justification for this was redistributive concerns; but these cross-subsidies also benefited the rich, and furthermore whether or not redistribution could be achieved by other, more efficient means (say, the income tax) was not discussed.

This price tinkering away from Ramsey-Boiteux principles was also sometimes motivated by the (correct) premise that regulators do not possess the information about cost and demand to fine-tune prices in a business-oriented fashion.

This, however, ignored the possibility of making use of decentralized information. The above-mentioned dichotomy between incentives and pricing opens the way for the use of business-oriented pricing. A price cap regulation, in which the firm must only comply with some cap on its weighted[16] average price, not only creates powerful incentives by making the firm accountable for its cost, but also sets the firm free to choose a business-oriented price structure.

A special case of this idea arises when one of the "products" supplied by the monopoly is an intermediate input, that is, the provision of access for rivals to an essential facility. By imposing access prices at marginal cost (assuming they can measure it), regulators de facto bias the price structure and focus markups on those final segments for which the essential facility owner faces no competition.[17] This is bound to be inefficient in general.

3. TWO-SIDED MARKETS

A particularly interesting choice of price structure arises in so-called two-sided markets. Two-sided "platforms" bring together multiple user-communities that want to interact with each other: gamers and game developers for videogames; users of operating systems and app developers for operating systems; "eyeballs" and advertisers for search and media platforms; cardholders and merchants for payment card transactions (Figure 4). The challenge for two-sided platforms is to find a viable business model that gets both sides on board.

Regardless of their market power, whether they are Google or a free newspaper like *Metro*,

- they choose to allocate a lower burden to the side (say side i) whose presence benefits most users on the other side. In equation (2), v_j represents how much a side-j user values an extra user on side i. This willingness to pay for an interaction with an extra user on side i can be recouped by the platform through a price increase on side j; the platform's real, or opportunity cost is therefore the platform's production cost c per interaction (perhaps equal to 0) minus v_j,
- like ordinary businesses, they choose a lower burden for the side which has a relatively elastic demand (a high η_i in the formula).

$$\frac{p_i-\left(c-v_j\right)}{p_i}=\frac{1}{\eta_i} \qquad (2)$$

Equation (2) often results in very skewed pricing patterns, with one side paying nothing (free search engine, portal, newspaper) or even being paid to

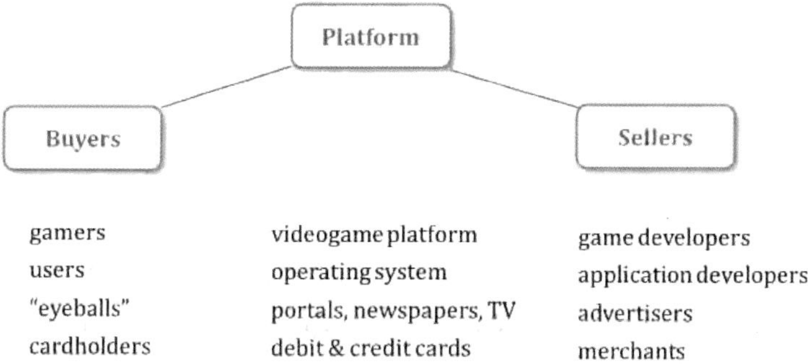

FIGURE 4.

enjoy the service (cardholders receiving cash-back bonuses[18]), while the other side is heavily taxed. The simplest example is that of sponsored-links/advertising-financed platforms: advertisers put a high value v_j on interacting with (especially well-to-do) buyers, while the latter attach little value to the presence of ads, or possibly perceive it as a nuisance.[19]

A regulator failing to understand the nature of two-sided markets might misleadingly complain about predation on the low-price side or even excessive pricing on the high-price side, despite the fact that such price structures are also selected by small, entering platforms. Regulators should refrain from mechanically applying standard antitrust ideas where they do not belong.

This does not mean that they should turn a blind eye when facing two-sided platforms. A case in point is provided by platforms that supply a service to their members, but are not the only route for a purchase (see Figure 5). For instance, American Express provides the cardholder with a service, but other payment methods such as cash, check, or other card systems are also available. A hotel or airline flight can be booked either through an online booking platform, such as Booking.com, or directly.

Such platforms usually charge a merchant fee and demand "price coherence" (the merchant is not allowed to surcharge for a transaction performed through the platform relative to a transaction that does not use it). While price coherence has sound justifications (it prevents surcharging hold-ups by the merchant[20]), it also comes with hazards; for, high merchant fees are in part passed through to third parties, namely consumers who do not use the platform. This may result in excessive merchant fees.[21] The market failure in this instance is not the skewed

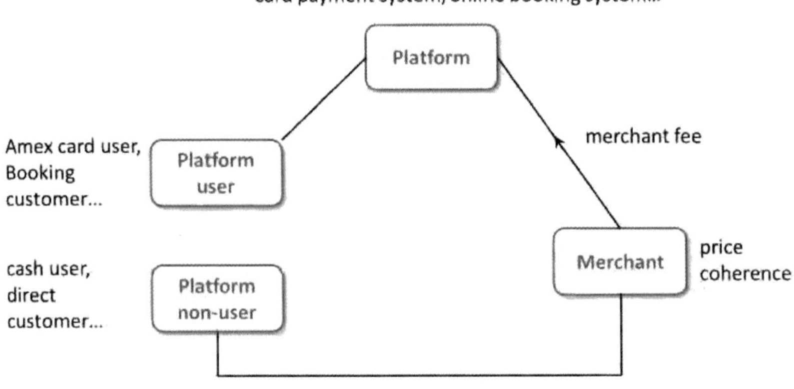

FIGURE 5.

pricing pattern (which is typical of two-sided markets), but the externality on non-contracting parties.

The analysis reveals that the merchant fee should obey the following Pigovian principle: In the case of card payments, the merchant fee should be equal to the benefit that the merchant derives from a card payment.[22] The consumer, who decides on the payment method, then exerts no externality on the merchant. This principle is now the European Commission's doctrine for regulating open systems Visa and MasterCard.

In this realm as in many others, neither laissez-faire nor a shotgun regulatory approach is warranted. Only sound economic analysis will do.

4. INTELLECTUAL PROPERTY

The rule-of-reason approach to competition policy requires some confidence as to which, of efficiency and anticompetitive effects, dominates. In this respect, simple rules can greatly strengthen our confidence in policy choices.

Consider intellectual property (IP), for which the shortage of data can be acute, with technologies not having yet hit the ground. Biotech and software technologies are often covered by a multiplicity of patents of varying importance and owned by different owners. This "patent thicket" is conducive to "royalty stacking" (or "multiple marginalizations" in the parlance of economics).

To understand royalty stacking, which was brilliantly formalized in 1838 by Antoine Augustin Cournot (1838) and more recently by Carl Shapiro (2001), it may be helpful to use an analogy (depicted in Figure 6) and return to medieval Europe, whose river transit was hampered by a multiplicity of tolls; for instance, there were 64 tolls on the Rhine River in the 14th century.[23] Each toll collector set his toll to maximize his revenue, oblivious of what this meant not only for the users but also for other toll collectors. Europe had to wait until the Congress of Vienna in 1815 and subsequent legislations to see the removal of toll-stacking.[24]

High technologies are currently witnessing an evolution toward more affordable prices, similar to that for river traffic in the 19th century. New guidelines have been set, so as to encourage the co-marketing of intellectual property through patent pools. Patent pools reduce the overall price of licensing complementary patents, benefiting both intellectual property owners and technology users.

Alas, patent pools and more generally co-marketing arrangements also may allow firms to raise price. For instance, the owners of two substitute patents (like the toll collectors on the two river branches in Figure 7) can raise licensing price

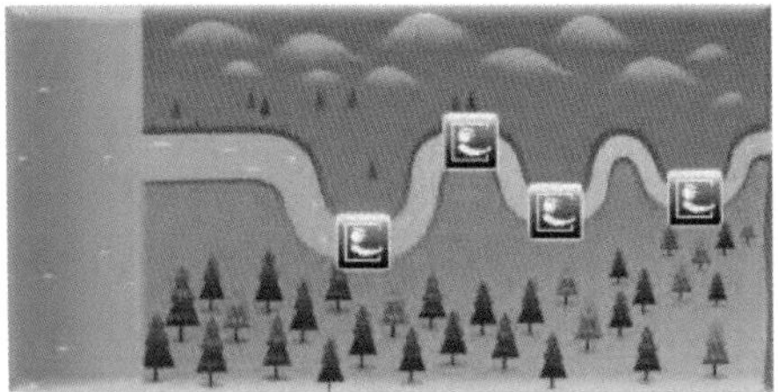

FIGURE 6.

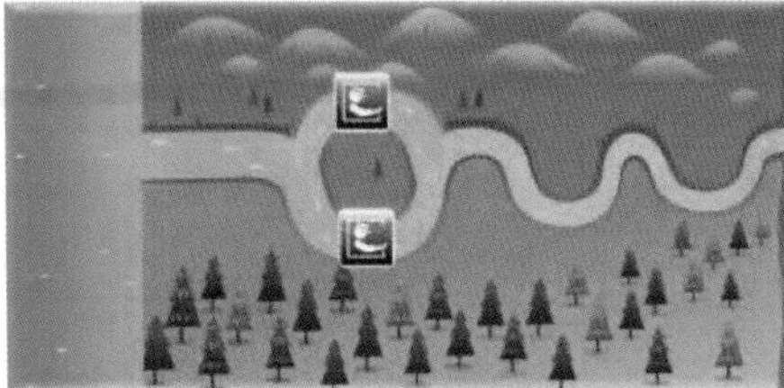

FIGURE 7.

to the monopoly level by forming a patent pool (setting a collusive toll for downstream access in the figure), akin to a cartel or a merger to monopoly.

A flashback is useful again. A little known fact is that, prior to 1945, most high-tech industries of the time were run by patent pools.[25] But the worry about cartelization through joint marketing led to a hostile decision of the US Supreme Court in 1945 and the disappearance of pools until the recent revival of interest.

But couldn't competition authorities just ban bad (price-increasing) pools and allow good (price-decreasing) ones? They unfortunately do not possess the relevant information: There is often no long history of licensing, and furthermore the pattern of substitutability/complementarity changes with the uses made of the technology[26].

However, simple regulations allow such sorting. First, "individual licensing" (the ability of individual owners to keep licensing their patents outside the pool, see Figure 8) re-creates competition when patent pools would otherwise have raised price. Patent pools with individual licensing therefore neutralize bad pools, while allowing good ones to achieve their price reduction.

The reasoning is best illustrated in the very simple case of two substitute patents. The competitive price for the licenses is then equal to 0 (assuming away any licensing cost). A pool has the potential to raise the price up to the monopoly price P^m, say. Suppose that the pool tries to sets a price $P(\leq P^m)$. Then each IP owner receives in dividends $PD(P)/2$, letting $D(.)$ denote the demand function

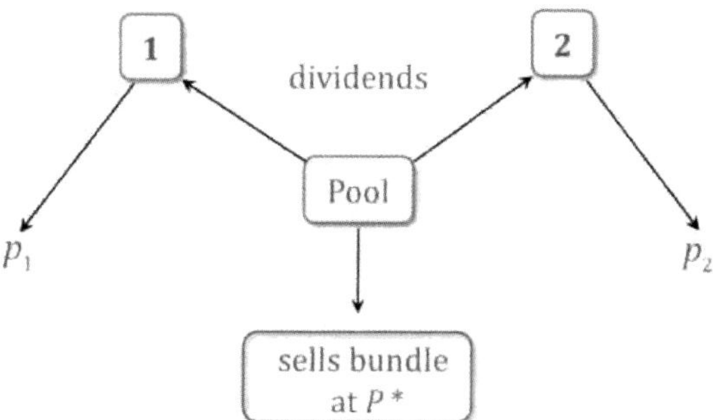

FIGURE 8.

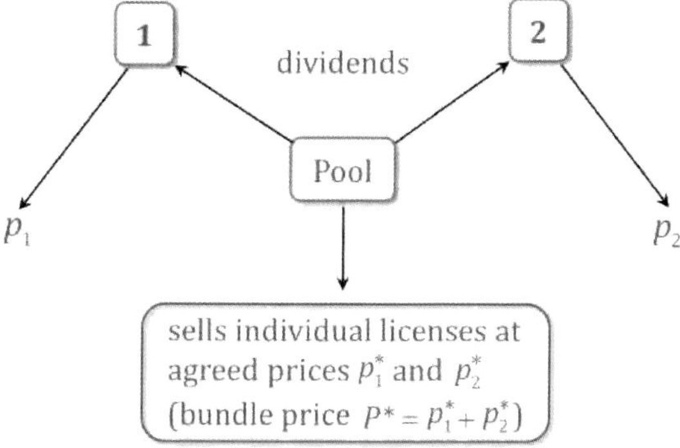

FIGURE 9.

for licenses and assuming equal sharing.[27] Rather than receive half of the pool's profit in dividends, each IP owner can undercut the pool slightly, and receive (approximately) the entire profit $PD(P)$ for itself.[28]

Second, and to counter the threat of tacit collusion (in the reasoning above, individual IP owners might forgo the short-run gain of undercutting the pool through a cheaper individual-license price, so as to prevent a price war and to keep sustaining the pool's high price in the future), it is wise to append a second, information-free requirement, called "unbundling": The users can buy individual licenses from the pool, and the pool price for multiple licenses is the sum of the individual prices (see Figure 9). Individual licensing together with unbundling implies that accepting a pool does not reduce welfare.[29]

Interestingly, both precepts derived from theory—independent licensing and unbundling—have been incorporated in the European guidelines (in 2004 and 2014, respectively); the US Department of Justice had required independent licensing in its Business Review Letters in the late 1990s already.

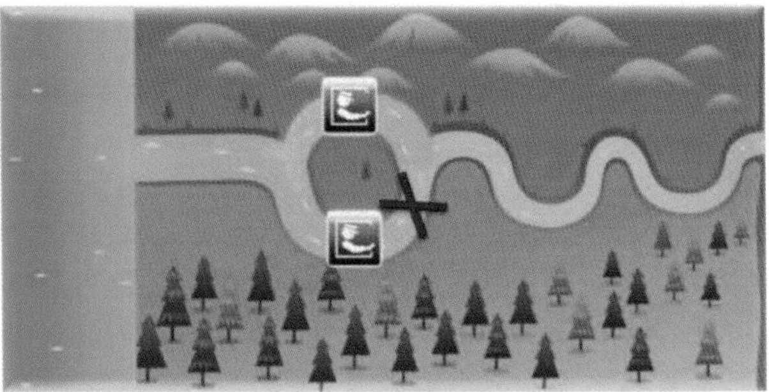

FIGURE 10.

Another information-free precept for the treatment of intellectual property originating from theoretical work is the suggestion that intellectual property owners commit to a cap on their licensing price before a standard is finalized. When a standard is designed, in many cases there are multiple routes to solving a given technological problem. Each one of these may be equally viable, but often a standard setting body will choose only one avenue (to pursue the analogy, the public authority may have enabled traffic on the upper branch of the river by building a lock on that branch; or the presence of a major city on the upper branch may have made this branch a superior alternative, as in Figure 10). After the decision has been made, however, the chosen patent becomes a "standard-essential patent (SEP)," and the patent owner can ask for a high royalty even though another patent could have offered comparable value, had the technology been designed differently.

To restrain firms from taking advantage of the fortuitous essentiality of their patents, an essentiality that resulted only from being included in a standard and not from technological merit, standard-setting bodies commonly require firms to commit in advance to license their patents on fair, reasonable and non-discriminatory (FRAND) terms. The problem with this approach is that FRAND commitments are very ambiguous: What exactly is a fair and reasonable rate? And in fact, large lawsuits regarding the meaning of the commitment proliferate all over the world.

One would not build a house on a piece of land whose price is not known in advance. The same obtains for technologies. We have proposed that intellectual property owners commit to their licensing conditions prior to the final choice of standard and we tried to explain why this commitment requirement is unlikely to result from competition among standard-setting bodies.[30]

5. CONCLUDING REMARKS

The theory of industrial organization has proved a very useful tool to think about one of the major challenges of our economies. It has fashioned antitrust and regulation. Recognizing that industries are different from each other and so one size does not fit all, it has patiently built a body of knowledge that has helped regulators to better understand market power and the effects of policy interventions, and firms to formulate their strategies.

Industrial organization has gone a long way, but much work remains to be done. An especially gratifying aspect is that the field of industrial organization is currently thriving, with many top young researchers producing exciting work.

Making this world a better world is the economist's first mission. I believe that the entire community of industrial organization researchers has contributed substantially to this mission. On behalf of this community, I was humbled, honored and grateful to be awarded the 2014 Sveriges Riksbank Prize in Economic Sciences in Memory of Alfred Nobel.

REFERENCES

1. Aghion, P. and P. Bolton. (1987). "Contracts as a Barrier to Entry," *American Economic Review*, 77(3): 388–401.
2. Armstrong, M. (1998). "Network Interconnection in Telecommunications," *Economic Journal*, 108 (448): 545–564.
3. Armstrong, M. (2006). "Competition in Two-Sided Markets," *RAND Journal of Economics*, 37(3): 668–69.
4. Armstrong, M. and J. Vickers. (2000). "Multiproduct Price Regulation under Asymmetric Information," *Journal of Industrial Economics*, 48: 137–160.
5. Baron, D. and R. Myerson. (1982). "Regulating a Monopolist with Unknown Costs," *Econometrica*, 50(4): 911–930.
6. Boiteux, M. (1956). "Sur la gestion des Monopoles Publics astreints à l'équilibre budgétaire," *Econometrica*, 24(1): 22–40
7. Bourguignon, H., R. Gomes and J. Tirole. (2014). "Shrouded Transaction Costs," mimeo, TSE.
8. Boutin, A. (2014). "Screening for Good Patent Pools through Price Caps on Individual Licenses," mimeo, ULB.
9. Caillaud, B. and B. Jullien. (2003). "Chicken & Egg: Competition among Intermediation Service Providers," *RAND Journal of Economics*, 34(2): 309–328.
10. Cournot, A.A. (1838). *Recherches sur les Principes Mathématiques de la Théorie des Richesses*.
11. Dupuit, J. (1844). "De la mesure de l'utilité des travaux publics," *Annales des Ponts et Chaussées*, Paris.

12. Edelman, B., and J. Wright. (2014). "Price Coherence and Adverse Intermediation," mimeo.
13. Freixas, X., Guesnerie, R., and J. Tirole. (1985). "Planning under Incomplete Information and the Ratchet Effect," *Review of Economic Studies*, 173–191.
14. Hart O., and J. Tirole. (1990). "Vertical Integration and Market Foreclosure," *Brookings Papers on Economic Activity*, Washington: Brookings Institution, vol. 1990, "Microeconomics," 1990, p. 205–286.
15. Laffont, J.J., P. Rey and J. Tirole. (1998). "Network Competition: I. Overview and Nondiscriminatory Pricing; II. Price Discrimination," *RAND Journal of Economics*, 29(1): 1–37; 38–56.
16. Laffont, J.J. and J. Tirole. (1986). "Using Cost Observation to Regulate Firms," *Journal of Political Economy*, 94: 614–641.
17. Laffont, J.J. and J. Tirole. (1988). "The Dynamics of Incentive Contracts," *Econometrica*, 56: 1153–1175.
18. Laffont, J.J. and J. Tirole. (1990). "The Regulation of Multiproduct Firms, I: Theory; II: Applications to Competitive Environments and Policy Analysis," *Journal of Public Economics*, 43: 1–36; 37–66.
19. Laffont, J.J. and J. Tirole. (1993). *A Theory of Incentives in Procurement and Regulation*, MIT Press.
20. Laffont, J.J. and J. Tirole. (1994). "Access Pricing and Competition," *European Economic Review*, 38(9): 1673–1710.
21. Lerner, J. and J. Tirole. (2004). "Efficient Patent Pools," *American Economic Review*, 94(3): 691–711.
22. Lerner, J. and J. Tirole. (2015). "Standard-Essential Patents," *Journal of Political Economy*, 123: 547–586.
23. Loeb, M., and W. Magat. (1979). "A Decentralized Method of Utility Regulation," *Journal of Law and Economics*, 22: 399–404.
24. Rey, P. and J. Tirole. (2007). "A Primer on Foreclosure," *Handbook of Industrial Organization*, vol. 3, ed. by M. Armstrong and R.H. Porter, North Holland, pp. 2145–2220
25. Rey, P. and J. Tirole. (2013). "Cooperation vs. Collusion: How Essentiality Shapes Co-opetition," IDEI Working Paper, n° 801.
26. Rochet, J.C. and J. Tirole. (2002). "Cooperation among Competitors: Some Economics of Payment Card Associations," *The RAND Journal of Economics*, 33(4): 549–570.
27. Rochet, J.C. and J. Tirole. (2003). "Platform Competition in Two-Sided Markets," *Journal of the European Economic Association*, 1(4): 990–1029.
28. Rochet, J.C. and J. Tirole. (2006). "Two-Sided Markets: A Progress Report," *RAND Journal of Economics*, 37(3): 645–667.
29. Rochet, J.C. and J. Tirole. (2011). "Must Take Cards: Merchant Discounts and Avoided Costs," *Journal of the European Economic Association*, 9(3): 462–495.
30. Sappington, D. (1982). "Optimal Regulation of Research and Development under Imperfect Information," *Bell Journal of Economics*, 13(2): 354–368.
31. Segal, I. (1999). "Contracting with Externalities," *Quarterly Journal of Economics*, 114(2), 1999, pp. 337–388.

32. Spaulding, R. M. (2011). "Revolutionary France and the Transformation of the Rhine," *Central European History*, 44(02): 203–226.
33. Whinston, M. (1990). "Tying, Foreclosure, and Exclusion," *American Economic Review*, 80(4):837–859.

ENDNOTES

1. Industrial organization economists have studied a variety of other market failures, involving information problems and a range of externalities (such as environmental damages or banking failures) which arise even in the absence of market power; small banks (such as the Cajas and the Landesbanken recently in Europe) often fail, leaving the deposit insurance fund/taxpayer to pay for bailouts, and firms without market power often pollute. This lecture focuses on market power, which limits the diffusion of a product, service or technology to downstream firms and end-users.
2. Chronologically, and very unfairly to the many others with whom I have had the chance to interact, Drew Fudenberg, Eric Maskin, Jean-Jacques Laffont—to whose memory this lecture is dedicated—as well as Patrick Rey, Jean-Charles Rochet, Paul Joskow, and Josh Lerner.
3. They must also account for enforcement costs.
4. The discussion here follows Hart-Tirole (1990) and Rey-Tirole (2007), to which we refer for the "loose ends" left over by this intuitive discussion. See also Segal (1999) for a broader treatment, which covers applications beyond industrial organization.
5. Antitrust practitioners are often reluctant to call a key patent an "essential facility"; for an essential facility is usually associated with an obligation to share. I nonetheless include key patents in the essential facility category as it fits the criterion "some input that cannot be reproduced or bypassed by others at a low cost." We will later discuss the obligation to share.
6. This quantity maximizes the "cake" to be divided between the two parties; the sharing of this cake will involve a monetary transfer between them.
7. Still another way of obtaining the monopoly profit is to offer the same following two-part tariff to all downstream firms: $T(q) = A + wq$, where w, the wholesale price, satisfies: $nq^C(w) = Q^m$, the monopoly quantity, and $q^C(w)$ is the Cournot quantity given unit cost w. The fixed fee A is then set so as to capture the resulting Cournot profit of each downstream firm.
   None of the schemes allowing the upstream firm to reap monopoly profit is robust to additional, private contracting: for there is always money to be made by the upstream firm by contracting for a higher quantity with an individual downstream firm as long as the latter's quantity lies below the Cournot reaction curve (for zero marginal cost). Thus, to sustain individual quantities below $q^C(0)$, all contracts must indeed be public.
8. For example, the antitrust authority may disapprove the handicapping of horizontal rivals, say, by making one's technology incompatible when no protection of intellectual property is at stake, by locking in customers through long-term contracts that have limited efficiency justification (as in e.g., Aghion-Bolton 1987), or by

committing to tough behavior through irremediable tying (as in e.g., the model of horizontal foreclosure of Whinston 1990).

9. To take two examples unrelated to market power, command-and-control in environmental regulation all over the world and judicial control of the business justification for layoffs in Southern Europe have backfired by imposing high costs on the industry and thereby casting doubts on the sustainability of these policies. The same principle holds for industrial organization.
10. Define "effort" as being costly for the firm (what is done beyond intrinsic motivation or career concerns), and $e = 0$ as the minimum effort. Then the cost-plus contract elicits $e = 0$ and yields a β– independent rent for the firm. Hence, the rent can be made small without jeopardizing the firm's participation.
11. See, e.g., Laffont-Tirole (1986). Precursors to my work with Jean-Jacques Laffont include Loeb-Magat (1979), Baron-Myerson (1982) and Sappington (1982). Under some conditions, the optimal regulatory scheme lets the firm pick within a menu of linear incentive contracts $t = a - b\,C$, each characterized by a pair of fixed-payment and cost-sharing parameters (a, b).
12. A broader list of caveats of high-powered incentives and their theoretical modeling can be found in Laffont-Tirole (1993).
13. This is the so-called "ratchet effect" (see, e.g., Freixas et al. (1985) and Laffont-Tirole (1988)).
14. Here we consider the case of independent demands; formulas must be adjusted to account for "cross-elasticities" in case of substitutes or complements.
15. See Laffont-Tirole (1990). The dichotomy does not hold in the absence of cost or profit measurement (Baron-Myerson 1982) as then a single instrument (the vector of prices) must accomplish two goals: capture the firm's rent and limit the departure from Ramsey-Boiteux principles.
16. This, of course, is very much of an idealization. In theory, the weights should be equal to the anticipated quantities at the Ramsey-Boiteux prices (not those that result from the firm's choice so as not to let it manipulate the weights); intuitively, an increase in price p_i generates a reduction of consumer surplus equal to the quantity of good i; a price cap based on the anticipated quantities therefore creates just the right "internalization" of consumer surplus. The caveat is of course asymmetric information: the regulator does not know the Ramsey-Boiteux quantities. More research is needed on this front (see Armstrong-Vickers 2000 for a contribution in this direction). Empirically, though, the use of price caps has had a substantial rebalancing effect toward a Ramsey-Boiteux-oriented price structure.
17. To see this, suppose that good i is supplied by a competitive downstream fringe at marginal cost c_D. The regulated firm owns the bottleneck input that allows the downstream fringe to operate. The upstream marginal cost is c_U. Let $c_i = c_D + c_U$. If access is given at access price $a = c_D$, then $p_i = c_i$ is lower than in the Ramsey-Boiteux formula. The fixed cost must then be recouped entirely through (very high) prices on goods for which the regulated firm faces no competition. For more on such "one-way" access pricing, see Laffont-Tirole (1994). Here I will not discuss "two-way" access pricing, in which owners of competitive bottlenecks (e.g., mobile phone

companies) give each other access; there is an abundant literature on this since the early work of Armstrong (1998) and Laffont et al (1998).

18. The case of payment cards is more complex than the other examples, since the card/cash payment decision is coupled with the decision as to whether to come to the store and inspect and purchase the good. This coupling implies that the merchant may be willing to take cards even if the benefit he derives from a card payment relative to a cash payment is smaller than the "merchant fee" that he has to pay for the card payment. The reason for this is two-fold: he may want to attract informed customers by accepting cards (Rochet-Tirole 2002) and he may be afraid that card refusal will lead to lost sales from unaware customers (Bourguignon et al 2014). Either way, the merchant perceives the card as a "must-take card."
19. There are many theoretical and empirical analyses of two-sided markets, including among the early theory pieces Armstrong (2006), Caillaud-Jullien (2003) and Rochet-Tirole (2003, 2006).
20. See e.g., Bourguignon et al (2014) and the literature on hold-ups/shrouded attributes.
21. See Rochet-Tirole (2002) and for a recent and elegant framework Edelman-Wright (2014).
22. This principle is called the "avoided cost test" or the "tourist test" (would the merchant rather have a customer pay by card rather than cash, given that the customer is in the shop, can pay by either means of payment and a tourist and therefore will not be attracted in the future by the merchant's accepting the card?). See Rochet-Tirole (2011).
23. There were 13 tolls between Mainz and Köln alone. Similar observations apply to the Elbe River or the French rivers (Rhône, Seine, Garonne, and Loire): see Spaulding (2011).
24. Actually, all tolls were abolished along the Rhine River.
25. These included airplanes, railroads, cars, TV, radio, chemicals, and many others.
26. Another issue is that patents may be complements at low prices (users will use the complete set at such prices and so an increase in a licensing price reduces the demand for the overall technology) and substitutes at higher prices.
27. Unequal sharing would imply that the IP owner with a lower share would have even more incentives to undercut.
28. The undercutting equilibrium still restores the pre-pool level of competition for a bad pool when there are more than two patents and/or when the patents are imperfect substitutes. But coordination problems then may lead to multiple equilibria (when $n > 2$). Boutin (2014) shows that appending the unbundling requirement (discussed below) selects the competition-restoring equilibrium.
29. See Rey-Tirole (2013).
30. See Lerner-Tirole (2015).

Economic Sciences 2015

Angus Deaton

"for his analysis of consumption, poverty, and welfare"

The Sveriges Riksbank Prize In Economic Sciences In Memory of Alfred Nobel

Speech by Professor Tore Ellingsen of the Royal Swedish Academy of Sciences.

Translation of the Swedish text.

Your Majesties, Your Royal Highnesses, Esteemed Nobel Laureates, Ladies and Gentlemen,

Immanuel Nobel was born on March 24, 1801. We know very little about his childhood, except that his schooling was short—at least to begin with. This was how most people in Sweden lived at that time, provided they were lucky enough to be among the sixty-five per cent who survived long enough to start school.

But Immanuel possessed exceptional technical talent and soon became an engineer and inventor. At the age of thirty, he was already a successful entrepreneur, married, with two children and his own house on the isle of Långholmen in Stockholm.

But his luck turned. Immanuel lost three barges filled with valuable cargo. The family's house burned to the ground. When a third son was born on October 21, 1833, his father's company had already gone bankrupt. Weak and sickly, Alfred Nobel arrived in a poor household. His gloomy childhood experiences marked him for life. Perhaps this is why, as a celebrated inventor and wealthy industrialist, Alfred later became a close friend of author Victor Hugo, portrayer of the unfortunate and poor—*Les Miserables.*

Through Hugo's tales of human adversities, those of us who are more fortunate can also begin to grasp the plight of the poor. But where the task of the writer ends, that of the researcher begins. Only by using the tools of science can we estimate the scale of poverty and understand how we can best fight it.

Scientific insights are rarely obvious, except in retrospect. How do you measure a poor person's income and living standard? What is typical of most genuinely poor people is the absence of ordinary employment and a steady recorded income. They live in an informal economy, characterised by subsistence living and barter. The life stories of poor people leave few traces in the national accounts.

Angus Deaton realised that material poverty is much better described from the expenditure side than from the income side. What do people eat, how much and how often? What is their housing like? How many children do they have? What clothes, sanitary conditions and health services are available to them? Thanks to decades of extensive household surveys, which Deaton helped design and analyse, today we can provide a scientific answer to the big question: Is material poverty around the world increasing or decreasing? The answer is that the percentage of the world's population living in deep misery is decreasing. Why? One important reason is that economic growth in the world's most populous countries, India and China, has improved living conditions even among the poorest.

But not all the findings from these household surveys are equally uplifting. People's living standard increases more slowly than recorded production. National accounts overestimate growth, since they ignore the fact that the informal sector shrinks as poverty falls.

One consistent theme runs through Deaton's research contributions. It is wrong to believe that people's various expenditures are strictly proportional to their income and wealth. Low income earners often consume entirely different goods than high income earners. Both save for the future, but the poorest save for partly other reasons than the richest. In many places today—as in the Sweden of 1833—the availability of safety nets, loans and credits is smallest when the need is greatest. If we want to understand what is happening at the macro level—in a local community, in a country or in the whole world—it is thus not enough to view the micro level as if it were an average or typical individual. Instead, Angus Deaton teaches us to carefully study how individuals living in a risky environment, like Immanuel Nobel, adapt to their different and constantly changing material conditions. Only then can we explain the interaction between consumption, saving and income in society as a whole. Only then can we understand how reforms affect the poor and the rich.

Dear Professor Deaton,

Your research spans innumerable aspects of consumption, great and small. Yet it is unified. You build new theories and discover unrecognised predictions of old ones, you master every detail of existing data, and you invent additional data through new measures and measurements.

You are an optimist, a skeptic, and a humanist. And above all, you are an empericist—always determined to confront what we believe with what we can know. Just like Alfred Nobel.

It is an honor and a privilege for me to convey to you, on behalf of the Royal Swedish Aademy of Sciences, our warmest congratulations. May I now please ask you to step forward and receive your prize from His Majesty the King.

Angus Deaton.

Angus Deaton

SCOTLAND

I was born in Edinburgh, in Scotland, a few days after the end of the Second World War. Both my parents had left school at a very young age, unwillingly in my father's case. Yet both had deep effects on my education, my father influencing me toward measurement and mathematics, and my mother toward writing and history.

The school in the Yorkshire mining village in which my father grew up in the 1920s and 1930s allowed only a few children to go to high school, and my father was not one of them. He spent much of his time as a young man repairing this deprivation, mostly at night school. In his village, teenagers could go to evening classes to learn basic surveying and measurement techniques that were useful in the mine. In Edinburgh, later, he went to technical school in the evening, caught up on high school, and after many years and much difficulty, qualified as a civil engineer. He was determined that I would have the advantages that he had been denied.

My mother was the daughter of William Wood, who owned a small woodworking business in the town of Galashiels in the Scottish Borders. Although not well-educated, and less of an advocate for education than my father, she was a great story-teller (though it was sometimes hard to tell the stories from gossip), and a prodigious letter-writer. She was proud of being Scottish (I could make her angry by saying that I was British, and apoplectic by saying that I was English), and she loved the Borders, where her family had been builders and carpenters for many generations. The region has a rich history; centuries of cattle-stealing along a lawless border left many good tales, and the memories of (mostly losing) battles against the English were well tended, particularly Flodden Field, fought in 1513 but which felt more like 1913. My mother knew and could sing many of the local songs. Sir Walter Scott's Abbotsford was nearby, and he is said to have

FIGURE 1. My great grandparents Alice, Thomas and sister Mairi Thurcroft c. 1955.

visited an ancestor in the cottage where we lived after we moved from Edinburgh; the house had once belonged to my great-grandmother. I have a vivid memory of a long walk in the woods near the River Tweed guided by the friend—a printer in Galashiels—who had introduced my parents to one another during the war. He had a spellbinding gift of turning his knowledge of local history into long rhyming ballads, composed in the moment, and he would point out places where someone had done something, or had something done to them ("and when her legs were cuttit off, she fought upon her stumps"), a mesmerizing treat for an eight-year old. In late afternoon, suddenly revealed in a clearing, but quite invisible from anywhere else, stood an enormous sandstone statue of Sir William Wallace. I suspect that today's relentless meritocracy, whatever its other benefits, would not leave my historian minstrel as a printer in a small Scottish town.

In Edinburgh, where we lived until I was nine, I attended James Gillespie's Boys School a few hundred yards from our home on the edge of the meadows, a large open space south of the center, then still dotted with wartime "allotments" where the locals grew vegetables. I didn't care for school much—it was very strict, corporal punishment in the form of the "tawse" was common and unpredictable, and I was often afraid—but I believe that I did well enough; indeed, my mother always regretted that I had not stayed long enough to become the "dux," as the best pupil was called. We learned a lot of history and geography, as well as arithmetic and reading, with lots of drill.

The educational highlights I remember were not in the classroom. My father spent a lot of time with me when he could. He taught me how to take square roots, a skill I have retained, but do not use often, except to check that I still remember. At weekends, he took me to Edinburgh's great zoo, to museums, to the botanical garden (with a giant hothouse, and whose bus stop was right by Robert Louis Stevenson's childhood home) and to the harbor at Granton, which had a fishery fleet (trawlers unloading fish and loading ice and salt), a lighthouse supply ship (the Pharos), and which imported esparto grass from Portugal for making high quality paper. Looming in the distance over the eastern end of the botanical gardens was an enormous castle, adorned with hundreds of grotesque gargoyles, which my father wistfully explained was Fettes College, Scotland's most exclusive (and expensive) school where he had (impossible) dreams of sending me. I was lonely when my father had to go on long civil-engineering assignments away from home, and I remember being even more lonely, and desperately bored, when I caught scarlet fever, and had to spend seven weeks in a darkened room, with no books and only an infinitely dull radio for entertainment. I detested Mrs. Dale's Diary ever after, and was glad to hear of its end in 1969. Even my beloved jigsaw puzzles were off limits. Boredom and loneliness have been familiar visitors throughout my life, though I have come to (reluctantly) accept that the turning inwards that they bring is linked to creativity, at least for me.

In those days, children could walk unattended to museums and libraries, as well as being sent to the local grocery store to buy food, or as we said to "do the messages." What was then called the Chamber Street Museum was a mecca of exotica, mummies, totem poles, taxidermy, science, exhibits that moved when a button was pressed, clocks, ships, and mines. The children's library on George IV Bridge had both delights and dangers; my parents did not read and could not guide me, though they once tried to cut off my Biggles addiction. I read much that terrified a seven-year-old, Edgar Alan Poe's *Pit and the Pendulum* and Dickens *Christmas Story*, as well as the much more reliably enjoyable Stevenson. I dreamed of coral islands, with or without treasure, of adventures in the South

Seas, and tried to imagine how long it would be before I would visit Africa and India, still (mostly) colored a proud pink on the maps of the 1950s.

In 1955, my father qualified as a civil engineer, and we moved to the village of Bowden in the Borders. The village is old; it has a 12th century church. The ruins of a fundamentalist Free Church were still present in the center, but the pub had closed a century before, though it was often referred to. I loved the escape from the city, and Dave Preston, a plumber who worked for my father and who was a member of Scotland's international fly-fishing team, took me fishing. Like nearly all other fly-fisherman I have ever met, he was far too busy fishing to teach me; it is not for nothing that many states in the United States have laws that prohibit paid guides from fishing themselves. Fly-fishing, like boredom, which it frequently resembles, has provided me with thousands of hours of dreamtime, where the inchoate muddle in my head is given a chance to sort itself into something that might resemble an idea. Fly-fishing in Scotland, at least for trout, was inexpensive, though not free, and I recall that the cost of the license was an occasional source of conflict at home. There never was much money and my father worried about it often.

My sister Mairi and I went to the local school in Newtown St. Boswells. I passed the dreaded exam at 11 plus, and went to High School in Hawick, a knitwear manufacturing town about 15 miles away. (Those who did not pass the exam were doomed to three years of gardening, cooking, or car repair depending on sex. Mairi, four years younger, elected to go to High School in Kelso.) At Hawick I learned Latin (a Bowden villager explained to my father, there were three languages on the curriculum, Latin, French, and "Algeebra") and its precision greatly impressed me. The declension in Latin frees word order from the burden of carrying meaning as it must in English and so gives great flexibility to poetry and rhetoric. The powerful idea that precision and beauty could be combined came from my Latin classes, though Algebra and the King James Bible played a part too, even if the Bible was less strong on the precision.

It turned out that Fettes College admitted two Foundation Scholars a year (out of a class of about 90), and several teachers at Hawick High School donated their time to train me for the competitive examination. They must have done this out of dedication to teaching; certainly my father had no money to pay them. I worked very hard over many months, becoming quite sick at the time of the exams, but won one of the scholarships. Even then, the incidental expenses were a strain for my family, and there was some difficulty as I tried to keep up with much richer boys. I remember being the only boy with a Scottish accent (though it seems likely now that there were a few others) and the social life was not always easy, especially at first. Fettes strengthened an older feeling that ordinary Scots like me were not full citizens in our own country, compared with a landholding English elite who spoke with a different accent, and who set boundaries that I could not cross (though perhaps I was too much influenced by the access rules for trout fishing). In any case, the feeling of being an outsider is one that still comes more easily to me than it should. And it is not without advantages; it helps me not back down when I am trying to argue a position that only I believe. (Of course, it is less helpful when that position is wrong.)

The teaching at Fettes opened up new landscapes in many directions. I specialized in mathematics and physics after two years, but that only opened up time for other activities. I continued to play the piano (with some ability), the pipe organ (not so well), and the double bass (not well at all, but it got me into the orchestra.) I played rugby seriously for a while, which helped get me into Fitzwilliam College at Cambridge, but I probably spent most time in (entirely optional) English classes. This lack of forced learning was of great benefit to me; I learned to browse, working only on things that seemed interesting, guided only by my (sometimes temporary) enthusiasms and by always willing and talented teachers. When I later became an economist in Britain, I had the same freedom; in the United States, newly minted economists must first find a field and a peer group, and then stick to them relentlessly in order to get a job, and to keep it. In Britain, I never had a field, I took no courses in economics, and escaped going to graduate school, so I could continue to work as I had done at Fettes, browsing across areas, learning new things that often seemed irrelevant, but were always interesting, new, and which with (perhaps not so) surprising frequency, would eventually come together to open up new insights. For many years, I regretted my lack of formal training, envying my peers who had taken tough courses, and who understood things that I did not know existed, but feel now that those regrets were misplaced. When I learn something that I want to learn, and do it my own way, I often make mistakes and it is usually slow, but when it is done, it tends to stick (like taking square roots), and there is always the chance that I find something that is not so well known after all. Fettes also taught me that people like to share what they know, and that they love to be asked. Being willing to confess ignorance and to listen is a fast and joyful way to learn; I sometimes worry that our competitive American graduate schools make such confessions difficult for many students.

CAMBRIDGE

This happy story fell apart when I got to Cambridge. Mathematics, it turned out, was not what I wanted to do if I had to do it fulltime, especially in a teaching program that was appallingly badly organized, and with fellow students who were better and much more dedicated mathematicians than I. Shopping around among other areas was fine if you were doing well in the subject that counted, but I was not. Rugby collapsed too in the face of the wanton and sometimes sadistic violence of those who took rugby seriously in my college. I requested a transfer to history of science, but was denied by a risk-averse advisor; I still think that it would have been a good choice for me, even though I would not be writing this particular biography. Eventually, in desperation, my tutors told me that I had to stop doing mathematics and take up what they clearly thought of as a last resort for ne'er-do-wells, a previously unconsidered option called economics. I did so, with no expectation of anything other than a degree, and the lights came back on.

When I left Cambridge, I worked briefly at the Bank of England as part of their new graduate intake. But the Bank did not know quite what to make of graduates in 1967, and they did not have anything very useful for me to do. So I learned, perhaps incorrectly, that I didn't want to be a banker, and I have never since left academia. I returned to Cambridge as a Research Assistant for my college economics tutor, Jack Revell, who was constructing wealth accounts for Britain. I spent several months in dusty archives, copying down information on the assets of friendly societies; I did not mind the work, and sometimes even regret today's easy availability of data. It is impossible not to think about the numbers, however dusty, to wonder what they mean, to look for patterns, even to test half-formed hypotheses, and when they are assembled into something that can be analyzed, I am protected from some of the stupider mistakes that are all too easy when I know nothing about the data. Today's equivalent—and it is undoubtedly better as long as it is done—is the ability to use computer graphics to visualize the data; I do not miss the graph paper, the erasers, and the endless starting all over again. But I never quite learned to use research assistants, or at least to sleep at night when they are working for me. It is not that I myself do not make mistakes, indeed I am a poor research assistant for myself, but someone else's mistake is not lodged deep in my brain where it can wake me up in the night.

My main reason for going back to Cambridge was not academic, but that I wanted to be with Mary Ann Burnside, an English major, originally from Wichita, Kansas, via Evanston, Wellesley and Berkeley. We were married before I left the Bank; we bought a small pretty house in the village of Barton outside of Cambridge (then reputed to have many Nobel laureates), and we had a daughter, Rebecca, and a son, Adam. Mary Ann died of breast cancer in 1975, and is buried in the old churchyard in Barton. Rebecca and Adam have families of their own now, Rebecca and her son Julian live in Chicago and Adam, his wife Sabina, and their daughters Celestine and Lark live in New York. Julian, Celestine and Lark,

FIGURE 2. Marriage to Mary Ann Burnside with parents and sister Cambridge 1968.

the Deaton *barnbarn*, had the times of their lives in Stockholm, where they were much photographed and televised.

All this lay far in the future. Soon after I arrived in Cambridge, Jack Revell left to take a chair in Wales, I was rescued from the dusty archives, and largely left to myself. Which was when Richard Stone brought me into his orbit. He led a larger project in which I was nominally employed, and he somehow decided that I was a kindred spirit who could be asked, not only to run regressions and fetch numbers, but also to come to dinner and, though he hardly designed it that way, to pattern myself on him. Stone had a passion for measurement, for modeling, and for clarity and transparency in writing. He had worked with James Meade and with Keynes on national income accounting during the war, for which work he received the 1984 Nobel Prize. It was under his guidance that I first started to think about saving and about demand analysis, but the guidance came by example, not by instruction. With my own students, I have tried to do the same, though if I had it to do again, I would probably give a little more purposive direction, at least on occasion.

In those days, Cambridge was still run by the Keynesians; Joan and Austin Robinson, Nicholas Kaldor and Richard Kahn were powerful figures. Meade and Stone were there, but were less than appreciated by the Keynesians. They had little taste for the often robust and frequently *ad hominem* arguments, and kept very much to themselves; the withdrawal of Cambridge's two future Laureates taught me one of the most important lessons of academic life: withdraw from the academic politics and get on with the work. The coffee room was a place of lively conversation, often very loud lively conversation; I remember Joan shouting, "What *do* you mean, Nicky, the international *pig* standard?" having misheard "pig" for "brick." Cambridge taught me much, and gave me an acquaintance with the ideas of the intellectual left. I didn't know until many years later that there were economists to the right of the Fabian socialists, and when I came across George Stigler's piece on why the professional study of economics makes one conservative, I thought that the *Journal of Political Economy* had committed an egregious typographical error. Joan Robinson was fond of saying that neoclassical economics was an apologia for American capitalism, and while I did not believe that then (nor today), it is a perspective that is often worth keeping in mind. It was later balanced at Princeton by a distinguished colleague's fondness for declaring that "government is theft;" it is a poor political slogan, but after 33 years in the United States, I am frequently reminded of its empirical relevance for some activities, such as crony capitalism.

Cambridge was full of good young economists around that time. James Mirrlees, Amartya Sen, Peter Diamond, Joe Stiglitz, Tony Atkinson, Christopher Bliss, Geoff Heal, Mervyn King, Hashem Pesaran, and Eric Maskin were all there or spent time there during my seven years. The first economics talk I ever attended was Tony Atkinson presenting his famous paper on inequality, and I expected all seminars to be of similar quality. When Tony went to Essex to become a professor at age 26, not only were his fellow young economists delighted at his achievement, but we were all energized by the possibilities for ourselves. My chance came in 1975, when I was offered and accepted the Chair of Econometrics at the University of Bristol. Mary Ann had died a few months before, I had two small children, and the additional income meant a lot to us.

I was still at Cambridge when I met John Muellbauer, who was a lecturer at the University of Warwick, and who had recently returned from completing his PhD in Berkeley; he had known Mary Ann there, which is how we met. We discovered a common interest in consumer behavior, and quickly found that we both knew a lot of not so well-known material, though from different perspectives, I by wrestling with the writings of Terence Gorman, then at the LSE, and he through the teaching of Dan McFadden at Berkeley; he was also much further along than I in his own writing. We became good friends, and worked together for nearly a decade.

Terence Gorman "adopted" me; he became a friend, and would talk to me for hours. I was both delighted and terrified; listening to Terence was always like a tantalizing glimpse through a mist, and feeling that, if I could only understand, many of the things I had puzzled over would be revealed. He would talk about things I'd thought about, like representations of additive preferences, which I knew I did not understand, but I would finish up knowing only that he understood it but could not explain. Yet he never flagged in making it clear how highly he thought of me, and that, if I did not understand, it was his fault, not mine. When he invited me to talk at the London School of Economics, very early in my career, I could not have been more petrified; it was my first talk, and the audience contained not only Terence himself, but many luminaries including Frank Hahn, Dennis Sargan, Jim Durbin, Amartya Sen, Michio Morishima, Partha Dasgupta, David Hendry, Ken Wallis, Richard Layard and the eccentric but brilliant John Wise. My paper was much better than I could have known (it later won the inaugural Frisch medal from the Econometric Society), but almost all I can remember is the terror. The now Lord Layard remembers that talk too, and recalls wondering where this self-possessed young man that no one had ever heard of could possibly have come from, so I must have managed to put on a brave face.

BRISTOL

At Bristol, I was once again fortunate with my colleagues. The chair, Esra Bennathan, became a close friend, and was a stalwart supporter of my appointment in the face of the skepticism of those who had been professors since before I was born. Martin Browning came to Bristol as his first academic job, and we worked together on labor supply and consumer demand over the life cycle. We also hired Ian Jewitt, one of the funniest people I know, and a thinker of startling originality, as well as John Broome, who was still trying to decide whether to be an economist or a philosopher (in the end, he chose the latter). From John I learned how to think about the ethical issues underlying economics and public policy; he and Amartya Sen are responsible for a part of the way I think about the world. The drifting apart of economics and philosophy, which were close in the 60s and 70s, has surely brought harm to both; recent signs of a rapprochement are to be welcomed.

After I visited Princeton for a sabbatical year, Orley Ashenfelter came to Bristol to visit in turn, and those years were the beginnings of a lifelong friendship.

Bristol, with its long history of wine importation and many wine merchants was the first inspiration for Orley's path-breaking interest in the economics of wine. Orley's work is as original as he is and he has an uncommon curiosity about everyday phenomena, whether it be labor markets, wine, hamburgers, or prohibition. His empirical skepticism and commitment to matching theory and data marked us as kindred minds from the first time we met, at a conference in Urbino in 1976. Orley brought a young graduate student with him to Bristol, David Card, who eventually went home in frustration with Bristol's computer facilities, only to be deported to Canada at the US border. The computer arrangement was indeed imperfect, and I wrote a number of theory papers there.

At Bristol, my collaboration with John Muellbauer flourished, there, and in London, where John had moved to Birkbeck College. We worked on the development of the Almost Ideal Demand System, tinkering with candidate functional forms, trying to shape one that would be "ideal;" we came close. We also realized that we could bring a unified and relatively new approach to consumer behavior that would be useful to others. I had good students in Bristol to try out the material, and the eventual result was our book *Economics and Consumer Behavior*. I remember that the first few key chapters were written very quickly, over a few months, and typed by our expert typing pool (how I miss the typing pool!). Each of us focused on the *other's* main areas of expertise; if we did not understand each other's ideas, how could we expect our readers to do so? Of course, we hit diminishing returns, and some of the later chapters held us up for a long time. The collaboration with John is one of the highpoints of my intellectual life. Our time together was full of learning from each other, from threshing out things that it turned out neither of us fully understood, and the exhilaration of kids who thought we were going to show the world. We knew more than we deserved to know, or so it seems it retrospect.

Bristol is a wonderful place to live. I, my children, and my second wife Helge lived in a tea-merchant's house built in the 1840s, not as elegant as some in Bristol or nearby Bath, but whose architecture came from the age of upstairs-downstairs. There was a servants' staircase, a basement kitchen and laundry, with an "area" that gave tradesmen access to the servants. The city is small, with theater and concert halls nearby, fine wine merchants, and the spectacular countryside is very close, especially the Mendips to the south and the Wye Valley in South Wales to the west; London is a fast train ride away. But at the end of my time there, money was short in the university, departments were being closed, and a lot of unpleasant time was spent in figuring out who would be next. Princeton seemed like an idyllic paradise with fabulous colleagues, students, and wealth. As indeed it was.

PRINCETON

Almost the first person I met in Princeton, at a party after giving my job talk, was Anne Case. It was a memorable meeting for both of us, but it was only fourteen years later, in 1997, after winding and separate journeys for both of us, that we became a couple and were married. It is impossible today for me to imagine a life in which we are not joined at the hip; we have offices a few doors apart, we often travel together, we sometimes—but not always—work together, we cook together, we go to the opera together, and best of all, we fly-fish together. In both cooking and fly-fishing, I was originally the teacher, but have been long surpassed by the pupil; on a river, Anne has an apparently natural but deeply mysterious gift for sensing just what is about to happen. Off the river, we have recently been working together on an important and large scale project on mortality and morbidity among middle-aged white people in the United States. A marriage that encompasses all of our lives is a rich gift.

As promised, Princeton brought collaborations with both students and colleagues. Christina Paxson came to Princeton not long after I did; she had always wanted to work in development economics, but had not been able to do so in graduate school. So we decided she would come to Princeton and that we would learn development economics together, which we did. We had a mutual interest

FIGURE 3. Marriage to Anne Case with children Adam and Rebecca 1997.

in saving, and we worked on life-cycle consumption in rich and poor countries. We also wrote about health, mortality, consumption inequality, and a series of food puzzles. Our work is prominently discussed in the Nobel citation. Chris is now President of Brown University. This is sad for me, but not for her; she always wanted to be an administrator and she has a great talent for it.

John Campbell was also a junior faculty member at Princeton. He had worked with Bob Shiller at Yale, and had written a breakthrough thesis about saving for a rainy day and opened up many new ideas. Together, we thought about the puzzles of consumption and saving that were then in the air; I remember a pleasant day at the Engineering Library as we tried to figure out what the spectrum at zero might be, and how it might be relevant for the relationship between earnings and consumption.

At Princeton, I joined the Research Program in Development Studies, which had been founded by Sir Arthur Lewis who, although retired, was still around on a regular basis, and who befriended me; he always called me "chief," though I have no idea why. Princeton thought of me as a partial replacement for Arthur, a daunting idea; I knew little about the subject, and my quantitative approach could not have been further from his deep historical wisdom that he had accumulated in the Caribbean, in England, and in Africa. He was unhappy in those years with how history had been marginalized in economics, and the mainstream's lack of interest in the persistence of poverty around the world, the topic that was central to his intellectual life. So it would have been understandable had he resented me, but his attitude was entirely the opposite. Central to the development group then was Mark Gersovitz, who had worked in every area that can lay claim to being part of development economics. He was my guide to the subject, and generously shared what he knew. Another great influence on my development work, especially in India, has been my friend and collaborator Jean Drèze. Jean is a scholar and activist, who argues and agitates for policies to help the poor. He brings to our joint work an unequalled knowledge of the life of farmers and laborers in India; he is also one of the finest analytical economists I know.

Over the last decade, I have worked with the Gallup Organization, occasionally advising on data collection, but more often simply analyzing the data that they have collected on wellbeing in almost every country in the world. Gallup is an impressive and unusual company that is deeply interested in the intellectual underpinnings of its work, and in making its own contributions to science. I was introduced to them by Danny Kahneman, then my Princeton colleague, who was working on and thinking about wellbeing, and had advised Gallup on measuring life evaluation and hedonic effect. Danny and I worked together on Gallup's data, most famously on a project that showed that, in the US, hedonic

FIGURE 4. At the Nordic museum Stockholm 2015.

effect improved with income, but only up to about $75,000 a year, while life evaluation continued to respond to income even beyond that limit. Gawker.com deftly summarized the project: science shows poverty sucks.

I have had a long relationship with the World Bank, beginning even before I moved to Princeton. The Bank's work constantly throws up good problems. Most are insoluble, but occasionally it is possible to come up with a better measure, or to see that something is not being thought about in the best way. For me, it is always useful to be presented with other people's problems, an escape from the risk in academia of small group self-referential research. In the early 1980s, I worked with Graham Pyatt, who was part of Richard Stone's team in the early days of the growth project, and who was starting the Living Standards Measurement Surveys, a still ongoing program to develop household surveys throughout the world. When Nick Stern, a friend since college, was Chief Economist, he asked me to think about the Bank's methods of measuring poverty, which greatly stimulated my interest in the topic. Most recently, I have worked with the technical advisory group of the International Comparison Program (ICP), which is currently hosted by the World Bank. The ICP is perhaps the world's most ambitious statistical undertaking, and it presents immense (and not fully solved) theoretical and empirical difficulties, all the way from index number and statistical theory, through to which prices to collect and how. The people who work on the ICP include national income accountants, subject specialists (e.g. construction, or education), survey statisticians, as well as economists. I have made several good friends and mentors in the program, especially Alan Heston, one of the founders of the ICP, and Bettina Aten, now at the Bureau of Economic Analysis.

Finally, two institutions and their leaders have helped shape my work. One is the National Bureau of Economic Research whose President, Martin Feldstein, generated vast public goods for economics as a whole, and was a lifelong supporter of me and of my work. Much of my research on consumption and saving first saw the light of day at the Bureau, either in the macro seminars, or in David Wise's group on aging with which I have worked for more than 20 years. Marty's successor, Jim Poterba, continues the good work. At the National Institute on Aging in Washington, the late Richard Suzman's creative energy, ingenuity and enthusiasm was responsible for bringing a generation of social scientists into health research, including me; his legacy is the change and advance that he brought to both fields. His friendship is sorely missed.

I will become an Emeritus Professor at Princeton in June of 2016. To Princeton, and to its units to which I belong, the Economics Department and especially the Woodrow Wilson School of Public and International Affairs, I express my gratitude for providing me with such a profoundly supportive environment and home for most of my working life.

Measuring and Understanding Behavior, Welfare, and Poverty

Prize Lecture, December 8, 2015

by Angus Deaton
Woodrow Wilson School, Princeton University, USA.

1. INTRODUCTION

The work cited by the Prize Committee spans many years, covers areas of economics that are not always grouped together, and involves many different collaborators. Yet, like the committee, I believe that the work has an underlying unity. It concerns wellbeing, what was once called welfare, and uses market and survey data to measure the behavior of individuals and groups and to make inferences about wellbeing. Often, little more than counting is involved, as in the estimation of the fraction of the population whose spending is below a cutoff, or the calculation of the fraction of newborn children who die before their first birthday. Measurement, even without understanding of mechanisms, can be of great importance in and of itself—policy change is frequently based on it—and is necessary if not sufficient for any reasoned assessment of policies, including the many that are advocated for the reduction of national or global poverty. We are wise to remember the importance of good data, and not to neglect the challenges that measurement continuously poses.

More ambitiously, estimation of behavior can elucidate mechanisms and causes, and help to make predictions about the effects of policy, providing a guide to policy improvement. Indeed, the analysis of consumer behavior with a view to measuring wellbeing has long been a basic task of economists. Although, as directed by the Committee, this article is about my own work, I shall try to set the work in the context to which it belongs, allowing myself liberal use of hindsight.

The link between measurement, behavior and policy is a running theme. So is the necessity of telling a coherent story of what we observe. Another key idea is the distinction between individuals and aggregates, what the committee refers to as "consumption, great and small." Aggregation needs to be seen, not as a nuisance, but as a hallmark of seriousness, as well as a source of hypotheses and understanding. The link between behavior and wellbeing, when it holds at all, holds for individuals, not for aggregates. While we often must focus on aggregates for macroeconomic policy, it is impossible to think coherently about national wellbeing while ignoring inequality and poverty, neither of which is visible in aggregate data. Indeed, and except in exceptional cases, macroeconomic aggregates themselves depend on distribution. These arguments are much more widely accepted today than they were thirty years ago.

Much of what follows is based on the traditional (in economics) premise that people know what is good for them and act in their own interest. People reveal (something about) their preferences in their behavior, which allows us to infer (something about) wellbeing from the choices that they make. The validity of revealed preference is currently being robustly challenged by behavioral economics, though no new general operating link between behavior and wellbeing yet exists; this is surely a key task for economics in the years ahead. Here I stick to the traditional position, if only because of the many successes that approach has brought.

I start with household surveys, how they are used to document living standards, inequality, and poverty and, beyond that, to understand behavior. From there, it is a short step, in Section 3, to demand analysis, which looks at how consumption patterns respond to prices and incomes. Understanding such effects is necessary for the design of tax and pricing policies and is useful for much else. Much of the early work on demand was concerned with single-period models, but the same set of methods was gradually extended to help understand the dynamics of behavior. Subsections 3.1 and 3.2 consider those in turn.

2. USING HOUSEHOLD SURVEYS FOR MEASUREMENT AND FOR ANALYSIS

2.1 Documenting the lives of the poor

The documentation of how people live, how much they spend, and on what, has long been used as a political tool, to make visible the living conditions of the poor to those in power, to shock, and to agitate for reform. According to George Stigler (1954), the first surveys were those of David Davies (1795) and Frederick Eden (1797) in England. The wave of social unrest in Europe in the

1840s brought a wave of budget studies, including that of Édouard Ducpétieaux (1855) which was a predecessor of Ernst Engel's (1857) famous study. Engel was also influenced by Adolphe Quételet's arguments for the statistical analysis of social data, including Quételet's concept of *l'homme moyen*, an early avatar of the representative agent. At around the same time, the pioneers of social epidemiology were making parallel inquiries into the health and living standards of the working classes, for example Louis-René Villermé (1830) on the geography of mortality and poverty in Paris, and perhaps most famously, Friedrich Engels (1845), who documented mortality differences and living standards in Manchester and argued that the industrial revolution had immiserated the working classes, starting off a debate about the effects of the industrial revolution on wellbeing that continues to this day.

The descendants of these studies are today's randomly selected, stratified, and clustered household surveys that are run regularly by most statistical offices in the world. The statistical theory of random surveys was developed only after Jerzy Neyman (1934), with important practical contributions in India, see Prasanta Chandra Mahalanobis (1946) who established one of the first national sample surveys, see You Poh Seng (1951) and T. M. Fred Smith (1976). Today's household surveys typically collect information on household incomes and/or (often detailed) expenditures, as well as demographic, geographical and other characteristics of household members. Their official purpose is often to collect weights for consumer price indexes, but they are also used to calculate national and global estimates of poverty and inequality. The United States Agency for International Development funds the system of internationally comparable Demographic and Health Surveys (www.dhsprogram.com), each of which documents the health, anthropometric status, and mortality rates of infants and children. Collectively, they provide much of the infrastructure for comparisons of health between countries. As was the case in the 18th and 19th centuries, these estimates of poverty and of mortality are used today by national and international organizations, aid agencies, and NGOs to enliven the consciences of the privileged of the world and to agitate for pro-poor policies.

Within countries both rich and poor, household surveys are the basis for estimates of poverty rates, of income inequality, and of changes in real wages across percentiles of the distribution. Sometimes, this information is sufficient to evaluate an approximation to the welfare effects of policy changes; a familiar example is the calculation of the compensating variation of an increase in a tobacco or gas tax by examining expenditures on tobacco or gas in a household survey. Better approximations require estimation of the response of purchases to prices, on which more below. Another example comes from countries where staple foods are both produced and consumed, with some households (farmers) producing, and others consuming. If, for example, the country is a net exporter, the imposition of an export tax will harm net producers and help net consumers and for each the welfare equivalent variation can be approximated by the value of *net* consumption, which can be read off from a household survey. In both cases, the distributional effects of the policy change can be read off from a national survey, see Angus Deaton (1989a) for the example of rice in Thailand.

Among the most difficult and pressing problems with household surveys is the quality of the data; in some cases, the problems are severe enough to threaten even the most basic understanding of growth, poverty, and inequality. India is perhaps the most important illustration. Per capita consumption estimated from household surveys has long been less than per capita consumption estimated in the national accounts statistics (NAS), even when adjustments are made for conceptual differences in coverage, for example surveys do not collect data on imputations for rents or financial intermediation, nor on the cost of publicly provided education and healthcare. This discrepancy has long concerned Indian economists, e.g. Bagicha Minhas (1988), and has steadily worsened over time; in 1972-73 the survey estimate of consumption fell short of the NAS estimate by five percent, while in 2009–10, only a half of national accounts consumption showed up in the surveys, rising to two-thirds after adjustment for differences in definition, Government of India (2014, Tables 3.2 and 3.3). That per capita consumption as measured in the NAS grows more rapidly than per capita consumption as measured in the surveys happens not only in India, but in many countries including, over some periods, the United States, Deaton (2005). While the sources of the discrepancies are largely obscure—itself a testament to the lack of attention devoted to the topic by national and international agencies—it is clear that the national accounts cannot be held blameless; again in India, there is likely exaggeration of the rate of growth in the national accounts—governments whose legitimacy depends on high growth tend to be unenthusiastic about any revision that decreases measured growth—and, on the other side, surveys cannot easily penetrate gated communities, nor capture the increasing share of expenditure outside of the household and unobserved by the single respondent that surveys rely upon.

These discrepancies block any coherent account of poverty, inequality, and growth. The historically high rates of growth of (national accounts) consumption in India since the 1980s would appear to warrant a much larger reduction in poverty than is shown by the surveys. When growth brings little poverty reduction, the usual inference would be that inequality is rising, which may well be true and likely accounts for some of the difference, but the main reason today is not a failure of trickle-down, but a failure of measurement. Those who choose to believe the national accounts, and disbelieve the surveys—except to note that they show limited increases in inequality—believe that the rate of poverty reduction is grossly understated in India and, beyond that, in the world as a whole given that India accounted for a quarter of global poverty in 2012. By contrast, those who choose to believe the surveys believe that a large fraction of India's spectacular growth is illusory. The most basic economic data, the rate of growth, its distribution, and who is gaining and who is being left behind are inaccessible, so that people are free to choose their facts according to their political prejudices, unconstrained by reality, and a reasoned political debate about these central issues becomes impossible.

The measurement of global poverty has long been carried out by the World Bank, which, in its latest estimates that document 1984 to 2012, World Bank (2016), uses information from more than 1,000 household surveys from 131 developing countries and 21 high-income countries; 43 of the surveys for the 2012 estimates are from sub-Saharan Africa, which is the region where poverty is most prevalent. Yet household surveys in Africa are often weak, often outdated (the 2012 estimates use surveys as old as 2003), are sometimes inconsistent over time within countries, have non-matching definitions—different reporting periods, or are surveyed at different times of year, either over time or over countries—so that it is extremely difficult to assess progress over time, or to make comparisons of poverty or inequality between countries.

In many countries and in the world as a whole, large numbers of people live in the vicinity of the national or global poverty line. In consequence, small changes in the position of the line, for example through the choice of price index for updating, or small changes in survey practice, can have dramatic effects on the number of people counted as poor. A spectacular example comes from India, where the sample survey organization ran a large randomized controlled trial on the effects of different lengths of the reporting (recall) period. People in one arm reported their consumption over the last 30 days, in the other, over the last 7 days, Pravin Visaria (2000). Because the reported flow rate is higher with the shorter reporting period, switching from 30 to 7 days reduced the national poverty rate in 1998 *by almost half* and "removed" 175 million people from poverty, Deaton (2001). Statistical solutions to poverty are easier than real solutions.

Education and health are two important categories that are inconsistently treated in different countries because private provision is included in the surveys while public provision is not, so that poverty measurement is hostage to local arrangements, which vary across countries; in sub-Saharan Africa, for example, the private share of healthcare spending ranges from 27 percent to 74 percent.

An effective improvement in state provision of either education or health could do much to improve the lives of the poor, but if it crowds out private expenditures—which would be desirable in many settings where the quality of private care is poor—measured poverty would increase.

It is perhaps tempting to abandon measures of material wellbeing and move to other measures, such as anthropometrics, or mortality, and I believe that the material poverty measures have been assigned too much weight, given their inherent unreliability. Yet, while it is surely important to emphasize other aspects of poverty, particularly health and education, those other dimensions are not substitutes for measures of material deprivation. While different deprivations are often correlated, the extent of the correlations are different in different places and times; for example, Africans tend to do better than Indians on anthropometrics, but worse on income and on mortality, and in China, when economic growth brought massive poverty reduction after the mid-1970s, infant and child mortality, which had been falling rapidly, greatly slowed, Deaton (2013, 115). In the end, if we want to know about material poverty, we will have to measure it better.

Household surveys from around the world are the underlying source for measures of global poverty and global inequality, where the former is defined as counts of those living below some uniform cutoff. Inequality can refer to dispersion in income (or consumption) across all of the citizens of the world, or to dispersion of per capita incomes across nations, or to inequality of per capita incomes of nations weighted by population, see Branko Milanovic (2007); the first can only be estimated with household survey data. These global poverty and inequality measures require that the data from each country be first converted to a common currency using purchasing power parity exchange rates. These PPPs are multilateral international price indexes which, although widely used by the research community through the Penn World Table and other databases, have properties that are not always well understood.

The International Comparison Project (ICP), started in the 1970s and continuing and developing today, Irving Kravis, Alan Heston and Robert Summers (1978), Summers and Heston (1991), is one of the outstanding intellectual achievements of economic measurement, and one that has never been recognized by the Prize Committee, see the comments by Paul Samuelson (2004). A primer on current practice is Deaton and Heston (2010); what is not widely realized is that there are many unresolved theoretical and practical questions, and that successive rounds of estimates have often been disconcertingly incompatible. The ICP produces benchmark estimates of PPPs in each round, most recently in 1985, 1993/94, 2005, and 2011. Between rounds, PPPs are updated using domestic price indexes so that, for example, the PPP for consumption for India relative to the US, is the benchmark PPP between India and the US updated by the relative rates of increase in CPIs of the two countries since the benchmark. While this is an intuitive and sensible procedure, it is at best an approximation; even under ideal conditions, changes in multilateral indexes over time, which use weights from all countries, will not match the relative changes in national price indexes, which use weights from one country only, see e.g. Paul McCarthy (2013).

The problem here is not the existence of approximation errors, but that in the three most recent rounds, these changes have been large enough so as to seriously reconfigure the economic geography of the world. In both 1993/94 and again in 2005, the consumption and GDPs of poor countries were revised downward relative to those of rich countries; recall that the US is always the (arbitrarily chosen) numeraire, so the revisions are to relative, not to absolute standings. For example, ICP 2005 revised downward the GDPs of India and China by 36 and 39 percent relative to the US; for some African countries the downward revision was much larger. In 2011, by contrast, the *price levels* of poorer countries were on average revised downward, so that per capita consumption and GDP levels were revised upward, offsetting at least some of the 2005 revisions, although not consistently so. These large and unpredictable revisions wreak havoc with attempts to measure global poverty and global inequality, see Deaton (2010) on the 2005 revisions, and on the difficulties that they caused for the World Bank poverty estimates, and Deaton and Bettina Aten (2015) and Robert Inklaar and D. S. Prasada Rao (2014) for attempts to understand the 2011 revision. Francisco Ferreira et al (2015) adapt the World Bank's poverty count in the light of the new numbers.

The reasons for the PPP revisions are not fully understood. Given that each round is done anew, there are often substantial methodological revisions; these are the most likely causes of change, but there is no well-defined procedure for measuring the effects of any particular revision. There is also variation that comes from the sampling of prices and from the choice of which goods to sample, from the choice of index formula, and from the structure of relative prices in any given year, Deaton and Olivier Dupriez (2010). One gauge of uncertainty is the ratio of Laspeyres to Paasche indexes for pairs of countries; in ICP 2005, these ratios were 9.6 and 5.1 for Tajikistan and Kyrgyzstan relative to the US, and are 1.7 and 1.6 for important countries like India or China. (An unfortunate aspect of multilateral price indexes is that weak data in one place, such as Tajikistan, can in principle affect *all* PPP comparisons including, for example, those between the US and China, or between France and Senegal.)

More troubling still are the conceptual questions. On the one hand, we need to compare like with like, using only goods and services that are close to identical in different countries. On the other hand, we also wish to capture what people actually spend, so that we want to use goods and services that are widely consumed and representative of actual purchases. These two requirements often stand in sharp opposition; in the extreme case where consumption bundles have nothing in common, there is no basis for comparisons of living standards. We need to be more humble about what PPPs can do, more cautious in using them in analysis—especially when very different countries are included—and more skeptical about the measures that depend on them, including international comparisons of GDP and consumption as well as calculations of global poverty and global inequality.

Even given a good set of PPP exchange rates, there are further hurdles in the way of calculating global poverty. One is how to set a global poverty line that can be used across the world, from Chad to Chile, from Colombo to Canberra. In the past, the World Bank has used the national poverty lines of the poorest countries, converted to US purchasing power equivalent, and averaged to give a global line. The idea is to aim for a destitution level of income that can serve as a cut-off for absolute poverty, and this is the origin of the famous $1-a-day line, World Bank (1990). Yet it is not always clear where those national lines come from, or what sort of intellectual or political legitimacy they should be accorded. Beyond that, those national lines should arguably be converted at PPPs that are tailored to the spending patterns of poor people, though this makes much less difference than might at first be thought, Deaton and Dupriez (2011). Paradoxes can arise; for example, India's high growth gave it an income that disqualified it from the poorest group when the lines were reset after ICP 2005, Shaohua Chen and Martin Ravallion (2010). However, it turns out that India's national line is lower than its national income would predict, so that when its national line was dropped from the average that defines the global line, the global line increased. At this new, higher, line, the world, including India, was estimated to be poorer; in effect, India became poorer because India had become richer, Deaton (2010). While such paradoxes are clearly undesirable, it is unclear how to avoid them, and new approaches need to be developed, perhaps using the new linear-programming methods being developed by the economic historian Robert Allen (2016). There is also an argument for the multidimensional poverty indexes developed by Sabina Alkire and her coauthors (2015), in which material destitution is not given all of the weight.

In the meantime, both the World Bank and the US government are committed to eliminating global poverty by 2030, or at least to reducing it to below 3 percent of the world's population. Placing such a difficult to measure object at the center of international development policy seems ill advised, though, as always with such global and cosmopolitan measures, it is unclear who is actually responsible for meeting the target, or how (or indeed whether) anyone will be held accountable.

2.2 Surveys for understanding behavior and welfare

The behavioral analysis of household surveys with a view to welfare-improving policy often focuses on food, and goes back to Engel and his famous law, that the poorer the household, the larger share of its outlay must be expended for the procurement of food. Engel (1895) went far beyond the original law and claimed that the food share is itself an indicator of family wellbeing independently of family composition. He used this identification assumption to measure the "costs" of children, a topic of continuing policy importance given that various public benefits, and indeed private settlements, such as those associated with divorce, are typically conditioned on family structure. If $w_f(x, z)$ is the budget share of food for a family with total expenditure x and household composition z, Engel's assumption allows us to compare any household of interest, h with a "reference" household, 0. If the household of interest has structure z^h, we can calculate how much x it needs to be as well off as the reference household by finding that x that gives it the same food share as the reference household, i.e. by solving $w_f(x^h, z^h) = w_f(x^o, z^o)$. The ratio x^h/x^o is known as the "equivalence scale," so that if, for example, the reference household has 2 adults, the equivalence scale might be 3 for a household with 2 adults and 2 children; each child costs half of an adult.

That this beguiling procedure makes no sense was long ago noted by J. Leonard Nicholson (1976); if children consume mostly food, a fully compensated family with more children will still have a higher food share than one with fewer children and so would be overcompensated by Engel's procedure, see also Deaton and John Muellbauer (1986). Even so, Engel's method is still used, perhaps because of its simplicity, perhaps because of a misunderstanding that Engel's Law implies Engel's later assertion, or perhaps because of the seemingly attractive idea that if people behave identically, they must be equally well off. For example, that equal food shares imply equal welfare is sometimes used to calculate the welfare effects of changes in *any* background circumstance z, for example changes in unmeasured quality of consumer goods, so as to correct biases in consumer price indexes as suggested by Bruce Hamilton (2001) and Dora Costa (2001). As with Engels' original procedure, these methods require additional assumptions to be valid; as noted by Robert Pollak and Terrence Wales (1979), an (indirect) utility function of the form $\psi(x, p, z)$ for prices p, generates identical demand functions for each good in terms of p and z, as does the utility function $F[\psi(x, p, z), z]$ where F is monotone increasing in its first argument. Yet the two utility functions give different levels of utility; circumstances z can affect wellbeing without affecting observable market behavior—public goods whose costs are compensated could be an example—so that we cannot get from behavior to wellbeing without identification rules, essentially an exclusion restriction that z affects wellbeing only through its observable effects on behavior. It is not clear how such exclusion restrictions can be justified, and we know from Nicholson's discussion of Engel's own example that the exclusion cannot always be right. Direct observation of utility through happiness surveys would resolve the conundrum, provided that such observations do indeed correspond to standard concepts of utility, Daniel McFadden (2014).

Household surveys continue to provide insights and to pose puzzles, particularly about food, which has been a consistent focus since the beginning. Here are some.

There is a large body of evidence, primarily from differential mortality, that suggests that, in at least some of the countries of the world, girls are discriminated against in favor of boys. Amartya Sen's (1989) documentation of "missing women" is the most famous. We might reasonably expect to see evidence of such discrimination in household surveys. The obvious place to look is expenditure on food, but surveys rarely attempt to find out who eats what. However, there is an indirect approach. Long ago, Erwin Rothbarth (1943) suggested that we might look at goods that were bought only by adults, tobacco and alcohol being the most obvious, and that expenditure on such items should indicate the expenditure needs of children. Given that children do not bring additional resources at birth, space needs to be made for their needs in the family budget, and so we might expect expenditure on adult goods to fall. In Deaton (1989b), I suggested that, in the presence of discrimination against girls, Rothbarth's method should reveal that parents make more space in the budget for boys than for girls, so that, to take a concrete example, controlling for total expenditure, Indian parents of boys might spend less on their *bidis* than Indian parents of girls. Yet I found no difference, indeed relatively precisely so, a result that has been replicated in a number of settings, see Deaton (1997). It might well be that discrimination lies, not in food provision, but in the provision of medical care, for example—in countries with dowries, girls are long term liabilities and boys long term assets—but the method itself could (as usual) be challenged on various econometric grounds.

Another food puzzle is related to economies of scale, the idea that two people can live more cheaply together than apart, so that members of larger households with the same per capita resources should be better off. Once again, it would seem that this idea, if true, should leave traces in the survey data. If we compare a larger with a smaller household at the same level of per capita income or total expenditure, then the presence of economies of scale implies that the larger household has been overcompensated, is better off, and thus should spend more per head on normal goods, such as food. Yet when Deaton and Christina Paxson (1998) investigated using data from the UK, the US, France, Taiwan, Thailand, Pakistan and African households in South Africa, we found exactly the opposite, that per capita food expenditures are *lower* in the supposedly overcompensated larger households, and that the difference is largest in the poorest countries, South Africa, Thailand, and Pakistan, where the need to spend more on food would seem to be the most urgent. There are a number of possible explanations, none very convincing, though there is a possible connection with another food puzzle about growth and calorie consumption.

In spite of the historically unprecedented rates of growth in India since 1980, in spite of upward sloping calorie Engel curves, and in spite of its near record levels of child malnutrition, per capita consumption of calories and protein has been *falling*, Deaton and Jean Drèze (2009). At the same time, anthropometric measures show that around a half of India's children are severely malnourished; Indian women do not get enough to eat when they are pregnant, Diane Coffey (2015), and Indian adults are among the shortest in the world. Hence it seems obvious that with rapid economic growth, upward sloping calorie Engel curves, and severe nutritional need, people should be eating more calories, not less. Once again, the puzzle is unresolved. Perhaps the best story is that heavy manual labor is declining along with rising living standards, so that the need for calories as fuel is diminishing, even while people remain malnourished; it is straightforward to build a model in which utility depends positively on consumption and negatively on effort, for which calories are a direct and necessary input. In an intermediate phase of development, during which people are getting better off and the need for heavy manual work is falling, the demand for calories can decline, at least temporarily. Eventually, once people are sedentary, calories stop being fuel, will yield positive net marginal utility, and consumption will rise. This account finds some support from the fact that the most rapid declines are in fuel-like commodities, such as grains and particularly the less-valued "coarse" cereals in India such as sorghum, millet, and maize, and also from the fact that India's more developed states are those with the lowest per capita calorie consumption. Manual labor may also help explain the economies of scale puzzle if there are overheads of labor—for example fetching fuel or water, or farm tasks—that can be shared by additional household members.

In rich countries where transport is good, there is little spatial price variation in most commodities so that household surveys have limited or no ability to analyze how spending patterns change with prices. Yet price responses are required for a wide range of policy problems, and there is a literature that searches for assumptions that will allow bricks to be made without straw. One early attempt was by Arthur Cecil Pigou (1910) who noted that if preferences are additive (utility is a monotone increasing transformation of an explicitly additive function of single commodity sub-utilities), price elasticities are approximately proportional to income elasticities, see Deaton (1974a). Given this, only one additional piece of information—one price elasticity, or two cross-sectional surveys at different times with different prices—is required for budget surveys to identify price as well as income responses. Of course, additivity is a strong assumption, even for broad groups of goods, and it can be avoided if we have some other source of price variation. One such is the spatial variation in prices that exists in countries where transport is expensive. Many such countries, including India, collect data, not only on each household's expenditures, but also on the physical quantities purchased, at least for those goods, like many foods or fuels, where quantities are readily defined. The ratio of expenditure to quantity gives a unit value for each good for each household. These unit values contain a quality component as well as a price component—indeed in their classic treatment of household surveys, Sigbert Prais and Hendrik Houthakker (1956) used the fact that unit values are higher for better off households to indicate welfare and to calculate equivalence scales—but, with a suitable theory of quality choice, price and quality can be disentangled and price effects estimated, Deaton (1988, 1997). An important finding from such studies, at least for countries like India and Indonesia, is that the absolute values of the estimated own price elasticities tend to be (absolutely) large relative to those obtained from time series data. This is what might be expected if complementary capital goods—including possibly even tastes, David Atkin (2013)—adapt slowly to prices, but it also raises issues about the relevant periods for policy analysis; certainly the deadweight losses of distortions are likely to increase over time.

3. SAVING, CONSUMPTION, AND DEMAND ANALYSIS

3.1 Demand analysis

In the late 1960s and early 1970s, considerable attention was devoted to the construction of large-scale macroeconomic models, either for short-term forecasting and control, or for state planning that made a longer-term assessment of industrial structure, including manpower planning and investment. The Cambridge Growth Project, Richard Stone and Alan Brown (1962), used a model constructed around an input-output matrix, a consumption function, and a matched set of demand equations that used prices and incomes to map out the demand for commodities. The model used the linear expenditure system whose empirical analysis was pioneered in Stone (1954), perhaps the first case where the parameters of a utility function were estimated. Parenthetically, Stone seemed to be unaware of what is now (somewhat ironically) called the Stone-Geary utility function (Cobb Douglas with an affine shift of origin); the cost function was derived by Lawrence Klein and Herman Rubin (1947–48), with the direct utility function given in an accompanying note by Samuelson (1947–48), and then rediscovered by Roy Geary (1950–51).

When I was asked to work on the consumption part of the model in 1969, I was troubled by a number of issues, which eventually required or led to further developments. First, the linear expenditure system is linear in prices and income, but not in its parameters, and the Cambridge team had not managed to come up with satisfactory estimates. This was easily solved using the new methods then evolving in engineering and economics, particularly the algorithms by Donald Marquardt (1963) and by Stephen Goldfeld, Richard Quandt and Hale Trotter (1966). This was the computational frontier in economics in the 1960s. According to Cambridge legend, Prais and Houthakker (1956) was the first study in economics to use an electronic computer; in Stone (1954), the term is not computer, but computor, which refers to a person not a machine.

Second, the utility underlying the linear expenditure system is additive, and as such cannot handle the full generality of behavioral response that choice theory permits. Of course, strong restrictions were essential at a time when researchers were limited to a handful of time-series data points, but even so, assuming additivity from the start loses control of the choice of how much to measure and how much to assume, always a key to convincing applied work. Even then, there is more than one kind of additivity, and different functional forms for each, and the question of how to choose between them, issues I tried to address in Deaton (1974b).

Additivity is more plausible for broad groups of goods, such as food or clothing, but how should such groups of goods be defined? By what principles are commodities and services to be combined into groups, and how might those principles be implemented in practice? Perhaps it would make sense to have a model of two-stage or hierarchic preferences, in which additive preferences are used to allocate income into broad categories, and some other rule used to break up the aggregates into finer categories. Just as aggregation over goods was a problem, so was aggregation over people. What justified the use of the representative agent in the linear expenditure system? Was this just an assumption, or an implication of such a utility function? And more broadly, why were demand functions not influenced by the distribution of income? In Cambridge in the 1960s and 1970s, we all listened to the Cambridge Keynesians, their denunciations of the validity of the non-substitution theorem, and their insistence on the interdependence of equilibrium prices and income distribution; could it really be true that a sweeping increase in income inequality would leave consumer demands unchanged?

The theory that answered most of those questions had been already developed by W. M. (Terence) Gorman; on aggregation in Gorman (1953), on two-stage budgeting in Gorman (1959), and on separability in Gorman (1968). These papers, which made extensive use of dual representation of preferences, were not easily comprehensible by those with a standard economics education at that time; they are classic examples of papers that were so far ahead of their time that their influence and usefulness for applied work was recognized only after the results had become familiar from other work. One strand of that other work came from Daniel McFadden, then at Berkeley, whose lectures had an enormous influence on those who heard them, and which were eventually published as McFadden (1978). McFadden's work influenced a generation of researchers on production and demand, including John Muellbauer who attended his lectures, and with whom I collaborated in England after 1970. Together we could combine Gorman and McFadden, and develop our combined knowledge into a coherent body of work that was relevant for the empirical work that we were both trying to do; this program eventually led to our book on consumer behavior, Deaton and Muellbauer (1980b). It also enabled us to address the aggregation issues.

There were two key sets of results. One was Muellbauer's (1975) work on aggregation, which extended Gorman's results to a class of preferences, price independent generalized linearity (PIGL), in which the distribution of income played an essential role in the demand functions. Of particular empirical interest was a logarithmic case (PIGLOG), by which the budget share of each good was a linear function of log income for each household, which previous studies had suggested gave a good fit to the data. PIGLOG preferences allow the aggregation of demands, and again the aggregate budget shares are linear in log income, but log income is adjusted for a measure of income inequality. The other key came from another student of McFadden; this was Erwin Diewert's (1971, 1974) concept of a flexible function form. The concept provided a solution to the problem of assumption versus measurement; a system of demand functions is a flexible functional form if the demand functions are unrestricted beyond the general restrictions implied by choice theory, adding up, zero degree homogeneity in prices and income, and symmetry and negative semi-definiteness of the Slutsky matrix of compensated price derivatives. A flexible functional form is a utility-consistent set of demand functions that can provide a first-order approximation (at a point) to an arbitrary set of utility-consistent set of demand functions. Given that the demand functions are derivatives of the expenditure (or cost) function, the preferences underlying the flexible functional forms are second-order local approximations to arbitrary preferences. A number of notable flexible functional forms were developed, by Diewert himself, the Generalized Leontief system, Diewert (1971) and by Laurits Christensen, Dale Jorgenson and Lawrence Lau (1975), the translog system, and later, the Almost Ideal Demand System (AIDS) of Deaton and Muellbauer (1980a). The AIDS, which is a member of the PIGLOG class, was the result of many months of tinkering to try to combine the best features of the earlier models; it allows linear estimation of its parameters, at least under an often reasonable approximation, it has one income parameter per commodity, which controls whether or not the good is a necessity or luxury, and a matrix of own and cross price responses of the budget shares to the logarithm of prices. It is a flexible functional form, with an explicit indirect utility function. The modesty of the "almost" refers to the fact that the quasi-concavity of the cost function cannot be globally imposed without destroying the flexibility of the functional form. Even so, its convenience and consistency with price theory, as well as the availability of a quadratic generalization, James Banks, Richard Blundell and Arthur Lewbel (1997), has made it a widely used tool in work that requires inference from prices to welfare, for example in tax evaluation, regulatory, or anti-trust work. Note that the AIDS, in spite of its incorporation of distribution, retains much of the representative agent; the model works by choosing a convenient utility function that, if possessed by everyone, would lead to a representative utility with adjustment only to income. It is a much harder undertaking to start from more realistic models of heterogeneous individuals, each of whom buys a different collection of goods, and then explicitly aggregate them, a procedure that, in general, will not lead to aggregate behavior that is in any way analogous to individual behavior; see for example, Houthakker (1955–56) for a startling example from production theory where Leontief technology for each firm turns into Cobb-Douglas for the economy as a whole.

3.2 Saving and intertemporal choice

The two papers by Franco Modigliani and Richard Brumberg (1955a, 1955b [1990]) are the foundations for utility-based modeling of intertemporal choice.

I had the good fortune to be sent to read both (one of which was then unpublished) when I was an undergraduate, and they seemed to me then (and now) a template for how to do economics. They proposed a simple theoretical structure for choice over time, which gave a clear way of thinking about an issue of the first order of importance, both for individuals and for society. The theory was used to bring order and a coherent interpretation to a mass of contradictory and previously disorganized empirical evidence from many studies using both cross-section and time series; the theory had to match everything, or it was nothing. It provided clear new predictions that could be tested. In a later paper, Modigliani (1970) extended the theory to cross-country evidence, and derived the famous rate of growth effects on national saving. Even if each individual has no net saving over life, accumulating wealth in youth and running it down in old age, the economy will have a positive saving rate if there is either population growth or economic growth because the savers would be either more numerous or working on a larger scale than the dissavers. There is no representative agent, the aggregate is unlike any individual, and the explicit aggregation generates non-obvious hypotheses linking national growth and national saving. It is an abiding sadness of my career that it turns out that there is overwhelming evidence that these correlations, which are indeed in the data, and that Modigliani was the first to see, turned out *not* to be attributable to life-cycle rate of growth effects; there is simply not enough age-related life-cycle saving to drive the effects, Laurence Kotlikoff and Lawrence Summers (1981), Christopher Carroll and Summers (1991), and fluctuations in national saving are driven more by within age-group effects rather than by changes in either the population or economic size of the cohorts themselves, Barry Bosworth, Gary Burtless and John Sabelhaus (1991), Paxson (1996), Deaton and Paxson (1997, 2000).

In the 1970s, a major innovation to life cycle theory was the extension to consumption and labor supply simultaneously. James Heckman's (1971) Ph.D. thesis appears to have been the key here, and was followed by a book by Gilbert Ghez and Gary Becker (1975), as well as an empirical landmark paper by Thomas MaCurdy (1981). In these models, there is a subutility function for each period of life, in which current labor supply (or leisure) appears together with consumption, and lifetime utility is a discounted sum over all periods. Under certainty, labor supply and the commodity demands are functions of current wage rates and prices together with a quantity, interpretable as the marginal utility of lifetime wealth, which captures the budget constraint and links the periods together. Similar (though static) demand functions were first used by Ragnar Frisch (1932) so that functions of prices, wages, and the marginal utility of money have come to be known as Frisch demand functions, in distinction to Hicksian demands (functions of utility and prices) or Marshallian demands (of income and prices). MaCurdy noted that with suitable functional forms, the unobservable marginal utility of money, which was constant over the lifetime, could be treated as a fixed effect in panel data and differenced away, while, under uncertainty, the marginal utility of money behaved as a martingale difference, so that its difference was an unpredictable shock.

Deaton (1985) and Martin Browning, Deaton, and Margaret Irish (1985), extended this line of work. Panel data, such as those used by MaCurdy, were (and are) scarce while repeated (independently drawn) cross-sectional data are available in most countries. Deaton (1985) noted that it is possible to track birth cohorts through successive household surveys, so that, for example, the data on those aged 30 in year 1 can be pooled with those aged 31 in year 2, and so on. The validity of this depends on there being a fixed underlying birth cohort available for repeated independent sampling, which is problematic among older cohorts where mortality rates are high. Although the method cannot track individuals over time, it can track statistics of birth cohorts over time, not only means, but medians, variances, and higher moments, and although all such statistics are samples from the underlying birth cohort, the sampling scheme is known, and standard errors can be calculated following standard methods so that errors-in-variables (or instrumental variable) methods can be used to adjust estimators and correct attenuation bias, e.g. Wayne Fuller (1987). The method was first applied in Browning, Deaton, and Irish (1985) (BDI), and has been widely used in many subsequent studies of life cycle behavior.

BDI's findings, using British data, were not favorable for the model. Wage rates are hump-shaped over the life cycle, peaking in middle age. In the simplest form of the life cycle consumption story, and as proposed in the original Modigliani and Brumberg papers, the starting hypothesis was that consumption should be flat over life, and the essence of the model is the saving and dissaving that permits consumption smoothing over life. Yet in our data, as in subsequent findings, consumption tracks wages and earnings, also peaking in middle age. We also tested, and faulted, the hypothesis that the way that labor supply responded to wages over the life cycle was not consistent with the way that it responded over the business cycle, so that high frequency and low frequency smoothing were apparently not governed by the same set of parameters.

There have been two responses to such findings. One is to maintain the strict version of the model, and conclude that the life-cycle story really does not explain very much (which of course does not mean that thinking about consumption, saving, and pensions should not be done within a life cycle framework). The other is to generalize the model, noting, for example, that tastes or needs are different at different points in the life cycle, or to allow for precautionary motives, see for example Orazio Attanasio and Guglielmo Weber (2010) for a review of a large literature. A somewhat simpler story that is consistent with the findings in BDI is that consumption is much more closely tied to income than life-cycle theory predicts; for example, some fraction of people may live hand-to-mouth, consuming their earnings and whatever liquid assets they have on hand.

One way to think about hand-to-mouth consumption is to prohibit consumers from borrowing but leave other assumptions intact. For those who are patient enough to want to accumulate, the prohibition makes no difference because they do not want to borrow. Those who do want to borrow could simply consume their income, but can usually do better by accumulating and decumulating assets on their own, which helps smooth their consumption in the face of stochastic income or earnings; the classic example is a farmer in poor country, with little opportunity to borrow at affordable rates, and weather driven stochastic income.

A formal model of such a consumer is mathematically identical to the classic model of speculative commodity storage as originally developed by Robert Gustafson (1958), used by David Newbery and Joseph Stiglitz (1981), and, in the consumption and savings literature, by Jack Schechtman (1976), Schechtman and Vera Escudero (1977) and by Stephen Zeldes (1989). In similar vein, Deaton and Guy Laroque (1992) had been further exploring (and challenging) the empirical usefulness of the commodity model, the consumption version of which appears in Deaton (1991). Together with the similar model by Carroll (1997), in which precautionary motives prevent consumers from ever wanting to borrow, these models are now referred to as "buffer stock" models of saving. Consumers typically maintain some assets so as to buffer consumption against random fluctuations in income just as a smallholder will keep a stock of grain so that, even with a bad harvest, there will be something to eat. Eventually, after a series of sufficiently bad draws of income, the consumer will spend everything she has—current income plus assets—because the marginal utility of money now is higher than the expected marginal utility of money going into the next period without a buffer. These asset "stock outs" can be rare, so that, the consumer nearly always has *some* cash on hand. In spite of never being able to borrow, and in spite of almost always having assets, the behavior of these consumers is quite different from the behavior of a consumer who can borrow. In effect, the presence of the borrowing constraints changes the consumer's behavior—their policy function—even though the borrowing constraint almost never bites. These "hand-to-mouth" consumers are also different from those who simply spend their earnings each period; they do better at consumption smoothing and are better off with the same earnings process.

A final point is relevant for thinking about saving, development and poverty. Many buffer stock savers would not be made better off if somehow they were made to save and "escape" from their low-asset buffer-stock stochastic equilibrium; if they are given assets, they would be better off, but will eventually return to the buffer stock stochastic equilibrium. In that sense, they do not want to be rich. If borrowing restrictions were eased, for example by the opening of local banks charging low interest rates, they would borrow to raise their current consumption and move to their optimal trajectory of falling consumption over time. One might easily mistake such an increase in consumption as evidence that better credit reduces poverty, but the mechanism has nothing to do with escaping from poverty by borrowing for productive assets, which these consumers do not want. Instead, we are looking at a consumption boom that is financed by borrowing that, in the long run, will produce lower consumption (higher poverty as usually measured), even though these people are indeed better off, see Scott Fulford (2013).

The other decisive innovation of the 1970s was Robert Hall's (1978) reworking of the permanent income hypothesis (PIH) in the light of rational expectations; Hall derived the stochastic Euler equation relationship between consumption in adjacent periods, an approach that has dominated most of the subsequent literature. Marjorie Flavin (1981), under the assumption of certainty equivalent quadratic preferences, devised a workhorse version of the PIH that gave an explicit form for the change in consumption in terms of the changes in expectations of current and future labor incomes. In this model, which is a special case of Hall's, consumers do not change their consumption from one period to the next unless current or expected future labor income changes, and when there are such changes, there is an explicit formula that depends on the interest rate and the time horizon that gives the change in consumption that is warranted by the changes in earnings prospects. The implication that consumption change should be zero in the absence of new information—the famous random walk of consumption hypothesis—seemed absurd at the time, given that standard consumption functions for the previous 25 years had regressed consumption on large numbers of lags of income and lagged consumption. That Hall could barely reject the hypothesis was almost as stunning as if he had accepted it, and radically changed subsequent research in the field. As investigations continued, it became evident that, in US quarterly data, the change in consumption was in fact correlated with the lagged change in labor income, which became known as the excess sensitivity finding.

The explicit link between innovations in labor income and consumption change in the PIH allowed for the first time a precise characterization of the dynamics of consumption. In particular, if we know the dynamics of earnings, we can solve for the dynamics of consumption. Today, the data on earnings are infinitely better, and the estimates more sophisticated, see Fatih Guvenen et al (2015), but in the mid-1980s, the best practice approximation to mean quarterly labor income in the US was a first-order autoregressive process in growth rates, with a positive autoregressive parameter. When we plug this into the formula for the change in consumption, we get the counterintuitive result that consumption should respond more than one for one to innovations in earnings, so that consumption, far from being smoother than income, which is what the data say, and what the permanent income hypothesis had been designed to explain, should actually be *less* smooth than income. The PIH actually predicts the opposite of its most famous predictions and all the textbooks are wrong, Deaton (1987).

If innovations in earnings growth are positively autocorrelated, an unanticipated earnings gain is not only good in itself, but it signals that there is more to come next quarter. In consequence, people can spend not only their Christmas bonus, but also the Easter bonus that it signals.

How can we escape this paradox? First, it is derived under the assumption of certainty equivalence, so that there is no precautionary motive for holding back given that the Easter bonus is far from certain. Second, and more promising, is the possibility that earnings innovations have to be paid back, so that the bonus in the first and second quarters has to be paid back eventually, or even more than paid back. Earnings may be tied to some pre-determined path—for example, set by the personnel department on the day you join your company—so that the bonuses are always short-lived; people know this, and do not change their consumption by much. In the end, this possibility is hard to test, if only because the very long run ripples from earnings innovations can only be observed on very long run data.

A better resolution brings us back to one of the main themes of this article, which is to think about aggregation, about individuals versus aggregates, and about the amount of information that individuals might reasonably possess. The dynamic properties of average earnings come from averaging millions of individual earnings processes, and averaging does not preserve dynamics. In particular, the idiosyncratic component of individual earnings will be annihilated by the averaging and leave only any common or macro component. Yet this component may account for only a small fraction of the individual's earnings, small enough that she may not be aware of it. More generally, there can be a stochastic process, such as a random walk, or an autocorrelated growth process, that is common to all workers, but on top of which, each worker has their own idiosyncratic process, for example pure white noise. If each worker follows the PIH, consumption will be smoother than earnings for each individual. If the aggregate process accounts for only a small share of the variance for each individual, and if the individual cannot filter out the aggregate component her own earnings, then as formally shown by Jörn-Steffen Pischke (1995), aggregate consumption will fail to satisfy the PIH formula; it will appear to be too smooth relative to the aggregate earnings process, and will be correlated with previous information, as in the excess sensitivity finding. The plumber, who worries most about the year-to-year fluctuations in his earnings, has little reason to be concerned about a common macro process that is part of his earnings, but that accounts for a tiny fraction of it, and would be difficult to detect, even if he knew that it existed.

Note that aggregation issues exist even in Hall's original Euler equation version. Even if each person's consumption follows a random walk, births and deaths will generate predictable growth if the young are systematically richer than the old. Similarly, unless people (or dynasties) live forever, aggregate consumption will not satisfy the individual Euler equations.

The permanent income hypothesis also has implications for inequality in consumption, income, and wealth; these were developed in Deaton and Paxson (1994). Suppose, as in Hall, that each consumer in a birth cohort is random walking. Unless their consumption changes are perfectly correlated, the cohort members' consumption levels will move further apart as the cohort ages. Consumption inequality will increase with age within a birth cohort. Aggregate inequality in the economy depends on demographics, as in Modigliani's growth effects for saving. Note that this does *not* require that earnings inequality increase with age, though it is entirely consistent with it doing so. We can imagine a stationary distribution of earnings over people, in which each person has a person specific mean plus an individual specific stationary process; if the innovations to these individual specific processes are (at least partially) uncorrelated across people, and if people follow the certainty-equivalent PIH, then the changes in consumption will be less than perfectly correlated, and consumption inequality will widen over time within the birth cohort. This theory also implies that *income* inequality should also widen, whether or not *earnings* inequality is increasing (the difference between income and earnings being the return to assets) while wealth inequality will increase an order of magnitude more rapidly than consumption inequality, essentially because there is increasing inequality in the increments to wealth, so that individual asset levels are spiraling apart even more rapidly. Everything here is driven by the stochastic innovations to labor income, or luck, so that consumption, income, and wealth inequality can be thought of as the fossils of accumulated luck.

Paxson and I looked at the data on birth cohorts using the repeated cross-section method for three countries, the US, Britain, and Taiwan, and found that consumption inequality did indeed increase with age. While it is always gratifying when a new prediction is confirmed in the data, Popper's curse is always lurking in the background; we learn most clearly by refutation, not confirmation, so that if one theory fits the data, so will others. In this case, the obvious alternative explanation is one in which income inequality is increasing within a birth cohort as some members are more successful than others, and consumption is tied to income according to a buffer stock model. An acid test of the model against this situation would be one in which the cross-sectional labor earnings were stationary, with no inequality increase, and where consumption inequality is still increasing. I know of no such test.

Even so, and as Paxson and I noted, the "fanning-out" of consumption with age is a measure of the extent to which society fails to provide consumption insurance to its members. With perfect insurance, which is typically undesirable because of moral hazard, individual idiosyncratic luck would be neutralized by redistribution across people, and there would be no fanning out of consumption. Of course, society provides its citizens with insurance in many ways, through families, through unemployment, disability, and pension payments, and even through national defense. The spread of consumption inequality is potentially informative about all of these, and so is of great interest beyond a test of the PIH. For example, as noted by Lucas (2003), the fanning out of consumption and of earnings, though consistent with both the PIH and with the buffer stock model, in either case indicates that there is less than perfect insurance; insurance could operate on consumption, conditional on income, or through income itself. The extent of insurance is also closely tied to the other puzzles discussed above; John Campbell and Deaton (1989) showed that Hall's excess sensitivity finding can be seen as another aspect of the excess smoothness finding, or *vice versa*, and Attanasio and Nicola Pavoni (2011) show that both can be used to measure the extent of insurance. Blundell (2014) provides a general discussion and review of recent developments.

Explicitly modeling earnings at the individual level, separating out macro from idiosyncratic effects, assessing insurance, and thinking about macroeconomics as an aggregate of heterogeneous agents has become a (or perhaps even the) central topic in macroeconomics today, displacing the representative agent models that so troubled me at the beginning of my career. In one key paper Rao Aiyagari (1994) developed a general equilibrium model with buffer stock consumers; although each consumer is saving and dissaving, aggregate variables are unchanging, and there is no representative agent. Per Krusell and Anthony Smith

(1998) added macroeconomic shocks to this model resurrecting a representative agent. Even so, they make a range of special assumptions, and there is good ongoing work today exploring more realistic cases where, once again, aggregated and individual behavior are sharply different, for example Greg Kaplan, Giovanni Violante, and Justin Weidner (2014) and Kaplan, Benjamin Moll, and Violante (2016). According to the opening words of a recent review paper by Jonathan Heathcote, Kjetil Storesletten and Giovanni Violante (2009) "Macroeconomics is evolving from the study of aggregate dynamics to the study of the dynamics of the entire equilibrium distribution of allocations across individual economic actors." I am delighted if I have played a part in this evolution.

4. CONCLUSION: ON DISCOVERIES

The Prize Committee asks that this article include a discussion of my discoveries and how they happened. There are certainly many things that I know now that I did not know when I started though many of them are things that other people knew all along—I am thinking in particular of Daniel McFadden and Terence Gorman. My usual experience is that a "discovery" turns out to be wrong: it turns out to be a coding error, or a misinterpretation of theory or of data, or is not a discovery at all, but has long been known. Occasionally, discoveries are real, though most are personal, in the sense that they change what I think, but not what others think.

I cannot resist referring back to one of my first discoveries on consumption and saving. As a cash-strapped young father in Britain in the mid-1970s when the government had lost control of inflation (the British retail price index rose by 16, 24, and 17 percent in 1974, 75, and 76), I realized that, when I went shopping, mostly for one or two items at a time, I could not tell inflation from relative price increase, especially in the early months of the inflation, and especially for items like coffee which, for me then, was a luxury with a wildly fluctuating price. On the basis of this, I argued, in Deaton (1977), that in an economy with unanticipated inflation, there would be "involuntary" saving as each consumer, buying one good at a time, held off from that good on the mistaken supposition that it was only relatively expensive. I recall too that my Cambridge colleagues, who were kind to a young research assistant, thought this was interesting, but absurd; we all knew, after all, that inflation caused people to dissave, and that this was how hyperinflations worked. So I was as surprised as were my colleagues when the entirely unanticipated increase in the household saving rate was announced, and later when there were similar increases in a number of other countries, Erkki Koskela and Matti Virén (1982). That was also my first encounter with Popper's curse: if one story correctly predicts a new finding—however unexpected—many other stories can do so too, in this case wealth effects are candidates.

Beyond that, I look back with the greatest pleasure on three discoveries. None of these insights came from problems that I was working on, but from realizing that something apparently unconnected had implications elsewhere. The first is that it is possible to track birth cohorts through repeated cross-sectional surveys, and that this insight could be used to investigate life-cycle consumption and labor supply. The second is my work with Christina Paxson on the dynamic effects of luck. The way that people respond to luck is a mechanism that drives up consumption inequality within a birth cohort and that, in turn, allows us to assess the extent to which society insures its members. Third, in development, is my work with Jean Drèze and with Paxson on food puzzles, primarily in India. The economies of scale puzzle had its early origins in a conversation with Drèze on the effects on wellbeing of family size. In time, that led to our later work on food and nutrition in India, on how food Engel curves do not identify the effects of rising income on calorie consumption, and on how nutrition depends on many more factors than the intake of calories and protein. Even on the subject of food and wellbeing, one of the oldest topics in economics, much remains unresolved.

5. CITATIONS

Aiyagari, S. Rao, 1994, "Uninsured idiosyncratic risk and aggregate saving," *Quarterly Journal of Economics*, **109**(3): 659–84.

Alkire, Sabina, James Foster, Suman Seth, Maria Emma Santos, José Manuel Roche and Paola Bellon, 2015, *Multidimensional poverty measurement and analysis*, Oxford. Oxford University Press.

Allen, Robert C., 2016, "Absolute poverty: when necessity displaces desire," http://www.economics.ox.ac.uk/Oxford-Economic-and-Social-History-Working-Papers/absolute-poverty-when-necessity-displaces-desire.

Atkin, David, 2013, "Trade, tastes, and nutrition in India," *American Economic Review*, **103**(5), 1629–63.

Attanasio, Orazio, and Nicola Pavoni, 2011, "Risk sharing in private information models with asset accumulation: explaining the excess smoothness of consumption," *Econometrica*, **79**(4): 1027-68.

Attanasio, Orazio, and Guglielmo Weber, 2010, "Consumption and saving: models of intertemporal allocation and their implications for public policy," *Journal of Economic Literature*, **48**(3): 693–751.

Banks, James, Richard Blundell, and Arthur Lewbel, 1997, "Quadratic Engel curves and consumer demand," *Review of Economics and Statistics*, **79**(4), 527–39.

Blundell, Richard, 2014, "Income dynamics and life-cycle inequality: mechanisms and controversies" *Economic Journal*, **124** (May) 289–318.

Bosworth, Barry, Gary Burtless, and John Sabelhaus, 1991, "The decline in saving: evidence from household surveys," *Brookings Papers on Economic Activity*, 183–241.

Browning, Martin, Angus Deaton and Margaret Irish, 1985, "A profitable approach to labor supply and commodity demands over the life-cycle," *Econometrica*, **53**(3), 503–543.

Campbell, John Y., and Angus Deaton, 1989, "Why is consumption so smooth?" *Review of Economic Studies*, **56**(3): 357-74.

Carroll, Christopher D., 1997, "Buffer-stock saving and the life cycle/permanent income hypothesis," *Quarterly Journal of Economics*, **112**(1), 1–55.

Carroll, Christopher D. and Lawrence H. Summers, 1991, "Consumption growth parallels income growth: some new evidence," in B. Douglas Bernheim and John B. Shoven, eds., *National saving and economic performance*, Chicago. University of Chicago Press for NBER.

Chen, Shaohua, and Martin Ravallion, 2010, "The world is poorer than we thought, but no less successful in the fight against poverty," *Quarterly Journal of Economics*, **125**(4), 1577–1625.

Christensen, Laurits R., Dale W. Jorgenson, and Lawrence J Lau, 1975, "Transcendental logarithmic utility functions," *American Economic Review*, **65**(3), 367–83.

Coffey, Diane, 2015, "Pregnancy body mass and weight gain during pregnancy in India and sub-Saharan Africa," *Proceedings of the National Academy of Sciences of the USA*, **112**(11), 3302–7.

Costa, Dora, 2001, "Estimating real income in the United States from 1988 to 1994: correcting CPI bias using Engel curves," *Journal of Political Economy*, **109**(6), 1288–1310.

Davies, David, 1795, *The case of labourers in husbandry stated and considered in three parts*, Bath. Cruttwell for Robinson, London.

Deaton, Angus, 1974a, "A reconsideration of the empirical implications of additive preferences," *Economic Journal*, **84** (334), 338–48.

Deaton, Angus, 1974b, "The analysis of consumer demand in the United Kingdom, 1900–1970," *Econometrica*, **42**(2), 341–67.

Deaton, Angus, 1977, "Involuntary savings through unanticipated inflation," *American Economic Review*, **67**(5), 899–910.

Deaton, Angus, 1985, "Panel data from time series of cross-sections," *Journal of Econometrics*, **30**, (1–2), 109–26.

Deaton, Angus, 1987, Life-cycle models of consumption: is the evidence consistent with the theory?" in Truman Bewley, ed., *Advances in econometrics: fifth world congress*, Vol. 2, New York. Cambridge University Press. 1221–48.

Deaton, Angus, 1988, "Quality, quantity and spatial variation of price," *American Economic Review*, **78**(3), 418–30.

Deaton, Angus, 1989a, "Rice prices and income distribution in Thailand: a non-parametric analysis," *Economic Journal*, **99**, S1-37.

Deaton, Angus, 1989b, "Looking for boy-girl discrimination in household expenditure data," *World Bank Economic Review*, **3**(1), 1–15.

Deaton, Angus, 1991, "Saving and liquidity constraints," *Econometrica*, **59**(5), 1221–48.

Deaton, Angus, 1997, *The analysis of household surveys*, Baltimore, MD. Johns Hopkins Press for the World Bank.

Deaton, Angus, 2001, "Counting the world's poor: problems and possible solutions," *World Bank Research Observer*, **16**(2), 125–47.

Deaton, Angus, 2005, "Measuring poverty in a growing world (or measuring growth in a poor world)" *Review of Economics and Statistics*, **87**(1), 1–19.

Deaton, Angus, 2010, "Price indexes, inequality, and the measurement of world poverty," *American Economic Review*, **100**(1), 5–34.

Deaton, Angus, 2013, *The great escape: health, wealth, and the origins of inequality*, Princeton, NJ. Princeton University Press.

Deaton, Angus and Bettina Aten, 2015, "Trying to understand the PPPs in ICP2011: why are the results so different?" NBER Working Paper 20244 (March).

Deaton, Angus and Jean Drèze, 2009, "Food and nutrition in India: facts and interpretations," *Economic and Political Weekly*, **44**(7), 42–65.

Deaton, Angus and Olivier Dupriez, 2011, "Purchasing power parity exchange rates for the global poor," *American Economic Journal Applied*, **3**(2), 137–66.

Deaton, Angus and Alan Heston, 2010, "Understanding PPPs and PPP-based national accounts," *American Economic Journal Macroeconomics*, **2**(4), 1–35.

Deaton, Angus and Guy Laroque, 1992, "On the behavior of commodity prices," *Review of Economic Studies*, **59**(1), 1–23.

Deaton, Angus and John Muellbauer, 1980a, "An almost ideal demand system," *American Economic Review*, **70**(3), 312–26.

Deaton, Angus and John Muellbauer, 1980b, *Economics and consumer behavior*, New York. Cambridge University Press.

Deaton, Angus and John Muellbauer, 1986, "On measuring child costs: with applications to poor countries," *Journal of Political Economy*, **94**(4), 720–44.

Deaton, Angus and Christina Paxson, 1994, "Intertemporal choice and inequality," *Journal of Political Economy*, **102**(3), 437–67.

Deaton, Angus and Christina Paxson, 1997, "The effects of economic and population growth on national saving and inequality," *Demography*, **34**(1), 97–114.

Deaton, Angus and Christina Paxson, 1998, "Economies of scale, household size, and the demand for food," *Journal of Political Economy*, **106**(5), 897–930.

Deaton, Angus and Christina Paxson, 2000, "Growth and saving among individuals and households," *Review of Economics and Statistics*, **82**(2), 212–25.

Diewert, W. Erwin, 1971, "An application of the Shepherd duality theorem: a generalized Leontief production function," *Journal of Political Economy*, **79**(3), 481–507.

Diewert, W. Erwin, 1974, "Applications of duality theory," in M. Intriligator and D. Kendrick, *Frontiers of quantitative economics*, 2, 106–71. Amsterdam. North-Holland.

Ducpétiaux, Édouard, 1855, *Budgets économiques des classes ouvrières en Belgique, subsistances, salaires, population*, Brussels. Commission Centrale de Statistique.

Eden, Frederick Morton, 1797, *The state of the poor or, an history of the laboring classes in England, from the Conquest to the present period*, London, Davis. [Cambridge. Cambridge University Press replica republished, 2011.]

Engel, Ernst, 1857, "Die productions- und consumtionverhältnisse des Königreiches Sachsen," reprinted with Engel, 1895.

Engel, Ernst, 1895, "Die Lebenskosten belgischer Arbeiter-Familien früher und jetzt," *International Statistical Institute Bulletin*, **9**(1), 1–124.

Engels, Friedrich, 1845, *Die Lage der arbeitenden Klasse in England*, Leipzig. Wigand. (English translation, New York, 1887.]

Ferreira, Francisco H. G, Shaohua Chen, Andrew Dabalen et al. (2015), "A global count of the extreme poor in 2012: data issues, methodology and initial results," *World Bank Policy Research Working Paper* No. 7432, Washington DC (October).

Flavin, Marjorie A., 1981, "The adjustment of consumption to changing expectations about future income," *Journal of Political Economy*, **89**(5), 974–1009.

Frisch, Ragnar, 1932, *New methods of measuring marginal utility*. Tubingen. J C B Mohr.

Fulford, Scott, 2013, "The effects of financial development in the short and long run," *Journal of Development Economics*, **104**, 56–72.

Fuller, Wayne A., 1987, *Measurement error models*, New York. Wiley.

Geary, Roy C., 1950–51, "A note on 'A constant-utility index of the cost of living,'" *Review of Economic Studies*, **18**(1), 65–6.

Ghez, Gilbert R. and Gary S. Becker, 1975, *The allocation of time and goods over the life cycle*, New York. NBER.

Goldfeld, Stephen M, Richard E. Quandt and Hale F. Trotter, 1966, "Maximization by quadratic hill-climbing," *Econometrica*, **34**(3), 541–51.

Gorman, William M., 1953, "Community preference fields," *Econometrica*, **21**(1), 63–80.

Gorman, William M., 1959, "Separable utility and aggregation," *Econometrica*, **27**(3), 469–81.

Gorman, William M., 1968, "The structure of utility functions," *Review of Economic Studies*, **35**(4), 367–90.

Government of India, 2014, *Report of the expert group to review the methodology for measurement of poverty*, Planning Commission, June.

Gustafson, Robert L., 1958, *Carryover levels for grains*, US Department of Agriculture, Technical Bulletin 1178.

Guvenen, Fatih, Fatih Karahan, Serdar Ozkan, and Jae Song, 2015, "What do data on millions of U.S. workers reveal about life-cycle earnings risk?" Cambridge, MA. NBER Working Paper No. 20913, January.

Hall, Robert E., 1978, "Stochastic implications of the life-cycle permanent income hypothesis: theory and evidence," *Journal of Political Economy*, **86**(6), 971–87.

Hamilton, Bruce W., 2001, "Using Engel's Law to estimate CPI bias," *American Economic Review*, **91**(3), 619–30.

Heathcote, Jonathan, Kjetil Storesletten and Giovanni L.Violante, 2009, "Quantitative macroeconomics with heterogeneous households," *Annual Reviews of Economics*, **1**, 319–54.

Heckman, James J., 1971, "Three essays on the supply of labor and the demand for market goods," PhD dissertation, Princeton University.

Houthakker, Hendrik S., 1955–56, "The Pareto distribution and the Cobb-Douglas production function in activity analysis," *Review of Economic Studies*, **23**(1), 27–31.

Inklaar, Robert, and D. S. Prasada Rao, 2014, "Cross-country income levels over time: did the developing world suddenly become much richer?" Groningen Growth and Development Center Research Memorandum 151, Groningen, Netherlands (Dec.)

Kaplan, Greg, Benjamin Moll, and Giovanni L. Violante, 2016, "Monetary policy according to HANK," Cambridge, MA. NBER Working Paper No. 21897.

Kaplan, Greg, Giovanni L. Violante, and Justin Weidner, 2014, "The wealthy hand-to-mouth," *Brookings Papers on Economic Activity*, Spring, 77–138.

Klein, Lawrence R. and Herman Rubin, 1947–48, "A constant-utility index of the cost of living," *Review of Economic Studies*, **15**(2), 84–7.

Koskela, Erkki, and Matti Virén, 1982, "Saving and inflation: some international evidence," *Economics Letters*, **9**(4), 337–44.

Kotlikoff, Laurence J. and Lawrence H. Summers, 1981, "The role of intergenerational transfers in aggregate capital accumulation," *Journal of Political Economy*, **89**(4), 706–32.

Kravis, Irving B., Alan W. Heston, and Robert Summers, 1978, "Real GDP *per capita* for more than one hundred countries," *The Economic Journal*, **88**(2), 215–42.

Krusell, Per and Anthony A. Smith, 1998, "Income and wealth heterogeneity in the macroeconomy," *Journal of Political Economy*, **106**(5), 867–96.

Lucas, Robert E., 2003, "Macroeconomic priorities," *American Economic Review*, **93**(1), 1–14.

MaCurdy, Thomas E., 1981, "An empirical model of labor supply in a life-cycle setting," *Journal of Political Economy*, **89** (6), 1059–85.

Mahalanobis, Prasanta Chandra, 1946, "Recent experiments in statistical sampling in the Indian Statistical Institute," *Journal of the Royal Statistical Society*, Series A, **109**, 326–70.

Marquardt, Donald W., 1963, "An algorithm for least-squares estimation of nonlinear parameters," *Journal of the Society of Industrial and Applied Mathematics*, **11**(2), 431–41.

McCarthy, Paul, 2013, Extrapolating PPPs and comparing ICP benchmark results," Chapter 18 in *Measuring the real size of the world economy*, Washington, DC. World Bank.

McFadden, Daniel, 1978, "Duality of production, cost, and profit functions," Chapter 1.1 in Mel A Fuss and Daniel McFadden eds., *Production economics: a dual approach to theory and applications*, Amsterdam: North Holland. 3–109.

McFadden, Daniel L., 2014, "The new science of pleasure: consumer choice behavior and the measurement of well-being," Chapter 2 in Hess, Stephane and Andrew Daly, *Handbook of Choice Modeling*, Elgar, 7–48.

Milanovic, Branko, 2007, *Worlds apart: measuring international and global inequality*, Princeton, NJ. Princeton University Press.

Minhas, Bagicha S., 1988, "Validation of large-scale sample survey data: case of NSS estimates of household consumption expenditure," *Sankhyā: the Indian Journal of Statistics*, 50, Series B, (3 Supplement), 1–63.

Modigliani, Franco, 1970, "The life-cycle hypothesis and intercountry differences in the saving ratio," in W. A. Eltis, M. FG. Scott, and J.N. Wolfe, eds., *Induction, growth and trade: essays in honour of Sir Roy Harrod*. Oxford. Oxford University Press. 197–225.

Modigliani, Franco and Richard H. Brumberg, 1955a, "Utility analysis and the consumption function: an interpretation of cross-section data," Chapter 15 in Kenneth K Kurihara ed., *Post-Keynesian Economics*, London. George Allen and Unwin, 388–436.

Modigliani, Franco and Richard H. Brumberg, 1955b, [1990], "Utility analysis and aggregate consumption functions; an attempt at integration," in Andrew Abel, ed., *The*

Collected Papers of Franco Modigliani: Volume 2, The Life-cycle hypothesis of saving, Cambridge, MA. The MIT Press, 128–97.

Muellbauer, John, 1975, "Aggregation, income distribution and consumer demand," *Review of Economic Studies*, **42**(4), 525–43.

Newbery, David M. G., and Joseph E. Stiglitz, 1981, *Theory of commodity price stabilization: study in the economics of risk*, Oxford. Oxford University Press.

Neyman, Jerzy, 1934, "On the two different aspects of the representative method: the method of stratified sampling, and the method of purposive selection," *Journal of the Royal Statistical Association*, 97, 558–625.

Nicholson, J. Leonard, 1976, "Appraisal of different methods of estimating equivalence scales and their results," *Review of Income and Wealth*, **22**, 1–11.

Paxson, Christina, 1996, "Saving and growth: evidence from micro data," *European Economic Review*, **40**(2), 255–88.

Pischke, Jörn-Steffen, 1995, "Individual income, incomplete information, and aggregate consumption," *Econometrica*, **63**(4), 805–40.

Pigou, Arthur Cecil, 1910, "A method of determining the numerical value of elasticities of demand," *The Economic Journal*, **20** (80), 636–40.

Pollak, Robert A., and Terence J. Wales, 1979, "Welfare comparisons and equivalence scales," *American Economic Review*, **69**(2), 216–21.

Prais, Sigbert J., and Hendrik S. Houthakker, 1956, *The analysis of family budgets*, Cambridge. Cambridge University Press.

Rothbarth, Erwin, 1943, "Note on a method of determining equivalent income for families of different composition," Appendix 4 in Charles Madge, *War-time pattern of saving and spending*, Cambridge. Cambridge University Press for National Institute of Economic and Social Research.

Samuelson, Paul A., 1947–48, "Some implications of 'linearity'," *Review of Economic Studies*, **15**(2), 88–90.

Samuelson, Paul A., 2004, "The first fifteen Nobel Laureates in economics, and fifteen more might-have-beens," in Peter Badge, *Nobel Economists*, Foundation Lindau Nobel Laureates Meetings.

Sen, Amartya K., 1989, "Women's survival as a development problem," *Bulletin of the American Academy of Arts and Sciences*, **43**(2), 14–29.

Seng, You Poh, 1951, "Historical survey of the development of sampling theories and practice," *Journal of the Royal Statistical Society*, Series A, **114**(2), 214–31.

Schechtman, Jack, 1976, "An income fluctuation problem," *Journal of Economic Theory*, **12** (2), 218–41.

Schechtman, Jack and Vera L. S. Escudero, 1977, "Some results on 'an income fluctuation problem'," *Journal of Economic Theory*, **16** (2) 151–66.

Smith, T. M. Fred, 1976, "The foundations of survey sampling: a review," *Journal of the Royal Statistical Society*, Series A., **139**(2), 183–204.

Stigler, George J. 1954, "The early history of empirical studies of consumer behavior," *Journal of Political Economy*, **62**(2), 95–113.

Stone, Richard, 1954, "Linear expenditure systems and demand analysis: an application to the pattern of British demand," *Economic Journal*, **64**(255), 511–27.

Stone, Richard, and Alan Brown, 1962, *A computable model of economic growth. A programme for growth, Volume 1*. London, Chapman and Hall.

Summers, Robert, and Alan Heston, 1991, "The Penn World Table (Mark 5): an expanded set of international comparisons, 1950–1988," *Quarterly Journal of Economics*, **106**(2), 327–68.

Villermé, Louis-René, 1830, "De la mortalité dans les divers quartiers de la ville de Paris, et des causes qui la rendent très différente dans plusiers d'entre eux, ansi que les divers quartiers de beaucoup de grandes villes," *Annales d'Hygiène Publique et de Médecine Légale*, 3, 294–341.

Visaria, Pravin, 2000, "Poverty in India during 1994–98: alternative estimates," Institute for Economic Growth, New Delhi, processed.

World Bank, 1990, *World Development Report: Poverty*, New York. Oxford University Press.

World Bank, 2016, PovcalNet: an online analysis tool for global poverty monitoring, http://iresearch.worldbank.org/PovcalNet/ (Accessed, January 20, 2016.

Zeldes, Stephen P., 1989, "Optimal consumption with stochastic income: deviations from certainty equivalence, *Quarterly Journal of Economics*, **104**(2), 275–98.